MILLER'S
CollectableS
PRICE ◆ GUIDE

Compiled and Edited by
Judith and Martin Miller

General Editor: Robert Murfin

MILLERS PUBLICATIONS

MILLER'S COLLECTABLES PRICE GUIDE

Compiled, edited and designed by
Millers Publications
The Cellars, High Street
Tenterden, Kent TN30 6BN

Compiled and edited by
Judith & Martin Miller

General Editor: Robert Murfin
Editorial co-ordinator: Sue Boyd
Artwork: Stephen Parry, Jody Taylor
Photographic co-ordinator and advertising executive: Elizabeth Smith
Display Advertisements: Trudi Hinkley
Index compiled by DD Editorial Services, Beccles
Additional photography by Ian Booth and Robin Saker

Copyright © 1992 Millers Publications

First published as *Miller's Collectables Price Guide 1992-93*

Reissued 1994

A CIP catalogue record for this book is
available from the British Library

ISBN 1-85152-681-1

Typeset by Mainline Typesetters, St Leonards-on-Sea
Illustrations by G.H. Graphics, St. Leonards-on-Sea
Colour origination by Scantrans, Singapore
Printed and bound in England by William Clowes Ltd
Beccles and London

CONTENTS

Key to Illustrations

Each illustration and descriptive caption is accompanied by a letter-code. By reference to the following list of Auctioneers (denoted by *) and Dealers (●), the source of any item may be immediately determined. In no way does this constitute or imply a contract or binding offer on the part of any of our contributors to supply or sell the goods illustrated, or similar articles, at the prices stated. Advertisers in this year's directory are denoted by †.

AA ● Ambeline Antiques, By George Antique Centre, St. Albans, Herts. Tel: (0727) 53032/081-445 8025

AAM ● Anything American (Chris Pearce), 33-35 Duddenhill Lane, London NW10. Tel: 081-451 0320

ABS ● Abstract, 58-60 Kensington Church Street, London W8. Tel: 071-376 2652

ACC †● Albert's, 113 London Road, Twickenham, Middx. Tel: 081-891 3067

ACL ● Academy Costumes Ltd., 25 Murphy Street, London, SE1. Tel: 071-620 0771

AG * Anderson & Garland, Marlborough House, Marlborough Crescent, Newcastle-upon-Tyne. Tel: 091-232 6278

AGM †● The Button Museum, Kyrle Street, Ross-on-Wye, Hereford & Worcs. Tel: (0989) 66089

AH * Andrew Hartley, Victoria Hall, Little Lane, Ilkley, W. Yorks. Tel: (0943) 816363

ARB ● Arbour Antiques Ltd., Poet's Arbour, Sheep Street, Stratford-on-Avon, Warks. Tel: (0789) 293453

ARC ● Architectural Antiques, West Ley, Alswear Old Road, South Molton, Devon. Tel: (07695) 3342

ASA ● AS Antiques & Decorative Arts, 26 Broad Street, Pendleton, Salford 6, Manchester. Tel: 061-737 5938

ASc ● Ascott Antiques, Narborough, Leics. Tel: (0533) 863190

ASH ● Ashburton Marbles, Grate Hall, North Street, Ashburton, Devon. Tel: (0364) 53189

B * Boardman, Station Road Corner, Haverhill, Suffolk. Tel: (0440) 703784

Bea * Bearnes, Rainbow, Avenue Road, Torquay, Devon. Tel: (0803) 296277

BEV ● Beverley, 30 Church Street, London NW8. Tel: 071-262 1576

BG ● Brenda Gunn, Antiquarius, Stand N13/N14, 135 King's Road, London SW3. Tel: 071-352 8882/4690

BGA ● By George Antique Centre, 23 George Street, St. Albans, Herts. Tel: (0727) 53032

BHE †● British Heritage Telephones, 11 Rhodes Drive, Unsworth, Bury, Lancs. Tel: 061-767 9259

BLO ● New Century, 69 Kensington Church Street, London W8. Tel: 071-376 2810/071-937 2410

Bon †* Bonhams, Montpelier Galleries, Montpelier Street, Knightsbridge, London SW7. Tel: 071-584 9161

BOW †● Simon Bowler, Smith Street Antique Centre, Warwick. Tel: (0926) 400554/021-783 8930

BS ● Below Stairs, 103 High Street, Hungerford, Berks. Tel: (0488) 682317

BST ● Barbara Stone Rare Books, Antiquarius, 135 King's Road, London SW3. Tel: 071-351 0963

BWe * Biddle & Webb of Birmingham, Ladywood Middleway, Birmingham. Tel: 021-455 8042

BY ● Bygones, Collectors Shop, 123 South Street, Lancing, Sussex. Tel: (0903) 750051/763470

C * Christie, Manson & Woods Ltd., 8 King Street, St. James's, London SW1. Tel: 071-839 9060

CA ● Crafers Antiques, The Hill, Wickham Market, Suffolk. Tel: (0728) 747347

CCC †● The Crested China Co., The Station House, Driffield, E. Yorks. Tel: (0377) 47042

CD †● The China Doll, 31 Walcot Street, Bath, Avon. Tel: (0225) 465849

CEN ● Central Antique Arms & Militaria, Smith Street Antique Centre, 7 Smith Street, Warwick. Tel: (0926) 497864

CHa ● Carol Hammond, Unit 8, Kensington Church Street Antiques Centre, 58/60 Kensington Church Street, London W8. Tel: 071-938 4405

A 5-shot 120 bore Adams model 1851 self-cocking percussion revolver, engraved 'Deane, Adams and Deane, 30 King William St., London Bridge', No. 10310R, London proved, 9in (23cm). **£1,300-1,750** *WAL*

CHA †● Chapel House Antiques, Pendre, Cardigan, Dyfed, and 32 Pentood Industrial Estate, Cardigan, Dyfed. Tel: (0239) 614868 and 613268

ChL †● Chelsea Lion, Steve Clark, Chenil Galleries, 181/183 King's Road, London SW3. Tel: 071-351 9338

CLA ● Classic Costumes, Northcote Road Antique Market, 155a Northcote Road, Battersea, London SW11. Tel: 081-764 8858

CLH ● Clem Harwood, The Old Bakery, Keevil, Trowbridge, Wilts. Tel: (0380) 870463

COB †● Cobwebs, 78 Northam Road, Southampton. Tel: (0703) 227458

COL †● Collectables, 335 High Street, Rochester, Kent. Tel: (0634) 828767

CNY * Christie, Manson & Woods International Inc., 502 Park Avenue, New York, NY 10022, USA. Tel: 212546 1000 (including Christie's East)

CP †● Cat Pottery, 1 Grammar School Road, North Walsham, Norfolk. Tel: (0692) 402962

CS †● Christopher Sykes Antiques, The Old Parsonage, Woburn, Bucks. Tel: (0525) 290259/290467

C(S) * Christie's Scotland Ltd., 164-166 Bath Street, Glasgow. Tel: 041-332 8134

CSC ● The Chicago Sound Company, Northmoor House, Colesbrook, Gillingham, Dorset. Tel: (0747) 824338

CSK †* Christie's (South Kensington) Ltd., 85 Old Brompton Road, London SW7. Tel: 071-581 7611

DEN * Denham Associates, Horsham Auction Galleries, Warnham, Horsham, W. Sussex. Tel: (0403) 55699/53837

DHO ● Derek Howard, The Original Chelsea Antiques Market, 245/253 King's Road, London SW3. Tel: 071-352 4113

DID ● Didier Antiques, 58-60 Kensington Church Street, London W8. Tel: 071-938 2537/(0836) 232634

DOL †● Dollectable, 53 Lower Bridge Street, Chester. Tel: (0244) 344888/679195

DOW ● Mrs M. Downworth, Great Western Antiques, Wednesday Market, Bartlett Street, Bath, Avon.

EHA ● Gloria Gibson, 2 Beaufort West, Bath, Avon. Tel: (0225) 446646

FA ● Frank Andrews, 10 Vincent Road, London N22. Tel: 081-881 0658

FOB ● Rosemary Fobister, Chelsea Antiques Market, 245/253 King's Road, London SW3.

FOR †● Forge Antiques (Paul Williams), Synod Inn, Llandysul, Dyfed. Tel: (0545) 580707/580604

FMN †● Forget Me Not Antiques (Heather Sharp), By George Antique Centre, 23 George Street, St. Albans, Herts. Tel: (0727) 53032/(0923) 261172

G&CC †● Goss and Crested China Ltd (Nicholas J. Pine), 62 Murray Road, Horndean, Hants. Tel: (0705) 597440

GAD ● Decodence, Gad Sassower, Shop 13, The Mall, Camden Passage, London N1. Tel: 071-354 4473/081-458 4665

GAK ● G. A. Key, 8 Market Place, Aylsham, Norwich, Norfolk. Tel: (0263) 733195

GAZ †● Gazelles, 31 Northam Road, Southampton. Tel: (0703) 235291/780798

GC * Geering & Colyer, now Michael Shortall Antiques Centres, Highate, Hawkhurst, Kent. Tel: (0580) 753463

GH * Giles Haywood, The Auction House, St. John's Road, Stourbridge, W. Midlands. Tel: (0384) 370891

GIL * Gildings, Roman Way, Market Harborough, Leics. Tel: (0858) 410414

GMC ● Gerry McClean, Stand No. R1-2, Chenil Galleries, 181-183 King's Road, London SW3. Tel: 071-352 8653/071-351 7170

GOL ● The Golf Gallery, Grays in the Mews B12, Davies Mews, London W1. Tel: 071-408 1239/081-452 7243

GRA ● Geoffrey Robinson, Alfie's Antique Market, 13-25 Church Street, London NW8.

HAL †● John & Simon Haley, 89 Northgate, Halifax, W. Yorks. Tel: (0422) 822148

HCH * Hobbs & Chambers, Market Place, Cirencester, Glos. Tel: (0285) 4736

HEW ● Muir Hewett, Halifax Antiques Centre, Queens Road Mills, Queens Road/Gibbet Street, Halifax, W. Yorks. Tel: (0422) 366657

HEY ● Heyford Antiques, 7 Church Street, Nether Heyford, Northampton. Tel: (0327) 40749

HOL ● Holmfirth Antiques (Ken Priestley), Halifax Antiques Centre, Queens Road Mills, Queens Road/Gibbet Street, Halifax, W. Yorks. Tel: (0484) 686854

HOW ● Howards Antiques, 10 Alexandra Road, Aberystwyth, Dyfed. Tel: (0970) 624973

HSS * Henry Spencer & Sons, 20 The Square, Retford, Notts. Tel: (0777) 708633

HUN ● Huntercombe Manor Barn, Henley-on-Thames, Oxon. Tel: (0491) 641349

IS †● Ian Sharp Antiques, 23 Front Street, Tynemouth. Tel: 091-296 0656

IW †● Islwyn Watkins, 1 High Street, 29 Market Street, Knighton, Powys. Tel: (0547) 520145/528940

JAS ● Jasmin Cameron, Antiquarius, J6, 131-141 King's Road, London SW3. Tel: 071-351 4154

Bears with bowls, 4in (10cm) wide. £15-20 *SP*

JH   *   Jacobs & Hunt, Lavant Street, Petersfield, Hants. Tel: (0730) 62744

JL   ●   Joy Luke, The Gallery, 300E Grove Street, Bloomington, IL 61701, USA. Tel: 309 828-5533

JMC   ●   J & M Collectables, The Cranbrook Antique Centre, High Street, Cranbrook, Kent. Tel: (0580) 891657

JMG   †●   Jamie Maxtone Graham, Lyne Haugh, Lyne Station, Peebles, Scotland. Tel: (07214) 304

JO   †●   Jacqueline Oosthuizen, The Georgian Village and 23 Cale Street, Chelsea, London SW3. Tel: 071-352 6071

K   †●   Keith Gretton, Unit 14, Northcote Road Antique Market, Battersea, London SW11. Tel: 071-228 0741/071-228 6850

KEY   ●   Key Antiques, 11 Horse Fair, Chipping Norton, Oxon. Tel: (0608) 643777

LAY   *   David Lay, ASVA, Auction House, Alverton, Penzance, Cornwall. Tel: (0736) 61414

LB   †●   The Lace Basket, 1a East Cross, Tenterden, Kent. Tel: (05806) 3923

LIL   ●   Liliana, Chelsea Antiques Market, 245/253 King's Road, London SW3. Tel: 071-352 5581/071-370 2979

A Corgi Chipperfield's Circus giraffe transporter, c1960, 4in (10cm) long.
£40-50   *HAL*

LR   ●   Leonard Russell, 21 King's Avenue, Mount Pleasant, Newhaven, E. Sussex. Tel: (0273) 515153

MA   ●   Manor Antiques, 2a High Street, Westerham, Kent. Tel: (0959) 64810

MAP   †●   Marine Art Posters, 42 Ravenspur Road, Bilton, Hull. Tel: (0482) 874700/815115

ML   ●   Magic Lantern (Josie Marsden), By George Antique Centre, 23 George Street, St. Albans, Herts. Tel: (0727) 53032

MSh   ●   Manfred Schotten, The Crypt Antiques, 109 High Street, Burford, Oxon. Tel: (099382) 2302

NA   ●   Nostalgia Amusements, 22 Greenwood Close, Thames Ditton, Surrey. Tel: 081-398 2141

NB   †●   Nicolaus Boston, Kensington Church Street Antique Centre, London W8. Tel: 071-376 0425/(0722) 326906

NCA   ●   New Century At Alfie's, 2nd Floor (S002), 13-25 Church Street, London NW8.

Nor   ●   Sue Norman, L4 Antiquarius, 135 King's Road, London SW3. Tel: 071-352 7217/081-870 4677

NP   †●   Neville Pundole, 1 White House Lane, Attleborough, Norfolk. Tel: (0953) 454106

OD   ●   Offa's Dyke Antique Centre, 4 High Street, Knighton, Powys, Wales. Tel: (0547) 528635

ONS   *   Onslow's, Metro Store, Townmead Road, London SW6. Tel: 071-793 0240

OSc   ●   Simon & Penny Rumble, Old School Antiques, Chittering, Cambridge. Tel: (0223) 861831

PBA   ●   Pryce and Brise, 79 Moore Park Road, Fulham, London SW6. Tel: 071-736 1864

PC   Private Collection

PCh   *   Peter Cheney, Western Road Auction Rooms, Western Road, Littlehampton, W. Sussex. Tel: (0903) 722264/713428

P(S)   *   Phillips, 49 London Road, Sevenoaks, Kent. Tel: (0732) 740310

PSA   ●   Pantiles Spa Antiques, 6 Union House, Eridge Road, Tunbridge Wells, Kent. Tel: (0892) 541377

P(O)   *   Phillips, 39 Park End Street, Oxford. Tel: (0865) 723524

RC   †●   Radio Crafts, 56 Main Street, Sedgebarrow, Evesham, Worcs. Tel: (0386) 881988

RdeR   ●   Rogers de Rin, 76 Hospital Road, Paradise Walk, London SW3. Tel: 071-352 9007

RE   ●   Ron's Emporium, 98 Church Lane, Sholden, Deal, Kent. Tel: (0304) 374784

RFA   ●   Rochester Fine Arts, 86 High Street, Rochester, Kent. Tel: (0634) 814129

An Art Deco advertising figure for Feather Light bicycle and motorcycle saddles, painted metal on a marble base, 11½in (29cm).
£40-60   *PC*

RGA • Richard Gibbon, Alfie's Antique Market, 13-25 Church Street, London NW8.

RO • Roswith, Stand F103, Alfie's Antique Market, 13-25 Church Street, London NW8.

RP • Robert Pugh, 2 Beaufort Mews, St. Saviour's Road, Larkhall, Bath. Tel: (0225) 314713

ROS • Roses, 60 King's Street, Sandwich, Kent. Tel: (0304) 615303

ROW • Rowena Blackford at Penny Lampard's Antique Centre, 31-33 High Street, Headcorn, Kent. Tel: (0622) 890682/861360

S * Sotheby's, 34-35 New Bond Street, London W1. Tel: 071-493 8080

S(AM) Sotheby's, 102 Rokin, 1012 KZ, Amsterdam, Holland. Tel: 31 (20) 627 56 56

SBA • South Bar Antiques, Digbeth Street, Stow-on-the-Wold, Glos. Tel: (0451) 30236

S(C) * Sotheby's Chester, Booth Mansion, 28-30 Watergate Street, Chester. Tel: (0244) 315531

SCO • Scot Hay House Antiques, 7 Nantwich Road, Woore, Shropshire. Tel: (063 081) 7118

SCR • The Scripophily Shop, Britannia House, Grosvenor Square, London W1. 071-495 0580

S(HK) * Sotheby's, 502-503 Exchange Square Two, 8 Connaught Place Central, Hong Kong. Tel: 852 524 8121

Sim * Simmons & Sons, 32 Bell Street, Henley-on-Thames, Oxon. Tel: (0491) 591111

SM • Stephen Maitland, Now & Then Telephones, 7-9 West Crosscauseway, Edinburgh. Tel: (0592) 890235/031-668 2927

SMA • Claire and Rosemary Smale, Alfie's Antique Market, 13-25 Church Street, London NW8.

S(NY) * Sotheby's New York, 1334 York Avenue, New York, NY 10021. Tel: 212 606 7000

Som • Somervale Antiques, 6 Radstock Road, Midsomer Norton, Bath, Avon. Tel: (0761) 412686

SP †• Sue Pearson, 13 Prince Albert Street, Brighton, E. Sussex. Tel: (0273) 29247

A Time is Money bank, Moore, by H. C. Hart & Mfg. Co., 5in (12.5cm) high.
£750-800 *CNY*

SRA †* Sheffield Railwayana Auctions, 43 Little Norton Lane, Sheffield, Yorks. Tel: (0742) 745085/(0860) 921519

S(S) * Sotheby's Sussex, Summers Place, Billingshurst, W. Sussex. Tel: (0403) 783933

STR • Strawsons Antiques, 39-41 The Pantiles, Tunbridge Wells, Kent. Tel: (0892) 30607

SWa • Stephen Watson, Alfie's Antique Market, 13-25 Church Street, London NW8. Tel: 071-723 0678

SWO * Sworders, G. E. Sworder & Sons, 15 Northgate End, Bishops Stortford, Herts. Tel: (0279) 51388

TAV * Taviners Ltd., Prewett Street, Redcliffe, Bristol. Tel: (0272) 265996

TBC • The Bramah Collection, PO Box 79, Eastleigh, Hants SO5 5YW.

TED †• Teddy Bears of Witney, 99 High Street, Witney, Oxon. Tel: (0993) 702616

TH • Tony Horsley. Tel: (0273) 732163

TOR †• Tortoiseshell (Pixie Taylor), Trebedw Guest House, Henllan, Llandysul, Dyfed, Wales. Tel: (0559) 370943

TP †• Tom Power, The Collector, Alfie's Antique Market, 13-25 Church Street, London NW8. 081-883 0024

VB • Variety Box, 16 Chapel Place, Tunbridge Wells, Kent. Tel: (0892) 31868/21589

VH • Valerie Howard, 131e Kensington Church Street, London W8. Tel: 071-792 9702

VS †* T. Vennett-Smith, 11 Nottingham Road, Gotham, Nottingham. Tel: (0602) 830541

WAL †* Wallis & Wallis, West Street Auction Galleries, Lewes, E. Sussex. Tel: (0273) 480208

WIL * Peter Wilson, Victoria Gallery, Market Street, Nantwich, Cheshire. Tel: (0270) 623878

WIN • Winstone Stamp Co., Great Western Antique Market, Bartlett Street, Bath, Avon. Tel: (0225) 310388/445520

WRe • Walcot Reclamations, 108 Walcot Street, Bath, Avon. Tel: (0225) 66291/63245

WW * Woolley & Wallis, The Castle Auction Mart, Castle Street, Salisbury, Wilts. Tel: (0722) 212711

YV • Yvonne Willcocks, K3 Chenil Galleries, 183 King's Road, Chelsea, London SW3. Tel: 071-352 7384

A Pye black plastic and chromed metal electric radio, modelled as a lady's handbag, with original label, 10in (25cm).
£220-300 *CSK*

Acknowledgements

The publishers would like to acknowledge the great assistance given by our consultants.

AERONAUTICA,	**Peter Card, Malcolm Welford,** *ADT Auctions Ltd,*
AUTOMOBILIA, RAILWAYS	*Prospect House, The Broadway, Farnham Common, Slough*
& SHIPPING:	**David Baldock,** *Chequers Garage, North Road,*
	Goudhurst, Kent
	Robert Brooks, *Brooks, 81 Westside, London SW4*
	Adrian Hamilton, *Duncan Hamilton & Co Ltd, The Square,*
	Bagshot, Surrey
	Malcolm Barber, *Sotheby's, 34-35 New Bond Street,*
	London W1
	Patrick Bogue, John Jenkins, *Onslow's, Metro Store,*
	Townmead Road, London SW6
ART DECO:	**Beverley,** *30 Church Street, London NW8*
POTTERY:	**Islwyn Watkins,** *1 High Street, Knighton, Powys*
ROYAL DOULTON:	**Tom Power,** *The Collector, Alfies Antique Market,*
	13-25 Church Street, London NW8
GOSS & CRESTED WARE:	**Nicholas Pine,** *Goss & Crested China Ltd, 62 Murray Road,*
	Horndean, Hants
MALING WARE:	**Ian Sharp,** *23 Front Street, Tynemouth*
EPHEMERA:	**Trevor Vennett-Smith, FRICS, FSVA, CAAV,**
	11 Nottingham Road, Gotham, Nottingham
FISHING:	**Jamie Maxtone Graham,** *Lyne Haugh, Lyne Station, Peebles,*
	Scotland
MONART GLASS:	**Frank Andrews,** *10 Vincent Road, Wood Green, London N22*
MILITARIA:	**Roy Butler,** *Wallis & Wallis, West Street Auction Galleries,*
	Lewes, East Sussex
MEDALS, BUTTONS &	**Jim Bullock,** *Romsey Medal Centre, 5 Bell Street,*
BADGES:	*Romsey Medal Centre, 5 Bell Street, Romsey, Hants*
ROCK & POP:	**Sotheby's,** *34-35 New Bond Street, London W1*
JEWELLERY:	**Valerie Howkins,** *39, 40 & 135 King Street, Gt. Yarmouth,*
	Norfolk
COFFEE POTS:	**Edward Bramah,** *PO Box 79, Eastleigh, Hants SO5 5YW*

INDEX TO ADVERTISERS

A Corgi mechanical Bedford, boxed, c1950, long.
£40-50 *HAL*

A switcher 0–4–0 steam engine, No. 1656, no lens, with bell tender 6403B, marked Lionel Lines, excellent condition.
£185-250 *JL*

11

 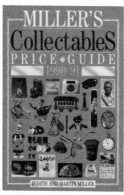 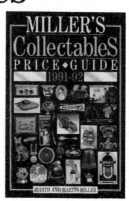

Introduction

The general antiques and art market has suffered another quiet year with objects in the middle price range being very slow moving. However, anything which is absolutely right, original and of good condition with a genuine provenance does not appear to have a problem finding a buyer. Neither for that matter does anything at the top of the market. There have been several good private collections offered for sale this year, notably the Zeppelin Collection featured in the aeronautica section. By the way, if you visit Frankfurt, Germany, we highly recommend a visit to the Zeppelin Museum. It is only a mile or two from the airport and staffed by descendants of the pioneer airmen.

Dolls have enjoyed a very good year, particularly German dolls, with the top German makers at last being recognised. The prices attained during the past year have shown that they are finally on a par with the top French manufacturers, a disparity which we have felt unfair for many years.

In our continuing efforts to bring you new collectable areas we have, amongst others, highlighted the less well-known, the unusual and a couple of as yet undiscovered collections, such as crisp and snack packets, which we can all start collecting now for free, as well as doing our bit for the environment.

Bicycle lamps, featured here for the first time, show a fascinating insight into the scientific development of vehicle lighting and they can be collected for a fraction of the cost of automobilia.

Following the success of our Coffee Making section in last year's Collectables, we have turned our attentions to Tea, showing both the history and development of tea making and the wonderful diversity of items that can be collected around a general theme.

Twentieth Century collectables do not appear to be affected by the current economic climate. Although pottery and porcelain have levelled off, there are still some undiscovered factories – look out for the 'Homemaker' series from the 1950s. Anything to do with films and television seems to be eagerly sought. Haute couture and fashion accessories have also been achieving good auction and sale results, but as with most things condition is paramount. Swatch watches are another example of how 'modern' collectables are already very popular, functional and, in some instances, valuable.

An area of quiet interest at present is waxed pictures, Osbornes, beautifully detailed and still available, affordable and surely undervalued.

As this, our fourth Collectables Price Guide demonstrates, we do take notice of your comments, so please keep writing to us and sending your suggestions, collections and comments, and finally, as always, good luck and good hunting.

Judith H. Miller

Aeronautica

The past 12 months have seen a gentle rise in both interest and prices of aeronautica. The Battle of Britain 50th Anniversary celebrations created considerable interest in aviation collectables and the market has been sustained by several good collections coming up for sale. The Kubis collection of Zeppelin and airship memorabilia was a unique selection of records, ephemera and documentation on Zeppelin design development and history. The Hindenburg items fetched remarkable prices, perhaps we will see a rise in airship disaster memorabilia to parallel the interest in shipping disasters.

A section from a Messerschmidt Me 109 tail fin, original blue grey camouflage, and a fragment from the Me 110 flown by Rudolf Hess, with plaque.
£600-650 *CSK*

A Second World War Luftwaffe bomber air crew white metal Pokal, inscribed I. Unteroffizier Jurgen Liedtke Am 2.10.42, 1939, 8in (20cm) high.
£550-600 *CSK*

A 10ct gold and enamel RFC pilot's wing brooch, 2in (5cm) wide. **£350-375** *C*

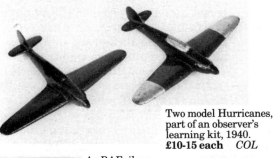

Two model Hurricanes, part of an observer's learning kit, 1940.
£10-15 each *COL*

An RAF silver condiment set, 1940s.
£45-50 *COB*

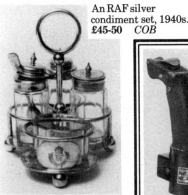

Two control column handgrips from Bf-109s, both with embossed plaques, 7½ and 10in (19 and 25cm) high.
£350-375 each

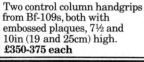

A pottery mug, decorated with an F-86 Sabre and the crest of 18 Fighter Bomber Wing, 4in (10cm) high. **£45-55** *C*

A gong formed from a Monosopape rotary engine, with mahogany mount, carved from a propeller boss, with hammer, 20in (51cm). **£120-150** *C*

A model five-cylinder radial spark ignition aluminium aero engine, 5in (13cm) diam.
£600-650 *C*

An Anzani full sized V-twin aero engine, crankcase No. 5435, believed to be c1912, 24in (61cm) wide including stand.
£1,600-1,850 *C*

An enamelled public house sign, The Old Airport, Wm. Hancock & Co., Ltd, some chips, mounted on wood, 44 by 35½in (111.5 by 90cm).
£500-550 *CSK*

Clocks

A Simplex alarm clock, by The Ansonia Clock Co., USA, with carved mahogany wings, plinth with brass plate engraved AIRCRAFT/1921/DEPOT/1926, 50in (127cm) wide. **£200-225** *C*

An oak cased RAF sergeant's mess timepiece, by T. W. Elliott Ltd., England, 1930, 14in (36cm) high.
£265-285 *CSK*

An RAF Operations Room sector clock, with painted dial divided into divisions, mahogany case with brass bezel, with fusee movement stamped 6160 Made by T.W. Elliott Ltd., England 1939, 18in (46cm) diam.
£2,750-3,250 *CSK*

Dress

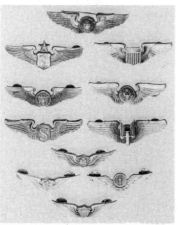

A black silk zip-up jacket, Marukin, by Kinjo Co., Okinawa, embroidered with a caricature and motto.
£330-350 *CSK*

A collection of 11 United States aircrew badges.
£100-125 *CSK*

A selection of flying boots, goggles and helmets, and a leather flying helmet mounted on a porcelain head.
£390-425 *CSK*

An RFC captain's tunic and forage cap with badge, and belt issued to Captain D. A. L. Davidson, MC, No. 9 Sqn., KIA 30.4.1917, aged 25.
£600-650 *CSK*

Ephemera

A selection of aviation postcards.
£1.50-4.50 each *COB*

A collection of 8 Biggles novels, by Capt. W. E. Johns, and 20 other aviation related novels.
£160-240 *CSK*

A collection of 27 aviation and flying text books and novels.
£385-425 *CSK*

Pre-war aviation magazines.
£5-7 each *COB*

A WWI RFC pilot's archive including log book, Training Brigade transfer card, Army form B 2079, RFC Graduation Certificate, Officer's Training Corps record sheet, F.S. Publication 34, personal photograph album, 'Cinquante Quatre' 1918 and 2 other books.
£3,000-3,500 *C*

A Luftwaffe camera gun with magazine, the tail section of a German 250kg bomb, a parachute flare and a Battle of Britain film prop gun.
£440-480 *CSK*

Instruments

A US Army Air Corps Link bubble sextant, model A-12, by Link Aviation Devices Inc. Binghampton, New York, 13in (33cm) wide, and a photocopy of an original instruction book.
£70-90 *CSK*

A programme for The First Aerial Derby, dated June 8th, 1912.
£145-160 *CSK*

A WWII period Luftwaffe flak battery range finder and tripod.
£310-330 *CSK*

A black crackle and satin chrome finish balloon theodolite, Hilger & Watts Ltd., and a balloon height indicator, each in mahogany fitted cases.
£210-250 *CSK*

Model Aircraft

A scale flying model of the Fokker DRI, Serial No. 152/17, built by H. T. Duffey, 49in (124.5cm) wingspan.
£500-550 *CSK*

A detailed scale flying model of the Supermarine Spitfire, Serial No. F2737, with single cylinder glow-plug engine, some damage, 82in (208cm) wingspan.
£770-850 *CSK*

This model is believed to have been built for use in a film, possibly The Longest Day.

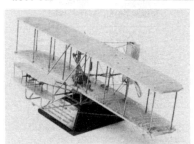

Three aluminium static display models, paint distressed.
a. BOAC Comet I
b. RAF Air Support Command Comet I
c. TWA Boeing 707.
£500-550 *CSK*

A hallmarked sterling silver and gilt presentation model of the Wright Brothers pusher bi-plane Kitty Hawk, 15in (38cm) wingspan.　**£3,550-3,750** *CSK*

A 1:72 scale aluminium model of the Mk I Spitfire, P9398, flown by Fl. Lt. Deere, 1940, by Doug Vaan, 6in (15cm) wingspan.
£220-250 *C*

A 1:36 scale aluminium model of James Capel's de Havilland Tiger Moth, Daily Mail London-Moscow 1989, by Doug Vaan, 9½in (24cm).
£330-360 *C*

A collection of 21 WWII period scratch built wood and metal model aircraft, in various scales.
£175-200 *CSK*

A plated mascot in the form of the Short Mayo S20/S21 Composite Mercury/Maia aircraft, mounted on a wood stand, 9½in (24cm) wingspan, and 3 others.
£245-280 *C*

A detailed static display model of the Pitts S2A, by F. E. Phelps, old damage, tail wheel missing, 15in (38cm) wingspan.
£250-280 *C*

A static display model of the BAC One-eleven super jet, in British Eagle Airways livery, with chrome stand and fitted carrying box, by Space Models Ltd., 44in (111cm) wingspan.
£600-630 *CSK*

A detailed ⅛th scale flying model of the Hawker Typhoon 1B, by D. Banham, 65in (165cm). **£770-820** *C*

Two ⅖ scale fibreglass models of the Supermarine Spitfires, mounted on mobile stands and with detachable wings, 144in (365cm) wingspan, Mk IA, Serial No. AR213. **£4,250-4,500** *C* Mk IIA, Serial No. N3192. **£1,900-2,000** *CSK*

A KLM travel agent's model, 1980s. **£45-50** *COB*

A stylised model of a Curtiss NC-4 flying boat, with brass decoration, lamp and switch by D.I.M., 15in (38cm) high. **£245-265** *C*

A travel agent's model, 1970s. **£30-35** *COB*

A detailed 1in:1ft scale wood and metal model of the Morane Saulnier Type N single seater fighter, as supplied to Nos 3 and 60 squadrons RFC, c1916, by P. Veale, Ditchling, 31in (79cm) wingspan. **£500-550** *C*

A Schneider wooden trophy, 1931. **£25-30** *COB*

A detailed brass model of the type 1402 Mk III radar aerial, on wooden mount, possibly ex W.D., some minor damage, 20in (51cm) wide. **£45-60** *C*

A chrome model of a Vicker's Viscount, 1950s. **£45-50** *COB*

Plaques & Medallions

A bronze medallion, embossed 'Lindbergh Medal of the Congress United States of America', and further embossed 'Act May 4 1928', 2½in (7cm), in plush lined box.
£165-190 *C*

A bronze medallion, the obverse with mythological representation of Bleriot's monoplane over Paris, signed E. Montagny, 2in (5cm), with non-original box. £110-130 *C*

A gilded bronze medallion, engraved 'Grande Médaille de L'Air 1927 Joseph Thoret', 3½in (9cm), with damaged original plush lined case.
£210-230 *CSK*

Posters

A gilded bronze plaque, engraved 'Au Lieutenant Thoret Performance la plus remarquable du Meeting de Vauville 1923', 4in (10cm) wide, with damaged original plush lined case.
£165-185 *CSK*

BEA, Fly Viscount, Muller-Brockman, offset lithograph in colours, minor tears, backed on linen, c1950, 51 by 36in (130 by 92cm).
£330-350 *CSK*

BOAC Stratocruiser Speedbird, lithograph in colours, printed by McCorquodale & Co. Ltd., London, minor defects, backed on linen, 24 by 37in (61 by 94cm). £640-660 *C*

Imperial Airways Argosy G-EBLF, English School, silk screen printed in colours, framed and glazed, 37 by 23½in (94 by 60cm).
£170-200 *C*

BEA Express Air Freight, lithograph in colours, by Harrison & Sons Ltd., London, tears and repairs, backed on linen, 40 by 25in (102 by 63cm).
£275-300 *C*

BEA, Forget Frontiers and Fly, lithograph in colours, minor defects, backed on linen, 1957, 40 by 24in (102 by 62cm).
£165-185 *C*

BOAC Speedbird, lithograph in colours, minor defects, backed on linen, 39 by 24in (99 by 61cm).
£385-400 *CSK*

BEA, Le Puy, lithograph in colours, printed by Publicontrol, Brussels, minor defects, backed on linen, 39 by 24½in (99 by 62cm).
£210-230   *C*

Air France, Proche Orient, Even, lithograph in colours, in excellent condition, backed on linen, 1950, 39½ by 24½in (100 by 62cm).
£165-185   *C*

Air France, Afrique Occidentale, A. Brenet, lithograph in colours, in excellent condition, backed on linen, 1950, 39 by 25in (99 by 63cm).
£250-275   *C*

Regie Air Afrique, F. Haudepin, lithograph in colours, printed by Fehrenbach & Cie, Paris, excellent condition, backed on linen, 31 by 23½in (79 by 60cm).
£250-275   *C*

An Air France travel poster, 1954.   **£15-20**   *COB*

Air Atlas, Renluc, lithograph in colours, in excellent condition, backed on linen, 1950, 39 by 24½in (99 by 62cm).
£150-175   *C*

Air France, Reseau Aerien Mondial, Plaquet, lithograph in colours, in excellent condition, backed on linen, 1950, 39½ by 25in (100 by 63cm).   **£220-250**   *CSK*

> **Cross Reference**
> Ephemera – Posters
> Shipping
> Railways

US Army, lithograph in colours, in excellent condition, backed on card, c1940, 34 by 25in (86 by 63cm).   **£385-425**   *CSK*

Air France, Amerique du Sud, lithograph in colours, printed by Perceval, Paris, creases and some repairs, backed on linen, 39 by 24in (99 by 61cm).   **£275-300**   *C*

Air France, Amerique du Sud, lithograph in colours, printed by Perceval, Paris, creases and some repairs, backed on linen, 39 by 24in (99 by 61cm).   **£275-300**   *C*

Two posters, Air France and Sabena.
£720-750   *CSK*

l. Afrique, Scandinavian Airlines System, reproduction in colours, printed by Aller Press, foxing, some small tears and repairs, backed on linen, 39 by 24in (99 by 62cm).
r. Air France, Orient, Extreme-Orient, Lucien Boucher, printed by Perceval, Paris, minor scratches, backed on linen, 39 by 24½in (99 by 62cm).   **£350-375**   *CSK*

A BEA fold-out poster, 1960s.   **£15-18**   *COB*

Prints & Paintings

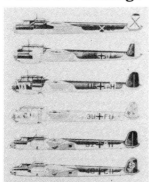

Constellation at Orly, Lucio Perinotto, signed, oil, 25½ by 36in (65 by 92cm). **£600-640** *CSK*

Dornier Do17, Dornier Do217 K2, Focke Wulf Fw 200 C-4, Junkers Ju 188 A and E, unframed, 16½ by 13½in (42 by 34cm), and larger original artwork by J. Doughty and 3 others. **£310-330** *CSK*

Hawker Siddeley Harrier, US Air Force, Avro Lancaster, Avro Manchester, Royal Australian Air Force, F.111-C and USAF F.111-A, unframed, 18 by 13in (46 by 33cm), and smaller by various artists, original artwork for Profile and other publications. **£160-175** *CSK*

Ju 88A.6 in readiness, Michael Turner, pencil, watercolour and bodycolour, signed and dated '85, 15 by 19in (38 by 48cm). **£530-575** *CSK*

Berlin-Johannisthal, Latham sur son Antoinette Passe au dessus de Berlin, Gamy, lithograph printed in colours, published by Mabileau & Co., Paris 1910, unframed, 35½ by 19in (90 by 48cm). **£165-185** *C*

1er Raid Paris-Bordeaux fait en six Heures le 3 Sept 1910 and Juvisy-Paris de Lambert sur biplan Wright-Aerial Magneto Lavalette Escmann, Gamy, lithographs printed in colours, finished by hand, published by Mabileau, Paris, 1909, unframed, 35 by 18in (89 by 45cm). **£390-420** *C*

The Airspeed Ambassador BEA Elizabethan class 'Zulu November' on take off, with her undercarriage half retracted, Gerald Coulson, signed watercolour and bodycolour, 21 by 30in (53 by 76cm). **£2,200-2,500** *CSK*

Two signed Keith Woodcock watercolours, with bodycolour, Ant 20 Bis reproduced in Aeroplane Monthly, August 1990, and Avro Lancaster of 61 Sqn. Skellingthorpe, 1944, reproduced on the book jacket of 'Avro Aircraft since 1908', published by Putnams. **£500-550** *CSK*

Spanish Conflict, Polikarpov I-16s and Fiat CR32, Spanish Civil War, Keith Woodcock, signed watercolour and bodycolour, September 1938, 10½ by 22in (26 by 56cm). **£220-250** *CSK*

Reproduced on the book jacket of 'Aircraft of the Spanish Civil War 1936-39'.

Allied Invasion – The Greatest Operation of its kind in History, Claude Page, signed and further signed and dated 1944, pencil, charcoal, and bodycolour heightened with white, unframed, 21 by 27in (53 by 68cm).
£330-360 *C*

Specially drawn for the Ministry of Information.

Rolls Royce, Frank Stratton, offset lithograph in colours, in excellent condition, backed on linen, 40 by 25in (101.5 by 63cm).
£385-410 *C*

Wilbur and Orville Wright, English School, silkscreen printed in colours, framed and glazed, 27 by 17in (68 by 43cm).
£220-250 *C*

A North American P-51D-10-NA Mustang on finals, Gerald Coulson, signed oil, 30 by 40in (76 by 101.5cm).
£1,650-1,850 *CSK*

Trimotor with classical figures, J. Cornelissen, oil on canvas, signed and dated 1928, 23 by 78in (59 by 199cm).
£880-920 *CSK*

Over the Alps, Dewoitine D.338, Keith Woodcock, signed watercolour and bodycolour heightened with white, 1939, 9 by 12in (23 by 30.5cm).
£420-460 *C*

Zero Encounter, after Robert Taylor, limited edition, colour reproduction, No. 338/1250, signed by the artist, and Joe Foss, Mar E. Carl, G. Ishikawa and Saburo Sakai, framed, 20 by 28in (48 by 70cm).
£250-275 *C*

Dawn Arrival, Fiat B.18V, Keith Woodcock, signed watercolour and bodycolour heightened with white, 1938, 9 by 13in (23 by 33cm).
£250-275 *C*

Dusk Arrival, Cams 53 Flying Boat, Keith Woodcock, signed watercolour and bodycolour heightened with white, 1935, 9 by 13in (23 by 33cm).
£210-240 *C*

The First of the Few, after Frank Wootton, colour reproduction, signed by the artist, and Alan Clifton, Jeffrey Quill, Arthur Rubbra and Sir Stanley Hooker, unframed, 26½ by 32½in (67 by 82cm). **£145-165** *C*

Propellers

A laminated mahogany two-blade propeller, the boss stamped 'DRG L5300 200 HP BR2 Salamander T.F.2 or Snipe G 623N67. D2780 6806 P2 G623.N67', 109½in (278cm) diam.
£880-920 *CSK*

A laminated mahogany two-blade propeller, the boss stamped 'DRG No. P 3033/11 R.R. Falcon 3 Bristol Fighter D2950 P2850 A4326 DFC/30', with painted metal leading edges, 116in (295cm) diam.
£1,450-1,550 *CSK*

A laminated mahogany two-blade propeller, the front of the boss engraved 'CRB Aug 1914 Nov 1918', the boss stamped 'Trevor Page & Co. Ltd., A208 D 2390 LP 160 HP Beardmore Armstrong Whitworth', the blades with manufacturer's transfers and calibration details, 115in (292cm) diam.
£420-460 *CSK*

A varnished laminated wood propeller, the boss lettered '110 HP Le Rhone 2300 Sopwith Aviation Co', 59in (150cm) diam, and 2 others.
£175-200 *C*

A single blade Everill laminated varnished wooden propeller, stamped DES 1/38A No. E37, ATC 593 by Everill Propeller Corp Lancaster PA USA, 38in (96cm) radius.
£100-125 *C*

A modern tinplate WWI twin-engined Gotha bomber, 15in (38cm) long.
£110-140 *C*

A modern painted tinplate WWI Fokker Eindecker fighter aircraft, 10in (26cm) long.
£75-100 *C*

A laminated mahogany two-blade propeller, the boss stamped 'IPC DG2366 D.2.4 P.2.05 HP 80 Gnome GW 35D 1910 Henri Farman', and bearing a transfer on each blade, 94½in (240cm) diam.
£725-775 *CSK*

Diecast & Tinplate Toys

Cross Reference
Diecast toys

A collection of 8 Tekno diecast toys.
£265-285 *CSK*

A pre-war Frog de Havilland 80A Puss Moth, with winding key, accessories and original box.
£275-310   *C*

A modern painted tinplate Fairey Swordfish torpedo bomber, by Tin Pot Toy Co., 14in (35cm) long.
£200-230   *C*

A lithographed tinplate clockwork single-engined cabin monoplane, with folding wings and battery operated port and starboard lights, one wheel missing, made in Germany, and an RAF fighter, by Wells o' London.
£200-230   *C*

A lithographed tinplate single engined clockwork airliner, made in England, and a clockwork aeroplane by Wells o' London.
£250-275   *C*

A pre-war Frog Interceptor Fighter Mark IV, with winding handle, accessories and instructions, in original box.
£100-125   *C*

<table>
<tr><td>**Cross Reference**
Toys – Tinplate</td></tr>
</table>

Trophies

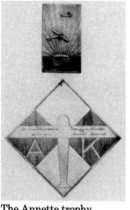

A modern painted tinplate Fokker DR1 single seater fighter, by Tin Pot Toy Co., 11in (28cm) long.
£100-125   *C*

A modern painted tinplate Avro 504K training aircraft, by Tin Pot Toy Co., 15½in (39cm) long.
£135-160   *C*

A bronze trophy depicting a man mounting a Pegasus, with description 'The Man, by the aid of his aeroplane, overcomes the attraction of the earth', and signed P. Moreau – Vauthier Sclp, and inscribed Susse Fes. Fondeurs Paris, damaged, 8½in (21cm).
£275-300   *CSK*

The Annette trophy, inscribed Sportsman Pilot Race, First Place Winner, pilot Benjamin Adomowicz May 29 1932 Floyd Bennett field, silver and gilt plated white metal, plinth missing, and a bronze plaque inscribed I.Zlot Do Inowroclawia Droju, and a silver metal plaque inscribed Biacom Adamouiczcom-Twyciezcom Atlantyku UX 1934 Aero Kub Krakouski.
£350-375   *CSK*

Ballooning

A bone ivory plaque of the French School commemorating the ascent of the Montgolfier Bros, Paris, 21 October 1783, 2in (5cm) diam, and a watercolour picture and a small oil on copper.
£310-340 *CSK*

Sadler's Balloon Ascent in 1811, English School, inscribed below, watercolour on vellum, signed and dated Parker '61, with inscription on reverse, 7 by 7in (17 by 17cm), Scientific Ascent of Mr. H. Coxwell London 9D 1862, gouache on vellum, signed with the initials R.G., inscribed label on reverse, framed and glazed, 5 by 8in (12.5 by 20cm), and 2 others.
£880-920 *CSK*

Second Happy Travel of Mr. Sadler between London and Nottingham, French School, gouache on vellum, signed and dated Ozanne, Lion 1830, framed and glazed, 7 by 10in (18 by 27cm), and 3 other prints.
£715-740 *CSK*

A representation of Mr. Lunardi's balloon, after F. G. Bryson, as exhibited in the Pantheon, 1784, by V. Green, aquatint by F. Jukes, with etching, published London 1785, unframed, 17 by 21in (43 by 54cm).
£250-275 *CSK*

Le Retour du Globe Aerostatique a Nantes le 6 Oct 1860, Mr. Gustave Lambert, M. H. Henderson, French School, watercolour over pencil, framed and glazed, 6 by 9in (15 by 23cm), and another.
£310-330 *CSK*

Monsieur Otto Lilienthal, Aeronaute, Berlin 25th June 1889, French School, gouache on paper, framed and glazed, 11½ by 8in (29 by 20cm), and 3 others.
£770-820 *CSK*

Montgolfier Balloons, English School, oil on brass sheet, one inscribed and dated 'Mr. Adorne 1784', the other 'Mr. Green 1845', 26½ by 18in (68 by 45cm). **£1,200-1,300** *C*

Francois Arban, French School, Aeronaut Professional Francais Expedition du bateau de secours, gouache over pencil, collector's label inscribed Saint Simon No. 60A, framed and glazed, 7 by 5in (17.5 by 12.5cm), and 4 other prints.
£600-650 *CSK*

Francois Arban lost his life after an ascent from Barcelona.

A handbill October 6, 1836
£75-85 *VS*

Mr. Gustave Lambert, Premiere Ascension Aerostatique du Ballon le pole nord exécutée le dimanche 27 juin 1860 ou profit de L'Expedition de Mr. Gustave Lambert, French School, gouache, framed and glazed, 7in (18cm) square, and 3 other prints.
£775-825 *CSK*

Zeppelins & Airships

A printed certificate, issued on board Hindenburg LZ 129, to certify an individual passenger's crossing of the International date line, 8 by 6in (20 by 15cm).
£185-210 *CSK*

An iron anchor from a WWI airship.
£375-465 *CSK*

A collection of menu cards and wine lists from Hindenburg LZ 129.
£1,800-2,250 *CSK*

A collection of airship, balloon and Zeppelin memorabilia, including an NSFK balloonist's badge.
£440-480 *CSK*

A porcelain part tea service from Hindenburg LZ 129, decorated in blue and gilt, with the Zeppelin-Reederei logo, printed mark for Heinrich-Elgenbein-Porzellan, and marked Eigentum Deutschen Zeppelin-Reederei.
£2,200-2,500 *CSK*

Graf Zeppelin LZ 130, a publicity brochure by Deutsche Zeppelin-Reederei GmbH, and various ephemera.
£950-1,000 *CSK*

A collection of original Deutsche-Luftschifahrt documents, papers and letters from the Kubis collection.
£2,900-3,300 *CSK*

Zeppelin-Weltfahrten, with frontispiece of Ferdinand Graf von Zeppelin, with foreword and history of balloon and airship construction, published by Zigarettenfabric Greiling A.G., Dresden, 1933-37, covers damaged.
£1,500-1,800 *CSK*

A porcelain commemorative bowl, by Heinrich & Co., the centre printed in blue with the Graf Zeppelin LZ 127 flying over the Bodensee, 7½in (19cm) diam.
£715-775 *CSK*

A pair of Zeiss 25 x 105 binoculars.
£550-600 *CSK*

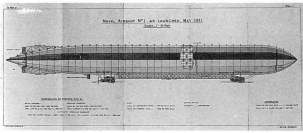

Naval Airship Nº1, as launched, May 1911.
Scale 1 = 24 Feet

A letter from Der Reichminister de Luftfahrt, Herman Goering, dated 3rd November 1933, expressing congratulations and warm appreciation to Kubis for his service and achievements on the occasion of the 50th Ocean crossing of Graf Zeppelin LZ 127, the original notepaper and envelope with watermark and early embossed version of the Luftwaffe emblem.
£330-350   *CSK*

Cross Reference
Ephemera

A collection of music sheets, Dr. Eckener Marsch von Richard Krauel Op. 17, and photograph of composer, dated 29.1.13.
£190-225   *CSK*

A steam driven airship with intrepid pilot racing a passenger train on a viaduct, mountains beyond, oil on board, framed and glazed, 22 by 19in (56 by 48cm).
£330-350   *C*

Four children's books.
£200-250   *CSK*

Handbook on IIM Airship, Rigid No. 9, issued by Airship Department, Admiralty, April 1918, original board, photographs, drawings and plans.
£200-225   *C*

Handbook on Rigid Airship No. 1, parts I and II, and Appendix 1913, issued by Admiralty, S. Branch, November 1913, Ref. S0281/13, original board, cloth, gilt photographs, drawings, and coloured plans.
£240-260   *C*

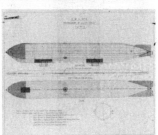

A collection of 11 ballooning and airship volumes and 18 aviation books.
£500-540
CSK

FURTHER READING
History of British Aviation, Brett R. Dallas, 2 vols. 1908-14 and 1913-14.
British Flying Boats and Amphibians, G. R. Duval, 1909-52. London 1953.
The Fighters: The Men and Machines of the First Air War, Thomas R. Funderburk, London 1966.
The History of Aeronautics in Britain, J. E. Hodgson, 1924.
Janes All the World's Aircraft — published annually.
Airmails 1870-1970, James A. Mackay, London 1971.
Combat Aircraft of the World, F. C. Swanborough, London 1962.
Aeromodelling, R. H. Warring, London 1965.

Americana

How to Hypnotize, c1930, 8½ by 11in (21 by 28cm). **£8-12** *AAM*

An Ambro type Civil War photograph, in original Union case, very fine condition. **£400-450** *AAM*

A copy of The New York Times, February 9, 1913. **£12-15** *AAM*

A pair of Wild West ceramic figures, c1940, 5½in (14cm) high. **£30-40** *AAM*

A Camel Cigarettes tin advertising sign, 10 by 20in (25 by 50.5cm). **£18-25** *AAM*

An oak barber's chair, with nickel fittings, by Token, restored but head rest missing, c1900. **£2,000-2,200** *AAM*

An Air King Bakelite radio, c1930, with original box. **£70-90** *AAM*

A Wild West cow girl figure, c1940, 13in (33cm) high. **£18-20** *AAM*

A Victorian 30-day mantel alarm clock, 10in (25cm) high. **£70-90** *ROS*

A Coleman's Ginger Ale tin sign, c1930, 12 by 24in (30.5 by 61cm). **£65-70** *AAM*

An arcade automaton, c1920s, 30in (76cm) high. **£350-400** *AAM*

A framed Chrysler advertisement, c1950. **£15-18** *AAM*

A Dexter cigars sign, 36 by 27½in (91.5 by 70cm).
£20-25 *AAM*

A Schlitz beer advertising light, 13in (33cm) diam.
£75-85 *AAM*

Two concrete door stops or yard ornaments, c1940s, 13in (33cm).
£120-130 *AAM*

An unused fruit crate label, 1930s.
£5-6 *AAM*

Children's Americana & Toys

A Westinghouse fan, c1920
£85-100 *AAM*

A Plasticville Diner toy, c1950, 9in (23cm) wide.
£22-25 *AAM*

The Diner is the most valuable item from the series.

> **Cross Reference**
> Toys

A child's tin rattle and a bell, c1950.
£6-8 each *AAM*

A child's 'clacker'.
£6-8 *AAM*

A National candy store cash register, only rings up to 90 cents, c1930.
£225-250 *AAM*

A child's tooled leather Western saddle, c1940s.
£65-75 *AAM*

This would be more valuable in the USA.

A pair of slippers, with original box, c1950.
£25-30 *AAM*

Money Boxes

Two money boxes, c1950, 6in (15cm) high.
£30-40 each *AAM*

A Pepsi-Cola clock, c1950, 15in (38cm) diam.
£125-130 *AAM*

Colas

A Pepsi-Cola tin advertising sign, 30 by 27in (76 by 68.5cm).
£45-55 *AAM*

A coin operated plastic musical money box, c1949, 6in (15cm) high.
£85-90 *AAM*

Coca-Cola

A Coca-Cola dispenser, 16in (40.5cm) high.
£85-90 *AAM*

Bubble Gum Machines

A Royal Crown Cola die cut advertising board, c1950.
£100-120 *AAM*

A Pepsi thermometer, 28in (71cm) high.
£30-35 *AAM*

A handbag mirror, engraved Coca-Cola, c1917, 3in (8cm) long.
£300-400 *AAM*

A gum ball machine with original gum, c1920, 16in (40.5cm) high.
£225-250 *AAM*

FURTHER READING
The Catalog of American Collectables,
Christopher Pearce, Mallard Press, New York.
Fifties Source Book, A Visual Guide to the Style of a Decade, Christopher Pearce, Virgin.
Vintage Juke Boxes, Apple Tree Press, 1988.

An advertising sign, c1940, 27 by 56in (69 by 142cm).
£200-250 *AAM*

Reproduction Coke trays from 1973, 6in (15cm) long.
£18-20 each *AAM*

An advertising board, c1940, 56in (142cm) wide.
£185-210 *AAM*

A cool box, c1950, 18in (45.5cm) wide.
£65-70 *AAM*

An advertising board, c1950, 50 by 30in (127 by 76cm).
£75-85 *AAM*

A cut out advertising sign, 30in (76cm) high.
£65-70 *AAM*

A salesman's training kit, c1960, 19in (48cm) wide.
£250-300 *AAM*

Coke miniatures, c1960, 1½in (4cm) high.
£6-8 *AAM*

A key ring.
£3-5 *COL*

A further selection of Coca-Cola is featured in previous editions of Miller's Collectables Price Guides, available from Miller's Publications.

American Kitchenalia

A toaster, c1950, 13in (33cm) wide.
£35-40   *AAM*

An ice crusher, c1930,
10½in (26cm).
£15-18   *AAM*

A plastic sieve, c1940,
4½in (11cm).
£3-5   *AAM*

Cross Reference
Kitchenalia

A flour dispenser, c1950,
7in (17.5cm).
£6-8   *AAM*

A Sunbeam
steam and dry
iron, c1950,
with original
box.
£25-30   *AAM*

Postcards.
£35-38
AAM

World's Fair

OFFICIAL SOUVENIR BOOK

NEW YORK WORLD'S FAIR 1939

Magazines, Railways.
£25-35
Pin-Up.
£15-20   *AAM*

Souvenir books, 1939.
£85-90 each   *AAM*

Borden's World's Fair
recipes.
£15-18   *AAM*

Salt and pepper shaker,
3½in (9cm) high.
£15-20   *AAM*

Automobilia

An Atlantis brass bulb box, c1920, 4in (10cm) diam, and a painted bulb holder, 4½in (11cm) diam. **£35-45 each** *BS*

A Victorian brass taxi horn, 16in (41cm) long. **£48-50** *ROS*

A Peugeot lithograph in colours, Leonetto Cappiello, backed on linen, 59 by 46in (149.5 by 116.5cm). **£550-600** *CSK*

A German Grand Prix poster, 29 by 19in (74 by 48cm), framed. **£240-260** *ONS*

A Dunlop printed zinc sign, 1913, 10½ by 36in (27 by 92cm). **£1,300-1,500** *ONS*

Le Mans, A. Galland, poster on linen. **£1,000-1,500** *ONS*

XVIIIe Grand Prix, Rene Lorenzi, 29th May, 1960, 12½ by 10in (32 by 25cm). **£510-550** *ONS*

Frank Clement was the company's first official works driver and a competitor in every Le Mans race entered by Bentley.

An Asprey's silver and gold slide action cigarette case, the inside inscribed 'From Bentley Motors Ltd., in appreciation of a great effort F. G. Clement 4th Grand Prix d'Endurance at Le Mans 18th-19th June 1927', hallmarked Asprey London 1923, 4in (10cm) high. **£3,000-3,400** *ONS*

A Lines Bros printed tin model of Captain George Eyston's Magic Midget, with original box and certificate, 15½in (39cm) long.
£760-840 *ONS*

A Rolls-Royce chromed car mascot, 5in (12.5cm).
£300-350 *BS*

Cross Reference
Tinplate Toys

Two signed photographs, Isle of Man, Hon. Brian Lewis winning in the Alfa Romeo, and Brooklands 1934 Whitney Straight in the Maserati.
£100-120 *ONS*

A Jep tinplate clockwork Delage racing car, with adjustable steering, plaster model of driver, and printed tinplate wheels, 18in (45cm) long. **£800-1,000** *ONS*

An Austin Motor Co., steelplate open pedal car, c1950, very good condition, 60in (152cm) long.
£1,800-2,000 *CNY*

A mahogany handmade scale model of an early 20thC motor saloon, 16in (40cm) long.
£28-35 *TAV*

A beechwood scale model of a DAV American truck, with handmade engine, fully fitted cab with individual living section, complete with separate petrol trailer, 101in (260cm).
£130-150 *TAV*

An album of motoring photographs Easter 1935-November 1935, containing many professional and some amateur photographs.
£1,500-1,800 *ONS*

When you ride ALONE you ride with Hitler !

Join a Car-Sharing Club TODAY !

Cross Reference
Posters

A war propaganda board, 28 by 22in (71 by 56cm).
£35-45 *AAM*

A further selection of Automobilia is featured in previous editions of Miller's Collectables Price Guides, available from Miller's Publications.

Art Deco

A WMF silver plated fruit bowl, c1930s, 12in (30.5cm) diam. **£85-95** *BEV*

A Sheffield silver plated tea set, teapot with ivory handles, 5½in (14cm) high. **£150-175** *BEV*

An English silver plated teapot, milk jug and sugar basin, teapot 7½in (19cm) high. **£100-120** *BEV*

A WMF fruit bowl, 14in (35.5cm) diam. **£250-300** *BEV*

A Harrods silver plated ice bucket, with liner, 5½in (14cm) high. **£75-85** *BEV*

A French silver plated bowl, 7in (17.5cm) diam. **£75-85** *BEV*

A Sheffield silver plated cake stand, with Bakelite stem, 9½in (24cm) diam. **£65-70** *BEV*

A Christofle silver plated vase, 16in (40.5cm) high. **£250-350** *BEV*

A silver plated fruit bowl, with 3 Bakelite feet, 9in (23cm) diam. **£45-55** *BEV*

A German silver plated fruit dish, 10in (25.5cm) diam. **£75-85** *BEV*

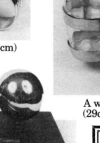

A chrome and marble inkstand, 14in (35.5cm) wide. **£85-95** *BEV*

A water set, with silver plated stand, 11½in (29cm) wide. **£85-95** *BEV*

A Danish silver plated dish, marked D & H, 9½in (24cm) wide. **£35-45** *BEV*

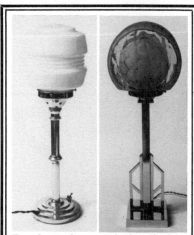

Two chrome lamps with glass shades, 18in (45cm) high. **£75-95 each** *BEV*

A silver plated dish, with Bakelite handle, 7in (17.5cm) square. **£40-45** *BEV*

Two Mappin and Webb silver plated bowls, largest 9in (23cm) diam. Large. **£55-65** Small. **£25-30** *BEV*

A WMF champagne bucket, 9in (23cm) high. **£150-160** *BEV*

A pair of Danish silver plated salad servers, in the style of Jensen, 12in (30.5cm) long. **£50-60** *BEV*

A chrome cake stand, with Bakelite handle, 8in (20cm) diam. **£55-65** *BEV*

A chrome tray, 14in
(35.5cm) wide.
£20-25 *BEV*

Three silver plated
ashtrays.
£22-25 each *BEV*

A silver plated ashtray,
4in (10cm) wide.
£22-25 *BEV*

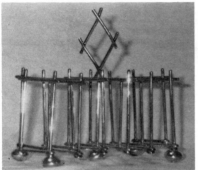

A silver plated
concertina-action toast
rack, marked with serial
number.
£35-45 *ROW*

A chrome bottle
opener, c1930.
£35-45 *BEV*

> **Cross Reference**
> Drinking

Two silver plated corkscrews, 1½ to 2in
£15-18 each *BEV*

A Mappin and Webb ice
bucket, 6in (15cm) high.
£65-75 *BEV*

A bell silver plate
cocktail shaker, with
Bakelite handle, 12in
(30.5cm) high.
£150-180 *BEV*

A chrome ashtray, 5in (12.5cm).
£35-40 *BEV*

A Sheffield silver plated fruit bowl, 7in
(17.5cm) diam. **£30-40** *BEV*

A cocktail set lacquered
in gold, red and black and
decorated with cockerels.
£30-35 *ROW*

A silver plated water
jug, 9in (23cm) high.
£55-65 *BEV*

A Mappin and Webb
silver plated sugar sifter
and cruet.
Cruet. **£40-45**
Sifter. **£45-50**   *BEV*

A Sheffield silver plated
vegetable or muffin dish,
with liner, by Yeoman,
11in (28cm) wide.
£80-120   *BEV*

A silver plated cocktail
shaker, American, 11in
(28cm) high.
£100-120   *BEV*

A silver plated coffee pot,
milk jug, sugar bowl and
tray, with Bakelite
handles, coffee pot 7in
(17.5cm) high.
£200-220   *BEV*

A silver plated ice bucket, 7in
(17.5cm) high.   **£45-50**   *BEV*

A Sheffield silver plated grape dish,
by Yeoman, 11½in (29cm) wide.
£75-85   *BEV*

A pair of chrome lights,
12in (30.5cm) high.
£85-95   *BEV*

A pair of chrome and
Bakelite nut dishes,
American, 8in (20cm)
wide.   **£20-25**   *BEV*

A St. James's silver
plated wine bottle holder,
8in (20cm) long.
£60-65   *BEV*

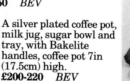

A German chrome ashtray, 7in
(17.5cm).   **£20-25**   *BEV*

A French silver plated biscuit barrel, 7in
(17.5cm) high.
£80-100   *BEV*

A chrome yacht, 12in
(30.5cm) high.
£45-55   *BEV*

Badges

Three Golden Shred Golly badges.
Round. **£1-2 each**
Figure shape.
£5-7   *COL*

Two Masonic badges.
Lapel pin. **50p-£1.50**
London District.
£5-7   *COL*

A Sandeman sherry badge, 1930s.
£9-12   *COL*

Three bowling badges.
Metropolitan Police
Bowling Association,
Cliftonville Bowling
Club and Jubilee Year
Kent County Bowling
Association 1961.
£4-6 each   *COL*

Football badges, Spurs
and Arsenal, 1940/50.
£6-8 each   *COL*

Speedway
badges.
**£2.50-3.50
each**
COL

A Boy Scouts lapel
badge, 1950s.
£7-9
Cloth badge.
£1-3   *COL*

Two badges, Pontin's and
Warner's.
£1-2 each   *COL*

A Donington motor
racing badge, 1970.
£2-4   *COL*

A selection of
children's badges.
50p-£1.50 each

Bakelite & Plastics

The word plastic comes from the Greek word 'plastikos' meaning to mould.

Some plastic substances occur naturally, for example: amber, horn, bone and tortoiseshell. Bois Durci is a mixture of woodflour and albumen, Gutta Percha is a resin from the palaquium tree and Shellac is a secretion of the lac beetle.

Chronology of Plastics:
- 1844 Hancock in England and Goodyear in USA perfected the vulcanisation of rubber by mixing it with sulphur. Vulcanite products appeared.
- 1862 Parkes exhibited Parkensine, made from cellulose nitrate, at the Crystal Palace International Exhibition.
- 1868 Hyatt Brothers in USA produced Celluloid from cellulose nitrate mixed with camphor. They developed the first plastics manufacturing techniques such as blow moulding, compression moulding and extrusion.
- 1907 Leo Baekeland produced phenol formaldehyde, the first truly synthetic plastic, which came to be known as Bakelite or oxybenzylmethylene-glycolanhydride. Compression moulded with fillers this gave the classic Bakelite mottled product, cast with pigments to resemble onyx, jade, marble and amber and came to be known as phenolic resin.
- 1924 Rossiter produced urea thiourea formaldehyde, marked as Linga Longa or as Bandalastaware by British Cyanides.
- 1933 ICI produced polythene.
- 1938 Du Pont produced nylon.
- 1939-45 War effort produced PVC, melamine, polyethylene, polystyrene and acrylic.

A miniature Bakelite penknife, in the shape of a sedan car, 2in (5cm) long.
£18-20 *GAD*

Two Bakelite night lights, c1930, 4 and 6in (10 and 15cm) high.
£20-30 each *GAD*

A phenol formaldehyde picture frame, c1930, 6½in (16cm) high.
£20-25 *GAD*

An American phenol formaldehyde and chrome cigarette dispenser, 1930s, 6½in (16cm) high.
£50-60 *GAD*

Three phenol formaldehyde lighters, French and American, 1930s, 3in (8cm) wide.
£15-20 each *GAD*

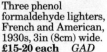

A carved phenolic walrus, c1930, 6in (15cm) wide.
£60-80 *GAD*

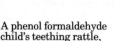

A phenol formaldehyde child's teething rattle, 1930s.
£30-40 *GAD*

Two French Celluloid corkscrews, c1930.
£6-7 each *GAD*

A phenol formaldehyde pen holder, c1930, 5in (13cm) wide.
£15-20 *GAD*

A Bakelite night light, c1930, 7in (18cm) high.
£30-40 *GAD*

A green phenolic resin desk set, made by Carvercraft, Hemel Hempstead, c1948, inkstand and letter rack.
£40-50 each
Blotter. **£20-25**
Ashtray. **£10-12**
GAD

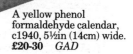

A yellow phenol formaldehyde calendar, c1940, 5½in (14cm) wide.
£20-30 *GAD*

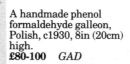

A Bakelite Lindenware ashtray.
£10-12 *GAD*

A handmade phenol formaldehyde galleon, Polish, c1930, 8in (20cm) high.
£80-100 *GAD*

A Bakelite miniature camera by Coronet, c1935, 2½in (6cm) high.
£50-60 *GAD*

A phenol formaldehyde majong set, American, c1930, 20in (51cm) wide.
£80-100 *GAD*

A urea formaldehyde and Bakelite ashtray, made by Roanoid, c1935. **£50-70** *GAD*

Cross Reference
Cameras

A phenol formaldehyde cigarette holder, in the shape of a St. Bernard dog, c1935, 6½in (16cm) long. **£20-25** *GAD*

A Celluloid locket, 1920s, 3in (8cm) high.
£25-30 *GAD*

A phenol formaldehyde paperweight, American, c1940, 3½in (8.5cm) diam. **£50-60** *GAD*

A Bakelite pipe stand, c1930, 7½in (19cm) high.
£10-12 *GAD*

A handmade phenol formaldehyde and perspex cigarette box, 5in (13cm) wide.
£30-35 *GAD*

A urea formaldehyde baby alarm, c1950, 7in (18cm) high.
£30-40 *GAD*

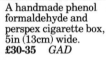

A Celluloid pin box with elephant, c1910, 3½in (9cm) wide.
£25-30 *GAD*

A Bakelite bowl on stand, c1930, 9in (23cm) diam. **£20-30** *GAD*

A French billiard table cleaner, c1920, 7in (18cm) wide.
£50-60 *GAD*

A pair of Bakelite candlesticks, by Lindenware, c1928, 15in (38cm) high.
£60-70 *GAD*

A Bakelite Coronet 3-D camera, English, c1950, 7in (17cm) wide.
£40-50 *GAD*

A Beetleware Edward VIII commemorative powder bowl and badge, c1936, bowl 4in (10cm) diam.
£20-25 each *GAD*

A Bakelite and chrome electric clock and night light, c1945, 21in (53cm) wide. **£200-250** *GAD*

A phenol formaldehyde Addison radio, Canadian, c1940, 10½in (26cm) wide. **£700-800** *GAD*

A carved phenol formaldehyde and elephant tusk ornament, Polish, c1930, 6½in (16cm) wide.
£60-70 *GAD*

A phenol formaldehyde and chrome candle holder, c1935, 8in (20cm) wide.
£30-40 *GAD*

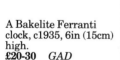

Cross Reference
Telephones

A Bakelite telephone, 200 series, c1935, 9in (23cm) wide.
£60-70
GAD

A Bakelite Ferranti clock, c1935, 6in (15cm) high.
£20-30 *GAD*

A Bakelite radio designed by Wells Coates, E. K. Cole model A75, c1940, 14½in (37cm) high.
£300-400 *GAD*

A urea formaldehyde clock and candlesticks set, c1927, clock 8in (20cm) wide.
£80-100 *GAD*

A phenol formaldehyde fish shaped barometer, American, c1940, 5in (13cm) wide.
£60-70 *GAD*

A Bakelite thermometer by Rototherm, c1970, 4in (10cm) high. **£10-12** *GAD*

A urea formaldehyde clock, German, c1928, 5½in (14cm) wide.
£40-50 *GAD*

A Bakelite Coca-Cola radio, sprayed red, c1948, 12in (31cm) wide.
£700-800 *GAD*

Cross Reference
Americana
Coca-Cola

Advertising

A urea formaldehyde Bathjoys stand, c1930, 10in (25cm) high.
£40-50 *GAD*

A Bakelite matchbox holder and striker, modelled as an Exide battery, c1935, 3½in (9cm) wide. **£40-50** *GAD*

A Smith's crisps sign, in Celluloid and marcasite, c1930, 5in (13cm) wide. **£40-50** *GAD*

Toiletries

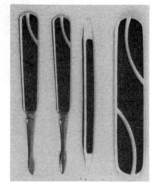

A Celluloid manicure set, c1930. **£20-30** *GAD*

A powder bowl made by Beetleware, with an impressed outline of Josephine Baker's face on the lid, c1930, 4in (10cm) diam. **£30-40** *GAD*

A selection of Celluloid combs, French and German, 1920s, 4in (10cm) wide.
£15-20 each *GAD*

Two carved phenolic perfume bottles, 5in (13cm) high. c1935, **£60-80 each** *GAD*

A phenol formaldehyde dressing table set, c1930, 11in (28cm) wide.
£60-70 *GAD*

A phenol formaldehyde shaving brush, c1935.
£15-20 *GAD*

A Celluloid manicure set, French, c1920, 8½in (21cm) wide.
£80-100 *GAD*

Bakelite table mats, c1925.
£20-25 *GAD*

A Californian Poppy perfume box with bottle, c1930, 3in (8cm) wide.
£25-30 *GAD*

Cross Reference
Toiletries

Household

Cross Reference
Kitchenalia

A phenol formaldehyde peg, c1950, 6½in (16cm) wide.
£20-25 *GAD*

A Bakelite sugar dispenser, c1940. **£8-10** *GAD*

A metalised Celluloid bottle opener, by Alfred Herbert, English, c1935, 4½in (11cm) high.
£30-40 *GAD*

A selection of Bakelite phenol formaldehyde napkin rings.
£10-12 each *GAD*

A Bakelite cake stand, English, c1935, 14in (36cm) high. **£25-30** *GAD*

A Bakelite lemon squeezer, 7in (18cm) wide. **£8-10** *GAD*

A set of 6 urea formaldehyde napkin rings, in a box, c1928. **£5-10** *GAD*

A shallow Lindenware Bakelite fruit bowl, c1930, 12in (31cm) diam. **£20-25** *GAD*

A Bakelite crumb tray and brush, 9in (23cm) wide. **£8-10** *GAD*

A plastic yellow and black Melaware cruet, c1950. **£10-15** *GAD*

A Bakelite flask by Thermos, c1927, 10½in (26cm) high. **£15-20** *GAD*

A yellow and green phenol formaldehyde cruet, c1935, 1½in (4cm) high. **£30-40** *GAD*

Bells

A set of phenol formaldehyde and silver plated fruit knives, English, c1930. **£8-10** *GAD*

A brass counter bell, 6½in (16cm) high. **£85-95** *BS*

A brass counter bell, c1900, 6in (15cm) high. **£110-120** *BS*

A rumbler bell, marked RW23, 19thC.
£120-130 *BS*

A large rumbler bell, in blacksmith made iron handle to form hand bell, marked RW28, by Robert Wells, Aldbourne, 18th/19thC.
£180-230 *BS*

A large rumbler bell, marked RW, late 18th/early 19thC.
£190-220 *BS*

A rumbler bell, marked RW30, 19thC.
£140-170 *BS*

A brass hand bell, 5½in (14cm) high.
£3-5 *RE*

Cross Reference
Horse Brasses & Harness

This bell was fitted with a blacksmith-made iron mount for fixing to a horse/oxen drawn wagon or cart.

A cast brass bell, plated, engraved A.M. 1940 below a crown, the mount stamped A.T.N. and a broad arrow, with clapper, 11in (28cm) high.
£1,200-1,500 *C*

A selection of rumbler bells, some marked RW, 18th/19thC.
£5-10 each *BS*

A servant's bell or team wagon bell, marked WC, William Cove, 18thC.
£50-60 *BS*

It is unusual to find a bell by this maker, and an unmarked bell similar to this would only be worth £5-10.

A wind up counter bell, on marble base, 19thC, 4in (10cm) diam.
£110-120 *BS*

A Victorian brass hanging bell, all original, 9½in (24cm) high.
£100-130 *RE*

Bicycle Lighting

Oil lamps specifically for bicycles and tricycles became commercially available in 1876, when the London firm of Salsbury patented a lamp that fitted inside the front wheel of an Ordinary (high wheeler) bicycle.

With the introduction of the equal sized wheeled Safety Bicycle in about 1886, oil lamps with parallel sprung rear brackets became popular. When the pneumatic tyre was economically manufactured and introduced five years later, oil lamps became smaller and neater in appearance and slowly but surely, cycling became more popular, particularly with the ladies. In consequence, manufacturers vied with each other to produce the most appealing novelties and some delightful and outrageous designs were produced.

By 1896 there were probably some 200 manufacturers of cycle lamps in the world and it was then that the first acetylene gas lamp was introduced. Called the Solar it heralded a wealth of calcium carbide fuelled lamps for the next 45 years.

Joseph Lucas produced the best quality lamps in this country with the companies of Powell and Hammer and H. Miller & Co., coming a close second. Lamps manufactured in Europe and America tended to be of a lesser quality but are well worth looking out for, even if only because of the fanciful names they gave their products to make them more appealing, like the Dandy, Little Darling and Boulevard.

A Coombes Brothers motorcycle or fore car lamp, built on cycle lamp principals, c1898.
£100-150 *PC*

An oil lamp, manufactured by H. Miller & Co., for Brown Brothers, c1895.
£40-50 *PC*

A Searchlight oil lamp, c1898.
£40-60 *PC*

An American kerosene lamp, designed to convert to a hand lantern, c1900.
£30-40 *PC*

A Midget oil lamp by J. Lucas Ltd., c1899.
£10-15 *PC*

A simple style hub lamp, manufactured from around 1876 to 1886, maker unknown, original condition.
£200-400 *PC*

A New Holophote nickel
plated oil lamp, with
correct brass name plate,
by J. Lucas & Son, c1898.
£50-80 *PC*

A safety bicycle oil lamp,
by H. Arthur Ward,
c1891.
£90-110 *PC*

A Plymouth oil lamp by
H. Arthur Ward, oil
reservoir missing, c1890.
£80-100 *PC*

A typical example of the
divided style hub lamp,
by Lucas, c1887.
£200-500 *PC*

An oil tricycle lamp, by
Rea Neale and Bourne,
c1880.
£100-150 *PC*

*Notice the absence of a
wick winder, it being
necessary to adjust the
wick with a stout pin.*

A safety bicycle oil lamp,
Invincible, by Salsbury,
London, damaged, c1891.
£100-150 *PC*

An Invincible oil lamp,
by Salsbury, with correct
side glasses and highly
polished lens, c1892.
£150-300 *PC*

A Perfecta acetylene gas
lamp, by Lohmann,
Germany, c1899.
£40-60 *PC*

A candle lamp, by
Riemann Bros, Germany,
c1901.
£150-200 *PC*

A Lucissime kerosene lamp, American, based on the patents of E. L. Williams.
£25-35 *PC*

An American sandwich style acetylene gas lamp, damaged, c1900.
£30-40 *PC*

An acetylene gas lamp, with water control valve, side jewels and deflector peak, c1909.
£50-80 *PC*

A late Victorian Neverout kerosene lamp, by Rose Manufacturing Co, U.S.A.
£20-40 *PC*

These lamps were imported but did not prove to be popular bearing in mind the high number of unused examples in existence.

A Carbo lamp, by H. Miller & Co., c1900.
£100-150 *PC*

The World Lamp, manufactured in Germany, c1904.
£80-120 *PC*

Catalogued between 1898-1910 and produced in 2 sizes.

A Luminator sandwich style acetylene gas lamp, by J. Lucas Ltd.
£200-400 *PC*

A Hine-Watt acetylene gas lamp, c1902.
£30-50 *PC*

A Lucas 'King of the Road' oil safety lamp, c1888.
£150-200 *PC*

A lamp by H. Miller & Co., c1911.
£60-90 *PC*

A King Holophote oil lamp, c1900.
£200-400 *PC*

A Burbury No. 2 oil
lamp, by J. Lucas Ltd.,
c1902.
£15-20 *PC*

*This model originally
sold for 2s 3d.*

A Solar acetylene gas
lamp, American, 1900.
£50-80 *PC*

A Microphote lamp,
designed by Augustine
Davidson for J. Lucas
Ltd., c1900.
£100-200 *PC*

A Searchlight sandwich
style acetylene gas lamp,
American, c1900.
£25-35 *PC*

An acetylene gas
motorcycle lamp, c1911.
£60-90 *PC*

A Horoscope oil lamp, by
Powell and Hanmer Ltd.,
c1903.
£25-35 *PC*

A Fairy oil lamp,
by Coombes Bros,
Birmingham, c1900.
£80-120 *PC*

A Dupee acetylene gas
lamp, with carbide in a
central compartment
jacketed by water,
American, c1898.
£40-60 *PC*

An American sandwich
style acetylene gas lamp,
c1900.
£40-60 *PC*

A cycle lamp,
manufactured in
Germany and inscribed
Ravenscroft and
Richards.
£20-30 *PC*

A Calcia Major lamp,
japanned and nickel
finished, 1928.
£35-45   *PC*

The Club Garda
acetylene gas lamp by
J. Lucas Ltd., with an ear
fitted to allow a red light
to shine to the rear, 1926.
£20-30   *PC*

A New Sultan acetylene
gas lamp, with rear
mounting adapted for the
Continental and Colonial
markets, by Powell and
Hanmer, c1922.
£50-80   *PC*

An original box for a
Lucas rear oil lamp,
1920s, soiled.
£8-12   *PC*

A Calcia Cadet lamp,
with acetylene gas rear
lamp connection beneath
the burner housing
valve, c1930.
£10-30   *PC*

A Radia acetylene gas
lamp, by J. Lucas Ltd.,
1914.
£25-35   *PC*

An oil rear lamp,
with box and
instructions for
use, by J. Lucas
Ltd.,
1920s.
£20-25   *PC*

A Colonia acetylene gas
lamp, by J. Lucas Ltd.,
with a deflector peak
fitted to the front rim,
1914.
£60-90
Standard model.
£35-45   *PC*

An unused oil lamp, with original
box, 1924.   **£20-30**   *PC*

A red reflector, boxed
and unused, by Lucas,
1920s.
£10-15   *PC*

Books

In forming a collection of rare books it is essential to remember that condition is everything. A modern first edition in fine condition with a pristine dustwrapper, can be worth 7-10 times as much as an equally fine copy lacking the dustwrapper. A fine signed limited edition of an illustrated book bound in a perfect morocco or vellum binding will be priced very much higher than a copy that is even slightly used.

Normally it is the first printing or edition of any title that is the most desirable, but with most authors some titles are much rarer than others, so the price varies accordingly.

For these reasons, it is extremely difficult to give a guide to the price of an individual volume. The very best way to start collecting is to browse and ask as many questions as possible, read and keep as many rare book catalogues as you can, and buy at a modest level initially.

Songs of Innocence, by William Blake, No. 41 of 51 facsimile copies, quarto, and Songs of Experience, No. 22 of 50 facsimile copies, quarto, with original wrappers, rebacked ex library, and modern slipcases.
£285-300   *C*

Breeches Bible, by Robert Barker.
£75-85   *HCH*

The Pied Piper of Hamelin, published by Oxford University Press 1962, 1st edition, with verse by Robert Browning, coloured illustration by Harold Jones, red cloth pictorially stamped in gilt, original dustwrapper, 10 by 7in (25 by 18cm).
£55-65   *BST*

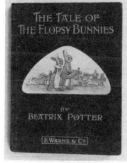

The Tale of the Flopsy Bunnies, by Beatrix Potter, published by Warne, 1909, 1st edition, with coloured illustrations by the author, dark green boards with coloured pictorial onlay, 6 by 4in (15 by 10cm).
£225-235   *BST*

Once in Royal David's City, published by Oxford University Press 1956, 1st edition, retold by Kathleen Lines, illustrated by Harold Jones, in original dustwrapper, 10 by 8in (25 by 20cm).
£55-65   *BST*

Fairy Tales, by Hans Andersen, published by T. C. and E. C. Jack, 1911, translated by H. Oskar Sommer, with 24 colour plates by Cecile Walton, black cloth pictorially printed in gilt, gold/black endpapers, front endpaper slightly chipped, 9½ by 7in (24 by 18cm).
£85-95   *BST*

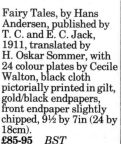

Travellers' Verse, published by Muller 1946, 1st edition, chosen by M. G. Lloyd Thomas, with 16 full page colour lithographs by Edward Bawden, colour lithographed illustrated cloth, 8½ by 5½in (21 by 14cm).
£55-65 *BST*

Chansons de L'ancienne France, published by Floury, Paris 1905, 30 woodcut illustrations by W. Graham Robertson, all coloured by hand through stencil and woodcut vignettes in black and white, 14 by 10in (36 by 25cm).
£225-235 *BST*

Four Tales from Hans Andersen, published by Cambridge University Press 1935, 1st edition, by R. P. Keigwin, illustrated by Gwen Raverat, 7 by 5in (18 by 13cm).
£38-50 *BST*

The Golden Cockerel, Zolotoi Petushok, by Alexander Pushkin, St. Petersburg 1907, with 8 pages of chromo litho illustrations by Ivan Bilibin, 13 by 10in (33 by 25cm).
£295-300 *BST*

The Book of Blokes, published by Faber and Faber 1929, by William Nicholson, with 32 pages of crayon portraits, 7½ by 5in (19 by 13cm).
£600-610 *BST*

The Hound of the Baskervilles, published by George Newnes 1902, 1st edition, by Arthur Conan Doyle.
£465-500 *C*

Aesop's Fables, published by Heinemann 1912, 1st edition, with introduction by G. K. Chesterton, 12 colour plates and 53 drawings in black and white by Arthur Rackham, green cloth pictorially printed in gilt, 8 by 6in (20 by 15cm).
£110-120 *BST*

Scenes Du Theatre Japonais, L'Ecole du Village, Hasegawa, Tokyo, 1900, Terakoya a historical drama in one act translated into French by Karl Florenz, 11 by 8½in (28 by 21cm).
£275-285 *BST*

The Cunning Little Vixen, published by Farrar, Strauss and Giroux, New York 1985, 1st edition, by Rudolf Tesnohlidek, illustrated by Maurice Sendak, 9½ by 8in (24 by 20cm).
£35-40 *BST*

The Story of Naughty Kildeen, published by Harcourt, Brace, New York, c1922, by Marie, Queen of Rumania and illustrated with drawings by JOB, coloured by hand, 13 by 11in (33 by 28cm).
£275-285 *BST*

The Lord of the Rings, 3 volumes, 1st by J. R. R. Tolkein, editions 1954-55, original red cloth dust jackets.
£2,400-2,500 *C*

Pinocchio, published by Saalfield Publishing Co., Akron, Ohio 1924, by Carlo Collodi, with coloured frontispiece, border drawings in green to each page, and many black and white drawings by Frances Brundage, 9½ by 7in (24 by 18cm).
£55-65   *BST*

Pinocchio, published by Garden City Publishing Company, New York 1932, by Carlo Collodi, with title and 4 colour plates and pictorial endpapers by Maud and Miska Petersham, 9 by 6½in (23 by 16cm).
£55-65   *BST*

November.

An Almanac of Twelve Sports, library edition printed on Japanese vellum, large quarto, 1897, 12 lithographed plates by William Nicholson.
£420-450   *C*

Punch Library of Humour, c1915, 25in (64cm) wide.
£140-150   *HEW*

Pinocchio, published by Platt, Munk New York 1940, by Carlo Collodi, edited by Watty Piper, 11 by 8½in (28 by 21cm).
£48-50   *BST*

The Rubaiyat of Omar Khayyam, by Willy Pogany, with 24 coloured plates.
£175-185   *BST*

Pinocchio, published by Italgeo Editrice, Milan 1944, by Carlo Collodi, with 12 full page colour plates, 13 by 10in (33 by 25cm).
£250-260   *BST*

Petrulus Hirrutus, published by Rutten and Loening, Frankfurt 1956, 1st edition, by Heinrich Hoffmann, 10 by 8in (25 by 20cm).
£100-110   *BST*

Winnie-the-Pooh, published by E. P. Dutton & Company 1926, by A. A. Milne, with illustrations by Ernest H. Shepard, No. 24 of 200 numbered paper copies signed by Milne and Shepard, original cloth backed pictorial boards, dust jacket, original box.
£530-560 *C*

A collection of 28 books in French and English including Cinq Semaines en Ballon, Collection Hetzel 1906, 1st edition, by Jules Verne, with 2 tinted wood engraved plates, illustrations, original polychrome cloth, spine slightly faded, De la Terre à la Lune, Autour de la Lune, 2 parts in one, Hetzel 1904, 1st edition, wood engraved illustrations, modern crimson half morocco by Sangorski & Sutcliffe, and Les Exilés de la Terre, J. Hetzel 1888, by André Laurie, with 22 wood engraved plates, illustrations, after George Roux, original polychrome pictorial cloth.
£300-325 *C*

The Novels, published by Dana Estes and Company, Boston, by Edward Bulwer, 26 volumes.
£1,000-1,200 *C*

A set of the Christmas Books, by Charles Dickens, all 1st editions in original cloth, comprising:
A Christmas Carol, 1st issue, Chapman & Hall, 1843, faded,
The Chimes, with vignette title in the second state, Chapman & Hall, 1845,
The Cricket on the Hearth, Bradbury & Evans, 1846,
The Battle of Life, 4th issue, Bradbury & Evans, 1846, and
The Haunted Man and The Ghost's Bargain, Bradbury & Evans, 1848.
£7,000-7,500 *C*

Illsée Princesse de Tripoli, H. Piazza and Cie., 1897, by Alphonse Mucha and Robert de Flers, No. 78 of 180 copies.
£1,250-1,300 *C*

My Man Jeeves, published by George Newnes 1919, 1st edition, by P. G. Wodehouse, and 4 others.
£330-350 *C*

The World Before the Flood, by James Montgomery, 3rd edition, 1814.
£500-525 *C*

Dickens Works, Library edition, Chapman & Hall, 30 volumes.
£825-850 *C*

Book Illustrations

Edward Ardizzone, 1900-79, Man yawning by his bedside, a pair, pen, black ink and pencil drawing, 4 by 3in (10 by 7cm).
£440-460 *C*

Ronald William Fordham Searle, b.1920, No Pets Allowed, signed twice, once with initials, extensively inscribed and dated 1953, 8 by 7in (20 by 18cm).
£600-630 *C*

William Heath Robinson, 1872-1944, The Everready Bedside Bomb Extinguisher, signed and inscribed as title and further inscribed For extinguishing incendiary bombs in the bedroom without leaving your bed, signed and inscribed on the reverse, pencil, pen and black ink heightened with white, unframed, 16½ by 13in (42 by 33cm).
£2,400-2,500 *C*

Donald McGill, 1875-1962, 2 illustrations, 'This Place gives me such an Appetite, I can eat Anything that's put on the Table' and 'My Husband never gets in till 5 o'clock in the Morning, What would you do? – Take me home to your place and I'll show you!!', both signed, inscribed on the reverse, pencil, watercolour and bodycolour heightened with white, 8 by 6in and 8½ by 6in (20 by 15cm and 21 by 15cm).
£990-1,000 *C*

Mary V. Wheelhouse, 1895-1933, 7 illustrations to Little Women and Good Wives, each signed and extensively inscribed, some dated 1911, pen and black ink and watercolour, 9½ by 6in (24 by 15cm).
£770-800 *C*

William Heath Robinson, When Tea as well as Sugar is Rationed an elegant Contraption for smart Occasions, signed and inscribed, signed and inscribed on the reverse, pencil, pen and black ink and grey wash, 15½ by 12in (39 by 31cm).
£2,800-2,950 *C*

Cross Reference
Ephemera
Autographs

Donald McGill, 'Be a Sport – Don't look while I'm dressing', signed, inscribed as title on the reverse, pencil, watercolour and bodycolour, 7 by 6in (18 by 15cm).
£700-725 *C*

Ronald William Fordham Searle, b.1920, Blood Sports at St. Trinian's, signed, extensively inscribed and dated 1954, with studio stamp on the reverse, pen and black ink heightened with white, unframed, 11 by 10in (28 by 25cm).
£2,000-2,150 *C*

Sir Max Beerbohm, 1872-1956, Portrait of Mr Robert Hichens, signed and inscribed, pencil, pen and black ink and grey wash, unframed, 12 by 7½in (31 by 19cm).
£1,550-1,600 *C*

Henry Mayo Bateman, 1887-1970, Teacher and Schoolmarm, a pair, each signed and inscribed to Mary Parker with best regards and To Mary E. Parker respectively and dated 1955, pencil, pen, black ink and watercolour, 9 by 5½in (23 by 14cm).
£880-900 *C*

Mark Boxer, 'Marc', 1931-88, A. J. P. Taylor, signed and inscribed, pen, brush and black ink, 11 by 8in (28 by 20cm).
£330-350 *C*

Victor Weisz, 'Vicky', 1913-66, Portrait of Stalin, signed, pencil, pen, brush and black ink, 12 by 9½in (31 by 23cm).
£245-260 *C*

DID YOU KNOW?
Miller's Collectables Price Guide is designed to build up, year by year, into the most comprehensive reference system available.

Bottles

A Gordon Straw Hat Dye bottle.
£5-10 *PC*

An American soft drink bottle, c1945, 8½in (21cm) high.
£8-10 *AAM*

A Club Soda bottle and contents, 1950, 8in (20cm) high.
£5-6 *AAM*

A hot water bottle, Combex, made in U.S.A. and England, c1950, 21in (53cm) high.
£40-50 *GAD*

Cross Reference
Americana

Three stoneware ink bottles.
£1-5 each *PC*

Cross Reference
Writing Accessories

Boxes

An inlaid mahogany box, the interior fitted to hold 12 glasses, containing 6, early 19thC, 10in (25cm) wide.
£200-300 *S(C)*

A brass cased veterinary bottle, 6½in (16cm) high.
£40-50 *BS*

Three stoneware pots, front centre is an ink well, the other 2 possibly used for wax or paint.
£2-8 each *PC*

A selection of stoneware bottles, possibly used for storing gum, washing blue and ink.
£2-8 each *PC*

A child's hand painted hat box, c1890, 7in (18cm) diam.
£40-60 *LB*

Cross Reference
Tea Caddies

A Victorian oak stationery cabinet, in the form of a pillar box, the interior with racks, 2 ink pots, and a drawer to the frieze, 14½in (37cm) high.
£715-750 *CSK*

A Victorian miniature oak pillar box, with a hinged brass aperture for letters, and a drawer in the base, 18in (46cm) high.
£1,850-1,950 *CSK*

A George IV rosewood, mahogany and brass inlaid travelling dressing case, the fittings hallmarked London 1822, with label inscribed J. Bramah and Sons, manufacturers, 124 Piccadilly, London, 14½in (37cm) wide.
£560-600 *P(S)*

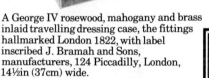

Cross Reference
Toiletries

A mahogany and brass bound lap desk, mid-19thC.
£180-200 *GAK*

A Bakelite box, with Aztec design on lid, 6½in (16cm) wide.
£30-35 *HEW*

Cross Reference
Bakelite

Button Hooks

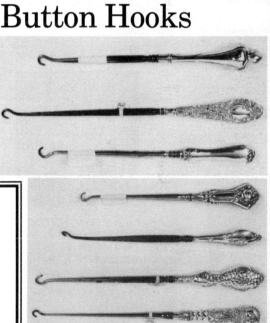

A selection of Victorian silver handled button hooks, 7 to 9in (18 to 23cm) long.
£22-40 *HOW*

A further selection of button hooks is featured in previous editions of Miller's Collectables Price Guides, available from Miller's Publications.

Buttons

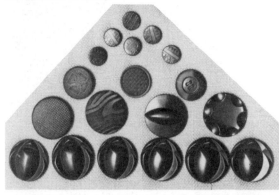

Enamelled flower buttons, late 19th/early 20thC.
£1-10 each   *AGM*

Dom/Corozo nut buttons, 20thC.
15-25p each   *AGM*

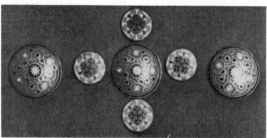

A selection of Continental enamel buttons, late 19th/early 20thC.
£1-10 each   *AGM*

Champlevé buttons with hand painted roses, late 19th/early 20thC.
£1-10 each   *AGM*

A selection of children's novelty and souvenir buttons, in wood, plastic, Celluloid and metal, 1930s, 40s, 50s and 60s.
15-25p each   *AGM*

Enamel buttons, early 19thC.
£10-15 each   *AGM*

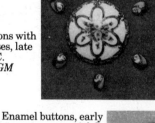

Brown and gold enamel buttons, with pearled enamel set into edge and blue enamel on back.
£1-10 each   *AGM*

Modern terracotta craft buttons.
15-25p each   *AGM*

Black enamel buttons with flowers.
£1-10 each   *AGM*

Continental silver buttons, on card.
£5-20 each   *AGM*

A white metal button, with hand painted enamel centre and paste edge, late 19thC. **£10-20** *AGM*

FURTHER READING
The Complete Button Book, Lilian Smith Albert and Cathryn Kent, London 1952.
The Collector's Encyclopedia of Buttons, Sally C. Luscomb, New York 1967.
Buttons for the Collector, Primrose Peacock, Newton Abbot 1972.
Buttons: A Guide for Collectors, Gwen Squire, London 1972.

A champlevé button, with hand painted centre, late 19thC. **£10-20** *AGM*

Stamped and tinted brass buttons, mounted in metal with japanned backs. **£1-10 each** *AGM*

A Shakespeare button, made to commemorate the 400th anniversary of the granting of the charter to the Corporation of Stratford, 1953. **£1-10** *AGM*

A selection of stamped metal buttons. **£1-10 each** *AGM*

Embossed Celluloid buttons with black tinting, and mounted in brass. **£1-10 each** *AGM*

Hand painted wooden craft work buttons, 1930s and 1940s. **15-25p each** *AGM*

Buckles

A Continental silver buckle, 3 by 2½in (8 by 6cm). **£25-35** *PSA*

A further selection of buckles is featured in previous editions of Miller's Collectables Price Guides, available from Miller's Publications.

Cameras

A mahogany box with tripod screw and camera mounting plate containing a quarter plate mahogany body and brass fitted folding camera, unmarked.
£1,100-1,200 *CSK*

The camera is mounted onto the box for use. The camera and 2 plate boxes are contained within the box.

A 4 by 6in (10 by 15cm) tropical Deck Rullo camera, Contessa-Nettel, Germany, with polished teak body, tan coloured leather bellows and trim and a Voigtländer Heliar 18cm f4.5 lens, film pack adaptor and 2 tropical double dark slides, in a Sands, Hunter & Co., fitted leather case.
£450-500 *CSK*

A 13 by 18mm Sola subminiature camera, Schatz & Sons, No. 666, with a Schneider Kinoplan f3, 2.5cm lens, waistlevel finder, sportsfinder, 2 film cassettes, in leather pouch.
£1,200-1,400 *CSK*

The Sola was patented on 29th October, 1934, and started sales in late 1938 or 1939.

A half-plate polished mahogany body Rover detective camera, J. Lancaster & Sons, Birmingham, with a brass bound lens with integral see-saw shutter and leather case.
£550-600 *CSK*

A 2 by 2½in (4.5 by 6cm) rollfilm Roland miniature camera, Plasmat GmbH, with a Rudolph f2.7, 70mm lens, in a rimset Compur-Rapid shutter, in maker's box.
£800-900 *CSK*

A 5 by 3.5mm approx. decoratively engraved camera disguised as a finger ring, with internal shutter, centre mounted lens, four-click iris diaphragm, internal film holder and Russian marks on back section.
£11,000-12,000 *CSK*

A ring similar to this is alleged to have been made for the KGB.

A Compass camera outfit, Le Coultre et Cie, Switzerland, comprising a 35mm Compass II camera No. 2931, with a CCL3B anastigmat f3.5, 35mm lens with focusing back engraved 'To Sir Bertram H. Jones. With the compliments of The Board of Compass Cameras Ltd.,' with accessories and fitted Compass pigskin case.
£2,000-2,100 *CSK*

A 3½ by 3½in (9 by 9cm) wet plate mahogany body sliding box camera with removable focusing screen and a brass bound lens with rack and pinion focusing.
£725-750 *CSK*

FURTHER READING
Subminiature Photography, White, 1990.

A 5 by 4in (13 by 10cm) Micro technical camera, with Schneider-Xenar f4.5, 180mm lens, a Schneider Tele-Xenar f5.5, 270mm lens, and 4 double book type plate holders, in canvas case. **£320-350** *C(S)*

A 2 by 4½in (5 by 12cm) stereoscopic binocular camera, W. Watson & Sons, with removable plate magazine section, engraved W. Watson & Sons 313 High Holborn London, Opticians, Patented in England and Abroad, in maker's fitted leather case. **£1,350-1,400** *CSK*

A 5 by 4in (13 by 10cm) tropical Improved Artists reflex camera, London Stereoscopic Co., with polished teak body, a Ross, London/Zeiss Tessar 7½₀, f4.5 lens. **£1,200-1,300** *CSK*

A 5 by 5in (13 by 13cm) mahogany body Transitional wet-dry plate bellows camera, with square cut leather bellows, a brass bound lens with rack and pinion focusing, brass lens cap, lens barrel signed Jabez Hughes, 379 Oxford St., London, No. 4101. **£1,800-2,000** *CSK*

Hughes was listed as a photographic apparatus manufacturer at 379 Oxford Street, W. from 1860-72, although his connection with photography predates this.

A quarter plate folding Frena camera, R. & J. Beck Ltd., with removable camera section and a Beck-Steinheil Orthostigmat 4¼in lens. **£290-320** *CSK*

A 5 by 4in (13 by 10cm) naturalist Graflex camera, Folmer & Scwing Division, Rochester, USA, with later two-position viewing hood and a Ross, patent Telecentric f6.8, 17in (43cm) lens, in a fitted leather case. **£950-1,100** *CSK*

The serial number dates the camera to c1918. The two-position hood was introduced in 1908.

A folding Ruby quarter plate tropical camera, Thornton Pickard, with Zeiss Tessar f4.5, 15cm lens, in teak and lacquered brass mounted case, with 6 wooden brass double book type slide holders, in leather carrying case. **£275-300** *C(S)*

A 5 by 5in (13 by 13cm) mahogany sliding box camera, J. B. Payne, Manchester, with removable focusing screen, wet plate dark slide, and a brass bound J. B. Payne lens, and a Thornton-Pickard roller blind shutter. **£1,300-1,500** *CSK*

> **Cross Reference**
> Photographs

A 2½ by 3½in (6 by 9cm) wood body camera body with lens mounting flange, c1910. **£45-50** *CSK*

A 35mm Alpa Alnea
model 5 camera, Pignons
S.A., Switzerland, with a
Schneider Alpa-Xenon
f1.9, 50mm lens, c1955.
£280-300 *CSK*

A 35mm Janua camera,
San Giorgio, Italy, with
San Giorgio Essegi f3.5,
5cm lens.
£725-750 *CSK*

*Approximately 3,000
units were made between
1948-51.*

A 35mm Nikon binocular
camera, Nichiryo
Trading Co., comprising
a 7 x 50 pair of binoculars
and combined 35mm
camera with a 165mm
f3.5 lens, in maker's case.
£275-300 *CSK*

A 1 by 1½in (3 by 4cm) rollfilm
Piccolo camera, Photo-Opera,
Paris, with simple meniscus lens,
pivoting stops, time and instant
shutter, direct vision finder and
close grained leather body covering.
£275-300 *CSK*

A 7 by 3½in (17 by
8.5cm) stereoscopic hand
and stand plate camera,
with red leather bellows,
polished wood interior,
wood ground glass screen
holder and a pair of
lenses set into a shutter,
retailer's label
J. Demuenynck-Racons,
Ostend.
£270-290 *CSK*

A 127-rollfilm Vollenda
camera, Nagel,
Germany, with a Leitz
Elmar 5cm f3.5 lens, in a
rimset Compur shutter,
in maker's leather case.
£150-165 *CSK*

A 2½ by 2½in
(6 by 6cm) Rolleiflex
f2.8 camera, Franke
and Heidecke, with
a Heidosmat 80mm
f2.8 viewing lens,
and a Carl Zeiss
Planar 80mm
f2.8 lens, set into a
Synchro-Compur
shutter, in maker's
leather ever ready
case.
£625-650 *CSK*

Canon

A 35mm Canon 7
camera, with a Canon
50mm f0.95 lens.
£575-600 *CSK*

A 35mm Canon S-II
camera, with a Canon
Camera Co. Serenar f3.5,
5cm lens, in maker's
leather ever ready case.
£180-220 *CSK*

A 35mm Canon NS
camera, Seiki Kogaku,
Japan, with pop-up
viewfinder, and a
Nippon-Kogaku Nikkor
f3.5, 5cm lens and cap, in
maker's leather ever
ready case marked
Canon and Seiki.
£3,400-3,600 *CSK*

*Approximately 100 units
were made from 1940-42,
with majority of serial
numbers ranging from
10800-11900.*

Kodak

Leica

A 116 rollfilm No. 1a Gift Kodak camera, with brown leather covered body, brown painted and nickelled fittings, Art Deco styled lens panel and baseplate, in maker's cedar wood box, with maker's stylised cardboard box. **£465-485** *CSK*

A 120 rollfilm Boy Scout Brownie camera, with green body covering, olive green paint and chrome styled front with Boy Scouts of America emblem. **£140-150** *CSK*

The 120 rollfilm version of the Boy Scout Brownie is extremely rare having been made for a short time in 1932. In that year Kodak introduced 620 rollfilm and the camera was changed to take the new film. It was then re-named the Six-20 Boy Scout Brownie.

Cross Reference
Art Deco

A 35mm black Leica M4-P camera, instruction book, passport and a Leitz, Canada, Summicron-M f2, 50mm lens and lens hood, in maker's box. **£650-680** *CSK*

A 35mm Leica copy camera, M. Olsztynski, Poland, with an E. Ludwig Victar f3.5, 5cm lens. **£350-375** *CSK*

A 35mm single wind Leica M3 camera, with a Leica Meter MC and a Leitz Summarit 5cm f1.5 lens, flange defective, in maker's ever ready case. **£450-475** *CSK*

A 35mm 24 by 24mm Leica copy camera, with a Cy Tillon f1.0, 50mm lens with top mounted finder, shutter speed. **£220-260** *CSK*

A 35mm Leica IIIc camera, converted to a black dial IIIf, with a Leitz Summitar 5cm f2 lens, in maker's leather ever ready case. **£180-200** *CSK*

A 35mm Leica IIIc camera, with a Leitz Elmar 5cm f3.5 lens, barrel engraved Luftwaffen-Eigentum, lacking vulcanite body covering, in maker's leather ever ready case, camera c1941, lens c1940. **£475-500** *CSK*

A 35mm black Leica M6 camera, in maker's presentation case, with instruction book, Leica passport and a Leitz, Canada bayonet-fit Summicron-M f2, 35mm lens, in maker's box. **£1,100-1,250** *CSK*

A 35mm grey body Leica IIIc camera, with a Leitz Summitar 5cm f2 lens. **£620-660** *CSK*

An experimental Mooly motor with an M-series baseplate fitting. **£1,750-2,000** *CSK*

A Reid & Sigriste Ltd., Leica copy 35mm Reid III camera, with a Taylor-Hobson Anastigmat 2in f2 lens, in maker's leather ever ready case.
£340-360 *CSK*

A 35mm black Leica M4 camera.
£725-750 *CSK*

A 35mm black paint Leicaflex 1 camera.
£1,150-1,250 *CSK*

The black Leicaflex camera is extremely rare. This is the second version with the round film counter.

A 35mm black Leica M4 MOT camera, with motor, lacks vulcanite, with AA battery pack, c1969.
£2,900-3,000 *CSK*

A total of 904 Leica M4 MOT and M4M were made between 1968-71.

A 35mm double wind Leica M3 camera, with a Leitz, Canada, Summilux f1.4, 35mm lens, black crackle finish spectacles and lens hood, in maker's leather ever ready case, c1954.
£1,500-1,650 *CSK*

This camera is from the first batch of Leica M3 and within the first 800 made in 1954. This example features the red slotted film rewind knob.

Zeiss

A 5 by 7in (13 by 18cm) tropical Tropica folding baseboard camera, with polished teak body, and a Carl Zeiss Jena Tessar f6.3, 21cm lens.
£2,500-2,600 *CSK*

The 13 by 18cm model is the rarest of 3 sizes made.

A 35mm Leica Ia camera, with a Leitz Elmar f3.5, 50mm lens, c1928.
£625-650 *CSK*

A 35mm dummy black dial Leica IIIf camera, with a removable dummy Leitz Summitar 5cm f2 lens.
£550-580 *CSK*

A 35mm chrome Leicaflex camera, with a chrome Leitz Summicron-R f2, 50mm lens.
£1,250-1,400 *CSK*

This camera was part of the first batch of Leicaflex cameras produced in 1964 and features the pie-shaped frame counter. The chrome Summicron lens is extremely rare: it is part of 300 of the first batch of lenses produced before production was standardised with a black anodised finish.

A 35mm Leica M2 camera, with lever rewind and a Leitz Summicron f2, 50mm lens, in maker's leather case.
£675-700 *CSK*

A 35mm twin lens Contaflex camera, with a Carl Zeiss Jena Sucher-Objective f2.8, 8cm viewing lens, and a Carl Zeiss Jena Sonnar f2, 5cm taking lens.
£775-800 *CSK*

FURTHER READING
An Age of Cameras, Edward Holmes, 1974.

Cinematographic Cameras

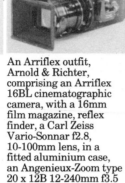

A 35mm Empire No. 3 cinematograph camera No. 41, W. Butcher & Sons Ltd., with polished mahogany body, with Taylor, Taylor & Hobson lenses, marked Prestwich Manfg Co., Tottenham, London, Patent No2102, camera with plaque Empire Cinematograph camera No.3. Manufactured by W. Butcher & Sons Ltd., Farringdon Avenue, London, E.C., in maker's fitted leather case.
£1,250-1,350 *CSK*

An Arriflex outfit, Arnold & Richter, comprising an Arriflex 16BL cinematographic camera, with a 16mm film magazine, reflex finder, a Carl Zeiss Vario-Sonnar f2.8, 10-100mm lens, in a fitted aluminium case, an Angenieux-Zoom type 20 x 12B 12-240mm f3.5 lens, on a tripod mounting, with accessories.
£2,100-2,500 *CSK*

A 16mm cine Kodak A camera, with black and polished metal body, hand crank and a Kodak Anastigmat f1.8, 25mm lens, in maker's fitted leather case.
£325-350 *CSK*

An Eclair cinematographic outfit, comprising 35mm metal body Cameraeclair camera, with reflex finder, 6 lens turret with Taylor-Hobson Cooke anastigmat Series 0 2in f2 lens, a Cooke Speed Panchro 28mm f2.8 lens, a Cooke Panchro anastigmat 40mm f2.5 lens, an Astro GmbH Pictorial Tachar f1.8, 75mm lens and a Ross Teleros f5.5, 240mm lens, the camera backplate engraved Syst,J. Méry Bté S.G.D.G., with Eclair electric motor, 2 handcranks, 5 Eclair 35mm camera film magazines, filters and copy instruction booklet, in a fitted metal bound leather case, c1933.
£300-325 *CSK*

A 35mm hand cranked, wood body Superb cine camera, with brass fittings, crank and 2 internal film holders, camera body stamped 51.
£340-360 *CSK*

A 16mm RCA sound cinematographic camera, type PR-25 No. 1156, with a Taylor-Hobson Cooke Cinema 1in f3.5 lens, on a 3 lens turret, crank and internal sound mechanism, in maker's fitted leather case.
£725-750 *CSK*

The camera is the world's first sound on film camera.

A 35mm Ensign cinematograph camera, Houghton-Butcher Mfg. Co., with black leather covered body, brass fittings, hand crank and an Aldis-Ensign Anastigmat 2in f3.1 lens.
£575-600 *CSK*

Lenses

A 16mm Bolex H16 Reflex camera, Paillard-Bolex, Switzerland, with a 3 lens turret, a Kern Vario-Switar f2.5, 18-86mm lens, filters and a Bolex H16-H6 Guide, in a fitted leather case, and a Paillard tripod.
£275-300 *CSK*

A Hektor 12.5cm f2.5 lens, E. Leitz, with front back reversible lens hood and scarce 'saucer' back cap, c1955.
£420-460 *CSK*

A Rollei-bayonet fit Magnar 4x lens, Carl Zeiss, with clip-on tripod mounting arm, in maker's fitted leather case, with instruction booklet.
£310-330 *CSK*

A prototype Carl Zeiss bayonet-fit Hologon f8, 15mm lens, and Hologon direct vision finder with built-in spirit level.
£2,750-3,000   *CSK*

The Hologon 15mm f8 lens became available in a bayonet mount for the M-series Leica camera in 1972.

A Leitz Contax-fit Thambar 9cm f2.2 lens, with nickelled Contax-fit mount.
£450-475   *CSK*

A Leitz Visoflex-fit Tele-Elmarit f2.8, 180mm lens, with integral lens hood and front and back caps, c1966.
£1,050-1,150   *CSK*

A prototype Leitz Hektor 120mm lens, in a 400mm Telyt-type mount.
£1,250-1,350   *CSK*

Magic Lanterns

A mahogany and brass body Cycloidotrope magic lantern slide with lacquered brass fittings, 2 by 3in (5 by 8cm) diam glasses, 2 sets of instruction leaflets, in maker's fitted wooden box with paper label, 11 by 5in (28 by 13cm).
£625-650   *CSK*

A mahogany and brass fitted biunial magic lantern with metal chimney, lacquered brass lens section with a pair of brass bound lenses, each with printed label E. H. Wilkie (late Royal Polytechnic), 114 Maygrove Road, West Hampstead and 3 slides, in fitted wooden box.
£950-1,000   *CSK*

A Lapierre metal bodied Salon magic lantern, with red, green, blue and yellow lacquered panels, lens, chimney and internal electric illuminant, with a quantity of hand painted strip slides, in maker's fitted box.
£200-250   *CSK*

A pressed and pierced metal magic lantern, with fluted chimney and lens, 11½in (29cm) high.
£160-190   *CSK*

Stereoscopes

A Negretti & Zambra mahogany body pedestal Scott's Patent stereoscope, mounted on a turned mahogany stand, stereoscope with plaque Scott's Patent Stereoscope, Negretti & Zambra, Cornhill & 11 Hatton Garden, London No. 185.
£560-600   *CSK*

E. E. Scott was granted patent No. 2581 on 3rd November, 1856, for Improvements in stereoscopes.

A Smith, Beck and Beck mahogany body table achromatic stereoscope, with a pair of focusing eyepieces and original mirror, 35 stereoscopic diapositives of French topographical views, in fitted wooden box.
£500-550   *CSK*

Miscellaneous

A burr walnut shaped Brewster pattern stereoscope, with hinged lid and a pair of fixed lacquered brass barrelled lenses and inset plaque Negretti & Zambra, Hatton Garden, 122 Regent St 59 Cornhill. **£140-160** *CSK*

A burr walnut pedestal stereoscope, with hinged top section, shaped eyepiece section, with stereo-positives of horses and horse racing subjects. **£550-600** *CSK*

A shaped wood hand-held stereoscope, H. Burfield, with hinged lid, rear glass screen and a pair of fixed, lacquered brass barrelled lenses and inset maker's plate, H. Burfield, 180 Strand, corner of Norfolk St. **£125-150** *CSK*

A metal red painted Flickergraph optical toy with viewing lens, handle, lid, one picture reel, printed paper labels 'For Use with the Animated Pictorial' and 'The Flickergraph daylight cine. British Made. Pat: App: For'. **£310-340** *CSK*

A cardboard body novelty Kodak advertising camera, with pop-up doll's head and opening drawer marked Kodak. **£425-450** *CSK*

A Polyrama Panoptique viewer, with diced green paper covered body, with 13 day and night views of various European scenes, 8 by 5½in (20 by 14cm). **£660-700** *CSK*

Zograscopes

A London Stereoscopic Co., 12in (30.5cm) diam black and cream painted Wheel of Life zoetrope, on a turned wood base, drum interior with printed paper label, with 9 coloured lithographic picture discs, 24 picture strips mostly with printed title, and printed label on the reverse. **£585-625** *CSK*

A mahogany body zograscope with 5in (12.5cm) diam magnifying lens and a mirror in a mahogany frame, with brass fittings, on an extending turned mahogany stand. **£575-625** *CSK*

Cross Reference
Signs & Advertising
Posters

Candlesticks

A pair of Victorian miniature brass chambersticks, 3in (8cm) diam.
£25-35 *MA*

A pair of Victorian candlesticks, with lobed square nozzles, by Rupert Favell, London 1885, 6in (15cm).
£400-430 *CSK*

A pair of Sheffield plate chambersticks, with seamed conical extinguishers, 6½in (17cm) wide.
£150-160 *HSS*

A French brass candelabra, 19thC, 13in (33cm).
£150-160 *ARC*

A pair of George II brass candlesticks, with knopped stems and petal bases, 7½in (19cm) high.
£400-425 *CSK*

A brass candlestick/table lamp, 12in (31cm) high.
£45-50 *WRe*

An early Victorian taperstick, with matching extinguisher, by Henry Wilkinson & Co., Sheffield 1841, 5½in (13.5cm) high.
£230-250 *HSS*

A pair of French brass candlesticks, 19thC, 10in (25cm).
£160-175 *ARC*

A George II silver taperstick, by James Gould, London 1736, 4½in (11cm), 4½oz.
£525-550 *P(S)*

A pair of German Art Nouveau pewter candlesticks, 7½in (19cm) high.
£150-175 *CSK*

A Canton chamber candlestick, with matching candle snuffer, chipped.
£300-350 *Bea*

A pair of late Victorian Corinthian column candlesticks, London 1895, loaded, 6in (15cm) high.
£425-450 *HSS*

A pair of French brass candle sconces, 19thC, **£150-160** *ARC*

Cross Reference
Oriental

Candle Extinguishers

Incorrectly known as 'candle snuffers' – snuffers are metal, scissor-like objects used to snuff out a candle – candle extinguishers are sometimes referred to as dousers and were an essential part of the 19thC home. No Victorian lady would be seen to actually blow out a candle, the extinguisher would always be employed with great delicacy and style.

Many subject matters were covered, as shown here, and quite a few of them were designed to raise a smile whilst being used. The clergy, in particular, were often the target of the manufacturers' jokes.

Most well known British ceramic manufacturers, notably Goss, Minton and Worcester, as well as many noted Continental factories, produced these highly collectable objects.

Mr. Punch, c1976, 4in (10cm).
£40-60 *TH*

Old Mr. Punch is very rare and would be worth about £2,000, but his dog is even rarer – Can you find one?

A hat, c1907, 3in (7.5cm) high.
£120-160 *TH*

Hats were originally made by Grainger's, then Worcester carried on after taking over their factory from c1890-1915.

Hush, c1976, 3½in (8.5cm) high.
£40-60 *TH*

The old models are easily recognisable with an arm behind the back, as they had been put together badly by the assemblers.

Worcester Budge and Toddy, based on characters from John Habberton's book, Helen's Babies, these children are trying on their grandfather's clothes, made until 1988, c1976, 4in (10cm) high.
£40-60 each *TH*

A parian extinguisher, c1870, 4½in (11cm).
£40-60 *CA*

Worcester young and old heads, c1976, 3½in (8.5cm) high.
£50-60 each *TH*

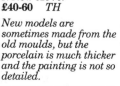

A Worcester mob cap, 1976, 3in (8cm) high.
£40-60 *TH*

A Worcester parian old head, not marked, 3½in (8.5cm) high. c1900.
£80-90 *TH*

The owl.
l. Old c1912.
£150-180
r. New c1976.
£40-60 *TH*

New models are sometimes made from the old moulds, but the porcelain is much thicker and the painting is not so detailed.

Three versions of Worcester French cooks, originally made by Kerr & Binns, c1925, 2½in (6cm).
£150-170 *TH*

Old mandarin, c1923, and Japanese lady, c1922.
£180-220 each *TH*
Modern mandarin and Japanese lady, 3in (7.5cm) high.
£50-70 each *TH*

The chopstick was changed to a mixing stick on the modern version because of the vulnerability.

The monk, 5in (12.5cm) high.
l. c1925. **£140-160**
r. c1976. **£60-80**

A Staffordshire frog, c1910, 2in (5cm) high.
£50-70 *TH*

A Copeland candle extinguisher with base, c1900, 4in (10cm) diam.
£100-120 *TH*

Old Mr. Caudle, c1893.
£120-150 *TH*

A Copeland bishop's mitre extinguisher, c1851, 5in (12cm) high. **£200-250** *TH*

A Goss Mr. Punch, with pearlised finish, c1900, 4in (10cm). **£120-140** *TH*

Three Continental extinguishers, 2 to 3in (5 to 7.5cm). **£40-100 each** *TH*

As with all ceramics, the condition is all important.

A Continental candle extinguisher, the top reverses to become a horse's hoof, 3½in (8.5cm) high. **£60-80** *TH*

Two Continental biscuit candle extinguishers, 3in (7.5cm) high. **£20-50 each** *TH*

A modern feather hat, c1976, 3½in (8.5cm) high. **£40-60** *TH*

A nun candle extinguisher for church candles, possibly Martinware, 4in (10cm) high. **£40-60** *TH*

Cruets

A silver plated cruet.
£18-25 *BGA*

A hand painted bird cruet, 1930s, 5in (13cm) wide.
£22-55 *BGA*

An American red and white plastic cruet, 4in (10cm) high.
£12-15 *AAM*

A foreign lustre cruet, c1930.
£12-15 *BGA*

Plastic Homepride pepper and salt pots, 3in (8cm) high.
£3-4 *PC*

A Shelley Dainty Shape cruet, 4in (10cm) high.
£65-75 *BEV*

Novelty pepper pots.
£4-5 each *HEW*

Carlton Ware pepper and salt pots, 3in (8cm) high.
£12-18 *HEW*

Foreign pepper and salt pots, 3in (8cm) high.
£10-12 *BGA*

A silver plate and glass cruet, 6in (15cm) wide.
£20-30 *BGA*

A Crown Ducal Chintz pattern cruet, 6in (15cm) diam.
£25-35 *BGA*

A Royal Norfolk hand
painted cruet, 1930s, 7in
(18cm) wide.
£20-40 *BGA*

A silver cruet, possibly
Indian, c1881, 6in (15cm)
high. **£150-180** *ROS*

A silver plated cruet, 6in
(15cm) high.
£40-50 *BEV*

A chrome cruet, in the shape of a guitar,
9½in (24cm) long.
£25-35 *BEV*

A foreign Brighton souvenir cruet, 8in
(20cm) wide. **£14-18** *ROS*

A blue and white cruet, Yuan pattern by Wood &
Son, 1930s, 6in (15cm) wide. **£20-25** *Nor*

A silver plated cruet, 1 to
3in (3 to 8cm) high.
£40-45 *FMN*

For further information on Cruets,
contact:
The British Novelty Salt & Pepper
Collectors Club
Coleshille
Clayton Road
Mold, Clwyd

CERAMICS

We have this year arranged our ceramics section for ease of identification as follows:

First we have listed factories and manufacturers that are clearly marked and then by areas that are collected, for example, cats and dogs, egg cups and ribbon plates.

The Art Potters, notably of the mid-20thC, the Art Deco period, continue to command top prices. It is worth remembering, however, that not everything marked Susie Cooper, Shelley or Clarice Cliff will be worth

fortunes. Top dealers are very choosey about the combination of the shape, pattern and colours used on a particular piece. This, of course, is good news as it enables us to start or add to our collections with less fashionable wares, and who knows, one day maybe they will become as sought after and hence as valuable.

Finally, there are a number of 1950s potters and manufacturers of household wares like 'homemaker' that are fast becoming collected, and although not ceramic – what about Melamine?

Barbola

A pair of candlesticks, 3½in (9cm) high.   £30-40   BEV

A pair of book ends, c1930, 7in (18cm) high.   £60-70   BEV

Beswick

The printed mark used from 1936 onwards is shown below. Beswick animals, particularly the wall mounted birds which only formed a small proportion of the wares produced by Beswick, are now most sought after. Their range of decorative household and kitchen ware has also appreciated noticeably in recent years.

Grouse, 6in (15cm) high.
£80-100   PC

An osprey, 7½in (19cm) high.   £40-60   PC

A magpie, lapwing and pigeon, 5in (13cm) high.
£20-40 each   PC

A set of 3 kingfishers, largest 8in (20cm).
£80-120   *PC*

A set of 3 swallows, largest 5in (12.5cm).
£60-80   *PC*

An eagle, 5 by 13in (13 by 33cm).
£60-80   *PC*

A woodpecker, 9in (23cm) high.
£30-60   *PC*

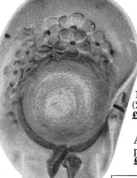

A wall vase, 1930, 10in (25cm) high.
£55-75   *MA*

A Double Diamond plaque, from a set of 3.
£130-150   *BEV*

Cross Reference
Signs & Advertising

Burleigh

A Pied Piper jug, c1930, 8in (20cm) high.
£85-95   *HEW*

A jug with squirrel shaped handle, 7in (18cm) high.
£50-60   *HEW*

A jug with parrot shaped handle, 7in (18cm) high.
£50-60   *HEW*

Clarice Cliff

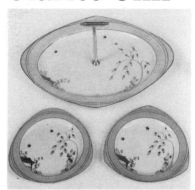

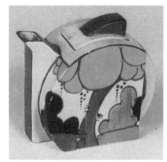

A Clarice Cliff,
Fantasque teapot, 5in
(12.5cm) high.
£150-200   *RE*

A Clarice Cliff sandwich set, with 6 plates,
c1939.   **£80-100**   *PC*

A Clarice Cliff Bizarre Aurea pattern bowl,
8½in (21cm) diam. **£75-85**   *PCh*

A Clarice Cliff
Rhodanthe pattern lotus
vase, painted with
orange, yellow and
brown on a cream
ground, factory marks
and facsimile signature
to base, 11½in (29cm)
high. **£235-275**   *P*

A Clarice Cliff Archaic
series vase, orange and
green ground with
orange lily, Fantasque
stamp to base, pattern
No. 374, 11½in (30cm)
high. **£500-600**   *TAV*

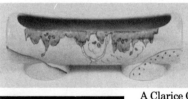

A Clarice Cliff posy
vase, 7in (18cm) wide.
£100-120   *HEW*

A Clarice Cliff, Royal
Staffordshire pottery,
Winston Churchill Toby
jug, with printed mark
and signature, numbered
118, 12in (30cm) high.
£660-680   *C*

Cross Reference
Commemorative
Toby Jugs

Devon ware

A Torquay cucumber dish, with cherry pattern, 10½in (26cm) wide. **£45-60** *JO*

A lavender bottle, 3in (8cm) high. **£20-30** *JO*

A Torquay mug, 3in (8cm) high. **£35-45** *JO*

Two inkwells, 3in (8cm) diam. **£30-40 each** *JO*

Cross Reference
Writing Accessories

A Watcombe tazza, 2½in (6cm) diam. **£15-20** *JO*

A plate, 7½in (19cm). **£45-55** *JO*

A vase with foot, 3in (8cm) diam. **£25-30** *JO*

A biscuit, cheese and butter dish, 8in (20cm) wide. **£95-110** *JO*

A Torquay chamberstick, 5in (13cm) wide. **£25-35** *JO*

An inkwell, 3in (8cm) diam. **£50-60** *JO*

A rooster hat pin holder, 4in (10cm) high. **£50-60** *JO*

Cross Reference
Hat pin holders

A Watcombe jug, 3in (8cm) high. **£35-45** *JO*

A vase, 4in (10cm) high.
£65-75 *JO*

A rooster plate, 6in (15cm) diam.
£45-55 *JO*

A rooster coffee pot, 8in (20cm) high.
£130-140 *JO*

A Dartmouth tray, 5 by 3in (13 by 8cm).
£15-20 *JO*

Crown Devon tea and coffee jars, 6in (15cm) high.
£5-10 each *ROS*

A jug, 3in (8cm) high and an ashtray, 5½in (14cm) wide.
£5-6 each *RE*

A plate, 6in (15cm) diam.
£45-55 *JO*

A cream jug, 2½in (6cm) high.
£15-20 *JO*

MAKE THE MOST OF MILLERS
Condition is absolutely vital when assessing the value of any item. Damaged pieces appreciate much less than perfect examples. However, a rare, desirable piece may command a high price even when damaged.

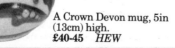

A Crown Devon mug, 5in (13cm) high.
£40-45 *HEW*

A rooster jug, 7in (18cm) high.
£140-160 *JO*

Carlton Ware

A fruit dish, 1930s, 10in
(25.5cm) long.
£40-50   MA

Carlton Ware
MADE IN ENGLAND
"TRADE MARK"

A set of 6 Guinness
advertising figures, an
ostrich, tucan, kangaroo,
tortoise, seal and a
drayman, Carlton Ware
transfer mark, 3½ to 4in
(9 to 10cm).
£210-230   WW

Salad items.   Bowl **£30-35**
Lettuce bowl **£15-20**
Gravy boat, without
stand. **£10-15**
Small bowl **£5-10   PC**

A vase, 5in (12.5cm) high.
£90-100   HEW

A leaf dish, 1930s, 9in
(23cm) long.
£15-20   MA

A black and white
powder bowl, 5½in
(14cm) high.
£65-70   DEV

A vase, decorated in
brightly coloured
enamels and gilt on a
lilac and black ground,
with the Devil standing
beneath a Wisteria tree,
printed mark in black
and numbered 0/797?
over 376, 6in (15cm) high.
£350-380   HSS

Doulton

The Detective, No. 2359,
1977-83, 9in (23cm).
£130-150 *TP*

Rosebud, No. 1581,1933-38, 3in (7.5cm).
£250-300 *TP*

The Waning of the
Honeymoon, George
Tinworth, c1910.
£700-1,200 *TP*

l. Bather, No. 597,
1924-38, 7in (17.5cm).
£350-450
c. Celia, No. 1727,
1935-49, 12in (30.5cm).
£550-650
r. Swimmer, No. 1270,
1928-38, 7in (17.5cm).
£550-600 *TP*

Vera, No. 1729, 1935-38,
4in (10cm).
£425-475
Gladys, No. 1741,
1935-49, 5in (12.5cm).
£350-400 *TP*

Blue Bird, No. 1280,
1928-38, 5in (12.5cm).
£220-250 *TP*

The Mermaid, No. 97,
1918-36, 7in (17.5cm).
£375-425 *TP*

Windflower,
No. 1939,
1940-49, 7in
(17.5cm).
£230-260 *TP*

Bunny, No. 2214,
1960-75, 5in (12.5cm).
£80-110 *TP*

For further information on Royal
Doulton, contact:
The Royal Doulton International
Collectors Club
Minton House
London Road
Stoke-on-Trent
Staffs

Gilbert & Sullivan figures.
l. Pirate King, No. 2901, 1981-85, 10in (25cm).
c. Colonel Fairfax, No. 2903, 1982-85, 12in (30.5cm).
r. Ruth the Pirate Maid, No. 2900, 1981-85, 11in (28cm). **£250-300 each** *TP*

A Doulton stoneware three-handled loving cup, decorated by Hannah Barlow, with silver rim, 6½in (16cm).
£325-350 *Bea*

A Doulton Series ware sweet dish, c1935, 8in (20cm) wide.
£35-45 *TP*

A Royal Doulton Dickens Series jug, Oliver Twist, 6in (15cm).
£70-80
PCh

Royal Doulton character jugs, Captain Hook, 4 and 6½in (10 and 16cm). **£200-250 each** *JL*

A Doulton Lambeth pottery plaque, painted factory mark and indistinct monogram, 13½in (34cm) diam.
£200-220 *CSK*

Goss China

William Henry Goss started producing parian statuary in 1858, but the Company is perhaps better known for the range introduced by his son, Adolphus, who joined the firm in 1883.

The Goss china models he introduced, with their coats-of-arms hand painted with meticulous care, were the forerunners of today's picture postcards. Almost every town in Britain had a Goss agent appointed to sell these as souvenirs to day trippers and holiday makers. The quality of these was excellent until the factory changed hands in 1929. From then, until it ceased production in 1939, the items produced were less carefully made.

For further information collectors are recommended to read *The Concise Encyclopedia and Price Guide to Goss China*, by Nicholas Pine, available from Milestone Publications, 62 Murray Road, Horndean, Hants. The definitive biography: *William Henry Goss, The Story of The Staffordshire Family of Potters who Invented Heraldic Porcelain* by Lynda and Nicholas Pine is also available from Milestone Publications and provides fascinating reading for those interested in the history of the family and the factory.

Fonts. **£50-150 each** and cottages. **£150-500 each**   *G&CC*

A Staffordshire tyg, with bear and ragged staff transfer decoration. **£15-20**   *CA*

St Ives church font, white. **£50**   *G&CC*

A League of Goss Collectors model, Cirencester Roman ewer, 1918. **£80**   *G&CC*

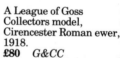

Goss matching crest models. **£30-45 each**   *CCC*

Assorted Goss models.   **£10-100 each**   *G&CC*

Examples of Goss from
all three periods.   **£20-200 each**   *G&CC*

Busts. **£50-150 each** and models with arms of
the nobility.
£10-20 each   *G&CC*

FURTHER READING
*The Concise Encyclopedia and Price Guide to
Goss China* and *The Price Guide to Arms and
Decorations on Goss China*, Nicholas Pine
(Milestone Publications), 62 Murray Road,
Horndean, Hants.
*William Henry Goss, The Story of the
Staffordshire Family of Potters Who Invented
Heraldic Porcelain*, Lynda and Nicholas Pine.

Pieces showing unusual Goss decorations. **£30-85 each**   *G&CC*

Busts of Sir Moses Montifiore, with and without hat.
£195 and £165   *G&CC*

A Goss coffee service in yellow.   **£230-280**   *CCC*

A Bournemouth bronze urn.   **£15**   *G&CC*

A selection of 1st period Goss.
£90-175 each   *CCC*

A selection of domestic ware with Goss transfers.
£35-65 each   *CCC*

A Rufus stone, with matching coat-of-arms.
£20   *G&CC*

The veiled bride.   **£950**   *G&CC*

A selection of Royal commemoratives.   **£20-50 each**   *G&CC*

Crested China

Many factories tried to emulate the success of the Goss factory in producing heraldic china in the early 1900s. The major ones were Arcadian, Carlton, Grafton, Savoy, Shelley and Willow Art. Standards were not so high, but the range of pieces produced was vast, including animals, Great War, buildings, figures, shoes and hats.

These potteries were mainly based in the Staffordshire potting towns around Stoke-on-Trent and most made their souvenir ware alongside tableware and sanitary ware!

Over the past five years the values of many crested shapes have increased in value, some far more so than Goss.

For further information, collectors are recommended to read *The Price Guide to Crested China* by Nicholas Pine, published by Milestone Publications, 62 Murray Road, Horndean, Hants. This contains the histories and marks for over 300 factories and lists every model recorded so far, together with over 1,000 illustrations.

A selection of wild animals.   **£20-90 each**   *CCC*

A selection of crested shoes.   **£6-20 each**   *CCC*

Arcadian crocodile.   **£75**   *G&CC*

A selection of traditional and national characters.
£10-45 each   *G&CC*

A selection of comical characters.
£65-175 each   *CCC*

A selection of crested figurines.   **£65-185 each**   *CCC*

A selection of crested statues.   **£25-80 each**   *CCC*

Carlton RMS Lusitania.   **£75**   *G&CC*

Two German ribbon plates, with colour scenes.   **£20-25 each**   *CCC*

A selection of sundials.   **£5-15 each**   *G&CC*

FURTHER READING
Crested China, Sandy Andrews.
The 1991 Price Guide to Crested China, Nicholas Pine (Milestone Publications), 62 Murray Road, Horndean, Hants.

A Mary Queen of Scots bed.   **£80**
and a selection of chairs.   **£10-25 each**   *CCC*

A selection of crested cats.   **£6-20**   *G&CC*

Leadbeater Art gate house, Stokesay Castle.
£150   *CCC*

Cross Reference
Ceramics – Ribbon Plates

A selection of teddy bears.
£20-30 each   *CCC*

World War I

A selection of war memorials.
£120-200 each   *CCC*

A selection of tanks.
£15-30 each   *CCC*

World War I submarine, E4 and E5.
£20-25 each
G&CC

An Arcadian British soldier.
£195-200   *CCC*

Cars. **£35-40 each**
Ships.
£45-95 each   *CCC*

A selection of WWI and a Boer War memorials.
£85-200 each   *CCC*

A selection of Red Cross vans.
£35-55 each   *CCC*

A selection of figures.
£80-150 each   *CCC*

Grays

Hancock

A coffee pot, 8½in (21cm) high.
£15-25   *MA*

A coffee pot, with blue and green stripes on a white ground, marked Hand painted Grays Pottery, Hanley England, second clipper mark, c1930, serial No. 4375 E, possibly designed by Susie Cooper, 8in (20cm) high.
£65-75   *ROW*

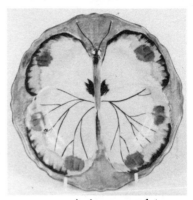

An ivory ware plate, c1930, 8½in (21cm) diam.
£35-40   *HEW*

| **Cross Reference** |
| Lighting |

A table light base.
£100-120   *HEW*

A Coronaware Cremorne hand painted bowl, 8in (20cm) diam.
£130-150   *PC*

A Rubeno ware jug, hand painted with pomegranates, 5in (13cm) high.
£70-80   *PC*

A hand painted bowl, F. X. Abraham, 8in (20cm) diam.
£150-160   *PC*

Maling Ware

A set of bridge ashtrays,
c1935.
£180-200 *IS*

A vase, 6in (15cm) high.
£65-75 *HEW*

A green lustre vase, with
pink flowers, 8in (20cm)
high.
£60-70 *BEV*

A bowl, 8in (20cm) diam.
£100-120 *HEW*

A Hayton Hunt jug,
modelled by William
Bradley, c1935, 9½in
(24cm) high.
£350-450 *IS*

*These jugs were used by
the Haydon Hunt,
Northumberland, of
which C. T. Maling was
Master.*

Lady Nicotine, a rare
figure, modelled by
Norman Carling, c1938,
6½in (16cm).
£600-800 *IS*

DID YOU KNOW?
Miller's Collectables
Price Guide is
designed to build up,
year by year, into the
most comprehensive
reference system
available.

FURTHER READING
Maling, The Trade Mark of Excellence, Steven
Moore, Tyne & Wear Museum Services, 1989.

Moorcroft

William Moorcroft initially worked for James MacIntyre & Co., and by 1898 was in charge of the Art Pottery Department. In 1904 he was awarded his first Gold Medal, but in 1913 MacIntyre's Art Pottery Department closed and he set up his own business at Cobridge where he worked until his son joined the Company in 1937. William Moorcroft died in 1945 aged 73, but his son, Walter Moorcroft continued making pottery until 1986. Despite financial problems the Company continues today.

A vase, with blue-green and pink forget-me-nots and poppies, printed mark and painted signature, glaze cracks, c1908, 8½in (21cm) high.
£775-800   *WIL*

A vase, painted with the Grape and Leaf pattern in colours on a blue ground, impressed marks and green signature, 9½in (24cm) high.
£325-350   *C(S)*

A bowl, designed for Tiffany and Co, with green trailing vine and blue grapes, on a pale yellow ground, covered in a lustrous glaze, signed in green W. Moorcroft, Tiffany & Co., c1908, 7½in (19cm).
£800-850   *S*

A Columbine bottle vase, with parchment ground rising to a mottled brown and covered in a semi-lustrous glaze, impressed W. Moorcroft signature and Royal Warrant, W.M. monogram painted in blue, c1949, 12½in (31cm).
£550-600   *S*

A Duck pilot plate, in blue, pink, brown and grey on a white ground, impressed factory mark with facsimile signature, and large printed paper Royal Warrant label, c1936, 10in (25cm) diam.
£850-900   *S*

Only two examples of this dish have been recorded.

A Blue Finch vase, 1990, 12in (30.5cm) high.
£350-375   *NP*

A banded Pomegranate vase, impressed Moorcroft Made in England, and signed in blue W. Moorcroft, c1925, 10½in (26cm). **£1,000-1,100** *S*

A Florian Ware jardinière, blue and green on a white printed ground, chipped and cracked, Florian Ware mark and signed W. Moorcroft des, c1903, 9in (23cm). **£500-550** *S*

A Florian bowl, in blue, green, mauve and yellow, 3 restored cracks, signed W. Moorcroft, impressed Moorcroft Burslem and shape number, c1919, 13in (33cm) diam. **£1,000-1,100** *S*

A MacIntyre Pomppeiian bowl, pattern, c1907,12in (30.5cm) diam. **£950-1,000** *NP*

A fruit bowl, impressed Moorcroft, and signed,10in (24.5cm) **£500-550** *HSS*

A Penguin plate, limited edition of 150, 1989, 10in (25.5cm). **£75-100** *NP*

A MacIntyre Flamminian vase, made for Liberty's, c1905, 5in (12.5cm). **£200-250** *NP*

A Big Poppy vase, with polished pewter rim, made for Liberty's, c1925, 5½in (13.5cm) high. **£300-325** *NP*

For further information on Moorcroft, contact:
Moorcroft Collectors Club
W. Moorcroft plc
Sandbach Road
Burslem
Stoke-on-Trent

A MacIntyre sugar basin, c1898, 5in (12.5cm) diam. **£250-275** *NP*

A Dandelion vase, limited edition of 250, 1991, 5in (12.5cm). **£95-125** *NP*

A Spring Flowers vase, c1955, 7½in (19cm) high. **£300-350** *NP*

Poole Pottery

A lamp base, 10in (25.5cm). **£50-70** *MA*

Two vases, 3½in (9cm). **£90-120 each** *JO*

A jug, with green decoration, 4in (10cm). **£145-165** *JO*

Rhead

A Charlotte Rhead charger, c1920, 17in (43cm) diam. **£400-450** *RO*

A Charlotte Rhead vase, 5½in (14cm) **£120-150** *HEW*

Radford ware

Like his father before him, Edward Radford joined the Pilkington Pottery and worked there until after WWI when he joined Messrs H. J. Wood Ltd. By 1930 he had left Wood and soon started his own business at Burslem, Staffordshire, the Radford Handcraft Pottery.

A wide range of pretty designs, usually floral, employing a technique of fusing the colours into the thin glaze were produced until about WWII. Edward Radford left Burslem after the war and ran a holiday home until his death in 1968.

Radford ware is easily recognised, very collectable and quite common. It is underpriced by some standards at present and certainly is an area to watch in the future.

A vase, with anemone pattern, 5½in (12.5cm) high. **£20-30** *BEV*

An anemone pattern jug, c1930, 9in (23cm). **£65-85** *MA*

A jug and a basket, hand painted with anemone design, c1935. **£80-100 each** *MA*

A group of Butterfly ware jugs, relief moulded with flowers and butterflies on a rocky ground, c1930. **£50-100** *MA*

An early Burslem vase, c1930, 8in (20cm). **£45-65** *MA*

An early Burslem jug, c1930, 13in (33cm). **£100-120** *MA*

A posy vase, painted with anemones, 1930s, 9in (23cm) diam.
£50-60 *MA*

A cream jug, sugar basin and vase; 1930s. **£20-40 each** *MA*

A 1930s vase, 4½in (11cm).
£35-55 *MA*

An early Burslem vase, 1930s, 6in (15cm) high.
£40-60 *MA*

A selection of posy vases, 5½in (14cm) high. **£15-25** *MA*

An early Burslem vase, 1930s, 5in (12.5cm) high.
£45-65 *MA*

A 1930s vase, with strawberry pattern, 10in (25.5cm). **£30-40** *MA*

An Indian Tree pattern vase, with vivid palette high glaze, c1930.
£90-120 *MA*

A vase, with pale green flowers, 5½in (14cm) high.
£65-75 *BEV*

An early Burslem Poppy jug, c1930. **£35-55** *MA*

A bonbon basket, 1930s, 8in (20cm) long.
£25-35 *MA*

A wall vase, c1930, 9in (23cm) high. **£90-120** *MA*

An early Burslem vase, damaged, c1930, 4½in (11cm) high.
£30-40 if perfect *MA*

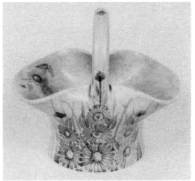

A basket, with Made in Great Britain back stamp, c1930, 5½in (14cm) high.
£35-55 *MA*

A posy vase, c1930, 5½in (14cm) diam. **£25-35** *MA*

A jug, hand painted with anemones, 10in (25.5cm).
£55-65 *BEV*

An early Burslem two-handled vase, with stylised tulips and silver lustre, c1930, 7in (17.5cm). **£80-100** *MA*

A selection of hand painted wall pockets, post-1940, 7½in (19cm).
£40-80 each *MA*

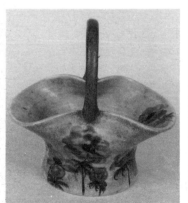

An anemone pattern basket, c1930, 8in (20cm) high.
£45-55 *MA*

An early Burslem hand thrown vase, 7in (17cm) high. **£45-65** *MA*

97

A pair of early Burslem candlesticks, c1930, 3½in (9cm) high. **£50-70** *MA*

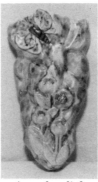

An early relief moulded Butterfly ware wall pocket, c1930, 8½in (21cm). **£80-100** *MA*

An early Burslem posy vase, c1930, 6in (15cm) square. **£30-40** *MA*

An anemone butter dish and cover, 1930s, 7½in (19cm) long. **£35-50** *MA*

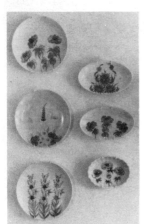

An anemone pattern Deco shape teapot, c1930, 5½in (14cm) high. **£85-100** *MA*

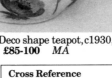

Cross Reference
Teapots

An early Burslem jug, c1930, 13½in (34cm). **£80-100** *MA*

A selection of hand painted plates, post-1940. **£30-50 each** *MA*

A hand painted Butterfly ware wall vase, c1930, 9in (23cm) high. **£90-120** *MA*

A pair of candlesticks, 1930s, 4in (10cm) diam. **£25-40** *MA*

A pair of early Burslem candlesticks, c1930, 4in (10cm) high. **£55-75** *MA*

An anemone posy vase, 1930s, 7in (17.5cm) high. **£50-70** *MA*

A square strawberry dish, 1930s. 6in (15cm) square,
£30-40 *MA*

A Butterfly ware teapot, c1930, 6½in (16cm) high.
£100-120 *MA*

A Butterfly ware jug, c1930, 9in (23cm).
£100-120 *MA*

A moulded two-handled fruit bowl, c1935, 12in (31cm).
£65-85 *MA*

An anemone flower urn, with grille, 1930s, 12in (31cm) wide. **£40-60** *MA*

A vase, with pale blue flowers, 9in (23cm) high.
£55-65 *BEV*

A hand painted ashtray, 6in (15cm) wide.
£10-15 *BGA*

A wall plate, 9in (22cm) diam.
£25-35 *MA*

A wall plate, c1930, 8in (20cm) diam. **£25-35** *MA*

A selection of hand painted wares, including a rare candle lamp, 1930s.
£45-65 each *MA*

An early Burslem anemone jug and toast rack, c1930. **£35-55** *MA*

Samson

Emile Samson (1837-1913) was a famous maker of reproduction porcelain, especially of the fine 18thC European manufacturers, including Sèvres, Crown Derby, Dresden and Meissen. He also produced a deceptively accurate range of Chinese Export Ware.

Not all Samson is marked, but among the marks used are pseudo Oriental on the Chinese Export copies and counterfeit marks of European factories appear. Dresden copies carry the crossed swords and initial 'S'. The letter 'H' with '39' is found on groups copied from Strasbourg faience, the 'H' is supposed to be the initial of the potter. Copies of Delft carry counterfeit Delft marks. The initial 'S' has been seen on 20thC Samson animals as well.

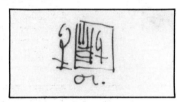

A bowl, 7in (18cm) diam.
£220-230 *JO*

A vase with armorial design, 10in (25cm) high.
£120-180 *JO*

Sugar sifter, with screw top, 6in (15cm) high.
£90-110 *JO*

> **Cross Reference**
> Cups & Saucers

An armorial plate, 9in (23cm) diam.
£480-510 *JO*

A pair of sugar casters, 7in (18cm) high.
£300-360 *JO*

A tankard, 5½in (14cm) high.
£290-310 *JO*

A pair of busts, Louis XV, 6in (15cm) high and Madame Dubarry, 5½in (14cm) high. **£200-250** *JO*

An urn and cover, 7½in (19cm) high.
£210-230 *JO*

A cup and saucer, cup 3in (8cm) high.
£70-90 *JO*

A powder bowl, with pseudo
Chinese mark, 4in (10cm) diam.
£110-150 *JO*

A mug, 5in (12.5cm) high.
£145-165 *JO*

A leaf shape bowl and
cover, 4½in (11cm) wide.
£120-150 *JO*

Shelley

A cup, saucer and plate, in antique
shape. **£30-35** *BEV*

A 1 pint tankard,
depicting an RAF WWI
Barrage Balloon, 4½in
(11.5cm) high.
£30-35 *TAV*

A pair of
vases, 6in
(15cm) high.
£90-100
HEW

CHINA
SHELLEY
ENGLAND

Sylvac

A rabbit match striker,
4in (10cm) high.
£20-25   *HEW*

A dog, 8½in (21cm)
high.   **£40-45**   *HEW*

A dog, with barrel, 5in
(13cm) high.
£10-15   *HEW*

Cross Reference
Cats & Dogs

A dog, 4in
(10cm) high.
£15-20
HEW

An Art Deco jug, in
orange, green and blue,
marked Wade Heath
Ware, Regd shape
No. 787794 Made in
England, c1934, 6in
(15cm) high.
£45-55   *ROW*

Wardle

A child's plate, 8in
(20cm) diam.
£10-15   *HEW*

A jug, 7in
(18cm) high.
£15-25
BEV

Wade Heath

An Orcadia Ware vase,
in green and orange,
c1934, 7in (18cm).
£55-65   *ROW*

A jug, with
squirrel, 4½in
(11cm) high.
£8-12   *BEV*

Cross Reference
Children's Ceramics

A blue ewer, with yellow
design, 8in (20cm) high.
£90-100   *BEV*

An Orcadia Ware vase,
in green, orange and
blue, 5½in (14cm) high.
£25-35   *BEV*

A blue vase, with pink
and green design, c1930,
8in (20cm) high.
£90-100   *BEV*

FURTHER READING
*The Sylvac Story, The History and Products of
Shaw and Copestake Ltd,* Susan Jean Verbeek,
Pottery Publications 1989.
An Introduction to Sylvac, Mick and Derry
Collins.

Welsh Pottery

Job Ridgway (1759-1813), was an English potter and the son of Ralph Ridgway who owned a pottery at Chell, nr Burslem, He began by working at the Swansea Potteries and then at the Leeds Potteries. With his brother George he established a factory at Hanley in 1794, moved to Cauldon Place, Shelton, in 1802, producing stone china and also porcelain. After his death this concern was run by his sons John (1785-1860), who became first mayor of Hanley in 1856, and William (1788-1864). Their stone china, known as Cauldon ware, became very popular; much of it was exported to the USA and some patterns were made specially for this purpose, e.g. the blue and white Beauties of America table service, decorated with prints of notable American buildings. William set up his own establishment at Bell Bank in 1830 producing similar wares including a service decorated with views of American rivers. Both factories made polychrome as well as blue and white wares. The Cauldon factory made lavishly gilded porcelain tablewares and also garden fountains and what were described as 'sanitary vessels' when exhibited at the Great Exhibition of 1851. This concern was eventually absorbed by the Coalport China Company.

A Royal Cauldon plaque, c1920, 18in (46cm) diam.
£250-275 *HEW*

A Llanelli pottery bowl, with potato print of swags of roses and border, poor condition, 5½in (14cm) diam.
£40-50 *CHA*

A hand painted and potato printed bowl, c1920, 6½in (16cm) diam.
£30-40 *CHA*

An impressed basket ware bowl, with sponged decoration, c1840, 6in (15cm) diam. **£50-60** *CHA*

A pottery bowl, decorated with blue rings, c1880, 6in (15cm) diam.
£20-30 *CHA*

A Royal Cauldon vase, in Chang pattern, c1930, 7in (18cm) high.
£40-50 *HEW*

A potato print bowl, c1900, 7in (18cm) diam.
£30-40 *CHA*

A pair of Llanelli pottery hand painted bowls, marked, c1920, 5in (13cm) diam.
£50-60 *CHA*

A Royal Cauldon jug, in Chang pattern, 10in (25cm) high.
£60-70 *HEW*

Winstanley Cats

The first Winstanley cats appeared in 1955 and have all been created by Jenny Winstanley. They are cast by hand in hard-fired earthenware, individually painted and glazed in a unique style. The eyes are individually made from cathedral glass and fitted after firing. Each animal is marked as below.

The Winstanley mark.

A kitten lying on its back with raised paws, marked J. Winstanley, England, 2, 7in (18cm) long.
£12-15   *CP*

A seated cat, marked designed J. Winstanley, Made in England, 26, with gold sticker on base Fifth Avenue, c1976, 8½in (21cm) high.
£20-25   *CP*

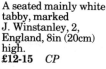

A seated mainly white tabby, marked J. Winstanley, 2, England, 8in (20cm) high.
£12-15   *CP*

A crouching kitten, marked J. Winstanley, England, 1, 4in (10cm) high.
£13-15   *CP*

A yellow and black tabby, lying down, c1979, marked J. Winstanley, 54 Made in England.
£35-40   *CP*

A black cat lying down, marked 2, J. Winstanley, 8in (20cm) long.
£12-15   *CP*

A standing tabby, and a seated tabby, marked J. Winstanley, England, 8 and 6 respectively, 11in (28cm) high.
£40-45 each   *CP*

A prone tabby, with white feet, marked J. Winstanley, 4, England, 4½in (11cm) high.
£22-26   *CP*

A prone tabby, on a circular cushion, marked J. Winstanley, England, 7, 12in (31cm) diam.
£12-15   *CP*

A seated dark-topped tabby, marked 2, J. Winstanley, 7in (18cm) high.
£12-15   *CP*

A Siamese 'sniffing' cat, marked J. Winstanley, England, 5, 6in (15cm) high. **£27-30** *CP*

A seated tortoiseshell cat with white paws, looking over right shoulder, marked J. Winstanley, 4, England, 9½in (24cm) high. **£22-25** *CP*

A Siamese cat, with organically painted eyes, faded, marked Designed J. Winstanley, Kensington, 48, 1970s, 12in (31cm) high. **£30-35** *CP*

A grey tabby with white paws, lying down with raised head, marked 7, J. Winstanley, England, 29.8.91, 6½in (16cm) high. **£35-40** *CP*

A seated ginger and white kitten, with raised left paw, made for the Japanese market and believed to be a good luck charm, 8in (20cm) high. **£20-25** *CP*

A seated dark tabby, with white paws, marked J. Winstanley, England, 4, 9½in (24cm) high. **£22-26** *CP*

A tabby lying down, marked J. Winstanley 7, England, 20.9.91, 7in (18cm) high. **£35-40** *CP*

Bowls & Dishes

A Quimper dish, 19thC, 12in (31cm) long.
£320-360 *VH*

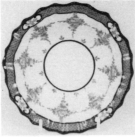

A Mintons china dish, 1930s, 5½in (14cm) diam.
£20-30 *MA*

A Glynn Colledge bowl, 1950, 9½in (24cm) diam.
£25-35 *MA*

A Savoie lead glazed bowl, c1915, 12in (31cm) diam.
£70-75 *VH*

Sixteen pieces of Copeland dessertware, the red ground gilt bordered with fleur-de-lys decoration and gilt centres, late 19thC.
£140-150 *PCh*

A Worcester blue and white fluted bowl, with Plant and Bird pattern, late 18thC, 4in (10cm) diam.
£40-45 *PCh*

Chamber Pots

An Edwardian hand painted chamber pot, 9½in (24cm) diam.
£35-40 *FMN*

A transfer printed chamber pot, 1920s.
£20-25 *BGA*

A Victorian blue and white transfer printed chamber pot.
£35-45 *BGA*

A Victorian blue and white chamber pot.
£35-45 *BGA*

A Victorian transfer printed chamber pot, with blue and floral pattern.
£35-40 *FMN*

A Royal Doulton green chamber pot.
£20-25 *BGA*

An Edwardian chamber
pot, embossed with green
and yellow flowers.
£25-35 *BGA*

A Victorian green
transfer printed chamber
pot.
£35-45 *BGA*

A Victorian brown
transfer printed chamber
pot, reg. 149280 Wren,
8½in (21cm) diam.
£35-45 *FMN*

An Edwardian
transfer
printed
chamber pot.
£25-30
BGA

A Paragon rectangular
dish, Edward VIII, 1937,
11in (28cm) long.
£120-140 *Bon*

Commemorative

A Staffordshire cup and
saucer, commemorating
Queen Victoria's Jubilee,
dated 1887.
£40-50 *HOW*

A Doulton jug, to
commemorate the last
meeting at Wimbledon of
the National Rifle
Association, 1860-89,
6½in (16cm) high.
£85-90 *PSA*

A loving cup, prematurely
commemorating the
Coronation of Edward VIII,
12th May 1937, 6in (15cm) high.
£85-95 *Bon*

A George VI/Queen
Elizabeth Coronation
vase, 1937, 6in (15cm)
high.
£20-30 *MA*

An Empire Exhibition
1924 dish, 4½in (11cm)
diam. **£40-50** *HEW*

A Crown Devon pottery
tankard, with moulded
profile of Edward VIII,
4in (10cm) high.
£120-140 *Bon*

A pair of Carlton Ware figures, coronation George VI/Queen Elizabeth 1937, plaque missing from one, 8 to 9in (20 to 23cm) high.
£600-800 *CHa*

A Paragon dish, Ocean Yacht Race Newport-Bermuda, 1978, 5in (13cm) diam.
£8-12 *MA*

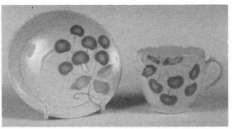

A T. G. Green cup, saucer and plate, c1930, saucer 5½in (14cm).
£8-10 *ROS*

Three Royal Doulton pieces:
l. Captain Cook liqueur.
£55-65
c. Plate, 1930.
£150-175
r. A Figurine, c1980-84.
£250-300 *TP*

A pansy transfer print cup and saucer, unmarked, saucer 3½in (9cm).
£10-12 *ROS*

A giant tea cup and saucer, 19thC, saucer 9in (23cm).
£30-40 *ROS*

Cups & Saucers

A Phoenix Ware cup, saucer and plate, 1930s, saucer 5½in (14cm).
£15-18 *ROS*

A Paragon cup and saucer, saucer 5½in (14cm).
£12-15 *ROS*

All Saints Church, Orpington, made in Germany, saucer 6in (15cm).
£20-25 *MA*

A French Art Nouveau cup, saucer and plate.
£25-35 *BEV*

A Shelley cup and saucer. **£45-55** *BEV*

A Shelley napkin ring.
£25-35 *BEV*

'Going to the Mill', 23rd August 1872, saucer 6in (15cm).
£15-20 *ROS*

A Shelley baby plate, 6in (15cm).
£35-45 *BEV*

A Shelley baby plate, 8in (20cm). **£35-45** *BEV*

Children's Ceramics

Mabel Lucie Attwell

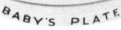

A Shelley plate.
£35-45 *HEW*

Shelley figures, 3 to 3½in (7.5 to 9cm) high.
£200-250 each *BEV*

A Shelley cereal bowl, 6in (15cm).
£20-25 *HEW*

It is very unusual to find these figures in turquoise.

Three Shelley plates, 6in (15cm).
£35-45 each *BEV*

General

A pair of Paragon children's mugs, with circus theme, 3in (7cm).
£35-40 each   *BEV*

A set of 4 Sylvan Pottery plates, 5in (12.5cm).
£15-20   *OD*

A relief moulded and transfer printed plate, 'The Evening Duty', attributed to Middlesbro' Pottery, c1845, 6in (15cm).   **£65-75**   *HOW*

A Muffin the Mule tea set.   **£90-100**   *HEW*

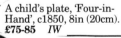
CROWN WORKS
BURSLEM
ENGLAND

An Osborne circus plate, 5in (12.5cm).
£10-15   *ROS*

A child's plate, 'Four-in-Hand', c1850, 8in (20cm).
£75-85   *IW*

A
SUSIE COOPER
PRODUCTION.
CROWN WORKS.
BURSLEM.
ENGLAND

A Susie Cooper child's plate, 8in (20cm).   **£45-50**   *BEV*

A Middlesbrough Pottery plate, c1860, 8in (20cm).   **£60-80**   *IW*

Egg Cups

Two Royal Doulton Merryweather egg cups, in yellow, 2½in (7cm).
£20-25 each   *GRA*

A limited edition egg cup, c1970.
£30-50   *CHA*
Cost £7.50 when first produced.

Figures
Continental

A pair of porcelain
figures, some damage,
1920s.
£45-55 *LIL*

A porcelain figure group,
1920s, 6in (15cm).
£20-30 *LIL*

A porcelain figure,
1920s, 5in (12.5cm).
£25-35 *LIL*

A porcelain figure,
c1900, 4½in (11cm).
£45-55 *FOB*

A figure, c1900, 4in
(10cm).
£35-45 *LIL*

A porcelain figure,
c1900, 4in (10cm).
£55-65 *LIL*

A porcelain figure,
c1895, 5in (12.5cm).
£110-115 *LIL*

Honey Pots

Two foreign honey pots,
possible Portuguese, 4½
and 5in (11 and 12.5cm)
high.
£10-15 each *PC*

Two brown glazed hives,
3 and 4½in (7.5 and
11cm) high.
£10-15 each *PC*

Household Ceramics

Two foreign honey pots,
5in (12.5cm) high.
£10-15 each *PC*

Two Czechoslovakian
honey pots, 4 and 5in (10
and 12.5cm) high.
£10-15 each *PC*

Two foreign honey pots,
4½ and 6in (11 and 15cm)
high.
£10-15 each *PC*

A Dutch napkin ring, 4in
(10cm) high.
£10-12 *HEW*

A Belleek nautilus
shell moulded
cabaret set,
printed mark
in black.
£375-400 *HSS*

A porcelain duck, 4in
(10cm).
£6-8 *HEW*

A Goebels napkin ring,
4in (10cm) high.
£38-40 *BEV*

Cross Reference
Teapots
Cups & Saucers

A rabbit napkin ring, 3in
(7.5cm).
£12-14 *HEW*

Cross Reference
Kitchenalia
Glass

DID YOU KNOW?
Miller's Collectables
Price Guide is
designed to build up,
year by year, into the
most comprehensive
reference system
available.

Two beehive pots, Portuguese, 4½ and 5in
(11 and 12.5cm). **£10-15 each** *PC*

A Kensington cruet set,
c1930, 5½in (14cm) long.
£10-20 *MA*

A set of 5 Wade porcelain tortoises, 1½ to 3in (4 to 7.5cm) long.
£10-12 *BEV*

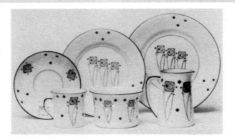

A Foley bone china part tea and coffee set, designed by George Logan, decorated with the Glasgow School rose motif, printed in green and lilac enamels, damaged, printed factory marks.
£575-600 *CSK*

A Copeland Spode Italian pattern pepper pot, c1900, 3in (7.5cm).
£10-20 *MA*

An Austrian bulldog mask, 6in (15cm) high.
£75-85 *HEW*

A Czechoslovakian vase, c1930, 6in (15cm) high.
£15-20 *HEW*

A cruet set, 7in (18cm) long.
£5-10 *MA*

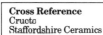

Cross Reference
Cruets
Staffordshire Ceramics

A pair of peppers, 6in (15cm).
£70-80 *GIN*

A common version.

A selection of Staffordshire Toby pepper pots, c1865, tallest 6in (15cm) high.
£63-125 each *HEY*

A porcelain pot with lid, 4in (10cm) wide.
£10-12 *BEV*

Two peppers.
l. An unusual variation.
£220-250
r. A naval man.
£180-200 *GIN*

A dressing table set, with atomiser, c1930, 7in (17.5cm) wide. **£10-15** *ROS*

Two Prattware transfer printed meat paste jars, 3in (7.5cm) high. **£20-30 each** *CHA*

A Royal Dux sculptured piece, with gold trim, 1950s, 11in (28cm) high. **£40-45** *BEV*

A pair of Prattware meat paste jars, 'The Garden Party', 3in (7.5cm) high. **£65-70 each** *CHA*

An early Victorian sardine box and cover on stand, 7½in (19cm) wide. **£40-45** *ROS*

A Coronet ware caravan biscuit barrel, 6½in (16cm) wide. **£45-55** *BEV*

A Spode supper dish, with Trophies Etruscan pattern, cracked and stained, printed and impressed mark, c1820, 8in (20cm) diam. **£70-90** *CSK*

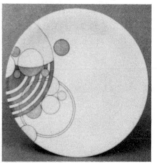

A Rye hand made boar, c1950, 6in (15cm) wide. **£14-18** *FOB*

A mask, marked C & Co., c1930, 7in (17.5cm). **£60-70** *HEW*

A Crown Ducal comport, 19thC, 9½in (24cm) diam. **£40-50** *ROS*

A Rubian Art Pottery hand painted toast rack, c1935, 7in (17.5cm). **£18-20** *ROW*

A Noritake porcelain tazza, designed by Frank Lloyd Wright, printed in yellow, orange, green and grey, printed factory marks, post-1922, 8½in (21cm). **£125-130** *CSK*

A set of porcelain cups, c1915. **£45-55** *BEV*

A Royal Winton sauceboat and small dish.
£35-45 each *BEV*

A pair of unglazed terracotta wall plaques, impressed Watcombe Torquay, signed TW, c1890, 9in (24cm). **£30-50** *ROW*

A pair of Czechoslovakian book ends, 6in (15cm) high. **£65-75** *BEV*

An Adderley coffee set, incorporating 6 cups and saucers, c1920. **£65-75** *FOB*

A Midwinter Stylecraft dish, designed by Hugh Casson, 1950s, 10in (25cm) wide.
£15-20 *HEW*

Jugs

A George Jones hunting jug, 4½in (11cm) high.
£15-25 *MA*

A transfer printed jug and bowl set, slight damage, 14in (36cm) high.
£40-45 *ROS*

Two jugs, c1830, 3½ and 4½in (9 and 11cm) high. **£5-25 each** *CHA*

A Victorian jug, 8in (20cm).
£28-30 *ROS*

Lustre Ware

Lustre is a shiny surface produced by coating the pottery with a metallic pigment, generally copper or silver, but occasionally gold or platinum, which by means of a reducing atmosphere in the kiln, is not allowed to oxidise.

A copper lustre mask jug, with relief moulded flowers in enamel colours, c1845, attributed to Staffordshire, c1845, 6in (15cm) high.
£130-140   *HOW*

A copper lustre jug, with pink and white enamel painted flower decoration, c1840, 7in (17.5cm) high.
£130-140   *HOW*

A Sunderland jug, printed with 'The Sailor's Farewell', 9in (23cm) high. **£325-350**   *AG*

Majolica

A George Jones dish, in the form of a cabbage leaf with a handle in the form of a rabbit, 8½in (22cm) long.   **£500-550**   *Bea*

A Tyneside orange lustre child's mug, 1850s, 2½in (6cm) high.
£20-30   *IS*

A taper holder, with frog, 3½in (9cm) high.
£50-60   *NB*

A penguin, 7in (18cm) high.
£50-60   *NB*

A copper lustre loving cup, c1880, 3½in (9cm) high.
£35-40   *CSA*

A mustard and pepper pot, 3 and 4in (7.5 and 10cm) high.
£15-20 each
NB

A Portuguese majolica frog, 6in (15cm) wide. **£80-100** *NB*

A jug, with elephant, 6½in (16cm) high. **£50-60** *NB*

A wild boar, 7in (18cm) wide. **£75-85** *NB*

A pair of Sarreguemines frog jugs, 10½in (26cm) high. **£180-200** *NB*

An owl jug, 8½in (21cm) high. **£100-125** *NB*

A pair of Holdcroft mugs, with lily design, 3in (7.5cm). **£130-150** *NB*

A corn-on-the-cob jug, on stand, 11in (28cm) high. **£100-125** *NB*

A corn-on-the-cob jug, with pewter lid, 6in (15cm). **£30-40** *NB*

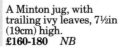

A Staffordshire fish jug, in green, brown and pink, c1880, 11in (28cm). **£70-80** *HOW*

A Minton jug, with trailing ivy leaves, 7½in (19cm) high. **£160-180** *NB*

117

A monkey musician, with violin, 9in (23cm) high.
£100-120   *NB*

A jug with face design, 10in (25cm) high.
£80-100   *NB*

A jug, with blackberry and bark design, 8½in (21cm) high.
£60-70   *NB*

A pair of miniature Satsuma ware vases, with hardwood stands, 5in (12.5cm) high.
£75-80   *TAV*

A Cantonese circular footed bowl, 16in (41cm) diam.   **£360-380**   *GH*

A Minton tower jug, 10in (25cm) high.
£200-300   *NB*

Oriental
Ceramics

A Chinese blue and white oval tapered vase, 17in (43cm) high.
£375-395   *AG*

An Oriental pattern tankard, decorated with exotic birds and flowers, 4½in (11cm) high.
£225-250   *PCh*

A Friar Tuck Toby jug, 6½in (16cm) high.
£40-50   *NB*

Cross Reference
Toby Jugs

A pair of Cantonese dished plates, 13in (33cm) diam.
£375-400   *GH*

An Imari circular dished plate, with scolloped rim, 18in (46cm) diam.
£400-450   *GH*

Printed Pot Lids

About 400 pot lid designs have been identified. These have been documented and numbered by A. Ball in his invaluable reference work *Price Guide to Pot Lids* which all collectors should possess. The listing which follows contains a representative selection of the pot lids most likely to be encountered by the general collector. The number refers to the listing system devised by Mr Ball in his book.

Harriet Beecher Stowe (172).
£700-1,000 *P*

No. Description
1. Alas! Poor Bruin.
   £80-100
2. Bear attacked by Dogs.
   £500-700
3. Bear's Grease Manufacturer, lettering on marbled border.
   £2,000-3,000
4. Bear Hunting.
   £150-200
5. Bears Reading Newspapers.
   £600-700
6. The Bear Pit.
   £65-85
9. Bears at School.
   £80-100
11. Bear with Valentines.
    £1,800-2,400
13. Shooting Bears
    £25-30
15. The Ins.
    £100-150
16. The Outs.
    £100-150
17. Arctic Expedition.
    £400-500
18. Polar Bears.
    £100-140
19. Bear, Lion & Cock, white surround.
    £75-95
20. All but Trapped.
    £1,000-1,400
21. Pegwell Bay.
    £600-800
23. Pegwell Bay.
    £600-800
24. Lobster Fishing, damaged.
    £80-120
25. Pegwell Bay, Lobster Fishing.
    £100-120
26. Pegwell Bay – Four Shrimpers.
    £30-40
27. Belle Vue Tavern.
    £200-230
28. Belle Vue Tavern – with Carriage.
    £30-40
29. Belle Vue Tavern.
    £220-250
30. Belle Vue without bay window.
    £70-100
31. Shrimpers, damaged.
    £60-80
32. S. Banger, Shrimp Sauce Manufacturer.
    £300-400
33. Shrimping.
    £60-80

34. The Dutch Fisherman.
    £1,000-1,200
35. Still Life – Game.
    £100-120
37. Ramsgate, Farmyard Scene.
    £60-80
38. Landing the Fare – Pegwell Bay.
    £50-60
41. Royal Harbour.
    £50-60
42. Royal Harbour, Ramsgate.
    £40-50
43. Nelson Crescent, Ramsgate.
    £80-100
45. Walmer Castle.
    £50-60
47. Walmer Castle.
    £150-180
48. Pretty Kettle of Fish.
    £75-95
49. Lobster Sauce.
    £40-50
50. 'Injury' untitled registration mark.
    £120-140
52B. Shell.
    £45-55
53. Examining the Nets.
    £50-60
55. Landing the Catch.
    £30-40
57. The Fish Market.
    £35-45
58. The Fish Barrow.
    £45-55
60. The Net-Maker.
    £200-250
62. Foreign River Scene.
    £50-60
63. The Shrimpers.
    £40-60
64. Sea Nymph and Trident.
    £200-250
65. Swiss Riverside Scene.
    £60-90
66. Dutch River Scene.
    £100-120
67. Jar – Pegwell Bay and Cliffs without Vessel in Cliffs.
    £70-80
70. Jar – Mending The Nets.
    £70-80
76. Charge of the Scots Greys at Balaklava.
    £120-140

78. Fall of Sebastopol.
    £120-140
81. Paste Pot, Meet of The Foxhounds.
    £75-100
86. Paste Pot, Milking The Cow.
    £110-130
91. Paste Pot, Uncle Tom & Eva, set of three.
    £450-650
97. The Bride.
    £120-150
98. An Eastern Repast.
    £100-120
101. The Mirror.
     £100-120
104. Reflections in Mirror.
     £350-400
106. Lady with Hawk.
     £90-100
107. Lady with Guitar.
     £60-70
110. Lady Fastening Shoe.
     £150-200
111. Lady Brushing Hair.
     £160-200
114. The Matador.
     £350-450
116. Jenny Lind.
     £1,200-1,500
118. The Trysting Place.
     £70-100
119. The Lovers.
     £60-90
123. Musical Trio.
     £80-100
132. Bunch of Cherries Coral Tooth Paste.
     £180-220
133. Grand International Buildings of 1851.
     £60-70
134. Exhibition Buildings 1851. Large with Acorn Border.
     £250-300
135. Grand Exhibition 1851.
     £40-50
137. The Crystal Palace.
     £150-180
139. Crystal Palace, interior.
     £260-300
143. Dublin Industrial Exhibition 1853.
     £90-110
144. International Exhibition 1862.
     £150-180
145. L'Exposition Universelle de 1867.
     £75-100
149. England's Pride.
     £125-155
150. Queen Victoria on Balcony, large.
     £250-300
152. Queen Victoria and Prince Consort, restored.
     £70-90

Napirima Trinidad.
£180-200   *RG*

No. Description
153. The Late Prince Consort.
£75-85
156. Napoleon III and
Empress Eugenie.
£100-120
157. Albert Edward, Prince
of Wales and Princess
Alexandra, on their
marriage 1863.
£75-100
159. Wellington with
Cocked Hat.
£1,500-2,500
160. Wellington – with clasped
hands, with order.
£180-220
160A. Wellington with
clasped hands.
£100-140
164. Tria Juncta in Uno.
£250-300
166. Balaklava, Inkerman, Alma.
£250-300
167A. Admiral Sir Charles
Napier C.B.
£220-250
168. The Allied Generals.
£90-100
170. Sir Robert Peel.
£200-230
171. Peabody.
£80-120
172. Harriet Beecher Stowe.
£700-1,100
174. The Blue Boy.
£80-100
175. Dr. Johnson.
£30-50
176. Buckingham Palace.
£90-120
179. Drayton Manor.
£50-80
180. Windsor Park, Returning
from Stag Hunting.
£120-150
181. Sandringham.
£60-80
182. Osborne House.
£50-80

---

183. New Houses of Parliament,
Westminster.
£190-250
185. St. Paul's Cathedral and
River Pageant.
£90-120
188. Strathfieldsaye.
£70-110
189. Westminster Abbey.
£200-250
190. Albert Memorial.
£100-120
192. St. Paul's Cathedral.
£150-200
193. Charing Cross.
£80-100

The Times (327).
£40-60   *RBE*

195. New Houses of
Parliament.
£100-150
201. Trafalgar Square.
£40-60
202. Holborn Viaduct.
£60-80
203. New St. Thomas's Hospital.
£50-60
204. Golden Horn.
£60-85
205. The Thirsty Soldier.
£60-80
206. Embarking for the East.
£60-80
209. Sebastopol.
£60-75
210. The Battle of the Nile.
£55-75
211. Meeting of Garibaldi
and Victor
Emmanuel.
£50-60
212. War – After Wouvermann,
hairline crack.

Derby Day, 4½in (11cm).
£60-70   *BRK*

£20-25
214. The Volunteers.
£90-120
216. The Redoubt.
£500-600
219. War.
£35-45
220. Peace.
£40-50
221. Harbour of Hong Kong.
£50-60
222. Ning Po River.
£80-100
223. Rifle Contest, Wimbledon 1864.
£50-60
224. Wimbledon, July 1860.
£45-55
226. Shakespeare's Birthplace –
exterior.
£40-50
227. Shakespeare's Birthplace –
interior.
£30-60
228. Anne Hathaway's Cottage.
£50-60
229. Holy Trinity Church.
£80-100
233. May Day Dancers at the
Swan Inn.
£30-50
236. The Parish Beadle.
£90-110

Albert Memorial (190).
£100-120   *RG*

237. The Children of Flora.
£70-80
238. 'Christmas Eve'.
£120-140
240. The Village Wedding.
£20-30
241. Our Home.
£100-150
244. The Bullfight, late issue.
£35-45
245. The Enthusiast.
£40-50
246. Blind Man's Buff.
£100-150
247. Master of the Hounds.
£30-40
248. Chiefs Return from
Deer-stalking.
£90-100
249. Dangerous Skating.
£50-70
277. The Skewbald Horse.
£60-70

289. The Sea Eagle.
£80-100
309. The Faithful Shepherd.
£60-80
310. H.R.H. Prince of Wales
visiting the Tomb of
Washington.
£80-120
311. I See You My Boy.
£35-45
312. French Street Scene, medium.
£25-35
312. French Street Scene, large.
£40-50
314. The Breakfast Party.
£90-100
315. Cattle and Ruins.
£50-70
318. The Old Water Mill.
£50-60
319. The Queen, God Bless Her.
£50-70
322. The Rivals.
£75-85
323. The Dentist.
£100-120
324. The Farriers.
£50-60
325. The Shepherdess.
£50-60
327. The Times.
£40-60

Back view of Pegwell
Bay Inn.
£65-75   RG
328. Uncle Toby.
£30-50
329C. The First Appeal.
£50-60
330B. The Second Appeal.
£70-90
331. Strasbourg.
£40-50
332. Transplanting Rice.
£45-55
333. Vue de la Ville de
Strasbourg Prise du Port.
£35-45
334. The Trooper.
£50-70
335. Fording the Stream.
£25-30
337. The Flute Player.
£30-50
340. On Guard.
£40-60
341. The Fisher-boy.
£50-70

346. Tam-o'-Shanter and
Souter Johnny,
damaged.
£35-45
347. Tam O'Shanter.
£90-110
348. Peasant Boys.
£50-70
349. The Poultry Woman.
£45-55
351. Preparing for the Ride.
£50-70
352. The Quarry.
£100-150
354. The Picnic.
£110-130

Harbour of Hong Kong
(221).
£50-60   RBE

355A. Royal Coat of Arms,
restored.
£70-90
358. Little Red Riding Hood.
£60-80
359. The Red Bull Inn.
£50-70
360. Letter from the Diggings,
medium.
£50-60
360. Letter from the Diggings,
large, mottled
border, restored.
£35-45
361. The Wolf and the Lamb.
£40-60
362. Charity.
£40-50
365. The Waterfall.
£60-80
385. The Wild Deer, complete.
£120-130
386. Donkey's Foal, lid and base.
£70-90

Little Red Riding Hood.
£65-75   RG

Derby Day and Pegwell
Bay Sea Shells.
£55-65 each   RG

396. The Traveller's Departure,
green border and
similar base.
£55-65
397. Tyrolean Village Scene.
£40-60
250. Fair Sportswoman.
£40-60
251. A False Move.
£150-200
252. A Pair.
£40-50
253. Snapdragon.
£70-90
254. The Best Card.
£25-30
255. Hide and Seek.
£25-35
256. A Fix.
£35-45
257. A Race or Derby Day.
£30-50
258. The Skaters.
£70-90
259. The Game Bag.
£40-50
260. The Game Bag.
£30-40
261. Pheasant Shooting.
£30-50
263. Children Sailing Boats in Tub.
£70-90
264C. Six Dogs.
£400-450
265. Good Dog.
£50-60
266. Contrast.
£60-70
267. Feeding the Chickens.
£50-60
269. Deerhound Guarding Cradle.
£130-160
270. The Begging Dog.
£70-90
272. Both Alike.
£45-65
273. Country Quarters.
£70-80
274. High Life.
£80-90
275. Low Life.
£80-90
276. The Snow-Drift.
£35-45

Ribbon Plates

Ribbon or pierced plates became popular in the Victorian era and are now becoming very collectable. This open work decoration can also be found on other items such as lids or vases and was copied from the metal working trade. Early pierced decoration in ceramics was difficult to achieve, and it was not until the 1800s that the technology changed, together with different techniques and clays used, enabling mass production, although a large number of plates would be lost in the firing stage due to the weak areas caused by the piercing.

Many countries produced pierced ware, including England, Germany, Austria and France. Some early examples date back to the 1770s. Generally these plates were not produced by the better factories, so they were considered poorer quality. They became part of the Victorian tourist trade with pictures and place names printed on them, especially by the popular seaside resorts like Brighton and Southend. The manufacture of these plates lasted until the early 1920s.

Originally pierced work was not intended to be threaded with ribbons, but in the late Victorian era the trend rapidly caught on, with pleasing results. The colours of the ribbons complementing the scenes in the centre of the plates. Most plates are transfer printed designs, but there are some to be found that are hand painted, and hence are more desirable and more valuable.

At the present time they are relatively inexpensive, the prices ranging from £18 for the smaller plates with little design to £50 for the more decorative, hand painted signed examples. The beauty of ribbon plates is that each plate can be 'individualised' by the colour of the ribbons threaded through the intricate hole pattern, and can therefore complement almost any existing decoration.

A Victorian plate, with transfer printed parrots, 9in (23cm).
£20-30   *FMN*

A hand painted plate, with ribbons, 9in (22cm).
£30-40   *FMN*

A Victorian plate, transfer printed with cherubs, and gilt trim, 8½in (21cm).
£50-60   *FMN*

A Victorian hand painted and transfer printed plate with ribbon, 8½in (21cm).
£30-40   *FMN*

A transfer printed plate with children and chickens, 7½in (19cm).
£40-45   *FMN*

A transfer printed plate, A present from Skegness, 8½in (21cm).
£20-30   *FMN*

Two hand painted violet pattern plates, one embossed, 8½ and 9in (21 and 23cm). **£30-40 each** *FMN*

A Victorian plate, with transfer printed deer and ribbon, 8in (20cm).
£25-35 *FMN*

A lustre plate, with transfer print, A Present from Maidenhead, and ribbon, c1900, 8½in (21cm). **£25-35** *FMN*

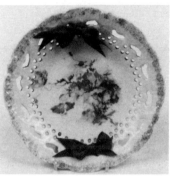

A Victorian transfer printed plate with ribbon, 8½in (21cm). **£25-85** *FMN*

A hand painted and gilded plate, 9in (22cm). **£35-45** *FMN*

An English hand painted plate, with gold inner circle, 9½in (24cm). **£50-60** *FMN*

A German hand painted plate, 8½in (21cm). **£30-40** *FMN*

A Victorian transfer printed plate, 8½in (21cm) diam. **£40-45** *FMN*

A Victorian transfer printed plate in rust and kingfisher blue, 8½in (21cm). **£25-35** *FMN*

An Austrian hand painted plate, 9in (23cm). **£35-45** *FMN*

A Victorian transfer printed plate with ribbon, 8½in (21cm). **£25-35** *FMN*

Spongeware

Most spongeware came from the Staffordshire potteries although Scottish and Welsh examples are quite common. Bright colours were stencilled on to pottery, usually with a sponge and supplemented with hand painting, occasionally potato prints were used. Spongeware is very collectable at the moment, especially in America.

Two pottery bowls, c1850.
£40-60 each *CHA*

A pottery tavern tankard, with terracotta base, probably Spanish, late 19thC, 6in (15cm) high.
£40-50 *CHA*

Three pottery bowls, the centre bowl with 3 bands in 3 colours all hand printed, probably child labour.
£60-65
l.&r. £35-40 each *CHA*

Children were taught to paint and stencil pottery and were used throughout the 19thC as a cheap alternative to adult labour.

A milk jug, 3½in (9cm) high.
£35-40 *CHA*

A jug, c1850, 4½in (11cm) high.
£40-50 *CHA*

A jug, chipped, 4in (10cm) high.
£30-40 *CHA*

Staffordshire Pottery

A mug, c1840, 3in (8cm) high.
£20-30 *CHA*

A jug with sheet pattern underglaze transfer of seaweed, c1835, 8in (20cm) high.
£75-85 *HOW*

A Bacchus type jug, with silver lustre and enamel painted face, c1820, 4½in (11cm) high.
£90-100 *HOW*

A jug, 4in (10cm) high.
£40-50 *CHA*

Cross Reference
Jugs

124

A jug in the form of a cottage painted in bright enamel colours, c1840, 5in (13cm) high.
£90-100 *HOW*

A black and white mug, showing a Welsh tea party, c1865, 4in (10cm) high. **£75-85** *HOW*

A railway mug, in green, brown and red, c1850, 4in (10cm) high.
£120-130 *HOW*

| Cross Reference |
| Railways |

A Napoleon jug, painted in black and yellow, c1825, 3in (8cm) high.
£100-120 *HOW*

A pottery savings bank, inscribed Albert Jenkinson, 14th Feb, 1873, in black, on 4 bun feet, some damage, 5½in (14cm) wide.
£360-380 *HSS*

| Cross Reference |
| Money Boxes |

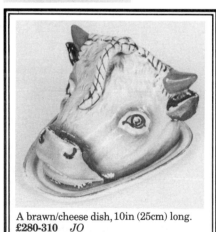

A brawn/cheese dish, 10in (25cm) long.
£280-310 *JO*

A dove tureen, in orange and green, c1860, 8in (20cm) wide.
£280-300 *HOW*

Staffordshire Animals

A pair of spaniels, with separately moulded legs, in red and white with gilt collars, c1855.
£300-330   *HOW*

A pottery figure of a seated cat, c1900, 8in (20cm) high.
£90-100   *HOW*

A set of 4 black furniture stands or sash window stops, 4½in (11cm) high.
£210-230   *PSA*

```
Cross Reference
Cats & Dogs
```

A pair of cows, 5½in (14cm) high.
£1,000-1,250   *JO*

A pair of zebras, on gilt line bases, glaze cracks, c1860, 8½in (21cm) high.
£360-380   *CSK*

A black and white cow with brown and white calf, 5½in (14cm) high.
£450-550   *JO*

A pair of Royal children and sheep, 8in (20cm) high.
£480-550   *JO*

A brown and white sheep, 4in (10cm) high.
£420-480   *JO*

A cow group with ducks, 5½in (14cm) high.
£450-550   *JO*

A pair of sheep, 3in (8cm) high.
£400-500   *JO*

Two sheep by Samuel Alcock, 5½in (14cm) high.
£350-450   *JO*

A tree-shaped spill holder, with sheep, 9in (23cm) high.
£1,550-1,650   *JO*

A pair of Lloyd of Shelton shepherd and shepherdess sheep shearing groups, 5½in (14cm) high.
£900-1,200   *JO*

A sheep and sunflower, 4in (10cm) high.
£300-350   *JO*

A sheep with lamb, 5½in (14cm) high.
£400-500   *JO*

A pair of sheep, the ewe with lamb, 4½in (11cm) high.   **£300-400**   *JO*

A ewe with lamb, 5½in (14cm) high.
£400-450   *JO*

A porcelain sheep, probably Samuel Alcock, 2in (5cm) high.
£70-80   *JO*

A shepherd and shepherdess, 5½in (14cm) high.
£550-650   *JO*

Staffordshire Figures

A young Welshman and woman, supporting a bucket on a milestone inscribed 'Langolen 1 Mile', some damage, 10½in (27cm) high.
£310-330 *Bea*

The Duke of Wellington and Napoleon, both 5in (13cm) high.
£110-130 *AG*

A group of Saul presenting his daughter to David, base titled in gilding, cracked and restored, c1850, 11in (28cm) high.
£140-150 *CSK*

Cross Reference
Welsh Ceramics

A female figure depicting Spring, on an oblong base, 8½in (21cm) high.
£190-210 *AG*

Death of Nelson, 3 male figures, 8in (20cm) high.
£240-265 *AG*

Death of Nelson, painted in colours, on a shaped oval base, titled in gilding, slight wear, c1840, 8in (20cm) high.
£390-420 *CSK*

Charlotte at the tomb of Werther, on oblong base, 18thC, 9in (23cm) high.
£250-270 *AG*

DID YOU KNOW?
Miller's Collectables Price Guide is designed to build up, year by year, into the most comprehensive reference system available.

Richard III seated in a tent with his right hand raised, 10in (25cm) high.
£280-300 *AG*

A pepper and a vinegar by Samson and Smith, with gold anchor mark, 5in (12.5cm) high.
£40-80 *GIN*

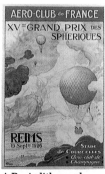

A Rapin lithograph poster, some damage. £1,500-2,000   C

A Drew & Sons two-person black leather picnic set, 1920s. £2,200-3,000   S

A Gerald Coulson oil on canvas, de Havilland DH 82A Tiger Moth airborne over South, signed, 28 by 36in (71 by 91.5cm). £3,500-4,000   C

A tinplate Vespa advertising sign. £30-40   K

A Ludwig Hohlwein lithograph, 1912. £3,500-4,000   CSK

A Kees Van Des Haan lithograph, minor tears and defects, backed on linen, 31 by 23in (79 by 58cm). £1,400-1,600   C

A Roger Perot lithograph. £3,000-3,500   CSK

A Charles Tichon lithograph. £3,000-3,500   C

A collection of 33 German World War II publicity photogravure prints, some creases. £600-700   C

A Coracle four-person picnic set, fitted with various cups and saucers, plates, cutlery, food boxes and a copper kettle with burner, 23½in (60cm) wide. £2,000-3,000   S

An Edwardian wicker four-person picnic hamper. £300-350   SWO

A Victorian mahogany caddy paint box, c1870, 9½in (24cm) long. **£485-550** *JAS*

A colour box by G. Rowney, with original water pot and boxwood tops on bottles, c1855, 10in (25cm) wide. **£800-1,000** *JAS*

A Regency Swiss colour box by Lebre Fab de Cartonnage à Lucerne, 6½in (16cm) wide. **£750-1,000** *JAS*

r. An oil palette, 14in (36cm) long. **£5-7** *PC*

A Victorian paint box, with original water pot, c1870, 9in (23cm) wide. **£485-550** *JAS*

r. A paint caddy box, by James Newman, London, almost complete, 1873, 12in (31cm) wide. **£700-1,300** *JAS*

A paint box, marked R. Ackerman, c1785, 10in (25cm) wide. **£475-550** *JAS*

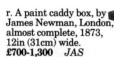

An artist's palette, with container for turpentine, c1880, 9½in (24cm) long. **£5-10** *PC*

A mahogany oil palette, mid-19thC, 20in (51cm) long. **£90-100** *JAS*

A Cyart perspex radio, USA, c1946.
£1,500-1,800 *GAD*

A phenol formaldehyde crib
toy, c1935, 4½in (11cm) high.
£60-80 *GAD*

A Royal Copenhagen ceramic dish,
with silver plated rim, hand
painted, 1937, 9½in (24cm).
£60-70 *RGA*

An Art Deco glass
vase, c1930, 7in
(18cm) diam.
£100-120 *PC*

An Art Deco handmade plastic designer buckle,
c1930. **£35-55** *K*

A Whitefriars bowl, 1930s,
8in (20cm) diam.
£30-40 *SWa*

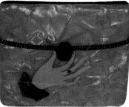

A Bandalastaware bowl,
c1927, 8in (20cm) diam.
£60-80 *GAD*

A French Celluloid cigarette
case, c1925. **£60-80** *GAD*

A Fada phenol formaldehyde radio,
c1939. **£700-800** *GAD*

A Scottie dog napkin ring, c1940,
3in (7.5cm) high. **£10-12** *GAD*

A urea formaldehyde cocktail
shaker, c1935, 10½in
(26cm). **£100-125** *GAD*

A Continental green and
opalescent vase, 1930s,
9in (23cm) diam.
£50-60 *SWa*

An Art Deco handmade plastic designer buckle,
c1930. **£35-55** *K*

Fifteen baseball pins, 2 scratched, the majority excellent to mint, 1910-40.
£2,750-3,250   *S(NY)*

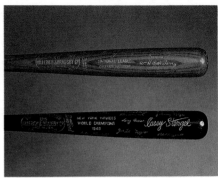

A run of World Series bats, including 2 bats for each year 1935-1988, virtually brand new with only minor wear or scratches.
£32,000-35,000   *S(NY)*

A Topps wrapper collection, 1951-85, 240 different wrappers, near mint condition.
£3,000-3,500   *S(NY)*

A Honus Wagner cigar label, c1910.
£2,750-3,000   *S(NY)*

36 Bowman Pacific Coast League cards, mint.
£4,000-4,500
S(NY)

Ty Cobb card, mint condition, 1910-11.
£8,500-9,000   *S(NY)*

A Babe Ruth candy wrapper, rare in this near mint condition, c1929.
£2,000-2,200   *S(NY)*

Chicago -v- Cleveland baseball programme, 1889. **£4,500-5,000**   *S(NY)*

A set of 96 Leaf Gum cards, 1948. **£12,000-12,500**   *S(NY)*

Helmar Turkish Trophies pillowcase premium, available by mail order offer, framed, 22in (56cm).
£3,000-3,500   *S(NY)*

A complete set of 48 Goudey Heads Up cards, 1938.
£13,500-14,000
S(NY)

A Dietz Gum Company of Chicago bubble gum wrapper, c1933, with 2 die-cut stand up numbered cards, near mint condition.
£9,000-10,000   *S(NY)*

A collection of strip cards, uncut strips of 5 cards each, blank backed, with drawings of baseball players, c1919, near mint condition. **£2,500-3,500** *S(NY)*

Spalding Guides, 54 copies from 1888-1941, near mint condition. **£6,000-6,500** *S(NY)*

A complete set of 280 Topps cards, 1953, near mint. **£10,000-12,000** *S(NY)*

A complete set of 224 cards, Bowman 1954, mint. **£5,500-6,000** *S(NY)*

8 Topps current all stars cards, 1951, near mint. **£3,000-4,000** *S(NY)*

A complete set of 6 cards, Sporting Life Cabinets, c1911, near mint. **£9,000-10,000** *S(NY)*

Bowman, No. 253 Mickey Mantle, 1951, mint condition. **£4,500-5,000** *S(NY)*

A complete set of 24 cards, Topps Test Comics, 1973, unissued original condition, mint. **£2,000-2,500** *S(NY)*

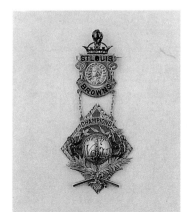

St. Louis Browns pendant, 1886, mint condition, 4⅓in (11cm) high. **£5,000-6,000** *S(NY)*

A Bowman uncut sheet of 36 cards, including card No. 253 Mickey Mantle, 1951, near mint condition. **£22,000-25,000** *S(NY)*

A Tunbridge ware writing slope of Hever Castle, 12½in (32cm) long.
£950-1,000 *STR*

Belgian pine condiment drawers with transfer printed tile fronts, 24in (61cm) wide. **£250-350** *CHA*

A Tunbridge ware double tea caddy of Glena Cottage, Ireland, on 4 bun feet, c1850, 8½in (21cm) wide.
£650-700 *STR*

A canteen of Walker & Hall cutlery comprising 94 pieces, 1930s.
£200-250 *JH*

A coromandel wood stationery box, the interior missing, c1870, 10½in (26cm) wide.
£200-250 *EHA*

A painted pine chest, central European, 17in (43cm) wide.
£450-550 *CHA*

A Japanese lacquered cabinet, with fitted boxes and a pair of pewter flasks, 15in (38cm). **£400-450** *JH*

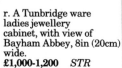

A Tunbridge ware box showing Edward VII as Prince of Wales, with a King Charles spaniel, c1860, 10½in (26cm) wide. **£900-1,000** *STR*

A mother-of-pearl glove box, c1860, 9½in (24cm) long. **£330-380** *EHA*

r. A Tunbridge ware ladies jewellery cabinet, with view of Bayham Abbey, 8in (20cm) wide.
£1,000-1,200 *STR*

A Zeiss Ikon 9 by 12cm tropical Adoro 230/7 camera, No. R19507, and a Carl Zeiss Jena Tessa f4.5 13.5cm lens. **£300-350** *CSK*

C. P. Goerz 9 by 12cm tropical Tenax folding plate camera, No. 298768. **£650-700** *CSK*

A Leitz reflex-fit Apo-Telyt f3.4 180mm lens. **£600-700** *CSK*

A Leitz 35mm cutaway Leica R4 camera No. 1614282. **£800-850** *CSK*

A Leitz 35mm replica UR-Leica camera, with lens. **£400-450** *CSK*

A Contessa-Nettel 6½ by 9cm tropical Adora camera, No. 215443. **£200-250** *CSK*

A Leica 35mm AF-Cl compact camera No. 34116248 with zoom lens. **£200-250** *CSK*

An Edison Bell Picturegram portable gramophone, with Edison Bell 'Era' soundbox, c1925. **£1,400-1,600** *CSK*

A 6½ by 9cm Sigriste jumelle camera, with E. Krauss, Paris, Planar/Zeiss f3.6 110mm lens, with 18 metal film sheaths. **£4,500-5,000** *CSK*

A Leitz 35mm Leica M4-P camera No. 1550707, in maker's original box. **£600-650** *CSK*

A mahogany cased Edison Gem phonograph, Model A, No. G99660, with combination gearing and K reproducer, with original aluminium horn. **£1,200-1,500** *CSK*

A Hansa Canon camera No. 1082, with pop-up viewfinder, with Nippon Kogaku Nikkor f3.5, 5cm lens No. 50712, in maker's ever ready case. **£9,000-10,000** *CSK*

An early Winstanley cat,
marked, 14in (36cm) high.
£65-75   *CHA*

A group of Winstanley cats.
£12-15 each   *CHA*

A Winstanley cat, c1990, 14in
(35cm) wide. **£40-50**   *CHA*

A Chinese porcelain
figure of a bird,
c1880.
£90-100   *HOW*

A Doulton Lambeth bear, by
Harry Simeon, c1900.
£120-150   *TP*

A Beswick game
cock, 9in (23cm).
£150-200   *PC*

A pair of Beswick turtle doves,
7in (17.5cm).
£100-150   *PC*

An older model
Winstanley cat,
No. 4, 8in (20cm).
£35-40   *CHA*

Two Beswick trout,
9½in (23cm) long.
£40-100 each   *PC*

A Beswick Cockatoo,
8in (20cm) high.
£80-120   *PC*

A group of Winstanley
cats, 4½in (11cm) high.
£12-15 each   *CHA*

'Saved', A Doulton Lambeth piece, possibly Leslie Harradine, c1910. **£200-250** *TP*

Rommel, A Doulton figure. **£150-170** *TP*

A Hannah Barlow Doulton figure. **£250-300** *TP*

'Scotties', 1928-38, 5in (12.5cm). **£400-500** *TP*

'Ard of 'Earing, Doulton Toby jug, 1964-67. **£450-550** *TP*

A Doulton fairy, 1929-38, 6in. **£400-500** *TP*

A Doulton Lambeth lemonade jug and beaker. **£250-300** *PCh*

Doulton Friar Tuck Toby jug, 1951-60, 6in (15cm). **£175-210** *TP*

Royal Doulton Dickens Series jugs, Sam Weller D6398 and Bill Sykes D6396. **£100-120** *PCh*

Simple Simon Doulton Toby jug, 1953-60. **£220-250** *TP*

Mephistopheles, Doulton character jugs, small 1937-48. **£350-450** large 1937-49. **£750-950** *TP*

Doulton Toby jugs with removable hats, c1920. **£1,200-2,000 each** *TP*

A pair of Royal Doulton vases, 13½in (35cm) high. **£160-200** *PCh*

Toby jugs from The Celebrity Collection, 1983-88. **£55-75 each** *TP*

A Crown Ducal bread plate, damaged, 1930s, 11in (28cm).
£25-30 if perfect *MA*

A Victorian ribbon plate, transfer printed with cherubs, 9in (23cm).
£50-60 *FMN*

A Victorian transfer printed ribbon plate, 'The Pheasant', signed, 8½in (21cm).
£50-60 *FMN*

A spongeware bordered hand painted plate, c1860, 9½in (24cm).
£130-150 *CHA*

A Victorian transfer printed ribbon plate, 9in (23cm).
£35-45 *FMN*

A Dutch pottery plate, made for the Welsh market, c1880.
£40-50 *CHA*

A Malicoine plate, c1900, 8in (20cm).
£50-60 *VH*

A Royal Worcester plate, c1875, 7in (17cm).
£12-15 *PSA*

A Royal Worcester Nelson commemorative plate.
£300-400 *PC*

A French faience plate, c1900, 8in (20cm). **£50-60** *VH*

A small Quimper plate, c1925-30. **£20-30** *VH*

A pair of faience plates, possibly Spanish, 18thC, 7in (17.5cm).
£115-130 *PSA*

Three German porcelain match strikers with comical heads, c1910.
£35-45 each   *HOW*

A Carlton ware footed bowl, 1930s, 9½in (24cm). **£200-300**   *CHa*

Two German match strikers, c1890. **£45-55 each**   *HOW*

A Carlton ware cruet, 8½in (21cm) diam.
£60-70   *BEV*

Carlton ware bells, Man about Town, The Vicar and The Bell Boy. **£25-60 each**   *BEV*

A Carlton ware moulded vase, 1930, 8in (20cm) high.
£50-70   *MA*

A Carlton ware vase, 1930s.
£500-600   *CHa*

A Carlton ware Fairy Shadow comport, c1925, 12in (25.5cm) wide. **£500-700**   *CHa*

A German novelty match striker, c1890. **£55-65**   *HOW*

A German match striker.
£45-55   *HOW*

Doulton match strikers, 4 to 5in (10 to 12.5cm) wide. **£60-70 each**   *BEV*

A Carlton ware vase, 8in (20cm).
£200-225   *CLH*

A pair of Carlton ware ashtrays.
£25-40 each   *BEV*

A Carlton ware farmyard cruet, 5½in (14cm) diam.
£60-65   *BEV*

Sailor figures as salt and pepper pots, 3in (7.5cm). **£30-35** *BEV*

Three animal figures egg cups, 2½in (6cm) high. **£8-20 each** *BEV*

A Shelley lemon squeezer, 4in (10cm) diam. **£20-30** *BEV*

A Japanese cruet in the form of a donkey and cart. **£18-20** *BEV*

A German pepper and salt, 5in (12.5cm) high. **£70-80** *BEV*

A foreign lemon squeezer, 5½in (14cm). **£25-30** *BEV*

A Czechoslovakian liquor bottle and cups, c1930. **£65-70** *BEV*

Three egg cups, 1930s, 2 to 2½in (5 to 6.5cm) high. **£3-6 each** *MA*

Three Carlton ware serviette rings, 4in (10cm). **£25-40 each** *BEV*

A set of 7 ceramic jazz musicians, probably German, c1930, 2in (5cm). **£75-90** *RGA*

A frog cruet, 4in (10cm) high. **£3-5** *BEV*

A pair of Swansea spongeware jugs, c1830. **£250-300**   *CHA*

A set of 3 Arabian Nights jugs, c1920. **£75-120 each**   *TP*

A Swansea hand painted pottery bowl, c1850, 6in (15cm) diam.   **£40-50**   *CHA*

A Swansea Cambrian hand decorated jug, c1800. **£80-120**   *RP*

A Crown Devon cup and saucer, 1930.   **£15-20**   *MA*

A spongeware and potato cut bowl, c1870. **£30-35**   *CHA*

A Welsh spongeware jug. **£30-50**   *CHA*

A Swansea hand painted lustreware bowl, c1860, 6½in (16cm) diam. **£40-50**   *CHA*

A Swansea lustreware jug, c1860, 5in (13cm) high. **£60-90**   *CHA*

A pair of Swansea pottery jugs, c1835, 5in (13cm) high. **£250-300**   *CHA*

A Cornish motto ware jug, 5in (13cm) high. **£25-35**   *MA*

A pair of Llanelli tea bowls and saucers. **£70-80**   *CHA*

A Cornish ware butter dish, T. G. Green, 6in (15cm) diam. **£12-18**   *MA*

A Poole painted terracotta vase, 6in (15cm) high. **£240-280**   *CHa*

A Llanelli pottery jug. **£100-125**   *RP*

A Llanelli potato print and hand painted bowl. **£50-60**   *CHA*

A Cornish motto ware mug, by Dartmouth Pottery. **£15-20**   *MA*

A pair of Llanelli jugs, c1840, 4in (10cm) high. **£350-400**   *CHA*

A copper lustre jug, possibly Staffordshire, c1845, 5in (13cm) high. **£100-120** *HOW*

An Adams dish and cover, 7in (18cm) long. **£20-25** *PSA*

A Staffordshire tavern frog mug, damaged, c1830, 5in (13cm) high. **£120-150** *CHA*

A Portabello jug, unmarked, c1850, 5in (13cm) high. **£240-250** *CHA*

Five Wedgwood Etruria egg coddlers, 4in (10cm) high. **£80-90** *ROS*

A Liverpool jug for the Delft pottery, c1800. **£180-200** *CHA*

A set of 3 Staffordshire face jugs. **£90-100** *CHA*

A French barber's bowl, rim chips, c1610, 12in (31cm) wide. **£1,000-1,200** *CHA*

r. A copper lustre jug, c1850. **£140-150** *HOW*

l. A Copeland Spode Italian trio, 1900. **£20-25** *MA*

A relief moulded jug, with enamel paint decoration, c1845, 8in (20cm) high. **£100-120** *HOW*

A Mason's Ironstone jug, 7in (18cm) high. **£195-220** *VH*

A Crown Ducal decorated jug, signed C. Rhead. **£150-160** *PCh*

A Wemyss tray, 9½in (24cm) long.
£280-320 *SBA*

A Crown Ducal egg cup set, c1930.
£50-60 *GRA*

A pair of frog pitchers.
£325-375 *NB*

A Kensington wall pocket, 1930s.
£45-56 *MA*

Twelve pieces of Gray's pottery coffee ware.
£20-30 *PCh*

A Staffordshire pottery piggy
bank, c1930. **£16-20** *HOW*

An Arcadian fireplace, 3½in
(9cm) high. **£22-25** *BGA*

Two Bewley pottery dishes,
c1940. **£10-12 each** *PSA*

A Glyn Colledge mug,
1950s. **£30-40** *MA*

A Ridgway child's mug.
£20-30 *PC*

A Shelley egg
cup.
£15-20 *BEV*

A Chameleon ware oil lamp.
£40-50 *TAV*

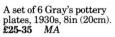

A set of 6 Gray's pottery
plates, 1930s, 8in (20cm).
£25-35 *MA*

A Copeland bust.
£85-100 *PCh*

A Copeland figure.
£280-300 *PCh*

An Edward Radford fruit bowl, c1930, 8in (20cm) diam. **£60-80** *MA*

An Edward Radford sugar sifter, c1930. **£25-35** *MA*

Two Edward Radford posy vases, late 1930s, 4½in (12cm) wide. **£15-20 each** *MA*

An Edward Radford Indian tree pattern charger, c1930. **£150-180** *MA*

An Edward Radford cruet, late 1930s, 4½in (11cm). **£15-18** *MA*

An Edward Radford early Burslem jug, c1930. **£40-60** *MA*

An Edward Radford fruit bowl, ranunculus pattern, c1930, 10in (25.5cm) diam. **£85-125** *MA*

An Edward Radford Indian Tree pattern jug, c1930, 8in (20cm) high. **£45-65** *MA*

An E. Radford early Burslem jug, c1928, 4in (10cm) high. **£50-70** *MA*

An Edward Radford teapot, ranunculus pattern, c1930, 6in (15cm) high. **£85-100** *MA*

A set of 3 Edward Radford coaching jugs, c1930, tall jug 11in (28cm) high. **£130-150** *MA*

An Edward Radford ranunculus pattern tray, 13in (33cm) wide. **£30-40** *MA*

A Staffordshire pottery commemorative plaque, c1815.
£180-220 *HOW*

A Paxton's two-handled tureen, with embossed leaves, 16½in (42cm) wide.
£140-160 *PCh*

An early 20thC fairing, 'Did you ring, Sir?'. **£25-30** *PCh*

A Staffordshire pottery commemorative jug, c1815.
£145-165 *HOW*

A Villeroy and Boch plat, 8½in (21.5cm).
£20-30 *NB*

A Staffordshire plaque, entitled 'The Case', the lawyer is milking the cow, painted with a matt finish, c1830, 13½in (34cm) wide.
£150-180 *HOW*

A German bisque pastille burner.
£350-400 *JL*

An ice pail, late 19thC, 8½in (21cm) high.
£100-130 *PCh*

A Pratt ware meat paste jar, 'Mending the Nets', 3in (7.5cm) high.
£65-75 *CHA*

A Continental bisque porcelain figure of a gallant gentleman, late 19thC. **£200-250** *TAV*

A Holdcroft oyster dish, 10in (25.5cm).
£90-110 *NB*

Two from a set of 3 Mason's Ironstone jugs, with Red Scale pattern, printed crown marks, c1830. **£525-575** *VH*

A Mason's Ironstone chamber pot, with floral decoration, 6in (15cm) high. **£50-75** *PCh*

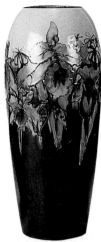

A Moorcroft Peacock Feather bowl, impressed marks. **£2,800-3,000** *S*

A Moorcroft Moonlit Blue vase, c1924. **£5,800-6,200** *S*

A Moorcroft Orchid vase, c1935. **£1,400-1,600** *S*

A Moorcroft Cornflower bowl. **£1,400-1,600** *S*

A Moorcroft vase and cover. **£900-1,000** *S*

A Moorcroft salt glazed vase, c1935. **£700-800** *S*

A Moorcroft salt glazed Honesty vase. **£1,300-1,500** *S*

A Moorcroft salt glazed Peacock Feather vase, impressed marks, c1934. **£1,900-2,200** *S*

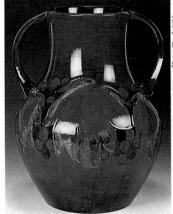

A Moorcroft flambé Leaf and Fruit vase, impressed marks, dated 1935, 15½in (39cm). **£3,000-3,500** *S*

A Boch Frères vase. **£400-500** *CHa*

A Moorcroft Persian tazza, c1915. **£900-1,000** *S*

A Minton's 14-piece Art Nouveau tile panel, with tube lined decoration, one corner chipped, moulded factory marks, 12 by 42in (30.5 by 106.5cm). **£500-550** *CSK*

A Satsuma Kyoto vase, seal mark, Meiji period, 10½in (26cm). **£180-220** *BOW*

A Satsuma vase, seal mark, signed Kyoto Yaki, Taisho period. **£45-55** *BOW*

A Satsuma dish, Taisho period, c1920, 7in (17.5cm). **£25-35** *BOW*

A Satsuma bottle, Edo period. **£80-90** *BOW*

A Satsuma box, gold shimazu mon and brown seal mark Daizan, Taisho period. **£90-110** *BOW*

A Satsuma tea set, Tokyo School, signed and black and gold seal mark. **£280-320** *BOW*

A Satsuma vase, seal mark in red, Taisho period. **£80-100** *BOW*

A Kutani saki cup, Meiji period, 3½in (9cm) diam. **£20-25** *BOW*

A Japanese shell dish, early 19thC. **£550-650** *BOW*

A Satsuma vase, signed Denzan, seal mark, Taisho period, 9½in (24cm) high. **£180-200** *BOW*

A cloisonné coffee pot, mid-19thC, 7in (18cm) high. **£80-100** *BOW*

A Canton tray, teapot, 2 cups and saucers, in Rose Medallion pattern, c1860. **£320-360** *BOW*

147

A Staffordshire Toby jug, c1800, 12in (31cm) high. **£2,500-3,000** *HEY*

Hearty Goodfellow Toby jug, some restoration, c1820. **£400-500** *HEY*

A pearlware Toby jug, c1795, 9½in (24cm) high. **£850-950** *HEY*

A pearlware Toby jug, with measure, c1790, 10in (25cm) high. **£800-1,000** *HEY*

A set of Doulton & Watts Nelson jugs, c1820. **£200-500 each** *TP*

A French Toby jug, Angoulême, c1920. **£110-130** *VH*

A miniature Toby jug, c1890, 4in (10cm) high. **£20-30** *PSA*

A Falstaff jug, by Edward Steel of Hanley, 1888. **£400-500** *HEY*

A Staffordshire Toby jug, restored, c1810, 10in (25cm) high. **£700-850** *HEY*

A Toby with impressed mark C.H. Brannam, c1900, 9in (23cm) high. **£350-450** *HEY*

A Yorkshire pearlware Toby jug, c1840. **£850-1,000** *HEY*

A bisque headed
clockwork musical
automaton.
£3,500-4,000 *CSK*

A bisque shoulder headed
character doll, marked 1727,
20in (51cm) high. **£880-1,000** *CSK*

An English
composition doll,
with 'Mama' box,
c1930.
£60-70 *PSA*

A Hermann Steiner jointed
doll, re-dressed, c1915.
£200-235 *PSA*

A boudoir doll, 1920s, 24in (61cm).
£130-160 *YV*

An Armand Marseille doll,
AM 390, c1905, 19½in (49cm).
£275-295 *PSA*

A Simon & Halbig bisque headed
doll, c1890, 26in (66cm) high.
£500-550 *DOW*

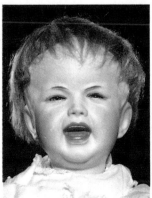

A painted felt doll,
Valentino, c1927.
£8,250-9,000 *CSK*

An early Jumeau
bisque headed doll.
£5,500-6,000 *CNY*

A bisque headed character doll,
impressed SFBJ 233 PARIS 8,
16in (41cm) high. **£2,500-3,000** *CSK*

A bisque headed
musical automaton.
£6,600-7,000 *CSK*

149

A printer's proof of cigarette cards, Stephen Mitchell & Son, issued 1939.
£70-100 *ACC*

Carreras set of 50, Film Favourites, 1938. **£40-60** *ACC*

State Express, set of 25, Proverbs, 1936. **£16-32** *ACC*

Wills's set of 50, Arms of Foreign Cities, 1912. **£30-60** *ACC*

Carreras set of 50, Film Stars, 1936.
£30-50 *ACC*

Wills's set of 50, Time and Money in Different Countries, 1906. **£65-130**
ACC

Wills's set of 50, Celebrated Ships, 1911.
£45-90   *ACC*

Wills's set of 50, Rugby Internationals, 1929.
£48-96   *ACC*

Abdullah set of 25, Feathered Friends, 1935.
£13-26   *ACC*

Wills's set of 50, The Coronation, 1911.
£48-96   *ACC*

Wills's set of 50, English Period Costumes, 1929.
£40-70   *ACC*

Wills's set of 50, Old English Garden Flowers, 1910.
£30-60   *ACC*

Wills's set of 25, Cinema Stars,
1928. **£23-46**   *ACC*

151

A late Victorian fan, with gold spangles on mother-of-pearl sticks.
£240-260 *YV*

A painted leaf fan, the sticks pierced and painted, the guardsticks carved, mid-18thC. **£850-1,000** *CSK*

A Canton fan, with ivory carved and pierced sticks and carved guardsticks, c1860, 11in (28cm). **£1,000-1,500** *CSK*

A mid-Victorian hand coloured litho fan.
£250-300 *YV*

A painted leaf fan, with carved and pierced mother-of-pearl sticks, c1750, 10in (25cm).
£880-1,000 *CSK*

A painted leaf fan, with carved and pierced ivory sticks, painted and decorated with red foil, c1740, 11½in (29cm).
£830-1,000 *CSK*

A hand coloured litho fan, with carved and silvered mother-of-pearl sticks, mid-19thC.
£250-300 *YV*

A painted leaf fan, with carved and pierced mother-of-pearl sticks, c1740, 11in (28cm).
£1,000-1,500 *CSK*

A painted silk leaf fan, with ribbonwork spangles and sequins and ivory sticks.
£770-1,000 *CSK*

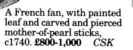

A painted leaf fan, with ivory sticks, early 18thC.
£900-1,200 *CSK*

A French fan, with painted leaf and carved and pierced mother-of-pearl sticks, c1740. **£800-1,000** *CSK*

An Empire fan, hand painted on silk, with carved and coloured sticks.
£250-300 *YV*

Staffordshire Transfer Printed Ware

A blue and white Basket of Flowers pattern plate, probably Wedgwood, c1835, 10in (25cm). **£40-50** *PSA*

A pair of Minton blue and white Genoese pattern plates, early Victorian, 9½in (14cm). **£50-100** *PSA*

A blue and white mug, early 19thC, 4in (10cm) high. **£70-80** *PSA*

A W. Adams & Son blue and white Damascus pattern dish, c1840. **£60-70** *PSA*

A J. & M. P. Bell & Co., blue Palestine pattern, c1840, 10in (25cm) diam. **£55-65** *PSA*

A J. R. J. Bevington, blue underglaze Monopteros pattern dish, 10in (25cm) diam. **£60-70** *PSA*

A set of 4 Johnson Bros blue and white transfer printed plates, small chips, c1920, 8½in (21cm). **£10-14 each** *PSA*

A blue and white Eton College pattern plate, probably by G. Phillips, c1840, 9½in (24cm). **£50-65** *PSA*

For a selection of Staffordshire Peppers, refer to previous editions of Miller's Collectables Price Guides, available from Miller's Publications.

A blue and white plate, 8in (20cm). **£85-95** *Nor*

A Thomas and Benjamin Goodwin meat dish, printed with Delhi Hindoostan, from the Indian scenery series, printed mark c1840, some staining, 16½in (42cm) wide. **£100-120** *CSK*

A blue and white whisky flask, 8in (20cm) high. **£110-125** *Nor*

A blue and white feeding cup, 4½in (11cm) diam. **£85-95** *Nor*

A blue and white underglaze Piping Shepherd pattern plate, c1820, 10in (25cm). **£80-90** *HOW*

A 'Neptune' plate, 10in (25cm). **£55-65** *Nor*

A pair of blue and white tureens, 8in (20cm) wide. **£175-200** each *Nor*

A blue and white jug, named, 8in (20cm) high. **£115-125** *Nor*

A blue and white underglaze plate, Sheltering Peasants pattern, c1820, 8½in (21cm). **£100-120** *HOW*

A blue and white dish, 7½in (19cm) long. **£125-135** *Nor*

FURTHER READING
Staffordshire Portrait Figures of the Victorian Age, Thomas Balston, London 1958.
Nineteenth Century English Pottery and Porcelain, Geoffrey Bemrose, London 1952.
English Pottery Figures, 1660-1860, Reginald G. Haggar, London 1947.
Commemorative Pottery and Porcelain, James A. Mackay, London 1971.
Staffordshire Saltglazed Stoneware, Arnold R. Mountford, London 1971.
Staffordshire Portrait Figures and Allied Subjects of the Victorian Era, P. D. Gordon Pugh, London 1971.
Staffordshire Pottery Figures, H. Read, London 1929.

Teapots

A Studio pottery teapot, monogrammed SD, 6in (15cm) high. **£30-50** *MA*

A blue tea set, produced for Westinghouse, U.S.A., by the Hall China Co., in the form of a train with carriage, milk tender missing, c1932, teapot 10½in (25cm) wide. **£275-320** *BEV*

These sets were given away with 'fridges.

A Maddox tea set, The First Cottage, teapot 7½in (19cm) wide. **£75-85** *BEV*

Cross Reference
Art Deco

A bunny teapot, made in England, 7½in (19cm) high. **£70-100** *HEW*

Toby Jugs

The Squire, by William Kent of Burslem, in underglaze colours, rust jacket, green waistcoat and yellow breeches, on a three-cornered chair placed on a seven-sided base, c1900, 11in (28cm) high. **£200-300** *HEY*

A pearlware Toby jug and cover, painted in Pratt type colours, some damage, c1810, 8in (20cm) high. **£310-330** *CSK*

Three mini Toby jugs, c1830.
£110-130 each *GIN*

The Gin Woman, decorated in overglaze enamel, with yellow hat and decorated in dark red and green, c1840, 9in (23cm) high.
£350-450 *HEY*

A Toby jug modelled as Admiral Nelson, in underglaze blue jacket and yellow flowered waistcoat, on a naturalistic base, c1870, 11½in (29cm) high.
£200-300 *HEY*

Peace, a Toby jug in highly glazed colours, black coat and hat, in yellows, browns and turquoise, 1919, 9½in (24cm) high.
£150-200 *HEY*

A Staffordshire Toby jug, holding an ale jug, handle to reverse, 19thC, 10in (25cm) high.
£475-500 *B*

A traditional Toby jug, decorated in translucent glazes, green coat, brown trousers, shoes and base, c1800, 10in (25cm) high.
£300-400 *HEY*

The Lady Toper, a Derbyshire majolica ware female Toby jug, coloured graduating from yellow to dark green at base, probably by Sharpe Bros & Co. of Swadlincote, c1880, 9in (23cm) high.
£350-450 *HEY*

A Yorkshire Toby jug, with figurehead handle, in underglaze green coat, plum breeches, on a deep base of green and brown sponging, restoration, c1870, 10in (25cm) high.
£150-250 *HEY*

The Nightwatchman, a Toby jug possibly by Enoch Wood, in rust enamel coat, black hat and boots, the spout formed from chair, the base in blue, red, yellow and black, c1810, 9in (23cm) high.
£350-450 *HEY*

A Royal Worcester china small jug and cover, depicting a jester in full motley, puce printed mark, shape 2856.
£250-300 *HSS*

Toothbrush Holders

A Donald Duck holder, 4½in (11cm) high.
£55-65
BEV

A pig with flute holder, 4½in (11cm) high.
£55-65 *BEV*

A pig with a fiddle holder, 4½in (11cm) high.
£55-65 *BEV*

A builder pig holder, 4½in (11cm) high.
£55-65 *BEV*

DID YOU KNOW?
Miller's Collectables Price Guide is designed to build up, year by year, into the most comprehensive reference system available.

Snow White, 6in (15cm) high.
£55-65 *BEV*

Grumpy.
£55-65 *BEV*

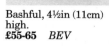

Doc, 4½in (11cm) high.
£55-65 *BEV*

Bashful, 4½in (11cm) high.
£55-65 *BEV*

Sleepy, 4½in (11cm) high.
£55-65 *BEV*

A Dopey holder, 4½in (11cm) high.
£55-65 *BEV*

These toothbrush holders were made for Maw & Son of London.

Toast Racks

Hand painted 'Yacht Ware' mid-1930s, sugar sifter 4½in (11cm) high, cruet 5½in (14cm) long, and toast rack 6in (15cm) long.
£25-35 each *PC*

A selection of Shorter Ware hand painted racks, 1950s, toast 5½ to 7½in (14 to 19cm) long.
£20-30 each *PC*

Cross Reference
Carlton Ware

Vases

A Grimwades Royal Winton floral wall vase, 1930s, 8½in (21cm) long.
£40-60 MA

A Watcombe Indian bottle vase, with saucer, top missing.
£190-210 *BLO*

A Royal Bonn two-handled vase and cover, with cream ground and floral decoration, incised mark, pattern No. 351, late 19thC, 15in (38cm) high.
£75-95 *PCh*

A Robert Heron & Son vase, 8in (20cm) high.
£150-200 *RdeR*

A pair of Edwardian pottery vases, 14½in (37cm) high.
£100-150 *RE*

A pair of German hand painted vases, 6in (15cm) high.
£35-40 *FOB*

DOLLS

The Doll market is very buoyant at present. Top quality dolls will always achieve good prices with, until recently, the French manufacturers leading. However, during the past few months there has been a marked increase in the top German makers, and the prices are now on a par with the French.

Middle range dolls remain much the same price-wise and remember that originality is as important as condition.

Bisque Headed Dolls

Bisque is porcelain at the initial biscuit stage of manufacture, before the glaze is applied. Delicate faces can be painted at this stage, the problem is, however, that bisque will easily sustain damage and wear with obvious effects on the price. Bisque can also be used for limbs and hands and feet, and in some cases for the complete doll. The finest French and German dolls have bisque heads.

A late Victorian miniature doll, with glass eyes, 4in (10cm) high. **£65-75** *DOL*

A character baby doll, with blue lashed sleeping eyes and composition body, damage to fingers, marked S PB in star H B 6, 21in (53cm) high. **£350-375** *CSK*

A character baby doll, with blue sleeping eyes, blonde mohair wig and toddler body, impressed Porzellanfabrik Burggrub Das Lachende Baby 1930 – 3½ D.R.G.M., 17in (43cm) high. **£400-425** *CSK*

A Bähr Pröschild character baby doll, c1920, 21in (53cm) high. **£475-500** *DOL*

A swivel headed doll, with blue eyes, gusseted kid body with individually stitched fingers and toes, marked 6 on head, FG and 6 on shoulder plate, 22in (56cm) high. **£1,250-1,300** *CSK*

A socket headed Paris bébé girl doll, with long light brown wig, brown glass eyes, composition body with fully jointed limbs, original lace and broderie anglaise garments and in original box, 23in (58cm) high. **£500-550** *HSS*

A child doll, with blue sleeping eyes and jointed wood and composition body, impressed 192 13, 28in (71cm) high. **£675-700** *CSK*

An early bisque clown, with clown's hairstyle and outfit moulded and painted, 4in (10cm) high. **£450-475** *CSK*

A socket head doll, with painted features, closing blue glass eyes, composition body and limbs, in full Scottish Highlanders costume, head impressed 192, early 20thC, 11½in (29cm) high.
£185-200 *HSS*

A turned shoulder doll, with gusseted kid leather body and separate fingers, dress frail, unmarked, c1885, 14in (36cm) high, with a miniature mahogany chair in Arts and Crafts style, 12½in (32cm) high.
£1,550-1,650 *S*

FURTHER READING
Delightful Dolls, Thelma Bateman, Washington 1966.
The American Doll Artist, Helen Bullard, Boston 1965.
Dolls: Makers and Marks, Elizabeth A. Coleman, Washington 1963.
The Collector's Encyclopedia of Dolls, Dorothy S., Elizabeth A. and Evelyn J. Coleman, New York 1968.
Dolls, Lady Antonia Fraser, London 1963.
Wonderful Dolls of Wax, Jo Elizabeth Gerken, Lincoln (Nebraska) 1964.
Directories of British, French and German Dolls, Luella Hart, Oaklands (Calif) 1964-65.
Dolls and Dollmakers, Mary Hillier, London 1968.
Dressing Dolls, A. Johnson, London 1969.
Dolls & Dolls Houses, Constance King, London 1977.
Dolls, J. Noble, London 1968.
Dolls of the World, G. White, London 1962.
European and American Dolls, G. White, London 1966.

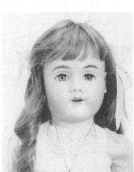

A bisque headed child doll, with blue sleeping eyes, straight limbed composition body and original outfit of red cotton bonnet, frock, stockings and shoes, marked DEP R O A, 16in (41cm) high.
£350-375 *CSK*

An all bisque bride doll, with glass eyes, all original, c1900, 5½in (14cm) high.
£140-160 *PSA*

A Halbig doll, with blue grey eyes, with replacement wig and eyelashes, small cracks, impressed 109, 15½ x 6½, 30in (76cm) high.
£675-700 *S*

A character baby doll, with brown sleeping eyes, bent limbed composition body dressed as a boy in brown checked suit, marked 604 10, by Bähr & Pröschild, 19in (48cm) high.
£575-600 *CSK*

A bébé, with brown yeux fibres, brown wig, wood and composition body, 3 tiny blemishes on forehead, marked 9 FG in cartouche, 23in (59cm) high. **£2,200-2,500** *CSK*

A Limbach doll, c1895, 7½in (19cm) high.
£100-150 *DOL*

A Nöckler and Tittel character doll, with intaglio blue eyes, pintucked broderie anglaise cream cotton dress and olive green velvet cape, impressed N & T 1 3, c1914, 12in (31cm) high.
£330-350 *S*

A French bébé Parise, all original, with original box, 14in (36cm) high.
£300-320 *PSA*

A bisque headed doll, with blue sleeping eyes and a jointed body, incised DEP, 20in (51cm) high.
£550-650 *CNY*

A Kling doll, c1860, 9in (23cm) high.
£200-250 *DOL*

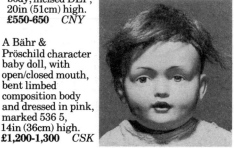

A Bähr & Pröschild character baby doll, with open/closed mouth, bent limbed composition body and dressed in pink, marked 536 5, 14in (36cm) high.
£1,200-1,300 *CSK*

A German shoulder bisque doll, with painted blue eyes, kid body with bisque lower arms, dressed as a sailor, unmarked, c1890, 18½in (47cm) high. **£175-200** *S*

A German doll, with cloth and sawdust body, c1890, 8½in (21cm) high.
£15-20 *DOL*

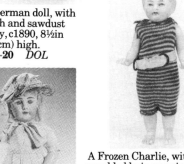

A Frozen Charlie, with blonde moulded hair, wearing original swimsuit, c1900, 4½in (11cm) high. **£90-95** *PSA*

An Alt, Beck and Gottschalck doll, with fixed blue glass eyes, ball jointed wood and composition body, impressed 1268 Dep N.8, c1892, 16in (41cm) high. **£1,100-1,250** *S*

A turned shoulder head doll, with fixed spiralled blue glass eyes, leather body with bisque lower arms, kiln dust to left temple and cheek, 5 fingers broken, impressed 8, c1890, 17in (43cm) high.
£425-450   *S*

A German two-faced doll, probably by Carl Bergner, with screaming and smiling faces, brown glass eyes, cardboard body, and composition lower limbs, inoperative voice box, c1895, 14½in (37cm) high.
£425-450   *S*

A German shoulder parian doll, with painted features, cloth body, bisque lower limbs, in original faded purple and lace dress, in box, c1880, 10in (25cm) high.
£275-300   *S*

A character doll, with weighted brown glass eyes, blonde painted hair, replacement curved limb composition body, unclothed, kiln dust to crown, impressed 166/10 Kley & Hahn for Hertel Schwab, c1912, 20in (50cm) high.   **£840-860**   *S*

A Frozen Charlie, in glazed china with light brown painted eyes, c1890, 14½in (37cm) high, and an all bisque doll with blue painted eyes, one leg possibly replaced, unmarked, c1900, 13in (33cm) high.
£350-375   *S*

A bisque headed doll, formed as a child's parasol, with composition arms and legs, marked Puppenfabrik, 20½in (52cm) high.
£200-250   *CSK*

A German shoulder bisque doll, with fixed blue eyes, fabric body and waxed composition lower arms, damage to rose in hair, impressed 150, c1880, 6in (15cm) high.
£1,100-1,150   *S*

A French Huret-style shoulder bisque doll, with fixed head and blue glass eyes, kid leather body with separately stitched fingers and blonde wig over cork pate, lightly impressed 3 to lower edge of shoulder plate, c1870, 15in (38cm) high.   **£840-860**   *S*

A French shoulder bisque doll, with fixed head and blue glass eyes, kid leather body with bisque lower arms and replaced real hair wig over cork pate, unmarked, c1870.   **£285-300**   *S*

Armand Marseille

Armand Marseille was a German manufacturer who made dolls between 1865 and about 1920. Although he produced some composition headed dolls he is best known for bisque heads.

A baby doll, 352, with top knot coming through its head, c1929.
£450-500 *DOL*

A character baby doll, wearing original clothes, mould No. 971, 10½in (26cm) high.
£200-225 *PSA*

A Nobbi Kid doll, all original, c1920, 8in (20cm) high.
£600-650 *DOL*

A Dream Baby doll, 351, c1928, 15in (38cm) high.
£225-250 *DOL*

A bisque headed character baby doll, modelled as an Oriental, with brown sleeping eyes, composition body and original shift, impressed AM 353/2K, 8in (20cm) high.
£560-580 *CSK*

A bisque socket head girl doll, with painted features, closing blue glass eyes, composition body and jointed limbs, head and neck impressed Armand Marseille, 390 n, Germany, A61/2M, 23½in (60cm) high.
£265-300 *HSS*

A jointed doll, AM 390, c1900, 18in (46cm) high.
£230-250 *PSA*

An Oriental doll, with weighted brown glass eyes and composition body, small chips to neck socket, c1926, 14in (36cm) high. **£575-600** *S*

Bergner

Carl Bergner was a German manufacturer who made dolls between 1890 and 1909 at Sonneberg. He is particularly noted for his two and three-faced dolls.

A three-faced doll, with squeaker, in mint condition, not wearing original dress, c1870, 15½in (39cm) high.
£1,300-1,500 *DOL*

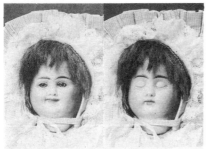

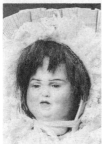

A Carl Bergner three-faced doll, the head turning by means of a ring inside, cardboard covered body with voice box, jointed wood and composition limbs, c1895, 12in (30cm) high.
£925-950 *S*

A bisque headed three-faced doll, the faces smiling, sleeping and crying, with fixed blue eyes, composition arms and legs, the shoulder plate stamped C.B., 15in (38cm) high. **£850-900** *CSK*

Bru

A bisque headed walking doll, with weighted blue glass eyes, composition walker body with straight wrists, dressed in later silk shift, some damage and 5 fingers missing, impressed BRU Jne/6, c1890, 16in (41cm) high.
£800-850 *S*

Gaultier

Gaultier was a porcelain factory in Paris which produced bisque dolls heads during the late 19th and early 20thC.

A pressed bisque doll, with fixed blue glass paperweight almond shaped eyes and papier mâché body with straight wrists, stringing loose, firing flaw to corner of mouth, incised F.4.G., c1870, 22in (56cm) high.
£1,500-2,000 *S*

A bisque doll, with open/closed mouth, fixed blue glass paperweight eyes, pierced ears, blonde real hair wig, and jointed wood body, impressed 5 F.G. in a scroll, 15in (39cm) high.
£1,000-1,050 *S*

MAKE THE MOST OF MILLERS
Condition is absolutely vital when assessing the value of any item. Damaged pieces appreciate much less than perfect examples. However, a rare, desirable piece may command a high price even when damaged.

Heubach

The German manufacturer Gebrüder Heubach first made dolls between 1820 and 1863. Later Ernst Heubach produced dolls from 1887 until about 1920. Heubach specialised in character dolls with fabric or composition bodies, and all Heubach dolls featured finely modelled bisque heads.

A Koppelsdorf 250 doll, c1910, 10in (25cm) high. **£165-185** *PSA*

A black baby doll, 399, c1920, 84in (21cm) high. **£250-300** *DOL*

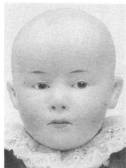

A bisque shoulder headed character doll, with closed mouth, blue intaglio eyes, moulded hair and stuffed body, impressed with the Gebrüder Heubach sunburst 7, 18in (46cm) high. **£500-550** *CSK*

A bisque headed character baby doll, with blue sleeping eyes, bent limbed composition body and dressed in original white frock and underclothes, marked with Gebrüder Heubach sunburst 9, 18in (46cm) high. **£790-820** *CSK*

A Dolly Dimple bisque character doll, for Hamburger and Company, impressed DEP H 3, c1910, 12in (31cm) high. **£1,000-1,100** *S*

A Koppelsdorf 320 doll, with toddler's body, c1925, 8in (20cm) high. **£100-150** *PSA*

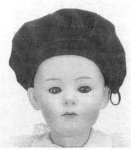

A bisque headed character baby doll, with closed mouth, blue sleeping eyes and jointed wood and composition body, impressed 8 with the Gebrüder Heubach sunburst, 16½in (42cm) high. **£525-575** *CSK*

Jumeau

Pierre François Jumeau made distinctive Jumeau Dolls between 1842 and 1899. Best known for his 'Parisiennes' and a particular Jumeau expression. The maker's marks vary and include:
BÉBÉ JUMEAU
Breveté SGDG Jumeau
Tête Jumeau
and later on DEP.

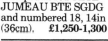

A bisque doll, with fixed blue glass eyes, and jointed wood and composition body, 2 fingers broken, slightly grainy complexion, stamped in red TETE JUMEAU BTE SGDG and numbered 18, 14in (36cm). **£1,250-1,300** *S*

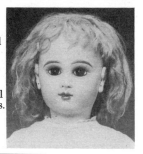

A bisque doll, with fixed brown glass eyes, damaged, inscribed to back of head in ink VI....O R, c1890, 24in (61cm) high, and a small collection of doll's clothes. **£725-775** *S*

A bisque headed bébé, with blue yeux fibres, brown wig and jointed wood and composition body, stamped in red Tête Jumeau, 18in (46cm) high.
£1,500-1,600   *CSK*

A bisque headed bébé, with fixed brown eyes, jointed wood and composition body with pull string voice box, stamped in red DÉPOSÉ TÊTE JUMEAU 11, 25in (64cm) high.
£2,100-2,200   *CSK*

A bisque headed bébé, with closed mouth, fixed blue eyes, jointed wood and composition body, stamped in red DÉPOSÉ TÊTE JUMEAU BTE S.G.D.G. 11, and stamped in blue on the body JUMEAU MEDAILLE D'OR PARIS, 23in (59cm) high.
£3,300-3,500   *CSK*

A bisque doll, with fixed brown glass eyes, the wood and composition body redressed, white leather modern shoes, kiln dust to face and chip at neck socket, impressed 1 at neck socket, c1890.
£225-250   *S*

A bisque headed bébé, with brown paperweight eyes, and jointed body with straight wrists, hairline crack at left temple, incised Déposé EJ, 26in (66cm) high.
£2,200-3,000   *CNY*

A bisque headed bébé, with brown paperweight eyes, and repainted jointed composition body with paper label marked BÉBÉ JUMEAU, original Jumeau box, lacking lid, with lithographed paper label BÉBÉ JUMEAU, PARLANT, 21½in (54cm) high.
£1,700-2,500   *CNY*

Kämmer & Reinhardt

Kämmer and Reinhardt was a German manufacturer who started producing dolls in about 1886. They also produced a range of character dolls in 1909. Their mark is a straightforward K & R.

A doll with five-piece body, and painted shoes and socks, 10in (25cm) high,
£200-230
and a small doll's trunk with removable tray and contents, c1900.
£60-70   *PSA*

A bisque headed doll, with brown sleeping eyes, and jointed body, head incised K * R Simon Halbig Germany, 31in (79cm) high. **£720-750**   *CNY*

A pair of bisque headed character baby dolls, with open/closed mouths, grey painted eyes and babies bodies, wearing contemporary baby clothes, impressed 36 K * R 100, 15in (38cm) high. **£950-1,000**   *CSK*

A bisque socket head girl doll, with blue grey glass sleeping eyes, composition body and jointed limbs, head and neck impressed K.R.53, 19in (47.5cm) high.   **£325-375**   *HSS*

A Kämmer & Reinhardt/ Simon & Halbig bisque character doll, with weighted blue eyes, jointed wood and composition body, lacking wig, impressed 116/a28, c1911, 13in (33cm) high. **£1,000-1,100**   *S*

A bisque headed character baby doll, with brown sleeping eyes, and composition baby's body, firing fault on left cheek, repairs to fingers, impressed K * R S & H 118/A 42.   **£730-750**   *CSK*

Kestner

J. D. Kestner was a German manufacturer from the early 19thC through until the early 20thC.

Although a small range of dolls was produced they are invariably of the highest quality. The most common Kestner mark is J.D.K.

A jointed body doll, 168, with plaster pate, c1910. **£500-550**   *PSA*

A bisque doll, with weighted brown glass eyes, and ball jointed wood and composition body, impressed F 10 162, c1892, 20in (50cm) high. **£825-850**   *S*

A character doll, 211, c1915, 18in (46cm) high. **£600-800**   *ChL*

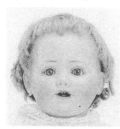

A bisque headed character baby doll, with blue sleeping eyes, baby's body and embroidered robe, impressed F10247 J.D.K.10, 12in (31cm) high. **£950-985**   *CSK*

A bisque headed character doll, with brown sleeping googlie eyes, water melon mouth, and jointed wood and composition toddler body, dressed in brown checked cotton, marked A.5.J.D.K.221, 10½in (26cm) high. **£950-985**   *CSK*

S.F.B.J.

S.F.B.J. was the 'Société de Fabrication de Bébés et Jouets' formed in 1899 from the leading French manufacturers including Bru and Jumeau. They produced an extensive range of products but the quality suffered. The mark was a simple S.F.B.J.

A bisque character doll, with fixed blue glass eyes, and jointed wood and composition body, redressed, some repainting, sparse flocking to head, impressed 235/6, c1910, 18in (46cm) high.
£725-775   *S*

A bisque headed character baby doll, with open/closed mouth, blue sleeping eyes and baby's body, impressed R.S.F.B.J.236 PARIS 10, 18½in (47cm) high.
£625-650   *CSK*

A bisque headed character doll, with blue lashed sleeping eyes, and jointed wood and composition toddler body, dressed in contemporary clothes, later wig, body overpainted, marked SFBJ 252 Paris, 14in (36cm) high.
£2,500-2,600   *CSK*

A bisque headed character boy doll, with fixed hazel eyes, and jointed composition body, left hand damaged, marked S.F.B.J., 227, Paris, 4,14in (36cm) high.
£1,750-1,800   *C(S)*

Simon & Halbig

Simon & Halbig was a German porcelain manufacturer with factories at Grofenhain and Ohrdruf who supplied dolls heads to doll makers from about 1870 until the early 20thC. The mark S & H or Simon & Halbig usually indicates a doll's head of high quality.

A bisque headed character doll, with blue sleeping eyes, blonde mohair wig and bent limbed composition body, impressed 1428 9, by Simon & Halbig, 15in (38cm) high, and a doll's trunk with linen.
£1,700-1,800   *CSK*

A pair of Franz Schmidt/ Simon & Halbig bisque character dolls, each with flirty blue glass eyes, in original cardboard boxes with paper Prima Charakter Baby labels, impressed 1296/36, c1912, 16in (40cm) high.
£1,750-1,800   *S*

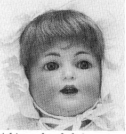

A bisque headed character baby doll, impressed K*R Simon & Halbig 122 32, 13in (33cm) high.
£675-700   *CSK*

A Simon & Halbig 1078 doll, c1910, 20in (51cm) high.
£450-500 *DOL*

A Simon & Halbig doll, mould No. 1078, c1895, 17in (43cm) high.
£400-425 *PSA*

A bisque headed child doll, with blue sleeping eyes, blonde mohair wig, and jointed wood and composition body in contemporary home made white clothes, impressed S 6 H 1009 DEP, 15in (38cm) high.
£525-550 *CSK*

A bisque headed character doll, with brown sleeping eyes, and jointed wood and composition toddler body, impressed K*R Simon & Halbig 115/A.
£1,800-1,900 *CSK*

A bisque Oriental doll, with weighted brown glass eyes, black mohair wig and jointed wood and composition body, impressed 1329 3, c1910, 14in (36cm) high.
£650-700 *S*

A bisque Gibson-girl style doll, with brown glass eyes, and ball jointed wood and composition body, unclothed and detached, one heel damaged, 4 fingers missing, some paint loss and rubbing, impressed 1158/3, c1894, 16in (41cm) high.
£650-675 *S*

A bisque headed character doll, with brown flirting sleeping eyes, blonde mohair wig, and jointed wood and composition toddler body, marked K*R Simon & Halbig 117n43, 16in (41cm) high.
£900-950 *CSK*

A Simon & Halbig shoulder bisque doll, with weighted brown glass eyes, and kid body with bisque lower limbs, impressed SH 1010-14, c1890, 28in (71cm) high.
£750-775 *S*

A shoulder bisque doll, with fixed spiralled brown glass eyes, moulded curly blonde hair, and leather upper arms and body, one ear chipped, the other glued, impressed S12H, c1890, 24½in (62cm) high.
£1,250-1,350 *S*

A Simon & Halbig/ Kämmer & Reinhardt bisque doll, with weighted blue glass eyes, ball jointed wood and composition body, and replaced blonde wig, 31in (78cm) high.
£475-500 *WIL*

A bisque headed character doll, with closed mouth, blue sleeping eyes and jointed toddler body, with new hands, impressed K*R Simon & Halbig 117 58, 21in (53cm) high.
£2,900-3,000 *CSK*

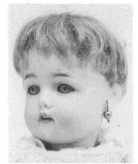

A bisque headed character baby doll, with blue sleeping eyes, short blonde wig and jointed body, impressed 1299 Halbig S & H 3½, 12½in (32cm) high.
£550-600 *CSK*

A bisque headed character doll, containing a voice box, hands replaced, impressed Simon & Halbig 117n 70, 28in (71cm) high.
£1,000-1,100 *CSK*

Steiner

A Jules Steiner doll, with fixed blue glass paperweight eyes, pierced ears, blonde mohair wig, papier mâché and kid body with keywind walking/talking mechanism, unclothed, 2 fingers repaired and arms repainted, c1880, 20in (51cm) high, together with extra dark real hair wig.
£875-900 *S*

Celluloid Dolls

A bisque headed bébé, with blonde mohair wig, straight limbed composition body and original outfit, silk distressed, marked J Steiner Fre A 3, 10½in (26cm) high.
£1,900-2,000 *CSK*

China Headed Dolls

A German china shoulder doll, with painted blue eyes, real brown hair wig, fabric body, bisque lower arms, wig sparse, 2 fingers damaged, c1850, 22in (56cm) high.
£425-450 *S*

A Celluloid baby doll sailor, 10in (25cm) high.
£50-60 *PSA*

A Berlin china shoulder doll, with glazed head, real hair wig, fabric body with blue leather lower arms, separately stitched fingers, mid-19thC,16½in (42cm) high. **£650-700** *S*

A china shoulder doll, with painted face, blue eyes, black painted hair, fabric body and bisque lower arms, tip of nose rubbed, kiln dust, German, mid-19thC, 20in (51cm) **£1,600-1,700** *S*

A selection of English Celluloid dolls, by Sydney Buckle, c1925. **£100-150** *DOL*

Composition Dolls

Composition dolls are made from a 'composition' of various materials including wood pulp, paper and paper pulp and size to build it together. Usually of a lesser quality than bisque porcelain.

An English composition doll, with tin covered sleeping eyes, and baby body, c1940.
£65-80 *PSA*

An English cloth doll, in original box, c1940.
£85-90 *DOL*

Felt Dolls

A painted felt doll, with blue side-glancing eyes, blonde mohair wig, and original frock, marked on foot Lenci, from the 450 Series, c1930, 13in (33cm) high, and a velvet covered ball with Lenci Miniature Series head, rabbit ears and felt hands, holding a felt rose, with inoperative squeaker, 7in (18cm) high.
£425-475 *CSK*

A Lenci felt Josephine Baker doll, with swivel limbs, some moth damage, late 1920s, 18½in (47cm) high.
£875-925 *S*

DID YOU KNOW?
Miller's Collectables Price Guide is designed to build up, year by year, into the most comprehensive reference system available.

Papier Mâché Dolls

A pair of French papier mâché pedlar dolls, affixed to wooden circular stands, mid-19thC, 8in (21cm) high.
£1,600-1,700 *S*

A German shoulder papier mâché doll, with moulded hair, blue painted eyes, and a kid body with painted wood hands and feet, head cracked, mid-19thC, 15in (38cm). **£400-425** *S*

A German shoulder papier mâché doll, with moulded coiffured hair, two-tone blue painted eyes, fabric body with blue leather lower arms and fabric lower legs, damaged, c1820, 25in (64cm) high. **£1,250-1,350** *S*

A German shoulder papier mâché doll, with fixed spiralled blue glass eyes, skin wig, fabric body, composition lower limbs with painted boots and stockings, some damage, c1870, 17½in (44cm) high. **£375-400** *S*

A German shoulder papier mâché doll, with fixed brown glass eyes, painted curly dark hair, fabric body and separately stitched fingers, some damage and repairs, c1840, 28in (71cm) high. **£1,500-1,600** *S*

Two papier mâché dolls, with painted features and blue eyes, with cloth bodies and wooden forearms, c1850, 20 and 23in (51 and 59cm) high. **£500-550** *S*

Peg Dolls

A Queen Anne period peg doll, completely original, c1700, 14in (36cm) high. **£1,200-1,400** *ChL*

A peg doll, c1910, 17in (43cm) high. **£140-150** *ChL*

Peg dolls were made from c1700-1950 using the same peg design.

Wax Dolls

'Wax dolls' are either made entirely of wax poured into a mould, or 'waxed', which is generally a composition or papier mâché doll dipped in wax to produce a better surface finish. Wax dolls made in England between about 1850 and 1900, with fine features and human hair, are highly prized and keenly sought by collectors.

A German all wax doll, c1860, 7in (18cm) high. **£400-450** *DOL*

A Prince Albert wax doll, 5in (13cm) high. **£200-250** *DOL*

An English poured wax doll, with blue glass eyes, applied blonde real hair, fabric body with poured wax lower limbs, face faded, c1880, 14½in (37cm) high. **£500-550** *S*

A German wax over composition headed doll, with sleeping eyes, light brown mohair wig, cloth and composition body with waxed limbs, c1880, probably by Cuno & Otto Dressel, 20in (51cm) high. **£350-375** *CSK*

An English poured shoulder wax doll, with fixed blue glass eyes, inserted blonde hair and cloth body with poured wax lower limbs and wearing original clothes, c1880, 16in (41cm) high. **£575-600** *S*

A wax headed pedlar doll, with bead eyes, wooden body, on chequerboard paper covered wood stand, with dome, c1840, 9½in (24cm) high. **£725-775** *CSK*

Wooden Headed Dolls

A gesso covered wooden shoulder head doll, peg jointed at elbows, shoulders, hips and knees, original dress, c1860. **£300-350** *DOL*

A miniature wooden doll, with black painted wig, articulated limbs, wearing original dress, late 18thC, 3½in (8.5cm) high. **£75-80** *HSS*

An early English wooden doll, gesso over wood, painted wooden torso with replaced wooden legs and one detached original wooden leg, re-dressed, 11½in (29cm) high. **£700-800** *CNY*

Dolls General

A Campbell baby, used to advertise Campbell's soups, c1930, 11in (28cm) high.
£100-150 *DOL*

A Bye-Lo Baby, designed by Grace Story Putnam, wearing original clothes, c1925, 9½in (24cm) high.
£500-520 *DOL*

A pair of Steiff character dolls, wearing Tyrolean costume, the boy with glass eyes and blonde mohair wig, both marked on left ear Steiff, 10½in (26cm) high.
£650-750 *CNY*

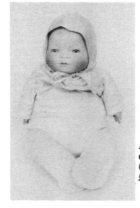

Two English dolls' heads, c1939, 3½in (9cm) high.
£8-12 each *DOL*

A doll's head mould, in copper and brass, 6½in (16cm) high.
£75-80 *RE*

A cloth Snow White and 2 dwarfs, 16 and 7in (41 and 18cm) high.
£100-120 *DOL*

A mask face cloth baby doll, with blue sleeping eyes, wearing original sewn on knitted clothes, still tied in original box, with label reading CHAD VALLEY "CARESE" Hygienic Doll, priced at 5/6, 13in (33cm) high.
£450-500 *CSK*

A Bye-Lo Baby, in original pink suit, 14in (36cm) long.
£590-620 *DOL*

A Norah Wellings gypsy doll nightdress case, 21in (53cm) high.
£15-20 *DOL*

An Effanbee cloth composition W. C. Fields doll, 19in (48cm) high.
£480-510 *CNY*

A Pedigree doll, wearing original clothes, c1940, 14in (36cm) high.
£10-15 *DOL*

A bisque shoulder headed musical marotte, with fixed blue eyes, white mohair curls, original braided streamers and cap, the head marked SPB in star H, 15in (38cm) high.
£575-600 *CSK*

A cardboard and paper dressing doll, with paper clothes, c1940, 8½in (21cm) high.
£18-20 *PSA*

A pair of Dollcraft composition and cloth Lone Ranger and Tonto dolls, in original lithographed boxes, c1938, 20in (51cm) high.
£1,400-1,600 *CNY*

An Ideal set of Snow White and the Seven Dwarfs stuffed dolls, with painted composition faces, including original boxes for all 7 dwarfs, 15½ and 7in (39 and 18cm) high. **£1,600-2,000** *CNY*

A papier mâché and cloth Jiggs nodder, with glass eyes, originally a store display, 21in (53cm) high.
£1,800-2,000 *CNY*

Jiggs is a character from the comic strip 'Bringing Up Father'.

A Happy Hooligan doll, with painted bisque face, 9½in (24cm) high.
£620-650 *CNY*

A pair of all bisque Kewpie dolls, with jointed arms, impressed O'Neill on the feet, in original boxes, 5½in (14cm) high. **£780-820** *CSK*

Dolls House Dolls

A group of 14 German miniature dolls, in original costumes, 1920s, the largest 7in (18cm) high. **£2,200-2,500** *S*

A bisque headed doll, with composition body, all original, c1910, 4½in (11cm) high. **£85-90** *PSA*

An original googlie eyed doll, with felt covered body, c1920, 4in (10cm) high. **£60-80** *PSA*

An all bisque French doll, 2½in (6cm) high. **£95-100** *PSA*

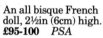

A china headed doll, with black painted hair, brown painted eyes and china limbs pegged to a wooden body, c1840, 5in (13cm) high, together with 2 Frozen Charlottes in contemporary clothes, 1 and 1½in (3 and 4cm) high, a cradle and a cane chair. **£770-800** *CSK*

Dolls Accessories

A doll with straw filled body, china head and limbs, c1880, 8in (20cm) high. **£50-60** *PSA*

An original Victorian doll's hat, 8½in (21cm) diam. **£125-150** *DOL*

A French doll's pram, all original, c1870, 19in (48cm) high. **£300-500** *ChL*

A doll with straw filled body, china limbs, black china hair and white face, c1880. **£60-65** *PSA*

An 'Alpha' baby's feeding bottle, in original box, 2½in (6cm) wide. **£12-15** *DOL*

A Victorian original
doll's bonnet, 8½in
(21cm) wide.
£125-150 *DOL*

A French wooden
chicken house, c1940, 7in
(18cm) high.
£20-25 *PSA*

A crib, 17in (43cm) long.
£15-30 *DOL*

An English painted wooden dolls
house, with some furniture, damaged,
late 19thC, 25½in (65cm) high.
£450-500 *S*

Dolls Houses

A dolls house, with some
furniture, late 19thC but
re-papered in 1930s, 29in
(74cm) high. **£1,400-1,500** *S*

A two-storey wooden
dolls house, with 4 rooms,
staircase and landing,
repainted and
redecorated, by G. &
J. Lines Bros., c1910,
37in (94cm) high.
£1,300-1,500 *C*

A printed paper on wood
dolls house, opening at
the front to reveal
4 rooms with staircase
and landing, with
original wall and floor
papers, by G. & J. Lines,
c1918, 26in (66cm) wide.
£550-650 *CSK*

An English two-storey
wooden dolls house, with
4 rooms, some kitchen
furniture and fittings
and 7 dolls house dolls,
late 19thC, 28in (71.5cm)
wide. **£600-700** *CSK*

A further selection of dolls houses is
featured in previous editions of Miller's
Collectables Price Guides, available
from Miller Publications.

A three-storey painted
wood dolls house, with
4 rooms, original kitchen
paper, dresser and fire
surrounds, front
paintwork overpainted,
numbered underneath 4,
28in (71.5cm) high.
£250-300 *C*

Dolls House Furniture

A marble fireplace, with grate, 5in (12.5cm) wide. **£45-65** *CD*

A lead gas stove. **£12-15**
Two chairs. **£3-5** *DOL*

A selection of shoes with cabinet.
Shoes **£15-30 each pair**
Cabinet **£16-18** *CD*

A kitchen sink, with copper water heater, 5½in (14cm) wide. **£90-110** *CD*

A bureau bookcase and fireplace, both 6in (15cm) high.
£20-25 each
A grandfather clock, 7in (18cm) high. **£5-8** *DOL*

A dressing table. **£12-15** *DOL*

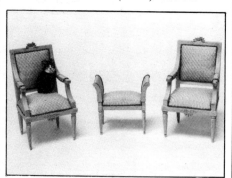

A wooden Aga stove, 3in (7.5cm) wide.
£140-160 *CD*

A japanned wardrobe and blanket box, by Judith Dunger, wardrobe 6in (15cm) high.
Wardrobe **£95-115**
Box **£45-55** *CD*

DRINKING
Corkscrews

A James Heeley & Sons
'A1' lever cork drawer,
c1890. **£35-55** *CS*

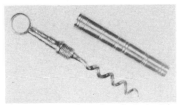

A steel pocket picnic
sheathed corkscrew,
c1830.
£60-80 *CS*

A German sprung stem
corkscrew, with bladed
worm, c1890.
£30-40 *CS*

A Victorian silver plated
folding pocket corkscrew,
by Wright & Bailey,
registered design of 1873.
£15-25 *CS*

A cast steel publican's
bar cork drawer, The
Original Safety, c1890.
£80-100 *CS*

A Victorian boar's tusk
corkscrew, with silver
cap and teeth on stem to
grip cork, c1880.
£120-150 *CS*

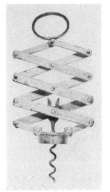

A bronzed steel
concertina corkscrew, by
James Heeley & Sons,
Weirs 1884 patent.
£50-80 *CS*

An English silver pocket
corkscrew with sheath,
c1790.
£180-260 *CS*

A Sir Edward
Thomason's 1802 patent
corkscrew, with Royal
coat-of-arms.
£270-320
Without Thomason
name.
£100-120 *CS*

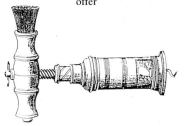

A bronze open frame corkscrew, by G. Twigg, patented in 1868.
£200-300 *CS*

A turned walnut handled 'T' bar corkscrew, with Henshall type button to steel stem, c1840.
£20-30 *CS*

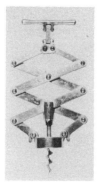

A French concertina cork drawer, stamped Ideal Brevete, 20thC.
£20-30 *CS*

A Victorian hotel or pub brass bar cork drawer, The Merrit.
£180-200 *CS*

An English brass bar cork drawer, The Rotary Eclipse, c1890.
£200-250 *CS*

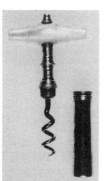

An English silver pocket corkscrew and sheath, with mother-of-pearl handle, c1810.
£170-220 *CS*

A German Hercules sprung stem corkscrew, c1900.   **£10-15** *CS*

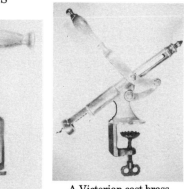

A Victorian cast brass publican's bar cork drawer, The Shamrock.
£120-180 *CS*

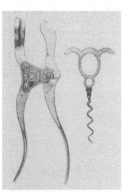

An all steel frame corkscrew, English version, The Victor, c1890. **£30-40** *CS*

A turned cherrywood 'T' bar corkscrew, with dusting brush, 1830. **£15-25** *CS*

An English cast iron cork drawer in 2 parts, The Patent Lever.
£30-50 *CS*

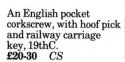

An English pocket corkscrew, with hoof pick and railway carriage key, 19thC.
£20-30 *CS*

A Victorian 'T' bar corkscrew, with dusting brush, c1870.
£10-15 *CS*

Drinking

A Victorian silver wine goblet by Hunt & Roskell, silversmiths to the Queen, c1872.
£250-300 *CS*

An English silver plate sommelier's wine taster, c1890, 3½in (9cm).
£30-40 *CS*

A German corkscrew with sprung stem, The Columbus, 19thC.
£35-45 *CS*

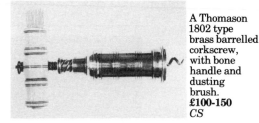

A Thomason 1802 type brass barrelled corkscrew, with bone handle and dusting brush.
£100-150 *CS*

Two Victorian turned ashwood plungers for inserting corks into wine bottles, c1880.
£25-30 each *CS*

A Staffordshire pottery publican's gin barrel, with brass tap and pottery lid, c1880. **£60-80** *CS*

A George III two-part
silver wine funnel, c1800.
£275-300 *CS*

A George III silver
wine goblet,
London marks.
£300-350 *CS*

A Booths countryside
cocktail dish, c1930, 12in
(30.5cm) diam.
£150-175 *HEW*

An English cut glass port
decanter, with mushroom
stopper, c1830.
£150-190 *CS*

A George III wine funnel,
with reeded edges,
maker's mark CH,
London 1791.
£300-325 *P(S)*

A Victorian silver
wine goblet, with
engraved decoration,
c1850.
£275-375 *CS*

Labels

A silver Punch decanter label or bottle
ticket, by John Robins, c1780. **£100-120** *CS*

A cast silver Hock decanter
label, c1830. **£60-80** *CS*

A selection of English
pottery wine bin labels,
usually made by
Wedgwood, Minton and
Copeland Spode, 19thC.
Sherry and Brandy.
£20-25 each
Dated Chateau wines.
£100-120 each
Silver plate port barrel.
£150-180 *CS*

A selection of late
Victorian fired enamel
on copper decanter
labels, c1890.
£20-30 each *CS*

A selection of silver wine
labels. **£70-210** *CSK*

A pierced silver Madeira
decanter label, c1830.
£50-60 *CS*

EPHEMERA
Autographs

A signed photograph of Mother Teresa, 8 by 10in (20 by 25cm), VG to EX.
£50-100 *VS*

A letter signed by Captain Scott, dated 15th July 1910, on British Antarctic Expedition notepaper, G.
£200-250 *VS*

A Charles Schulz printed cartoon of Snoopy, signed and inscribed, 8½ by 11in (21 by 28cm), VG.
£60-70 *VS*

Astronauts

Valentina Tereshkova signed photograph, 7 by 4½in (18 by 11cm), VG.
£65-100 *VS*

Neil Armstrong signed and inscribed half length photograph, 8 by 10in (20 by 25cm), VG.
£110-150 *VS*

Buzz Aldrin signed and inscribed colour photograph, 8 by 10in (20 by 25cm), VG.
£35-75 *VS*

Neil Armstrong signed colour photograph, 8 by 10in (20 by 25cm), but not signed by Aldrin or Collins, VG.
£100-150 *VS*

Valentina Tereshkova, the first woman in space, signed first day cover, commemorating the Space Shuttle Challenger, postally cancelled 18th June 1983, G. **£35-75** *VS*

Valentina Tereshkova, signed first day cover, commemorating the STS-7 Space Shuttle, postally cancelled 18th June 1983, VG.
£35-75 *VS*

Historical

A hand addressed and signed envelope by Robert Browning to the Secretary of the Athenaeum Club, postally cancelled London, 3rd March 1884, G to VG.
£110-150 *VS*

Emily Pankhurst autograph quotation, 'Human emancipation must precede social regeneration', on album page, VG.
£50-100   *VS*

Suffragette items are very collectable at present.

AMQS – Autograph Musical Quotation Signed
a.m.r. – Adhesion marks to reverse

Cetywayo, Zulu King who defeated the British at Isandhlwana, 1879, signed piece, in pencil, annotated to right edge in ink, in another hand, 'Written by Cetywayo, Feby. 80', slight smudges, G.   **£210-250**   *VS*

Lillie Langtry signed postcard with her married name Lillie de Bathe, and below Mrs Langtry, G to VG.
£110-150   *VS*

EX – Excellent
FR – Fair
G – Good
MT – Mint
P – Poor
VG – Very Good

Lillie Langtry card in signed blue crayon, a.m.r., G.
£30-50   *VS*

Jonathan Swift small signed piece 'Swift' attached to larger contemporary album page together with a newspaper extract of a letter from Swift to the Earl of Peterborough, stained, FR.
£550-600   *VS*

Henry Longfellow signed piece cut from letter and attached to contemporary album page alongside contemporary photograph, signature faded, FR.   **£50-100**   *VS*

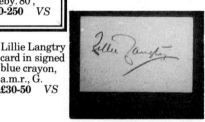

Military

Hiroshima, signed composite by Paul Tibbets, pilot of the Enola Gay, Jacob Beser, electronic counter measures, Theodore Van Kirk, navigator and Thomas Ferebee, bombardier, VG.   **£70-100**   *VS*

Cross Reference
Aeronautica

Willy Messerschmitt signed postcard of the Messerschmitt Me 264VI, May 1978, VG to EX.
£60-100   *VS*

Arturo Toscanini signed piece attached to album page, dated in another hand '18-10-1937', G.
£30-50 *VS*

Montgomery signed hardback edition of 'I was Monty's Double', by M. E. Clifton James, also signed by the author, 1966-67, lacking dustjacket, VG.
£100-150 *VS*

General George S. Patton signed typed letter, 21st May 1945, to Captain Paterson, slight creasing, slight a.m.r., G. to VG.   **£500-700** *VS*

Musical

Jerry Lee Lewis

Giacomo Puccini photograph signed and inscribed 'alla bella e gentile amica Signorina Ileana Leonidoff ricordo di Giacomo Puccini Vienna Gen 1919', some creasing and staining.
£750-850 *S*

Jerry Lee Lewis signed and inscribed photograph, 8 by 10in (20 by 25cm), VG to EX.
£25-50 *VS*

Henry Mancini signed and inscribed cartoon caricature of the Pink Panther, with additional A.M.Q.S. from the Pink Panther theme tune, VG to EX.
£40-50 *VS*

Louis Armstrong signed and inscribed photograph, 8 by 10in (20 by 25cm), slight crease, VG.
£120-150 *VS*

A signed photograph by Sir F. Pablo Tosti, Enrico Caruso and Antonio Scotti.
£1,000-1,200 *VS*

Political

Charles De Gaulle signed photograph together with a signed typed letter 18th December 1941, slight a.m.r., 8 by 10in (20 by 28cm), G.
£320-350 *VS*

Mikhail Gorbachev signed colour photograph.
£400-500 *VS*

Leon Trotsky signed and inscribed hardback edition of 'The History of the Russian Revolution'.
£1,000-1,500 *VS*

Nicolae Ceaucescu signed photograph together with a signed typed letter, VG.
£60-100 *VS*

Ronald Reagan signed and inscribed photograph, 8 by 10in (20 by 25cm), VG. **£90-100** *VS*

Royalty

Queen Victoria appointing Lewis Edmund Coker an adjutant in the Volunteer Forces, 30th July 1884, some creasing, G.
£100-150 *VS*

Edward VIII and others, a full length signed photograph of King Edward VIII, Albert, Duke of York, Henry, Duke of Gloucester and George, Duke of Kent, 10½ by 8½in (26 by 21cm). **£990-1,200** *CSK*

Extremely rare in this form as king.

Queen Victoria, William Hay Leith Tester, La Teste, 1870, end page inscribed by the Queen to her Lady In Waiting 'To dear Miss M. MacGregor with every wish for her speedy recovery from Victoria R., March 7, 1870', green cloth and gilt.
£120-180 *CSK*

Edward VIII as Prince of Wales shown in drag during one of the ship's plays. **£200-300** *VS*

Wallis, Duchess of Windsor, a photograph of the Duke and Duchess' residence in the Bahamas, signed by Wallis only, 5 by 4in (13 by 10cm), G. **£75-100** *VS*

King George V signed autograph two-page letter to Sir William Simmons, 14th December 1887, VG. **£100-150** *VS*

Queen Alexandra signed photograph by Alice Hughes of London, 8 by 11½in (20 by 29cm), G. **£100-150** *VS*

Show Business

Fred and Adèle Astaire, an early signed sepia, 7 by 5in (18 by 13cm), slight silvering and heavy a.m.r., slight wrinkling, G. **£80-100** *VS*

Brigitte Bardot signed photograph, 8 by 10in (20 by 25cm), VG to EX. **£45-65** *VS*

Fred Astaire signed reproduction, 8 by 10in (20 by 25cm), VG. **£50-100** *VS*

Gary Cooper signed and inscribed sepia, small tear, 8 by 10in (20 by 25cm), G. **£110-150** *VS*

Ronald Colman photograph of him and his wife and signed by Colman 'Benita and Ronald Colman', 8 by 10in (20 by 25cm), slight crease, G. **£40-50** *VS*

W. C. Fields signed photograph, 8 by 10in (20 by 25cm). **£300-400** *VS*

Walt Disney signed and inscribed photograph with large bloodhound, corner creasing, 11 by 14in (28 by 36cm), G. **£400-700** *VS*

Noel Coward signed photograph, 6 by 4in (15 by 10cm), G. **£80-100** *VS*

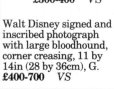

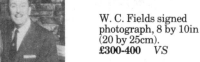

Basil Rathbone, signed
sepia, annotated in
another hand 'Died 21
July 1967', corner
creasing, G.
£100-120 *VS*

Bela Lugosi, signed
postcard as Count
Dracula, slight a.m.r.,
VG.
£200-250 *VS*

Groucho Marx, signed
and inscribed postcard,
signed in later years, VG.
£80-120 *VS*

Peter Sellers, signed and
inscribed postcard, VG.
£30-40 *VS*

Cary Grant, signed photograph,
December 1948, lightly laid down, G.
£120-150 *VS*

Lee Marvin, signed and
inscribed photograph
from 'The Man Who Shot
Liberty Valance', VG.
£50-60 *VS*

Ingrid Bergman, signed
postcard, Picturegoer,
No. W161, VG.
£60-90 *VS*

John Wayne, signed and inscribed
photograph from 'Donovan's Reef',
corner crease, VG.
£100-150 *VS*

Carole Lombard, signed
and inscribed Paramount
portrait, slight surface
crease, VG.
£150-200 *VS*

Margaret Rutherford, signed postcard, slight a.m.r., G.
£30-40 *VS*

Carole Lombard, signed postcard, a.m.r., G.
£100-120 *VS*

Gary Cooper, signed postcard, corner crease and slight a.m.r., G.
£60-80 *VS*

Robert Ryan, signed and inscribed, VG.
£40-50 *VS*

Ronald Colman, signed sepia postcard, a.m.r., G-VG.
£30-40 *VS*

David Niven, signed postcard, Picturegoer No. W932, VG-EX.
£40-50 *VS*

Laurel and Hardy signed and inscribed sepia, 7 by 5in (18 by 13cm), VG to EX. **£250-300** *VS*

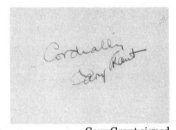

William Boyd signed 'Hoppy' sepia, 7½ by 9½in (19 by 24cm), corner crease, G. **£85-100** *VS*

Ingrid Bergman signed and inscribed hardback edition of Casablanca script and legend, by Howard Koch, G to VG. **£100-150** *VS*

Madonna signed magazine photograph, 8 by 10in (20 by 25cm), G to VG. **£55-70** *VS*

Judy Garland signed photograph outside the Verandah Grill Restaurant on board R.M.S. Queen Mary in 1952, 6 by 4½in (15 by 11cm), G. **£190-220** *VS*

Samantha Fox signed colour photograph, 8 by 10in (20 by 25cm), EX. **£50-100** *VS*

Cary Grant signed album page, VG. **£40-50** *VS*

Billie Holiday photograph signed and inscribed, 8 by 9½in (20 by 23cm), torn. **£500-800** *VS*

Dorothy Gish photograph signed and inscribed in pencil, 7 by 10in (18 by 25cm), VG to EX. **£40-50** *VS*

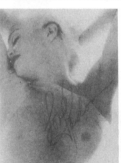

Madonna signed colour photograph, 8 by 10in (20 by 25cm), VG. **£125-150** *VS*

Boris Karloff photograph signed in later years, slight creasing and small tear, 7 by 5in (18 by 13cm), FR. **£85-100** *VS*

Alfred Hitchcock photograph signed in white ink, slight staining, neatly laid down, 12 by 9in (31 by 23cm), FR to about G.
£200-300 *VS*

Laurence Olivier photograph with full signature, 7 by 5in (18 by 13cm), EX.
£65-80 *VS*

The Munsters colour photograph signed by Al Lewis, Fred Gwynne, Yvonne De Carlo, Beverley Owen and Butch Patrick, 8 by 10in (20 by 25cm), EX.
£120-150 *VS*

Laurel and Hardy signed sepia photograph by Stax, slight discolouration, 7 by 10in (18 by 25cm), VG.
£600-650 *VS*

S. Haing Ngor signed photograph from 'The Killing Fields', 8 by 10in (20 by 25cm), EX.
£60-80 *VS*

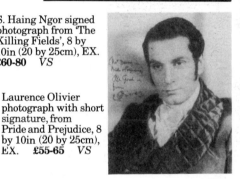

Laurence Olivier photograph with short signature, from Pride and Prejudice, 8 by 10in (20 by 25cm), EX. **£55-65** *VS*

Tyrone Power signed and inscribed photograph, 11 by 14in (28 by 36cm), VG.
£70-90 *VS*

Groucho Marx signed and inscribed photograph with first name only, in row with, but not signed by, Chico and Harpo, signed in later years, 8 by 10in (20 by 25cm), VG.
£100-150 *VS*

Phil Silvers signed photograph as 'Sgt Bilko', slight corner crease, 7 by 9in (18 by 23cm), VG.
£80-120 *VS*

Authentic signed photographs of Silvers as Bilko are extremely rare.

Florence Mills, black American dancer, famous in Blackbirds Revue, signed, 5½ by 8½in (14 by 21cm), slight scuffing, G.
£45-55 *VS*

Marie McDonald, The Body, photograph signed and inscribed, 8 by 10in (20 by 25cm), some corner creasing, G.
£60-80 *VS*

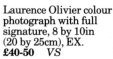

Star Trek photograph signed by William Shatner, Leonard Nimoy and De Forest Kelley, 8 by 10in (20 by 25cm), EX.
£55-65 *VS*

Laurence Olivier colour photograph with full signature, 8 by 10in (20 by 25cm), EX.
£40-50 *VS*

John Waters signed photograph, 8 by 10in (20 by 25cm), EX.
£45-55 *VS*

Jane Russell signed photograph, in classic pose from 'Outlaw', 8 by 10in (20 by 25cm), VG to EX.
£35-45 *VS*

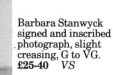

Darryl F. Zanuck signed and inscribed colour photograph, 8 by 10in (20 by 25cm), VG.
£40-50 *VS*

Sylvester Stallone signed photograph, from the original 'Rocky' film, corner creasing, 8 by 10in (20 by 25cm), G.
£40-50 *VS*

Barbara Stanwyck signed and inscribed photograph, slight creasing, G to VG.
£25-40 *VS*

Sporting

Gene Tunney, a signed and inscribed photograph by Apeda of New York, of the World Heavyweight Champion 1926-30, slight creasing, 8 by 10in (20 by 25cm), VG.
£40-60 *VS*

Jack Sharkey signed and inscribed sepia photograph by Bryant of New York, of the World Heavyweight Champion 1932-33, slight creasing, 8 by 10in (20 by 25cm), G.
£50-80 *VS*

Marty Servo photograph of World Welterweight Champion 1946, signed on reverse, 5½ by 4in (14 by 10cm), slight scuffing, G.
£45-55 *VS*

Hagler and Hearns, colour photograph signed by both, EX.
£60-90 *VS*

Cigarette Cards

Kimball's Dancing Women, set of 50, 1889.
£220-250 *Bon*

"GOLD FLAKE" TOBACCO.

A mild coarse cut Pipe Tobacco.

W. D. & H. O. WILLS, Limited.

A Wills's advertisement card, issued 1893.
£300-400 *ACC*

Kinney's Famous Gems of the World, set of 25, 1889.
£120-150 *Bon*

An American advertising card, issued 1887.
£60-120 *ACC*

Player's advertising cards, issued 1894.
£250-500 each *ACC*

A collection of 18 American cards, comprising: W. Duke & Sons Ltd., Gems of Beauties, 6/25, 1884, Stars Of The Stage, 1/25, 1891, French Novelties, 1/25, 1892, Beauties, folder, 3/25, 1886, Banner Tobacco Co., Beauties, 6/25, 1890, and P. Lorillard Co., Actresses, coloured, 1/25, 1888.
£150-200 *CSK*

Lambert and Butler's Waverley series, set of 25, 1904. **£120-150** *Bon*

Carreras Ltd., Highwaymen, set of 25, 1924.
£35-70 *ACC*

Duke's Holidays, set of 50, 1890.
£180-200 *Bon*

Churchman's Civic Insignia and Plate, set of 25, 1926.
£40-60 *ACC*

Turf Cigarettes Mythological Gods and Goddesses, set of 25, 1924. **£25-50** *ACC*

Ogden's Boy Scouts, set of 50, 1911. **£115-230** *ACC*

E. & W. Anstie Ltd., Aesop's Fables, set of 25, 1934. **£42-65** *ACC*

Wills's English Period Costumes, set of 25, 1927. **£40-70** *ACC*

Hill's War series, 25/25, 1915. **£170-200** *Bon*

Lambert and Butler's Wireless Telegraphy, 25/25, 1909, and Worlds Locomotives, 25/25, 1912. **£85-100** *Bon*

Carreras Ltd., The Nose Game, set of 50, 1927. **£11-17** *ACC*

Taddy & Co., Royalty, Actresses and Soldiers, 1/20, 1898, Natives of the World, 2/25, 1899, Edward Ringer & Biggs, Calendar, one, 1900, and Pritchard & Burton, Star Girls, 1/25, 1900. **£160-200** *CSK*

Ardath Tobacco Co. Ltd.,
Your Birthday Tells
Your Fortune, set of 50,
1937.
£24-36 *ACC*

Lea's, Chairman, Old
English Pottery and
Porcelain, 50/50, Old
Pottery and Porcelain,
2nd series, 50/50, 3rd
series, 50/50, 4th series,
50/50, 5th series, 46/50.
£95-120 *Bon*

Wills's Lucky Charms,
set of 50, 1923.
£11-22 *ACC*

Architectural

Wills's British Castles, set of 25, 1925.
£45-75 *ACC*

Cope Bros. & Co.,
Cathedrals, set of 25,
1939.
£20-30 *ACC*

A set of 25 framed cards
of British Lighthouses,
c1925, 17½ by 11½in
(44 by 29.5cm).
£130-150 *ROS*

Wills's Gems of Belgian
Architecture, set of 50,
1915. **£28-56** *ACC*

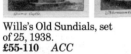

Wills's Old Inns, set of 50, 1939.
£48-96   *ACC*

Wills's Old Sundials, set of 25, 1938.
£55-110   *ACC*

Wills's Old Inns, set of 40, 1936.   **£80-160**   *ACC*

Equestrian

Gallaher's Racing Scenes, set of 48, 1938.
£16-28   *ACC*

Flora & Fauna

Wills's Life In The Tree Tops, set of 50, 1925.
£13-26
ACC

Franklyn, Davey & Co., Hunting, set of 25, 1925.
£16-32   *ACC*

Carreras' Horses and Hounds, set of 25, 1926.
£26-39   *ACC*

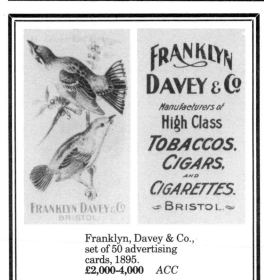

Franklyn, Davey & Co., set of 50 advertising cards, 1895. **£2,000-4,000** *ACC*

Wills's Garden Life, set of 50, 1914. **£25-50** *ACC*

Gallaher's Animals and Birds of Commercial Value, set of 100, 1921. **£36-72** *ACC*

Gallaher's British Birds, set of 100, 1923. **£55-95** *ACC*

Geographical

Wills's Garden Hints, set of 50, 1938. **£7-12** *ACC*

Player's Counties and their Industries, set of 25, 1914. **£25-50** *ACC*

Godfrey Phillips Red Indians, set of 25, 1927.
£55-85 *ACC*

Wills's Overseas Dominions, Australia, set of 50, 1915.
£25-50 *ACC*

Churchman's Holidays in Britain, set of 48, 1937.
£9-13 *ACC*

Heraldic

Wills's Borough Arms 2nd Edition, set of 50, 1906.
£30-60 *ACC*

Dexter's Borough Arms, set of 30, 1900.
£16-32 *ACC*

Wills's Borough Arms 2nd Series, set of 50, 1904. **£28-56** *ACC*

Military & Wartime

Godfrey Phillips Soldiers of the King, set of 36, 1939.
£16-24 *ACC*

Wills's Waterloo, never
issued.   **£100-150**   *ACC*

Edwards, Ringer & Bigg
Easter Manoeuvres, set
of 3, 1897.
£400-800   *ACC*

Wills's Britain's part in
the War, set of 24, 1917.
£21-42   *ACC*

Wills's Air Raid
Precautions, set of 50,
1938.
£14-24   *ACC*

Churchman's Air Raid Precautions, set of 48, 1938.
£11-17   *ACC*

Naval & Shipping

Wills's The World's
Dreadnoughts, set
of 25, 1910.
£45-95   *ACC*

199

Nicolas Sarony & Co., set of 50, Ships of all Ages, 1929.   **£18-28** *ACC*

Wills's Life in the Royal Navy, set of 50, 1939. **£11-22** *ACC*

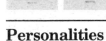

Wills's Ships' Badges, set of 50, 1925. **£16-32** *ACC*

Personalities

Wills's Musical Celebrities, set of 50, 1911. **£110-220** *ACC*

R. & J. Hill Ltd & H. Archer & Co., Our Empire, set of 30, 1929. **£7-11** *ACC*

Churchman's In Town Tonight, set of 50, 1938. **£8-14** *ACC*

Lambert & Butler London Characters, set of 25, 1934. **£48-78** *ACC*

Proverbs

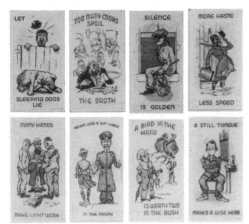

Bocnal Tobacco Co.,
Proverbs, set of 25, 1938.
£40-60   *ACC*

Ardath Tobacco Co.,
Proverbs, set of 25, 1936.
£16-32   *ACC*

Royalty

Senior Service Sights of
London, set of 12, 1935.
£8-15   *ACC*

Wills's Our King and
Queen, set of 50, 1937.
£9-18   *ACC*

Wills's The Life of Edward VIII, set of 50.
£550-750   *ACC*
These were never issued because of the Abdication.

Wills's The Reign of H.M. King George V, set of 50, 1935. **£20-40** *ACC*

Gallaher's The Reason Why, set of 100, 1924. **£48-96** *ACC*

Scientific

Wills's Engineering Wonders, set of 50, 1927. **£15-25** *ACC*

Wills's Do You Know...?, set of 50, 1924. **£10-20** *ACC*

Show Business

Godfrey Phillips Shots from The Films, set of 48, 1934. **£12-22** *ACC*

Carreras Famous Film Stars, set of 96, 1935. **£60-90** *ACC*

Gallaher's Shots from Famous Films, set of 48, 1935. **£22-36** *ACC*

Carreras Film Stars, set of 54, 1937.
£30-45 *ACC*

Wills's Radio Celebrities, set of 50, 1935.
£22-36 *ACC*

Wills's Cinema Stars, set of 50, 1931.
£60-120 *ACC*

Sporting

Wills's Cricketers, set of 50, 1928. **£50-100** *ACC*

Godfrey Phillips Sportsmen – Spot the Winner, set of 50, 1937. **£12-18** *ACC*

Godfrey Phillips International Caps, set of 50, 1936. **£36-56** *ACC*

Franklyn Davey Boxing, set of 25, 1924. **£45-90** *ACC*

Ardath Tobacco Co., National Fitness, set of 50, 1938. **£22-33** *ACC*

Churchman's Boxing Personalities, set of 50, 1938. **£90-180** *ACC*

Gallaher's Sporting Personalities, set of 48, 1936. **£12-20** *ACC*

Transport

Park Drive Champions, set of 48, 1935.
£10-15   *ACC*

Wills's Railway Engines,
set of 50, 1924.
£50-100   *ACC*

Churchman's Kings of Speed, set of 50, 1939.
£28-56   *ACC*

> **Cross Reference**
> Railways

Lambert and Butler Keep Fit, set of 50, 1937.
£24-40   *ACC*

Lambert and Butler
Aeroplane Markings, set
of 50, 1937.
£50-90   *ACC*

Lambert and Butler
Motor Cars, set of 25,
1922.
£60-120   *ACC*

Lambert and Butler
Motor Cycles, set of 50,
1923.
£150-300   *ACC*

Cross Reference
Aeronautica

Lambert and Butler
Motor Cars, set of 25,
1923.
£60-120   *ACC*

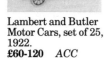

Carreras Vintage Cars,
with word 'Filter' in
white oval, set of 50,
1978.
£7-10   *ACC*

Cross Reference
Automobilia

Wills's Speed, set of 50, 1938.
£12-20   *ACC*

Silks

A quantity of silk cigarette cards in one box, subjects include flowers, flags, crests, Royalty, birds, butterflies and Indians.
£500-600   *CSK*

FURTHER READING
Card Photographs, A Guide to their History and Value, Lou W. McCulloch, Millbank Books UK. *The Guide to Cigarette Card Collecting,* Albert's, London, 1992.

Magazines & Comics

A 1962 Playboy.
£8-10   *AAM*

Picture Goer, Gregory Peck and Jennifer Jones, 1946.
£3-4   *ACC*

Picture Post Magazines, 1942-50s.
£1-2 each   *COB*

Picture Show Annuals, 1957 Yul Brynner and Deborah Kerr, The King and I, and 1956 Rock Hudson and Barbara Rush in Captain Lightfoot.
£10-15 each   *ACC*

1938 Boys' Magazines.
£2-3 each   *COB*

Preview annuals, 1951 and 1959.
£10-15 each   *ACC*

Eagle Comics, 1st September 1950, 29th September 1950, excluding Nos 1 and 2 of Volume 1.   **£8-12 each**   *ACC*

Picture Show, White Christmas, 1954 and David Niven, Ava Gardner and Stewart Granger in The Little Hut, 1957.
£3-4 each   *ACC*

Mickey Mouse Weekly, April 6th and September 7th, 1940.   **£10-15 each**   *ACC*

Child's Own Magazine with Fry's advert on back, coloured inside by a child reducing value, 8 by 6½in (20 by 16cm).
£5-6   *ROS*

Picture Show Annuals, Alan Ladd and Shelley Winters, 1955 and Forever Amber, 1952.
£10-15 each   *ACC*

Picture Post, August 1950.
£4-5   *ROS*

Posters

Automobile Club Show, lithograph printed in colours, printed by Waterlow and Sons Ltd., London, backed on linen, damaged, 30 by 20in (76 by 51cm).
£650-700   *CSK*

Leonetto Cappiello, Job, Papier a Cigarettes, lithograph in colours, printed by Vercasson, Paris, backed on linen, damaged, 1912, 62 by 47in (158 by 119cm).
£350-400   *CSK*

John Gilroy, My Goodness – A 200th Birthday Label!
£90-100   *ONS*

John Gilroy, Guinness for Strength, lithograph in colours, printed by Sanders, Phillips & Co. Ltd., London, framed, damaged, 29 by 20in (74 by 51cm).
£300-350   *CSK*

John Gilroy, My Goodness, My Guinness, offset lithograph in colours, c1940, printed by Sanders, Phillips & Co., London, excellent condition, 30 by 20in (76 by 51cm).
£350-400   *CSK*

A Velocette motorcycle poster, 1960s.
£70-75   *COB*

Cross Reference
Automobilia

Terrot poster, 1960s.
£40-45   *COB*

A G.W.R. Railway Auction Poster, 1870s.
£25-30   *COB*

A reward poster, includes Murder, 1826.
£50-60   *COB*

Five D. W. Burley, Chessington Zoo, lithographs in colours, printed by McCorquodale & Co., London, damaged, 60 by 40in (153 by 102cm).
£300-400 *CSK*

Elastic Sportszalag, published by Athenaeum.
£45-55 *ONS*

Alo, Chamonix-Mont Blanc, PLM, lithograph in colours, printed by Cornille & Serre, Paris, c1924, damaged, 42½ by 31in (108 by 79cm).
£600-650 *CSK*

Austin Cooper, London's Leisure Hours, by Underground, lithograph in colours, printed by The Baynard Press, backed on linen, damaged, 40 by 25in (101 by 63cm), and 2 other London Underground posters by A. Cooper.
£350-400 *CSK*

North Berwick, poster published by LNER, framed.
£600-650 *ONS*

Cross Reference
Railways

A Biba poster, 1970s.
£25-30 *COB*

These were only sold in Biba in London.

Travel

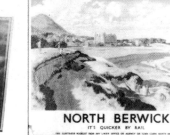

Anthony R. Barker, See Ireland First-On Shell, Giants Causeway, Ulster, Ballynahinch, Connemara, Happy Valley, Co. Down and Glandalough, lithographs in colours, printed by J. W. R. Ltd., London, damaged, 31 by 44½in (79 by 113cm).
£280-300 *CSK*

Cross Reference
Shipping

S. R. Badmin, Come and Explore, published by British Travel & Holidays Assoc.
£240-300 *ONS*

Christopher Richard Wynne Nevinson, A.R.A., One Way To Pleasure By Motor-bus, lithograph in colour, printed by the Avenue Press, backed on linen, damaged, 39 by 25in (99 by 63cm).
£350-400 *CSK*

LNER, Harwich For The Continent, printed by Dangerfield.
£550-600 *ONS*

D.N.A., Gourock and Ashton, CCR, lithograph in colours, printed by McCorquodale & Co., Glasgow, damaged, 40 by 25in (101 by 63cm) and Cambridge, by Fred Taylor.
£90-120 *CSK*

E. A. Cox, London's Country, No. 5, Hop Pickers in Kent, published by General.
£60-100 *ONS*

A Shipping poster, 1950s.
£50-60 *COB*

Donald Maxwell, The Lake District of Surrey, poster published by Southern Railway, framed.
£80-100 *ONS*

Brighton and Hove, published by LMS, 40 by 50in (101.5 by 127cm).
£850-900 *ONS*

Frank Sherwin, Kent, The Garden of England, published by BR(SR).
£200-225 *ONS*

Gyrth Russell, The Wye Valley, published by BR(WR).
£250-300 *ONS*

A Carr Linford, Oxford, published by BR(WR).
£150-200 *ONS*

On Early Shift, Greenwood Signalbox, New Barnet, published by BR, on linen.
£250-300 *ONS*

Jack Merriott, Wales, published by BR(WR).
£260-300 *ONS*

Fred Taylor, Heidelberg, published by LNER.
£220-250 *ONS*

Wartime & Military

A recruiting poster, 1916.
£70-80 *COB*

Quier, Mary Had An Air Force Lad Who Talked To Her of OPs, published by Counter Intelligence ASC-USSTAF, 12½ by 18in (32 by 46cm).
£90-110 *ONS*

Maurice Bennett, Keep It Dark, Careless Talk Costs Lives, and Night Attack Who Told Them Where To Find Her?, 15 by 10in (38 by 25cm).
£40-60 *ONS*

Gates Willson, Join the Women's Land Army, d.c.
£130-150 *ONS*

A recruiting poster, 1930s.
£7-10 *COB*

Noke, Talk Less, You Never Know, original artwork, signed, gouache, 22½ by 17½in (57 by 44cm).
£170-200 *ONS*

Cross Reference
Militaria

Careless Talk May Cost His Life, Don't Talk About Aerodromes or Aircraft Factories, 20 by 13½in (50 by 34cm).
£210-250 *ONS*

Keep Mum she's not so Dumb! Careless Talk Costs Lives, 15 by 10½in (39 by 26cm).
£85-120 *ONS*

The Pilot's Home because nobody talked!
£120-150 *ONS*

Don't Take The Squander Bug When You Go Shopping, 19½ by 14½in (49 by 37cm).
£55-75 *ONS*

Abram Games, Join The ATS, signed by the artist and model and dated 1941, d.c., together with a scrap book of photocopies and cuttings concerning the famous poster.
£3,000-3,500 *ONS*

There was much discussion of the suitability of ATS advertising. This poster was criticised in Parliamentary debate for being too glamorous and it attracted much notice in the press where it was nicknamed the 'Blonde Bombshell'. It was withdrawn and replaced by a less glamorous photographic image of an actual ATS private.

Measurements of posters:		
d.c.	double crown	30 by 20in (76 by 51cm)
q.c.	quad crown	30 by 40in (76 by 102cm)
s.s.	single sheet	60 by 40in (152 by 102cm)
d.r.	double royal	40 by 25in (102 by 64cm)
q.r.	quad royal	40 by 50in (102 by 127cm)

A 1915 recruitment poster, slight damage.
£35-40 *COB*

A WWI recruiting poster, 1915. **£45-50** *COB*

A French edition of piano music, c1925, 13 by 10in (33 by 26cm). **£5-8** *ROS*

She Knows What You Want, But She Wants What You Know, original artwork, watercolour, 20 by 14½in (51 by 37cm). **£170-200** *ONS*

Sheet Music

Elijah, for vocal and orchestral parts, c1920, 13½ by 10½in (34 by 26cm).
£5-8 *ROS*

Jewels from the Ballet, with an introduction by Robert Helpmann, c1950, 8½ by 11in (21 by 28cm).
£5-8 *ROS*

Ballantine's Complete School of Tuition for the Banjo, c1920, 14 by 10in (36 by 25cm).
£5-8 *ROS*

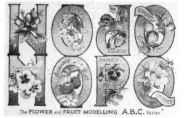

Barcarole for the piano, c1925, 14 by 10½in (36 by 26cm).
£5-8 *ROS*

Scraps

Raphael Tuck, cut outs, The Flower and Fruit Modelling A.B.C., Series 3402, A-D and E-I, EX.
£35-45 each *VS*

Raphael Tuck, cut outs, The Flower and Fruit Modelling A.B.C., Series 3402, J-M and N-Q, EX.
£35-45 each *VS*

Fans

An Italian fan, with painted chicken skin leaf, tortoiseshell sticks, the guardsticks set with locks of hair in lockets entwined with gilt serpents, and other gilt metal decorations including serpents, c1800, 9in (23cm).
£1,500-1,600   *CSK*

A trompe l'oeil fan, the leaf painted with paintings, drawings, music and papers, sticks of gilt metal, the guardsticks set with miniatures of children, mauve paste and enamelled in green, c1823, 7½in (19cm).
£1,650-1,850   *CSK*

Le Démènagement du Clerge, a printed fan, French, old repairs to leaf, 1789, 11in (28cm).
£1,000-1,100   *CSK*

Retrato Encantador, retrato de lo que adoro, a novelty fan with hand coloured etching of a girl dreaming as four putti carry a portrait of her lover, French for the Spanish market, c1825, 9in (23cm).
£1,200-1,300   *CSK*

The portrait is on a removable slide concealing a mirror with which the owner of the fan can mirror herself.

A printed Revolutionary fan, the leaf a hand coloured etching, with wooden sticks and bone fillets, French, c1790, 11in (28cm).
£1,100-1,200   *CSK*

A fan, with chicken skin leaf pen and ink drawing, tortoiseshell sticks, signed with initials A. H. fecit 1798.
£935-1,000   *CSK*

La Constitución Restable à la Union, a printed fan, with hand coloured engraving, the ivory sticks pierced, painted and gilt, Spanish, 1812, 9in (23cm).
£350-400   *CSK*

A French fan, the silk leaf painted with Louis XVI at the Altar of Love, framed with sequins, the ivory sticks pierced and gilt, with tortoiseshell filets, worn and repaired at folds, c1780, 11in (28cm).
£950-1,000   *CSK*

Collect pour les transport des paquet N.l., a printed fan, French, the ivory sticks possibly English, c1785, 10in (25cm).
£600-650   *CSK*

Reunion des Trois Ordres de l'Etat à l'Assemblée Nationale, a printed fan, French, c1787, repairs to leaf, 11in (28cm).
£1,100-1,200   *CSK*

S. M. El Rey D. Alfonso XII, a hand coloured lithographic fan, the wooden sticks cloutê with steel, 1875, 11½in (29cm).
£350-400   *CSK*

A French marriage fan, the silk leaf painted with The Marriage Contract, framed in sequins, the ivory sticks carved, pierced and gilt, worn and repaired at folds, c1780, 11in (28cm).
£825-875   *CSK*

A hand coloured lithographic fan of a bullfighting scene, the verso signed Eugenie, Souvenir de St Sebastian, 17 September 1857, with wooden sticks, lacks screw to pin, 1857, 11½in (29cm).
£200-300 *CSK*

A French marriage fan, the silk leaf painted with figures at the Altar of Love, framed in sequins, the ivory sticks carved, pierced and gilt, c1780, 11in (28cm).
£950-1,000 *CSK*

A printed fan, the leaf a hand coloured engraving with bone sticks, lower leaf damaged and stained, 1830, 8½in (21cm). **£700-750** *CSK*

A fan, with painted leaf and mother-of-pearl sticks carved, pierced and gilt, French, c1820, 8½in (21cm).
£825-925 *CSK*

A Carlist cockade fan, the linen leaf painted, the wooden handle carved with the cypher of Don Carlos VII and the Carlist motto in a cross, c1868, 9½in (24cm) open.
£350-450 *CSK*

Casamiento de Fernando VII con Maria Cristina de Napoles, a printed fan, the ivory sticks carved and pierced with lovers, the guardsticks carved with the Royal arms, 1829, 10in (25cm).
£570-625 *CSK*

A Canton brisé fan of carved and pierced tortoiseshell, c1810, 7½in (19cm).
£1,100-1,250 *CSK*

A fan, with painted leaf and painted mother-of-pearl pierced, gilt and carved, sticks, small repair, c1750, 11in (28cm).
£1,650-1,850 *CSK*

A fan, the leaf painted with Chinese figures riding and boating, the ivory sticks carved, c1760, 11in (28cm). **£800-850** *CSK*

A hand painted silk fan,
with mother-of-pearl
sticks, c1900.
£250-300 *YV*

A fan, the canepin leaf
painted, mother-of-pearl
sticks carved with birds,
flowers and insects and
backed with mother-of-
pearl, c1870, 10in (25cm).
£660-720 *CSK*

A folding pocket fan, the
leaf painted, the ivory
sticks gilt and hinged
below the mount to allow
the fan to be folded in two
when closed, c1855, 11in
(28cm).
£1,400-1,600 *CSK*

A brisé fan, intricately
pierced, silvered and gilt,
c1800, 5in (12.5cm).
£250-300 *YV*

A fan, the leaf painted,
signed F. Soubrony, the
mother-of-pearl sticks
carved and silvered,
6 of the 16 sticks are
arranged on the face of
the leaf, c1890, 13in
(33cm). **£1,100-1,250** *CSK*

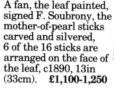

A printed fan, with
mother-of-pearl sticks
pierced and gilt, c1855,
10½in (26cm). **£220-250** *CSK*

A fan, the leaf painted,
the verso with a
shepherd, the ivory
sticks carved and
pierced, silvered and
gilt, c1760, 11in (28cm).
£1,000-1,100 *CSK*

A fan, inscribed d'après Watteau,
the verso with monogram V.
crowned with the Crown of Prussia,
with ivory sticks, the guardsticks
carved with roses and a bird's nest
and V. crowned, c1865, 11in (28cm).
£1,500-2,000 *CSK*

A Dutch fan, with
painted leaf, and carved
pierced and gilt mother-
of-pearl sticks, c1775,
11in (28cm).
£2,000-2,200 *CSK*

A fan, the leaf painted,
the ivory sticks carved,
pierced, silvered and
painted, c1750, 10in
(25cm).
£1,000-1,100 *CSK*

A printed fan, with hand
coloured lithograph leaf
of Queen Isabel II and
Don Francisco de Asis at
a bullfight in the Plaza
Mayor, Madrid, and the
verso with girls in
regional dress on swing,
inscribed with monogram
FR, the mother-of-pearl
sticks pierced and gilt,
c1845, 10½in (26cm).
£200-250 *CSK*

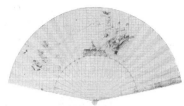

A fan, with painted canepin leaf, signed Japhet, and ivory sticks, the guardsticks carved as a dagger, late 19thC, 11in (28cm).
£1,200-1,250 *CSK*

Ne Pluribus Impar, a French printed fan, with bone sticks, c1785, 11in (28cm).
£1,100-1,200 *CSK*

Naissance du Duc de Normandie, a French printed fan, with wooden sticks, 1785, 11in (28cm).
£1,000-1,100 *CSK*

A Bill of Fare for a Wedding Dinner, a printed fan, the leaf a hand coloured etching published by Robt. Hixon No. 13 Bridges Street, Covent Garden, London and inscribed in a contemporary hand Nov. 12th 1794, 10in (25cm).
£700-900 *CSK*

The Prince and Princess of Wales, a printed fan, published by Sudlow, 191 Strand, with pierced wooden sticks, English, 1795, 10in (25cm).
£1,430-1,500 *CSK*

Commemorating the marriage of George, Prince of Wales, with Caroline of Brunswick in 1795.

A fan, with painted leaf, ivory sticks carved, pierced, painted and gilt and backed with mother-of-pearl, some damage, c1750, 10½in (26cm).
£2,200-2,500 *CSK*

A French printed fan, the leaf with a hand coloured oval vignette of the French taking an island fort and portraits of a French Grenadier and another, the reserves decorated with cut paper work, with wooden sticks, with bone filets, c1785, 11in (28cm).
£500-550 *CSK*

An Assignat printed fan, with wooden sticks, French, c1795, 12½in (32cm).
£1,000-1,100 *CSK*

A fan, with painted leaf and the mother-of-pearl sticks carved and pierced with putti and rocaille, c1850, 11½in (29cm).
£1,450-1,600 *CSK*

A Chinese fan in European style, the leaf painted with The Triumph of Bacchus, the ivory sticks carved with figures and birds, late 18thC, 13in (33cm).
£800-900 *CSK*

A Canton fan, with painted leaf and mother-of-pearl sticks carved on both sides with figures and buildings, mid-19thC, 11in (28cm).
£1,450-1,750 *CSK*

Fishing
Reels

A 3³⁄₁₆in Hardy, The Lightweight, Spitfire spool, c1950.
£40-60 *JMG*

A 2¼in Hardy brass reel, probably 1880s.
£150-200 *JMG*

A 3⅛in Hardy Uniqua reel, c1904.
£80-100 *JMG*

A 3¼in Hardy Spitfire type, unnamed, post WWII.
£60-80 *JMG*

A 3½in Hardy Uniqua, wide drum, 1920s.
£80-100 *JMG*

A 6¾in Scarborough sea reel, wood.
£25-35 *JMG*

A 3⅛in Hardy Cascapedia, one of only 12 made, 1930s.
£800-1,000 *JMG*

A 2¾in Malloch of Perth The Sun & Planet reel, with handle turning the spool, possibly 1920s.
£40-60 *JMG*

A 3¾in Malloch of Perth Sun and Planet reel, probably 1930s.
£50-70 *JMG*

A 4¼in Farlow spinning reel, c1910.
£80-100 *JMG*

A 2¾in Hardy Silex Multiplier, smallest size, 1930s. **£100-140** *JMG*

A 3¼in Hardy The Bouglé reel, 1930s.
£250-300   *JMG*

A 2⅝in Hardy The Field reel, c1900.
£150-200   *JMG*

A 3½in Hardy Super Silex Multiplier, 1930s.
£100-150   *JMG*

A 3¾in Hardy St. George Multiplier fly reel, 1930s, rare.
£80-100   *JMG*

A 3⅛in Hardy Perfect reel, wartime Spitfire model, by Jimmy Smith.   **£80-100**   *JMG*

A 2¾in all brass Hardy Perfect reel, c1895.
£400-500   *JMG*

A 5in all brass Hardy Perfect reel, c1891.
£500-800   *JMG*

A rare Scottish vintage fishing tackle dealer, c1924, with a deep knowledge of old reels, grey beard, ruddy-ish patina, and a most generous nature towards owners of fine tackle; buys up to £300   *JMG*

A 3¼in Malloch Sidecaster brass reel, with the Gibbs patent lock lever, 1930s.
£30-45   *JMG*

A 3⅛in Hardy Perfect, c1909, with American leather box. **£80-100** *JMG*

A 3¼in Hardy Special Perfect reel, 1930s. **£100-130** *JMG*

A 5in brass faced Hardy Perfect reel, c1909. **£180-200** *JMG*

A 2½in Perfect reel, with ivorine handle and leather case, c1900. **£120-150** *JMG*

An Allcock Ambidex Mark 9 reel, with blue finish, post war. **£20-30** *JMG*

A French reel, the Trio, post war. **£35-40** *JMG*

A French spinning reel, Centaure, post war. **£25-35** *JMG*

A 2½in brass and ebonite reel. **£40-50** *JMG*

A 4⅜in Edward Vom Hofe of New York sea reel, c1900. **£120-170** *JMG*

An Allcock Felton Crosswind reel, with black finish, 1930s. **£40-50** *JMG*

Very desirable in the U.S.A.

A 3¾in Anderson of Edinburgh Centabrake reel, 1930s. **£20-35** *JMG*

A 2⅝in brass The Moscrop reel, made in Manchester, c1900. **£60-80** *JMG*

A 3⅛in Army & Navy Stores fly reel, with early calliper check inside, with leather case, c1910. **£40-50** *JMG*

A Hardy Altex spinning reel, marked Patent Applied For, c1932. **£250-350** *JMG*

A 3½in Hardy Super Silex Multiplier, 1930s. **£120-170** *JMG*

A 3½in unnamed reel, possibly Allcock of Redditch, 1920s. **£20-30** *JMG*

A 3³⁄₁₆in Hardy The Lightweight reel, with steel check mechanism inside, 1936. **£50-80** *JMG*

A 3¾in Hardy St George Multiplier fly reel, pre-war. **£120-170** *JMG*

A 4½in Farlow of London, The Grenaby reel, possibly c1925. **£40-60** *JMG*

A 3⅛in Hardy Uniqua fly reel, with ivorine handle on fluted brass cup and check mechanism, c1904. **£50-80** *JMG*

A German spinning reel, the DAM Multirex, with green finish, 1950s. **£15-20** *JMG*

A 5in Milwards brass frogback sea reel, 1930s. **£50-70** *JMG*

An Italian fixed spool reel, the FSR, post war. **£10-15** *JMG*

Flies

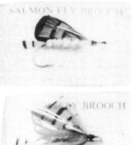

A 2¾in Dingley of Alnwick trout reel, c1915. **£20-30** *JMG*

Four salmon fly brooches, post war. **£2-3** *JMG*

A Farlow black japanned, salmon fly box, 1920s. **£30-40** *JMG*

A card of 12 gut-eyed flies, by S. Allcock, c1910. **£15-20** *JMG*

General

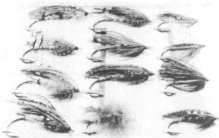

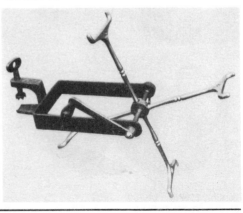

A very large black japanned fly box, by Malloch of Perth, containing some gut-eyed salmon flies, c1900. **£2-4 each** *JMG*

A Hardy line drier, green and gold, 1897. **£40-60** *JMG*

A Hardy multi-purpose tool, The Curate, used as tweezer or disgorger, gut cutter and stiletto, to apply oil or clean a hook, pre-war. **£30-40** *JMG*

A Hardy The Practical line drier, 1920s. **£40-50** *JMG*

A Malloch of Perth three-rod holder, for the back of the boat, possibly 19thC. **£80-100** *JMG*

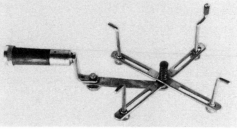

A Hardy Compact line drier, with wooden handle and 4 grooves in arms, c1930s. **£20-30** *JMG*

A Hardy rod holder, for the back of a boat, possibly 1920s. **£30-50** *JMG*

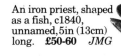

A rod holder, to put into the bank and hold the rod on top, possibly 19thC, 5in (13cm) long. **£20-30** *JMG*

A Bambridge of Eton leather fishing wallet, with all original pieces inside, c1910. **£25-30** *JMG*

An iron priest, shaped as a fish, c1840, unnamed, 5in (13cm) long. **£50-60** *JMG*

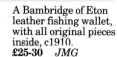

A Hardy The Boomerang, a priest for killing fish, for opening the fish's mouth and for carrying a dead fish, c1909. **£80-100** *JMG*

A Hardy trace-making black japanned box, with 3 tools inside, pre-war. **£20-30** *JMG*

Garden & Farm Equipment

An elm wheelbarrow, green painted, with wood and iron wheel, 60in (152cm) long.
£130-150 *AL*

A foot guard for use when digging, to protect base of foot. **£8-10** *IW*

A fruit picking ladder, 84in (213cm) high.
£65-70 *AL*

An iron and glass cloche, 22in (56cm) square.
£60-65 *AL*

A green painted wooden basket, 23in (59cm) wide.
£32-35 *AL*

An apple picking ladder, 120in (304.5cm) high.
£40-45 *AL*

A patent flower holder, Wakefield Floral Aid, 3½in (9cm) high.
£10-12 *AL*

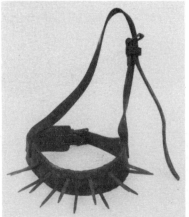

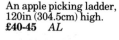

A florist's vase, in green enamel, 15in (38cm) high.
£12-14 *AL*

A calf muzzle to prevent suckling.
£15-20 *IW*

Two galvanised watering cans, with copper roses, 6½ and 9in (16 and 23cm) high.
£16-18 each *AL*

A wooden basket, 18in
(46cm) high.
£22-25 *AL*

A green painted lamp,
with copper base,
Blu-Lite, Birmingham,
possibly for greenhouse,
17in (43cm) high.
£60-65 *AL*

A green painted watering
can, 15½in (39cm) high.
£32-35 *AL*

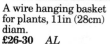

A galvanised watering
can, 14in (36cm) high.
£12-14 *AL*

An original Arnold & Son horse tooth rasp,
c1900, 14in (36cm) long. **£25-30** *BS*

A wire hanging basket
for plants, 11in (28cm)
diam.
£26-30 *AL*

A terracotta flower pot,
6½in (16cm) high.
£12-14 *AL*

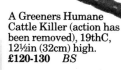

A horse gag, early 19thC,
14½in (37cm) long.
£30-35 *IW*

A Greeners Humane
Cattle Killer (action has
been removed), 19thC,
12½in (32cm) high.
£120-130 *BS*

A wire potato basket,
11½in (29cm) high.
£18-20 *AL*

A terracotta plant pot
and tray, 9½in (24cm)
high.
£30-35 *AL*

A wooden trug, 18in
(46cm) wide.
£32-35 *AL*

GLASS

A pressed glass plate to commemorate Queen Victoria's Jubilee, 9½in (24cm) diam.
£15-20   *ROS*

A pair of George III silver and cut glass condiment flasks, 5½in (14cm) high.
£190-200   *PSA*

A Daum Cadillac Imperial in crystal, 16in (41cm) long.
£450-475
ABS

Bowls

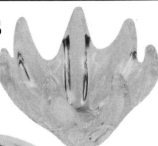

A French clear glass bowl, signed Vannes, c1955, 4in (10cm) diam.
£35-45   *GRA*

A Lalique opalescent shallow bowl, moulded with a spiral of fish around a bubble centre, 12in (30cm) diam.
£380-400   *Bea*

A Scottish jug and 4 glasses in mottled green and clear glass, c1940.
£25-35   *SWa*

A Scottish bowl in violet and clear glass, c1925, 9in (23cm) diam.
£45-55   *SWa*

A carnival glass dish, 9in (23cm) diam.
£30-35   *HEW*

A further selection of carnival glass dishes is featured in previous editions of Miller's Collectables Price Guides, available from Millers Publications.

Decanters

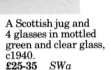

A Victorian glass paperweight pen and inkstand, chipped, c1840, 5in (13cm) long.
£30-40
If perfect.   **£150 plus**   *ROW*

l. A decanter with single neck rim, marked Rum, c1790, 8in (20cm) high.
£200-250
r. A green decanter of club shape, with gilt Rum cartouche and gilt lozenge stopper, c1790, 7½in (18.5cm) high.
£220-260   *Som*

Cross Reference
Writing Accessories

l.&r. A pair of blue square bottles with canted edges, pouring lips and gilt decoration Rum and Shrub with gilt ball stoppers, c1800, 6½in (16cm) high.
£550-600
c. A larger bottle, marked Rum, c1800, 7in (17cm) high.
£200-250 *Som*

l. A pair of ovoid decanters with wide base fluting and flute cut necks, with target stoppers, c1810, 8½in (21cm) high.
£550-650
r. A decanter engraved with looped ribbon, bows and Prince of Wales feathers, flute cut base and neck, lozenge stopper, c1780, 8in (20cm) high.
£150-220 *Som*

Three ovoid spirit decanters, c1810.
£85-95 each *Som*

l.&c. Two spirit decanters, with lozenge stoppers, c1810, 8in (20cm). **£85-95 each**
r. A decanter, with blaze printy and flute cutting, cut mushroom stopper, c1820, 8½in (21cm).
£220-250 *Som*

l. A Victorian spirit decanter, with broad flute cutting and cut stopper, c1845.
£45-55
c. A spirit decanter, with flute and diamond cutting, cut lozenge stopper, c1810, 8in (20.5cm).
£85-95
r. A spirit decanter, with flute, printy and diamond cutting, cut mushroom stopper, c1810, 7½in (18.5cm).
£85-95 *Som*

Two spirit decanters, c1825.
£80-120 each *Som*

l. A Continental ruby tinted cut glass and silver mounted crested hawk shaped claret jug, having import marks, 14in (36cm) high.
r. A cut glass claret jug of flattened oval shape, with Imperial Russian pheasant head silver colour mount, indistinct mark, hinge damaged, c1900, 11½in (29cm) high.
£850-950 each *GC*

l. A decanter with flute cut base, 3 cut neck rings, and target stopper, c1820, 9in (23cm) high.
r. An ovoid decanter with flute cut base and neck, 3 neck rings, and mushroom stopper, c1810.
£200-250 each *Som*

Two decanters with flute cutting, c1840, 9in (23cm).
l. **£200-250**
r. **£80-100** *Som*

Four blue oviform decanters, 2 with lozenge-shaped stoppers, painted with Brandy Hollands and Rum, the 2 stoppers inscribed B and H, one stopper badly chipped, 10in (25cm) high overall; and 2 others.
£365-385 *CSK*

l. A spirit decanter, with diamond cut neck rings and target stopper, c1810, 7in (18cm) high.
£85-95
c. A decanter with diamond and vertically scribed cutting, with small foot ring and star cut base, c1880, 8in (20cm).
£65-75
r. A spirit decanter, with broad vertical flute cutting and annulated neck rings, with hollow cut mushroom stopper, c1840, 7in (18cm).
£70-90 *Som*

A blue mallet-shaped decanter with ball stopper, painted with an imitation label for Rum, gilding rubbed, 10in (25cm) high.
£285-300 *CSK*

Drinking Glasses

Four dwarf ales with conical bowls, 5 to 6in (13 to 15cm).
£35-45 each *Som*

A cased centre vase designed as a footed goblet, with hunting scene decoration, clear glass stem, 6½in (16cm) diam. **£1,100-1,200** *GH*

A bell bowl champagne, with tear drop baluster stem and conical folded foot, c1720, 6½in (16cm) high. **£130-150** *WW*

A Bohemian amber flashed goblet, the bowl engraved with hounds in a forest glade, set on a knopped faceted stem and lobed foot, 9½in (24cm) high.
£325-350 *Bea*

A Minton gothic vase, by T. Steel, c1840, 9in (22cm).
£550-600 *BA*

l. A bonnet glass with double ogee moulded body and blue rim, c1780, 3in (7.5cm) high.
£250-300
c. A blue Wrythen North Country egg cup in soda glass with knopped stem and plain foot, c1800, 4in (9.5cm) high.
£50-100
r. A cream opaline egg cup with amethyst rim, c1830, 3½in (8cm) high.
£120-170 *Som*

Fire Grenades

Two Minimax amber glass phials for soda acid fire extinguishers, filled with sulphuric acid, 8½in (21cm) long. **£40-50 each** *BS*

An amber glass Haywards grenade, 7in (18cm) high. **£60-80** *BS*

Two blue glass fire grenades, usually filled with sodium bicarbonate solution, thrown at fire and smashed, 6½in (16cm) high. **£80-120 each** *BS*

Hats

A Cranberry overlaid hat, c1880, 3½in (9cm) high.
£145-150 *PBA*

l. A glass hat, 19thC, 2½in (7cm) high.
£30-40
r. A Nailsea glass hat, 19thC, 3½in (9cm) high.
£65-75 *PBA*

Two glass hats, 19thC, 3½ to 4in (9 to 10cm) diam. **£50-60 each** *PBA*

A turquoise blue hat, overlaid with white, c1850, 2½in (6cm) high.
£70-80 *PBA*

Perfume Bottles & Accessories

A Loetz glass powder bowl, with red lid, yellow base, black finial and feet, c1920, 5in (13cm) diam.
£110-130 *ROW*

An amber Fabergé perfume display piece, c1940, 11in (28cm) high.
£75-85 *GRA*

A black enamel and clear glass perfume bottle, on chrome and black glass base, c1930.
£125-135 *GRA*

Pressed Glass

A clear and amber pressed glass powder bowl, 1930s, 5½in (14cm) high. **£12-15** *SWa*

A John Derbyshire opaque matt black paperweight, modelled as a resting winged Sphinx, external trade mark and diamond reg. mark to base for 9th March 1876, 9in (22cm) long. **£1,800-1,900** *GH*

A Sowerby yellow semi-translucent plate, with scolloped rim and pierced ribbon border, with internal moulded basketweave decoration, unmarked, c1880, 8½in (21cm) diam. **£170-200** *GH*

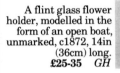

A flint glass flower holder, modelled in the form of an open boat, unmarked, c1872, 14in (36cm) long. **£25-35** *GH*

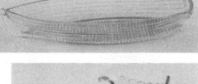

A pair of Davidson primrose pearline flared bowls, with wavy sides and moulded ribbed body decoration, unmarked, c1890, 4in (10cm) diam. **£30-40** *GH*

A flint glass jug and bowl to commemorate Queen Victoria's jubilee 1887, jug 4½in (11cm) high. **£15-25** *GH*

A John Derbyshire opaque black paperweight modelled as a resting lion, supported on an oval base, external trade mark to base, c1875, 6½in (16cm) long. **£180-200** *GH*

A pair of Sowerby dark blue translucent glass flower holders, modelled as open boats, internal trade marks and reg. no. to both 42947 for 10th February 1886, 10½in (26cm) long. **£40-50** *GH*

An opaque white jug, with external moulded Bacchanalian figure and grape vine decoration, unmarked, c1880, 3in (8cm) high. **£30-40** *GH*

A pair of Davidson primrose pearline bowls, with twin looped side handles, on splayed feet, unmarked, c1890, 3in (8cm) diam. **£30-40** *GH*

A Sowerby light blue translucent glass flower holder, modelled as an open boat, unmarked, c1886, 12in (31cm) long. **£40-50** *GH*

A Sowerby flint glass flower holder, modelled in the form of an open boat, internal trade mark and reg. no. 64086 for 22nd December 1886, 5in (13cm) long. **£10-15** *GH*

Vases

A celery vase by Joseph Webb, Stourbridge, dated 23rd June 1853, 9½in (24cm) high. **£70-75** *PSA*

A French frosted glass vase, signed Caravelle, c1930, 4in (10cm). **£35-40** *GRA*

A Lalique ovoid frosted glass vase, 'Archers', inscribed R. Lalique, France, with gilt brass light fittings, 10½in (26cm). **£2,750-3,000** *Bea*

Monart

A French opaline glass vase, with gilt metal rims, 9in (23cm). **£500-550** *Bea*

A Monart vase, the neck with blue, black and aventurine above a bulbous green and aventurine body, printed label III.R.D.364 and retailer's label for Watsons, Perth, 12½in (32cm) high. **£100-125** *C(S)*

A Monart vase, with multi-coloured swirling decorations on a clouded ground, 5½in (14cm) high. **£275-300** *C(S)*

Two handkerchief vases, c1930. **£16-18 each** *FOB*

An Art Deco vase, 4in (10cm) high. **£15-20** *RE*

A Monart table lamp and domed shade in pink, green, orange and white inclusions, with original metal fittings, printed label, VII.P./23.508, 14in (36cm) high. **£875-900** *C(S)*

Cross Reference
Lighting

MAKE THE MOST OF MILLERS
Condition is absolutely vital when assessing the value of any item. Damaged pieces appreciate much less than perfect examples. However, a rare, desirable piece may command a high price even when damaged.

Whitefriars

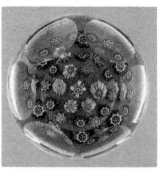

A Charles Kaziun faceted concentric millefiori colourground weight, signed with two 'K' canes, 2½in (6.5cm) diam.
£450-475
S(NY)

A sapphire blue engraved vase, 1930, 5½in (14cm) high. **£18-25** *SWa*

A clear and streaky grey glass vase, 1960s, 5in (13cm) high.
£18-28 *SWa*

Baccarat

A Baccarat garlanded double clematis weight, 3in (7.5cm) diam.
£1,200-1,500 *S(NY)*

A dish by E. Barnaby Powell, 11in (28cm) wide.
£45-65 *SWa*

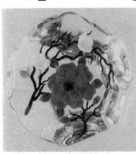

A Baccarat garlanded white double-clematis weight, mid-19thC, 2½in (6cm) diam.
£440-460 *C*

Paperweights

A Victor Trabucco faceted magnum floral weight, signed 'VT', 4in (10.5cm) diam.
£520-550 *S(NY)*

A Baccarat scattered millefiori weight, signed and dated 'B 1848', 3in (7.5cm) diam.
£1,200-1,500 *S(NY)*

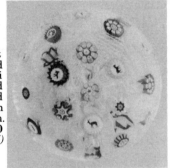

A bird and flower colourground weight, signed with a single 'S' cane and engraved B 378 1981 Ayotte & Stankard, 3in (8.5cm) diam.
£1,100-1,300 *S(NY)*

A Baccarat faceted close millefiori mushroom weight, 3in (7.5cm) diam.
£775-825 *S(NY)*

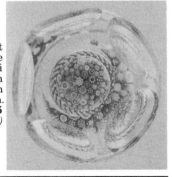

A Baccarat faceted clematis weight, mid-19thC, 3in (8cm) diam. **£4,400-4,600** *C*

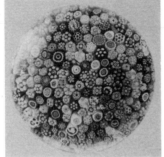

A Baccarat garlanded pansy weight, 3in (7cm) diam. **£1,100-1,300** *S(NY)*

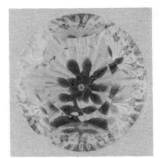

A Baccarat faceted garlanded double clematis weight, 3in (7.5cm) diam. **£640-660** *S(NY)*

A Baccarat signed and dated close millefiori weight, signed and dated 'B 1847', 3in (7.5cm) diam. **£1,200-1,500** *S(NY)*

A Baccarat patterned millefiori weight, 3in (7.5cm) diam. **£770-800** *S(NY)*

Clichy

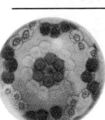

A Clichy pink ground patterned millefiori weight, mid-19thC, 3in (7.5cm) diam. **£1,200-1,500** *C*

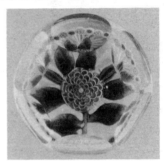

A Baccarat faceted garlanded pompom weight, 2½in (6.5cm) diam. **£1,100-1,300** *S(NY)*

A Clichy blue and white swirl weight, mid-19thC, 2in (5.5cm) diam. **£880-920** *C*

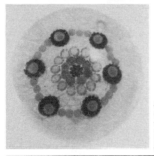

A Clichy turquoise ground patterned millefiori weight, mid-19thC, 3in (8cm) diam. **£1,300-1,400** *C*

A Clichy patterned concentric millefiori weight, mid-19thC, 2½in (6.5cm) diam. **£460-480** *C*

A Clichy green and white 'Barber's Pole' chequer weight, mid-19thC, 2½in (6.5cm) diam. **£2,800-3,200** *C*

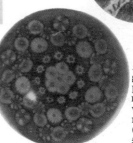

A Clichy green ground patterned millefiori weight, mid-19thC, 3in (8cm) diam. **£825-850** *C*

A Clichy blue ground patterned millefiori weight, mid-19thC, 2½in (5.5cm) diam.
£500-525 *C*

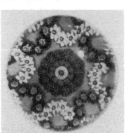

A Clichy turquoise ground patterned millefiori weight, mid-19thC, 3in (7.5cm) diam.
£2,400-2,600 *C*

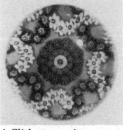

A Clichy style swirl weight, 2in (5.5cm) diam.
£200-225 *HSS*

A Clichy miniature blue ground concentric millefiori weight, mid-19thC, 2in (4.5cm) diam.
£680-700 *C*

A Clichy swirl weight, mid-19thC, 2½in (6.5cm) diam.
£880-920 *C*

A Clichy swirl weight, mid-19thC, 2in (5.5cm) diam.
£600-625 *C*

A Clichy garlanded patterned millefiori weight, mid-19thC, 3in (7.5cm) diam.
£1,220-1,250 *C*

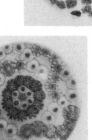

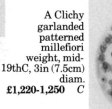

A Clichy pale turquoise ground patterned millefiori weight, mid-19thC, 3in (7.5cm) diam. **£500-525** *C*

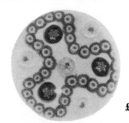

A Clichy white ground patterned millefiori weight, mid-19thC, 3in (7.5cm) diam. **£600-650** *C*

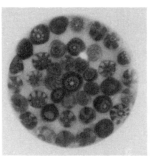

A Clichy 'sodden snow' ground spaced concentric millefiori weight, mid-19thC, 3in (8cm) diam.
£600-625 *C*

A Clichy purple and white swirl weight, mid-19thC, 3in (8cm) diam.
£680-700 *C*

Paul Joseph Stankard

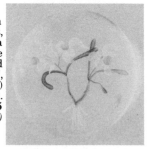

A cattleya orchid weight, signed with a single 'S' cane and engraved 4/75 219 77, 3in (7.5cm) diam.
£500-525 *S(NY)*

A triple orchid weight, signed with a single 'S' cane, 3in (7.5cm) diam.
£750-850 *S(NY)*

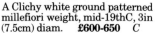

A compound violet weight, signed with a single 'S' cane and engraved Millicent Brocklebank A 470 1980, 3in (7.5cm) diam.
£700-800 *S(NY)*

A floral weight, signed with a single 'S' cane and engraved Especially for M. Brocklebank A 469 1980, 3in (7.5cm) diam.
£775-850 *S(NY)*

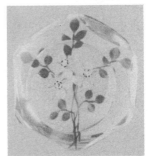

A faceted triple meadow wreath weight, signed with a single 'S' cane and engraved A 471 1980, 3in (7.5cm) diam.
£325-350 *S(NY)*

St Louis

A St Louis posy weight, mid-19thC, 2½in (7cm) diam.
£1,200-1,500 *C*

A St Louis fruit weight, 2½in (6cm) diam.
£450-475 *S(NY)*

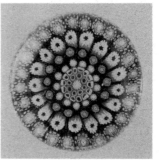

A St Louis concentric millefiori weight, 2½in (6.5cm) diam.
£580-620 *S(NY)*

A St Louis double clematis weight, 19thC, 2½in (7cm) diam.
£550-600 *C*

A St Louis pelargonium weight, mid-19thC, 2½in (6.5cm) diam.
£1,600-1,800 *C*

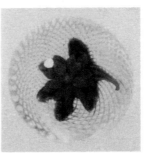

A St Louis weight, mid-19thC, 2½in (6cm) diam.
£800-825 *C*

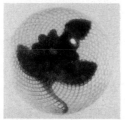

A St Louis double clematis weight, mid-19thC, 2½in (6cm) diam.
£700-725 *C*

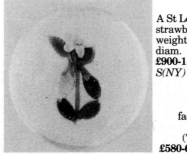

A St Louis strawberry weight, 3in (7.5cm) diam.
£900-1,100 *S(NY)*

A St Louis faceted dahlia weight, 3in (7.5cm) diam.
£580-620 *S(NY)*

Hatpins

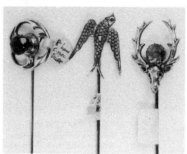

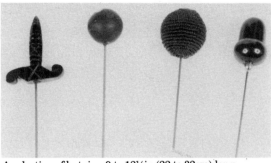

A selection of hatpins, 9 to 12½in (22 to 32cm) long.
£12-25 each   *AA*

Three unusual silver
topped hatpins with
hinges, c1900.
£40-50 each   *HOW*

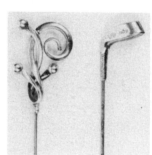

l. Two Charles Horner
silver hatpins, Chester
1908/9, 10in (25cm) long.
r. A silver butterfly
hatpin with amethyst
colour stone,
Birmingham 1910,
10½in (26cm) long.
£25-35 each   *HOW*

Two Charles Horner
silver topped hatpins,
Chester and
Birmingham, 1904, 10in
(25cm) long.
£25-35 each   *HOW*

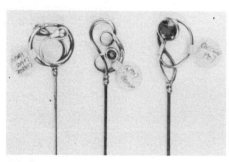

Three Charles Horner
silver topped hatpins,
Chester 1907, 10in
(25cm) long.
£20-40 each   *HOW*

An Art Deco Bakelite
hatpin, 9in (22cm) long,
and a gentian painted
bone with marcasite,
c1920, 7in (18cm) long.
£10-14 each   *AA*

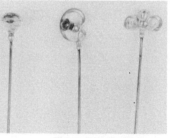

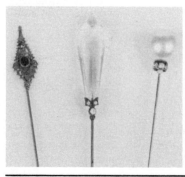

A selection of Edwardian
hatpins,
l. filigree, 10½in (26cm)
long.
£12-14
c. crystal, 4½in (11cm)
long.
£10-12
r. paste, 4½in (11cm)
long.
£8-10   *AA*

Three Charles Horner
silver hatpins with paste
and gem stones, 5 to
6½in (13 to 16cm) long.
£20-26 each   *AA*

A selection of Charles Horner silver Art Nouveau hatpins, Chester, c1910, 10 to 11½in (25 to 29cm) long.
£45-50 each *AA*

Two Victorian silver hatpins, one with mother-of-pearl, 7½in (19cm) long and one with leaf design, 11½in (29cm) long.
£20-35 each *AA*

Two Victorian hatpins, one star shaped cut steel, 4in (10cm) long, one opalescent glass, 7in (17cm) long.
£15-20 each *AA*

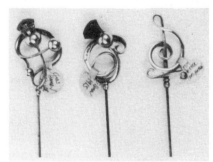

Three Charles Horner silver topped hatpins, Chester, c1907, 10 to 10½in (25 to 26cm) long.
£25-35 each *HOW*

A selection of hatpins with sequins, mother-of-pearl and paste decorations, 1930s-50s, 3 to 4½in (8 to 11cm) long.
£3-6 each *AA*

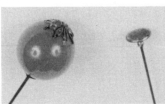

l. An agate hatpin, c1900, 9in (23cm) long. **£18-20**
c. Edwardian amethyst enamel on brass, 5in (12cm) long.
r. Mother-of-pearl, 6in (15cm) long.
£10-12 each *AA*

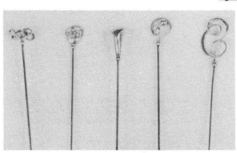

A selection of Charles Horner silver Art Nouveau hatpins, 6½ to 7½in (16 to 19cm) long.
£25-30 each *AA*

Hatpin Holders

An Edwardian hatpin holder, 5in (13cm) high.
£18-25 *AA*

An Edwardian hatpin holder with floral decoration, 5in (13cm) high.
£18-25 *AA*

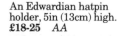

An Edwardian hatpin holder, 5in (13cm) high.
£18-25 *AA*

A Victorian hatpin holder, with gilt and floral decoration, 6in (15cm) high.
£18-25 *AA*

A Victorian hatpin holder, 5½in (14cm) high.
£20-25 *AA*

A blue and white hatpin holder, c1900, 5in (13cm) high.
£16-20 *AA*

A Victorian Indian tree design hatpin holder, 5in (13cm) high.
£20-25 *AA*

A silver hatpin holder, Chester, c1915, 4½in (11cm) high.
£38-45 *AA*

A hatpin holder, c1900, 5½in (14cm) high.
£20-30 *AA*

Inkstands

A brass inkstand with liner, 3½in (9cm) high.
£50-60 *PSA*

A French boulle and rosewood encrier, veneered in scarlet tortoiseshell, with Asprey retailer's imprint, 19thC, 9in (23cm) wide.
£700-800 *CSK*

A late Victorian
inkstand, with a pair of
diamond cut glass
inkwells, plated mounts
and hinged covers, 10in
(25cm) long.
£240-270   *HSS*

A Wm. Hutton & Sons
inkstand, with shaped
triform base, reed and
ribbon borders and
2 glass wells, Sheffield
1911, 5oz.
£325-375   *P(O)*

Cross Reference
Writing Accessories

A Kerr & Binns inkstand,
c1862, 6in (15cm) high.
£300-400   *TH*

A Victorian cast brass
inkstand, liner missing,
5in (13cm) square.
£35-40   *PSA*

A George V silver
inkstand, by the
Goldsmiths and
Silversmiths Company,
London 1923, 8in (20cm)
wide, 575 grammes.
£400-450   *HSS*

Juke Boxes

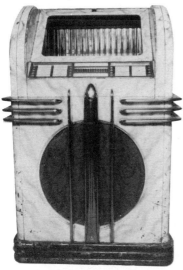

A Wurlitzer Model 700C,
Serial No. 583, with
24 selections of 78rpm
records, original plastics
and coin mechanism,
1940, 55in (139.5cm)
high.
£2,250-2,500   *CSK*

*The Wurlitzer 700 was
designed by Paul Fuller
and was part of
Wurlitzer's special drive
planned for the spring of
1940. In that year Paul
Fuller did his finest work,
producing 11 new models
of which 7 were distinct
concepts.*

A Wurlitzer 51
table top juke box,
with 12 selections,
in wood veneer
case, 20in (51cm)
high.
£2,250-2,500
CSK

An AMI Art Deco juke
box, in marbled wood and
plated metal, c1938, 49in
(124.5cm).
£6,000-6,500   *AAM*

A Wurlitzer Model 750, Serial No. 745286, with 24 selections of 78rpm records, original plastics and coin mechanism, 54in (137cm) high.
£4,300-4,500 *CSK*

A Wurlitzer star speaker, 1940s, 25in (64cm) diam.
£1,000-1,200 *AAM*

Cross Reference
Americana

A Symphony Bal Ami stereo juke box, Model S40, Serial No. 1156, 40 selections, 1952, 55in (139cm).
£600-800 *CSK*

A Wurlitzer 1100 juke box, 78rpm, unrestored, c1947, 58½in (148cm) high.
£4,000-4,500 *AAM*

A Wurlitzer 1600 High Fidelity, 45rpm, unrestored, c1953, 54in (137cm) high.
£2,000-2,500 *AAM*

Delft Jewellery

An Edwardian Delft and silver filigree butterfly, 1½in (4cm) wide.
£16-35 *AA*

A Delft and silver brooch,
1920s, 2in (5cm) wide.
£25-35 *AA*

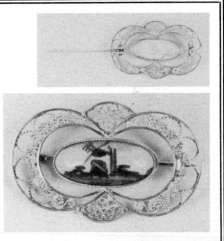

An Edwardian
filigree brooch, and
reverse view
showing mark,
1½in (4cm) wide.
£18-35 *AA*

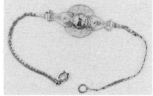

An Edwardian Delft and
silver bracelet.
£16-30 *AA*

A Delft and silver
necklace, c1930.
£16-20 *AA*

An Edwardian Delft and
silver daisy filigree
necklace.
£16-35 *AA*

Jewellery
Marcasite

Reproduction marcasite and silver bows.
£25-35 each *FMN*

Reproduction marcasite
alphabet brooches.
£15-22 each *FMN*

A silver and marcasite
fish brooch, c1920, 1½in
(4cm) long.
£50-60 *FMN*

A chrome and marcasite
head brooch, c1920, 2in
(5cm) long.
£25-35 *FMN*

Two silver marcasite bow brooches, 2in (5cm) long. **£40-50 each** *FMN*

Three reproduction marcasite animal brooches, elephants, 1in (3cm), fish 2in (5cm) and frog 1½in (4cm). **£25-35 each** *FMN*

A silver marcasite flower brooch, c1920, 2in (5cm) wide. **£35-45** *FMN*

A silver and marcasite necklace, c1920. **£45-55** *FMN*

A silver marcasite galleon brooch, c1920, 1½in (4cm) wide. **£30-40** *FMN*

Mexican

A Mexican silver bracelet. **£80-100** *CHa*

A Mexican silver brooch, c1940. **£80-100** *ASA*

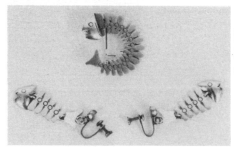

A Mexican silver brooch and earring set, marked Taxco. **£50-65** *CHa*

A Mexican silver bracelet with green stones. **£100-120** *CHa*

A Mexican silver bracelet. **£70-85** *CHa*

DID YOU KNOW?
Miller's Collectables Price Guide is designed to build up, year by year, into the most comprehensive reference system available.

A pair of Mexican silver earrings, marked Taxco. **£38-45** *CHa*

Mosaic Jewellery

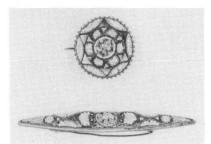

Two Victorian silver brooches, one with 9ct gold hearts and loveknot, Birmingham 1896, 2in (5cm) long
£40-45
and bar, Birmingham 1887, 2in (5cm) long.
£30-35 *HOW*

Two Victorian mosaic brooches, 1in (3cm) diam and 3½in (9cm) long.
£30-45 each *FMN*

Two Victorian 9ct gold brooches:
Top. With centre pearl, Birmingham 1897.
£95-110
Bottom. Yellow and rose gold, Birmingham 1888, both 2in (5cm) long.
£80-90 *HOW*

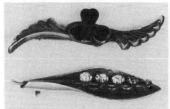

Two mosaic brooches, violin on brass, 2in (5cm), and a horseshoe, 1in (3cm) long, 1930s, these have more rounded edges than Victorian examples. **£20-30 each** *FMN*

A diamond bar brooch.
£310-330
HCH

Mosaic jewellery from Venice, Italy, was popular in the late Victorian era. The quality was good, using tiny pieces of glass and subtle colours, compared with the late 1930s revival.

Bar Brooches

Two Victorian silver brooches:
Top. Moss agate clover, Birmingham 1899.
Bottom. Enamel, Birmingham 1898, both 2in (5cm) long.
£35-45 each *HOW*

A silver and paste bar brooch, Birmingham 1920, 2in (5cm) long
£25-35
and a silver brooch with 9ct gold anchor motif, Birmingham 1897, 2in (5cm) long.
£30-40 *HOW*

Two Victorian silver brooches, each with 9ct gold flower onlay, 1895 and 1896, both 2in (5cm) long.
£45-55 each *HOW*

An Edwardian brooch, 9ct gold, with sapphires, 2in (5cm) long, and a Victorian 9ct gold bar brooch with diamond inset, 1½in (4cm) long.
£95-100 each *HOW*

A diamond and rose diamond cluster bar brooch, with palmette design terminals.
£600-700 *CSK*

243

A Victorian silver brooch with Grace and a yacht, very unusual to have a scene, 1½in (4cm) long.
£100-110 *FMN*

Two Victorian silver brooches, Birmingham 1887, 2in (5cm) long. **£30-40 each** *HOW*

Victorian Name Brooches

In the 1880s silver became popular for everyday wear, and was mass produced by machine. Most of the name brooches were bars in various designs. They were decorated with leaves, flowers, hearts and engraved designs, although some were round with cut out designs in the centre. Some were given as love tokens, others were given by the lady of the house to her servants. They were mostly made in Birmingham or Chester from 1870 to 1918. Although some gold brooches exist they are very rare.

A selection of silver Victorian name brooches, some with gold lettering, c1900, Maggie, Chester 1903, maker W.R.S., Ellen, Emily, and Louie, 1½ to 2in (4 to 5cm) long.
£30-45 each *FMN*

Alice, Dorothy, Esther, Mary and Nita, prettier and more desirable names, 1½ to 2in (4 to 5cm) long.
£50-65 each *FMN*

Two Victorian silver name brooches, Madge, Birmingham 1897, 1½in (4cm) long, and Edith, Birmingham 1898, 2in (5cm) long.
£35-45 each *HOW*

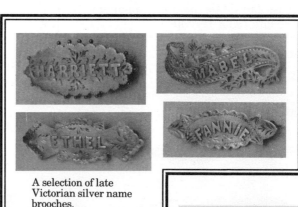

A selection of late Victorian silver name brooches.
£20-60 each *PVH*

Two Victorian silver brooches, one Baby, 1899, 1½in (4cm) long
£30-35
and Mizpah, Birmingham 1888, 2in (5cm) long.
£35-40 *HOW*

A Victorian silver name brooch 1½in (4cm) long.
£40-45 *FMN*

A Victorian gold
name brooch, Mabel,
1½in (4cm) long.
£70-90 *FMN*

Silver name brooches,
round, c1890, Lizzie,
Pollie, and Eliza, 1in
(3cm) diam.
£40-50 each
Edith, unusual but name
not so desirable, 2in
(5cm) long.
£40-50 *FMN*

*The price depends on the
name, i.e. Sarah,
Elizabeth, Emily,
Jennifer, Esther and
Lucy are more desirable,
so £70 each.*

Bracelets

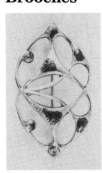

A Danish silver
and blue enamel
bracelet.
£50-55 *CHa*

A Continental mesh woven design bracelet.
£420-500 *CSK*

An 18ct two-colour gold
barrel link bracelet, with
diamond cross bands.
£300-400 *CSK*

A broad mesh bracelet, with sapphire and rose
diamond bar decoration. **£600-650** *CSK*

Brooches

A diamond set brooch.
£375-500 *C(S)*

A silver Art Nouveau
brooch, 1½in (4cm) wide.
£65-70 *PSA*

A diamond set floral
and leaf pattern brooch.
£420-450 *AG*

A David Anderson
enamelled fish brooch.
£75-100 *CHa*

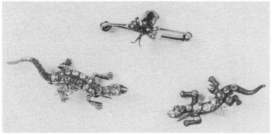

Three brooches.
£10-16 each *VB*

A diamond and rose diamond brooch.
£2,000-2,500 *CSK*

A diamond and pavé diamond crossover design double clip brooch, one stone missing.
£2,200-2,500 *CSK*

A yellow gold spray brooch, set with 40 diamonds and 36 square cut rubies.
£600-700 *AG*

A diamond double flowerhead clip brooch.
£850-900 *CSK*

Two silver brooches:
Top. Coronation, 1902, 1½in (4cm) wide.
£45-50
Bottom. A Greek brooch, c1902, 1in (3cm) diam.
£85-90 *HOW*

An oval shell cameo brooch.
£200-300 *CSK*

Two silver brooches:
Top. Shaped as a playing card, 1½ by 1in (4 by 3cm). **£35-45**
Bottom. A Victorian brooch, 1in (3cm) wide.
£40-45 *HOW*

A Victorian silver acorn brooch.
£15-25 *PVH*

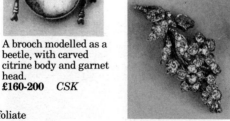

A brooch modelled as a beetle, with carved citrine body and garnet head.
£160-200 *CSK*

A diamond foliate pierced lozenge shaped brooch.
£470-550 *CSK*

A 19thC diamond and rose diamond brooch.
£575-675 *CSK*

An 18ct gold, diamond and square cut ruby leaf cluster brooch.
£80-150 *CSK*

Earrings

A pair of diamond nine-stone
cluster ear screws. **£700-800** *CSK*

A pair of diamond and
calibre emerald cluster
leaf design ear clips.
£2,700-3,200 *CSK*

A pair of oval shell cameo
earrings.
£420-500 *CSK*

General

A pair of
diamond
dress clips.
£2,200-2,500
CSK

A silver
charm tag,
2in (5cm)
long.
£140-160
LEW

Necklaces

An Edwardian diamond
graduated necklace, with
diamond two-stone
stylised laurel leaf
dividing links, in a fitted
case. **£7,000-7,500** *CSK*

A Continental loop-in-loop guard
chain, with beadwork decoration.
£1,750-2,000 *CSK*

An Edwardian 15ct gold,
turquoise and split pearl
necklace, incomplete, in
original case.
£500-550 *HSS*

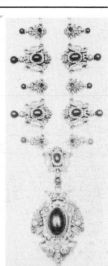

An Austro-Hungarian
lapis lazuli, garnet and
gem panel necklace.
£720-800 *CSK*

Pendants

A pair of Boucheron
cuff links, signed
Boucheron Paris,
numbered 32015,
in maker's case.
£500-600 *CSK*

An enamelled silver minaudiere,
decorated in colours, enclosing a
mirror and compartments, with
black cord and tassel, London
import marks for 1926, 3½in (9cm).
£350-450 *P*

An Italian gold and lapis
lazuli pendant brooch,
c1860.
£950-1,000 *S(S)*

A 19thC gold oval locket
pendant, the cover set
with an oval hardstone
cameo.
£470-550 *CSK*

Pins

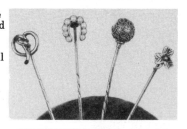

Four Victorian gold tie pins, one 15ct with seed pearls
£40-50
and 3 9ct, a knot, a ball
£35-45 each
and a clover leaf.
£20-30 *FMN*

Three stock pins, 2in (5cm) long. **£3-17 each** *VB*

Three Victorian tie pins, a silver boot, a silver signed and dated shield, and a gold on silver, Birmingham 1879, and one Edwardian brass dog tie pin, c1910. **£20-35 each** *FMN*

Three stock pins, 2½ to 3in (6 to 8cm) long. **£7-30 each** *VB*

Cross Reference
Hatpins & Hatpin Holders

Three stock pins, 2½ to 3in (6 to 8cm) long. **£7-15 each** *VB*

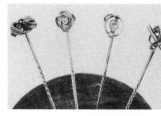

Four gold Victorian tie pins, a 15ct knot with ruby
£80-90
and a 9ct with diamond, peridot and pearl and sapphire.
£70-85 each *FMN*

Rings

A 9ct gold ring, with rectangular head of rose cut diamonds.
£220-300 *C(S)*

A platinum and diamond single stone ring, with baguette diamond single stone shoulders.
£1,200-1,500 *CSK*

A Cartier 18ct three-colour gold triple band ring and bracelet set, 79.7gr.
£770-900 *CSK*

A diamond and baguette diamond shaped oval cluster ring, with baguette diamond arch shoulders.
£1,300-1,500 *CSK*

A 9ct gold bee ring, the torso formed from a cabochon emerald and an opal. **£450-500** *C(S)*

A platinum square cut diamond single stone ring, with baguette diamond single stone shoulders.
£2,300-2,500 *CSK*

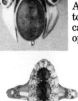

A diamond and sapphire marquise ring. **£485-550** *C(S)*

A ruby and diamond five-stone half hoop ring, with carved gallery and shoulders.
£1,000-1,200 *CSK*

A baguette diamond eternity ring.
£1,500-2,500 *CSK*

A Crown Milano satin glass bride's bowl decorated with flowers, on silver plated stand, 14in (36cm) diam.
£450-550 *JL*

A mid-Victorian blue satin glass night light, in 3 pieces, 6in (15cm) high.
£220-250 *PSA*

A wrythen moulded soda glass carafe, c1850, 7in (18cm) high.
£50-100 *Som*

A pair of ruby cameo glass vases, some damage, mid-19thC, 10in (25cm) high. **£250-300** *PCh*

A pair of Venetian glass candlesticks, 13½in (34cm).
£140-150 *ML*

A set of 3 blue spirit decanters, with gilt wine labels and lozenge stoppers, in a black and brass stand, c1790, bottles 7in (17cm) high. **£1,500-1,800** *Som*

A set of 3 green spirit bottles, c1820.
£1,000-1,500 *Som*

A Cranberry glass jug, 19thC, 7½in (19cm) high. **£150-170** *PSA*

A red lustre glass vase, Austrian, c1900, 11in (28cm) high.
£80-100 *RGA*

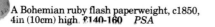

A Bohemian ruby flash paperweight, c1850, 4in (10cm) high. **£140-160** *PSA*

A vinegar bottle, c1880, 8in (20cm).
£70-100 *PSA*

A pair of Austrian green
and gilt glass vases,
with enamelled tulips,
c1900.
£300-400   RGA

A clear glass enamelled tazza, c1930,
7in (18cm) high.
£50-60   SMA

A Pilkington's Lancastrian vase,
with impressed mark, 7in (18cm)
high. **£110-125   CHa**

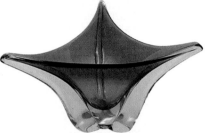

A Murano pink/green and clear glass
bowl, 1950s, 11in (28cm) wide.
£35-55   SWa

An Art Deco glass handkerchief
vase, 8½in (21cm) high.
£60-70   PSA

A Murano glass clown
liqueur bottle, c1930,
9½in (24cm) high.
£25-30   BEV

A Continental
glass vase,
with green and
white combed
pattern, 8in
(20cm) high.
£35-45   SWa

An orange with
blue spiral vase,
by M. Powolny for
Loetz, c1930, 4in
(10cm).
£85-95   GRA

A pair of Murano glass figures,
10½ and 12in (26 and 31cm) high.
£50-80   PC

A pink glass vase, by
John Walsh, c1930,
8½in (21cm) high.
£40-50   GRA

A Carnival glass water set
comprising a pitcher and
6 tumblers, in Milady pattern,
pitcher 11in (28cm) high.
£450-500   JL

A sand art souvenir bottle. **£100-150** *HOW*

A sand art souvenir bell, c1870, 5½in (14cm). **£70-80** *HOW*

A cut glass vase, c1930. **£45-55** *SWa*

An Anthony Stern dish, with blue and white swirl pattern, 1980s, 10in (25cm) diam. **£110-130** *SWa*

A yellow glass bowl, with black rim and clear foot, Austrian, c1920, 12in (31cm) diam. **£120-140** *SWa*

A Whitefriars vase, 1960s. **£20-30** *SWa*

A blue glass vase, c1955 **£25-35** *GRA*

A Continental moulded glass vase. **£25-35** *SWa*

A pink and green freeform vase, c1960. **£20-30** *GRA*

A pair of Whitefriars vases, pewter and clear glass, c1960. **£18-28 each** *SWa*

A Whitefriars bowl, 1960s. **£45-55** *SWa*

A pair of glass spirit decanters. **£140-180** *PCh*

A Monart globe lamp, on original wooden base, c1950. **£150-250** *FA*

A Tiffany lamp.
£2,400-3,000   *S(NY)*

A Pairpoint lamp,
c1915.
£3,800-4,000   *S(NY)*

A Tiffany lamp.
£2,200-3,000
S(NY)

A Tiffany
Favrile glass
lamp, c1910,
23in (59cm)
high.
£3,800-4,000
S(NY)

A Tiffany
Favrile glass,
Jack-in-the-
Pulpit vase,
inscribed L.C.
Tiffany-Favrile
3561D.
£20-22,000
S(NY)

A Tiffany Favrile
lamp, c1914.
£1,600-2,000   *S(NY)*

A Tiffany Favrile
glass lamp, c1910.
£38,000-40,000   *S(NY)*

Two Tiffany Favrile glass lamps,
c1910:
l. **£2,000-3,000**
r. **£12,000-15,000**   *S(NY)*

A Tiffany adjustable
desk lamp, c1914.
£2,000-2,200   *S(NY)*

A Tiffany Favrile glass
special order lamp, c1914.
£33,000-35,000   *S(NY)*

A Tiffany Favrile glass
vase. **£40,000-43,000**
S(NY)

A Pairpoint lamp, base impressed
PAIRPOINT MF'G CO/3091,
c1915. **£22,000-25,000**   *S(NY)*

A panelled slag glass
table lamp, with metal
base. **£230-250**   *JL*

A Tiffany Favrile glass vase,
cracked, c1915, 5½in (14cm)
high. **£16,000-18,000** *S(NY)*

A Pairpoint lamp,
c1915,   **£7,000-
10,000**   *S(NY)*

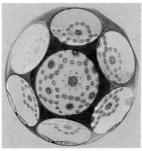

A Baccarat faceted ruby flash
overlay patterned millefiori
paperweight, 3in (8cm) diam.
£4,500-5,000   *S(NY)*

A Clichy faceted double overlay
concentric mushroom
paperweight. **£750-800**   *S(NY)*

A Baccarat faceted thousand
petalled rose paperweight.
£2,200-2,500   *S(NY)*

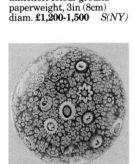

A Clichy patterned
millefiori colour ground
paperweight, 3in (8cm)
diam. **£1,200-1,500**   *S(NY)*

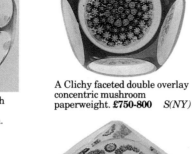

A Clichy faceted patterned millefiori
paperweight. **£1,500-2,000**   *S(NY)*

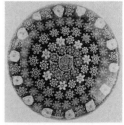

A Clichy concentric
millefiori paperweight,
3in (7cm) diam.
£4,500-5,000   *S(NY)*

A Baccarat faceted
concentric millefiori
mushroom paperweight.
£4,500-5,000   *S(NY)*

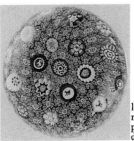

A Baccarat scattered
millefiori red carpet ground
paperweight, signed and
dated B 1848, 3in (8cm)
diam. **£9,000-9,500**   *S(NY)*

A St. Louis pear and cherry
paperweight, mid-19thC, 3in (8cm)
diam. **£2,200-2,500**   *C*

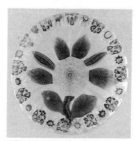

A Baccarat garlanded pompom
paperweight, with star cut
base, 2½in (6cm) diam.
£2,000-2,500   *S(NY)*

l. A Baccarat scattered
millefiori blue carpet ground
paperweight, signed and
dated. **£6,500-7,000**   *S(NY)*

A Baccarat flat bouquet
paperweight, with star cut
base, 3½in (9cm) diam.
£9,000-10,000   *S(NY)*

A Baccarat faceted garlanded red double clematis paperweight, on a star cut base, 2 small chips, mid-19thC. **£1,600-2,000** *C*

A St. Louis faceted bouquet hand cooler, the sides cut with 5 rows of graduated printies, mid-19thC, 2½in (6.5cm) long. **£1,600-2,000** *C*

A St. Louis pink ground pom-pom paperweight, mid-19thC, 3in (7cm) diam. **£2,600-3,000** *C*

A Clichy scattered millefiori moss ground paperweight, 2½in (6cm) diam. **£3,000-3,500** *S(NY)*

A St. Louis pom-pom paperweight, mid-19thC. **£3,500-4,000** *C*

A Clichy faceted close concentric millefiori mushroom paperweight, mid-19thC. **£1,400-1,800** *C*

A Clichy double overlay faceted concentric millefiori mushroom paperweight, mid-19thC, 3in (7cm) diam. **£8,000-9,000** *C*

A Clichy faceted sulphide paperweight, mid-19thC, 3in (7cm) diam. **£1,500-1,800** *C*

A St. Louis close concentric millefiori mushroom paperweight, mid-19thC, 3in (7.5cm) diam. **£1,200-1,500** *C*

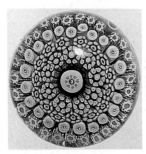

A St. Louis close concentric millefiori paperweight, mid-19thC. **£3,000-3,500** *C*

A Clichy 2-colour swirl paperweight, 3in (7cm) diam. **£900-1,500** *S(NY)*

A Pantin cherry paperweight, 2in (5cm) diam. **£8,500-9,000** *S(NY)*

A Victorian mosaic
on silver pendant,
2in (5cm) long.
£45-55 *FMN*

Victorian 9ct gold brooches,
pearl and sapphire. **£100-120**
sapphire. **£75-85** *HOW*

Two Victorian mosaic brooches.
£30-40 each *FMN*

A Victorian mosaic on brass photo
frame, 2 by 1in (5 by 3cm).
£80-95 *FMN*

A pair of silver Charles Horner
hatpins, Chester 1904, 10½in
(26cm) long. **£80-90** *HOW*

A Victorian brass backed mosaic
bracelet, 7in (18cm) long.
£30-45 *BGA*

Two Edwardian 9ct gold brooches,
with ruby and aquamarine stones.
£60-75 each *HOW*

Two Edwardian silver and enamel
brooches, peacock, 2½in (6cm),
and butterfly, 2in (5cm), c1910.
£70-95 each *HOW*

A Victorian 9ct gold brooch with
ruby and pearls and an
Edwardian almandine garnet
9ct gold brooch.
£90-100 each *HOW*

Two Victorian 15ct gold bar
brooches, one with pearl buckle,
2in (5cm) long.
£110-130 each *HOW*

Three Victorian mosaic brooches:
Bird, 2in (5cm). **£80-120**
Round, 1in (3cm) diam. **£30-40** and
Horseshoe, 1in (3cm). **£50-60** *FMN*

A silver and enamel Charles
Horner brooch, 1908. **£60-70** and
an Edwardian Welsh lady brooch
silver and enamel. **£25-35** *HOW*

A Seeburg Classic juke box, c1940. **£3,000-4,000** *AAM*

An AMI Continental 2 juke box, stereo with 200 record selection, 45rpm, made in USA. **£3,250-3,500** *CSC*

A Wurlitzer model 1800, produced in USA, plays 104 selections at 45rpm, both A and B sides, 1955. **£4,000-4,250** *CSC*

A Seeburg 148 Trashcan juke box, c1948. **£3,000-4,000** *AAM*

A Seeburg Symphonola juke box, 78rpm, restored, c1936. **£8,500-9,000** *AAM*

A Rock-Ola Commando juke box. **£10,500-12,000** *AAM*

An AMI Model I juke box, 200 selections at 45rpm, made in USA. **£3,500-3,700** *CSC*

A Rock-Ola 451 juke box, 100 selection at 45rpm, made in USA. **£450-550** *CSC*

A Wurlitzer 1100 juke box, 24 selections at 78rpm, A sides only, produced in USA, c1948. **£7,500-8,000** *CSC*

A Wurlitzer Victory juke box, unrestored, c1942-45. **£10,000-12,000** *AAM*

A Wurlitzer Lyric juke box, German, c1961. **£1,800-2,200** *CSC*

Christmas tree decorations,
c1940. **£10-12 each** *AAM*

A Sunbeam Bread embossed tin,
c1950, 46in (116.5cm) square.
£200-250 *AAM*

A Coca Cola tray, c1936.
£250-275 *AAM*

A Coca Cola office
cooler, C27, unrestored
£1,500-1,800 *AAM*

A tin menu board embossed
DAD'S, 27½in (70cm) high.
£60-70 *AAM*

A tin rattle,
3in (8cm) wide
£5-8 *AAM*

A Twinkle beverages
sign, c1950, 27in
(69cm) high.
£65-70 *AAM*

Worlds Fair booklets.
£12-20 each *AAM*

Humorous postcards.
50p-£2 each *AAM*

A Louis Marx tinplate
toy, 1930s.
£750-800 *SWO*

A 7up enamel sign, c1940.
£45-50 *AAM*

A US Army truck. **£75-85** *AAM*

An English painted enamel water jug, c1920. **£15-20** *CHA*

A painted churn with brass dairy number, Dutch, c1912. **£70-80** *CHA*

An Austrian cold painted bronze bird, c1900. **£110-130** *GMC*

An Art Nouveau copper jug. **£50-60** *PC*

An Austrian cold painted bronze elf, c1900, 3in (8cm) high. **£130-170** *GMC*

A brass wall sconce, Dutch, 18thC. **£200-300** *KEY*

A pair of Victorian brass candelabra. **£160-180** *ML*

An enamel milk can, 11in (28cm) high. **£15-20** *CHA*

Bronze mortars, c1680, l. **£70-90** c. **£300-350** r. **£40-50** *KEY*

An Art Nouveau silver toilet tray, Chester 1876, 13oz. **£220-250** *PCh*

A spelter cold painted figure, 19thC, 21in (53cm) high. **£70-80** *PCh*

A Swiss pewter flask. **£100-120** a German stone and pewter mug. **£200-225** and an English pewter beaker. **£30-35** *KEY*

Two pairs of pewter candlesticks, 9 and 10in (23 and 25cm) high. **£120-150 each pair** *KEY*

EARLY TECHNOLOGY

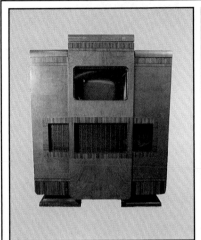

WE BUY & SELL, EXPORT & IMPORT

Cameras, Cine Projectors and Photographs, Television and Radio, Dentistry, Veterinary, Medical, Anaesthetics, Opticians' and Chemists' Items, Telephones and Telegraph, Barrel Organs and Mechanical Music, Typewriters, Dictaphones and Calculators, Scientific Instruments and Nautical Items, Slot Machines and Weighing Machines, Early Electric Motors, Light Bulbs, Fires, Toasters, Switchgear and Limelights, Exceptional Tools and Drawing Instruments, Keys, Locks, Weathervanes and Early Metalwork, Mechanical Spits, Early Kitchen and Laundry Items, Automata and Puppets, Unusual Clocks and Barometers, Wind-up Gramophones, Phonographs, Juke Boxes and Rare "78s", Sewing Machines, Magic Lanterns, etc.

(Callers strictly by appointment. 15 minutes from Edinburgh city centre.)

Monkton House, Old Craighall, Musselburgh, Midlothian EH21 8SF, Scotland, U.K.

Tel: 031-665 5753 · Fax: 031-665 2839

Also at Bow-Well Antiques, 103 West Bow (Grassmarket), Edinburgh EH1 2JP. Tel: 031-225 3335

A porcelain snuff bottle, c1825.
£1,500-2,500   *S(HK)*

A moulded fruit rind snuff bottle, c1840.
£850-1,000   *S(HK)*

A laque burgauté snuff bottle, Japanese, c1880.
£2,200-3,000   *S(HK)*

A calcite snuff bottle, c1840.
£1,000-1,500   *S(HK)*

A bamboo snuff bottle, carved in the form of a peach, c1840.
£1,400-1,800   *S(HK)*

A tortoiseshell snuff bottle and dish, c1840.
£4,000-5,000   *S(HK)*

A pewter snuff bottle, with ring handles, c1830. **£2,200-3,000**   *S(HK)*

An ivory snuff bottle, with matching stopper, c1865.
£6,000-7,000   *S(HK)*

A hair crystal snuff bottle, on a finished footrim, c1785. **£1,500-2,000**   *S(HK)*

An amber snuff bottle, Qianlong.
£2,000-3,000   *S(HK)*

A moulded porcelain snuff bottle, with a decorated panel each side, c1850.
£720-800   *S(HK)*

A cloisonné enamel snuff bottle and dish, small restoration to bottle, c1825. **£1,500-2,000**   *S(HK)*

A lacquer box and cover, fitted with a shallow tray, 19thC.
£5,000-5,500 *S(NY)*

A lacquer writing utensil box, fitted with inkstone, silver waterdropper, brush, knife, awl and ink holder, some restoration, 19thC. **£12,000-13,000** *S(NY)*

A lacquer 4-case inro, signed Kajikawa saku, 19thC. **£2,500-3,000** *S(NY)*

A lacquer 3-case inro, signed Jokasai, minor damage, 19thC, 3in (8cm). **£5,000-5,500** *S(NY)*

A lacquer 4-case inro, signed Kajikawa saku, minor damage, 19thC, 3in (8cm).
£2,500-3,000 *S(NY)*

l. A lacquer and Shibayama-style 6-case inro, minor damage, 19thC, 3½in (9cm).
£3,500-4,500 *S(NY)*

l. A lacquer writing utensil box, some damage and restoration, late 18thC.
£2,500-3,500 *S(NY)*

A boxwood snuff bottle and dish, c1840.
£850-900 *S(HK)*

l. A lacquer 5-case inro, signed Tessho with kakihan, 19thC, 3½in (9cm).
£4,500-5,500 *S(NY)*

A white jade snuff bottle, c1815.
£850-900 *S(HK)*

l. A lacquer Shibayama-style 5-case inro, 19thC.
£2,500-3,000 *S(NY)*

A cinnabar lacquer snuff bottle, Qianlong, small restorations.
£3,500-4,000 *S(HK)*

Jimi Hendrix's hat, in black felt, labelled
The Westerner, size 7½, this hat worn by him
until early 1968. **£14,500-16,000**   *S*

A Gibson Explorer used by
ZZ Top. **£900-1,200**   *CSK*

A Tommy Morrison boxing
outfit. **£100-150**   *CNY*

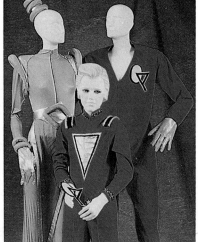

Two women's space suits for Mork and
Mindy, and a child's suit, 1978-82.
£400-600   *CNY*

Two pieces of a guitar smashed by Jimi Hendrix, 1967,
together with concert programme. **£30,000-31,000**   *S*

A Sylvester Stallone outfit for
Rambo III, Tri-Star, 1988.
£130-150   *CNY*

Madonna's gold basque, designed
by Jean Paul Gaultier, with
his label, and matching
panties. **£9,000-10,000**   *S*

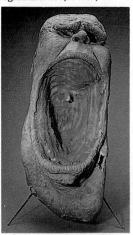

A foam rubber head of Slimer
for Ghostbusters, Columbia,
1984. **£330-400**   *CNY*

A selection of film lobby cards, with 8 cards to a set, 11 by 14in (28 by 36cm) each.
Top l. Ben-Hur, 1925.
£900-1,200
c. Rio Rita, 1929.
£400-500
Top r. The Mark of Zorro, 1920. **£1,000-1,500**
l. Speedy, 1928.
£1,600-2,000
r. Blood and Sand, 1922.
£1,300-1,500
Bottom l. Trader Horn, 1931.
£1,200-1,500
c. Her Wedding Night, 1930.
£850-1,000
Bottom r. All Quiet on the Western Front, 1930. **£1,000-1,250** *CNY*

The Ghost Breaker,
Paramount, 1922, linen
backed, 41 by 27in
(104 by 69cm).
£580-600 *CNY*

My American Wife,
Paramount, 1922, linen
backed, 41 by 27in
(104 by 69cm).
£1,900-2,200 *CNY*

Blood and Sand,
Paramount, 1922, linen
backed, 41 by 27in
(104 by 69cm).
£3,200-3,500 *CNY*

The New Frontier,
Republic, 1935, linen
backed, 41 by 27in
(104 by 69cm).
£3,300-3,500 *CNY*

The Trail Rider, Fox, 1925,
linen backed, 41 by 27in
(104 by 69cm).
£550-600 *CNY*

Forbidden Planet, MGM, 1956,
41 by 27in (104 by 69cm).
£2,400-3,000 *CNY*

Know Your Men, Fox, 1921,
linen backed, 41 by 27in
(104 by 69cm).
£950-1,200 *CNY*

Krazy Kat, Columbia,
1933, linen backed,
41 by 27in (104 by 69cm).
£1,100-1,300 *CNY*

Fantasia, Disney, 1940,
linen backed,
41 by 27in
(104 by 69cm).
£4,000-6,000 *CNY*

Dumbo, Disney, 1941,
linen backed,
41 by 27in
(104 by 69cm).
£2,600-3,000 *CNY*

Bambi, Disney, 1942,
linen backed,
41 by 27in
(104 by 69cm).
£1,100-1,300 *CNY*

Shall We Dance, RKO,
1937, linen backed,
41 by 27in (104 by
69cm). **£1,900-2,500** *CNY*

The War of the Worlds,
Paramount, 1953.
£650-750 *CNY*

Tarzan, The Ape
Man, MGM, 1932,
linen backed.
£3,200-4,200 *CNY*

Mutiny on the Bounty, MGM,
1935, jumbo window card,
28 by 22in (71 by 56cm).
£550-750 *CNY*

Godzilla, Toho,
1955, one sheet.
£850-950 *CNY*

Tarzan and his Mate, MGM,
1934, linen backed, 41 by
27in (104 by 69cm).
£3,300-4,000 *CNY*

Pitfalls of a Big
City, Pathe, 1923,
3-sheet, linen
backed.
£850-950 *CNY*

Platinum Blonde,
Columbia, 1930,
linen backed.
£2,700-3,500 *CNY*

That Hamilton Woman,
Alexander Korda,
1941, linen backed.
£1,600-2,000 *CNY*

The Hoodlum, First
National, 1919, linen
backed, 41 by 27in
(104 by 69cm).
£1,000-1,500 *CNY*

Our Blushing Brides,
MGM, 1930, rotogravure
one-sheet, linen backed.
£1,450-2,000 *CNY*

Circus Days, First
National, 1921,
double insert.
£400-500 *CNY*

A Walt Disney Celluloid from Pinocchio, 1940, inscribed on back, matted and framed, 8 by 10½in (20 by 26.5cm). **£20,000-22,000** *S(NY)*

A Walt Disney Celluloid from Lady and the Tramp, 1955, with watercolour background, signed, matted and framed, 9 by 12in (23 by 31cm). **£12,000-13,000** *S(NY)*

A publicity Celluloid of Lady and the Tramp, 1955. **£4,500-5,000** *CNY*

A Walt Disney gouache on multi-cel set up, Pinocchio, 1940. **£27,200-28,000** *CNY*

A Walt Disney gouache on full Celluloid, Peter Pan, 1953, with watercolour background, 11 by 15in (28 by 38cm). **£17,000-18,000** *CNY*

Warner Bros. Celluloid from Bugs Bunny on Broadway. **£2,000-2,500** *S(NY)*

Bart, Lisa and Maggie, There's No Disgrace Like Home, gouache on 6 Celluloid set up on matching production background, 9 by 12in (23 by 31cm). **£2,300-2,500** *CNY*

Bart, Lisa and Maggie, Simpsons Roasting On An Open Fire, gouache on 3 Celluloid set up on a matching production background, 9½ by 11in (24 by 28cm). **£2,500-3,500** *CNY*

Walt Disney, Fantasia, 1940, gouache on full Celluloid. **£1,450-2,000** *CNY*

Bart, Homer, Lisa and Maggie, gouache. **£2,700-3,200** *CNY*

Bart, Homer, Lisa and Maggie, gouache on an 8 Celluloid set up, 9 by 64in (23 by 162.5cm). **£3,000-4,000** *CNY*

l. Bart Auctions His Sister Maggie, gouache on 2 Celluloid set up. **£14,250-15,250** *CNY*

Walt Disney Celluloid from Bambi, 1942, signed Walt Disney and framed. **£15,500-16,500** *S(NY)*

Warner Bros. Celluloid from Box Office Bunny, 9 by 20in (23 by 51cm). **£1,300-2,000** *S(NY)*

Warner Bros. Celluloid from Bugs Bunny on Broadway, 10 by 13in (25 by 33cm). **£2,100-2,500** *S(NY)*

Walt Disney Celluloid from Snow White and The Seven Dwarfs, 1937. **£5,200-6,000** *S(NY)*

Walt Disney gouache on full Celluloid, applied to a water-colour production background, unknown production, c1940. **£3,300-4,000** *CNY*

Walt Disney Celluloid from Snow White and the Seven Dwarfs, 1937. **£3,200-4,000** *S(NY)*

Walt Disney Celluloid from Snow. White and the Seven Dwarfs, 1937, applied to airbrushed background, framed, 12½ by 9½in (32 by 24cm). **£5,200-6,000** *S(NY)*

Walt Disney Celluloid from Snow White and the Seven Dwarfs, 1937, on a watercolour production pan background, 11 by 20in (28 by 51cm). **£4,200-5,200** *S(NY)*

Walt Disney Celluloid from Snow White and the Seven Dwarfs, 1937. **£4,500-5,500** *S(NY)*

Walt Disney Celluloid from Cinderella, 1950, signed Walt Disney. **£21,000-23,000** *S(NY)*

Walt Disney gouache on Celluloid, Sleeping Beauty, 1959. **£2,500-3,500** *CNY*

Warner Bros. Celluloid from Box Office Bunny, 13 by 17in (33 by 43cm). **£4,800-5,500** *S(NY)*

A cut-out showcard, some damage, c1910. **£40-60** *K*

A selection of hotel labels, 1930s-40s.
£3-5 each *COB*

An enamelled iron kiosk sign, National Telephone Co., c1906.
£40-80 *SM*

A 1912 diary and almanack.
£7-10 *COB*

A tinplate Yeast-Vite sign, mint condition. **£30-60** *K*

A White Hawk Toffee tin, 11in (28cm) high.
£90-110 *ChL*

A showcard/poster for Cannon Ales and Stout, c1920.
£75-100 *K*

An early 20thC Lux insert.
£10-20 *K*

A pictorial tin, Bewlays Cigarettes, early 20thC. **£60-80** *K*

l. A Doulton Burslem advertising piece, c1936. **£250-300** *TP*

A Horner toffee tin, c1960. **£10-12** *ROS*

A Victorian Christmas chocolate tin, very good condition.
£40-60 *K*

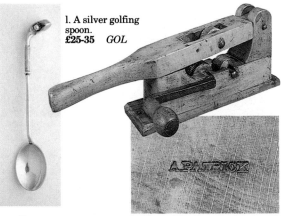

l. A silver golfing spoon.
£25-35   *GOL*

A gutty golf ball marker, stamped A. Patrick, c1870. **£35-36,000**   *C(S)*

The Manchester Golfer magazine, May 1911.
£15-25   *GOL*

A feather-filled golf ball, c1840.
£2,700-3,500   *C(S)*

A Strauss toy,
£350-400 and Jocko the golfer with box.
£350-450 each   *GOL*

A magazine cover, Sept 1933.
£25-35   *GOL*

l. A driver by McEwan, c1860.
£3,000-3,500   *C(S)*

A feather-filled golf ball, c1840. **£5,500-6,000**   *C(S)*

r. An unused feather-filled golf ball, c1840.
£11-12,000
C(S)

l. A feather-filled golf ball, c1840.
£4,200-4,500   *C(S)*

r. A feather-filled golf ball.
£7,000-8,000
C(S)

l. A Brassey postcard.
£8-12   *GOL*

r. A Carlton ware golfing tobacco jar.
£400-600   *MSh*

A rag work cushion cover, 1930s.
£10-20   *CHA*

A Victorian cross-stitch
purse, 3in (8cm) high.
£25-45   *PC*

A handmade silk cushion with antique
lace, 16 by 9in (41 by 23cm).
£20-25   *ROS*

A Welsh reversible woven wool
blanket. **£80-90**   *CHA*

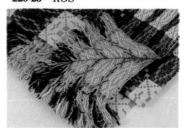

A Welsh reversible woven wool
blanket. **£80-90**   *CHA*

l. Victorian
beaded
Dorothy bags.
£40-60 each   *PC*

A Victorian beaded
Dorothy bag, slight
damage. **£30-50**   *PC*

r. A handmade
silk cushion
with antique
lace, 15 by 18in
(38 by 46cm).
£22-25   *ROS*

A Welsh wool blanket, hand woven
on old trestle looms.
£80-90   *CHA*

A Victorian beaded
Dorothy bag.
£50-70   *PC*

A polished cotton quilt in gold
and red. **£150-200**   *CHA*

A Welsh reversible woven wool
blanket. **£80-90**   *CHA*

A pure silk handmade
cushion, 9in (23cm)
square. **£18-20**   *ROS*

A Welsh reversible wool blanket,
woven on old trestle looms.
£80-90   *CHA*

Kanga and Eeyore, by Gund, c1964, 14in (36cm).
£50-70 each   *TED*

A 1930s teddy
bear. **£45-55**   *PSA*

A straw filled teddy bear, 7in
(18cm) high. **£30-40**   *PSA*

A selection of felt covered 20thC clockwork
toys. **£30-50 each**   *PCh*

Donald Duck, 1930s,
11in (28cm) high.
£110-130   *ChL*

A Chinese puppet, 1920s,
25in (64cm) high. **£55-75**   *ROS*

A Linemar tinplate Bubbling Bull battery
operated toy, 1950s. **£40-50**   *NA*

A two-faced golly, c1930, 19½in
(49cm) high. **£50-70**   *ChL*

A Lionel Donald Duck hand car,
worn paint. **£450-550**   *JL*

Tinplate toy boxers, hand
operated, c1930. **£15-18**   *PSA*

An E. H. Shepard final
study for the Pooh Cook
Book. **£3,000-3,500**   *CSK*

A Lionel operating fork-lift platform with car and lumber. **£150-200** *JL*

A 3in scale model of a six-wheeled undertype steam engine wagon. **£5,500-6,500** *CSK*

A Lionel pre-war Union Pacific train set, comprising one engine, 2 passengers, one observation car and 3 vestibules. **£500-550** *JL*

A Lionel Black Hudson steam engine, No. 5344, and whistle tender. **£1,500-2,000** *JL*

A Lionel GG1 engine marked Pennsylvania, in excellent condition, with original box. **£850-950** *JL*

A Lionel girl's train set, in excellent condition. **£2,500-3,500** *JL*

A Lionel 4–6–4 steam engine and coal tender, engine not working, condition excellent. **£800-1,000** *JL*

A Lionel Super Chief train set, with 2 diesel engines, 2 vista domes, 1 observation car and a Pullman. **£1,000-2,000** *JL*

A Lionel pre-war standard gauge Blue Comet train set. **£1,300-1,500** *JL*

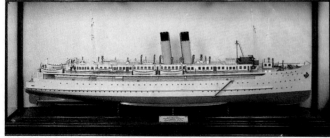

A detailed ¼in:1ft scale builder's model of the train ferry steamer Drottning Victoria, Trelleborg, built by Swan Hunter & Wigham Richardson Ltd., 105in (266.5cm) long. **£8,800-10,000** *C*

Kitchenalia

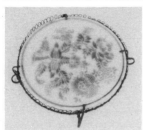

A teapot stand, 5½in
(14cm) diam.
£15-16 *SCO*

A breakfast companion, fitted
with a hand bell above a butter
dish and cover, 8in (22cm) high.
£180-200 *WIL*

A saltglazed bread crock,
with stick work interior,
mid-19thC, 15in (38cm)
diam. **£100-120** *CHA*

A further selection of irons is featured in
previous editions of Miller's Collectables
Price Guides, available from Millers
Publications.

A French charcoal iron,
with cockerel latch,
19thC.
£35-40 *CHA*

An oak and brass knife
sharpener, 30in (76cm)
high.
£35-40 *CHA*

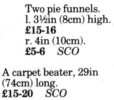

Two pie funnels.
l. 3½in (8cm) high.
£15-16
r. 4in (10cm).
£5-6 *SCO*

A carpet beater, 29in
(74cm) long.
£15-20 *SCO*

A Worcester
bird pie
funnel, 4½in
(11cm) high.
£12-14 *SCO*

A chrome tea caddy,
1930s, 5½in (14cm) high.
£15-20 *PC*

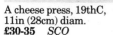

A cheese press, 19thC,
11in (28cm) diam.
£30-35 *SCO*

Cross Reference
Tea Caddies

273

A candle holder, 19thC,
5in (12.5cm) diam.
£12-15 *SCO*

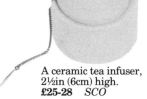

A ceramic tea infuser,
2½in (6cm) high.
£25-28 *SCO*

A brass scoop, 6in (15cm)
long.
£28-30 *SCO*

Cross Reference
Candlesticks

A Doulton strainer
funnel, 7½in (19cm) high.
£25-30 *SCO*

A stone storage jar and
lid, 10in (25cm) high.
£25-30 *SCO*

A butter stamp with
sleeve, 19thC, 5in
(12.5cm) long.
£38-40 *SCO*

A Doulton Lambeth
stoneware pot with lid,
4in (10cm) high.
£25-28 *SCO*

A brass hanging bracket.
£45-50 *SCO*

A selection of
horn beakers,
3-4in (7.5-10cm)
high.
£9-16 *SCO*

Coffee Equipment

A Victorian cast iron coffee
grinder, with ebony knob on
handle, c1870, 7in (18cm)
high.
£90-100 *HOW*

Two Turkish mill
grinders, 19thC and
20thC.
£20-100 each *TBC*

A Continental brass
coffee grinder, early
20thC.
£50-80 *TBC*

A French earthenware filter, 20thC.
£20-30   *TBC*

A Vardy & Platow maker,
early 20thC.   **£300-350**   *TBC*

A Rabauts replica coffee
maker. Original of 1825.
£1,000-1,500   *TBC*

A Parkers steam
fountain maker,
patented 1833.
£40-80   *TBC*

A French plated
percolator, late 20thC.
£100-120   *TBC*

Kitchenalia

THE SPECIALIST SHOP
FOR ANTIQUE
KITCHEN COLLECTABLES.

UNUSUAL AND INTERESTING
DECORATIVE ITEMS TO PUT
THE FINISHING TOUCH
TO YOUR KITCHEN.

'The Old Bakery', 36 Inglewhite Rd.
Longridge, Preston, Lancs. PR3 3JS.
Telephone: (0772) 785411

Madame Bleu, early 20thC.
£50-60   *TBC*

A copper biggin,
late 19thC.
£150-160   *TBC*

A coffee grinder, 19thC,
8½in (21cm) high.
£30-35   *ROS*

A grinder by A. Kenrick & Sons, West
Bromwich, early 20thC.   **£320-360**   *TBC*

For a further selection of coffee making
equipment please refer to Miller's
Collectables Vol. III, pp153-162.

A coffee mill, c1930.
£25-35   *TBC*

Cooking Utensils

A Victorian cast iron pot
with lid, 7in (17.5cm)
diam.   **£35-40**   *SCO*

An Edwardian sieve, 10in (25cm) long.
£5-8   *ROS*

A Victorian double
saucepan, 6in (15cm)
high.   **£30-35**   *SCO*

An iron hanging skillet,
11in (28cm) diam.
£8-10   *RE*

A tin fish kettle with
liner, 14in (35.5cm) wide.
£40-45   *SCO*

Enamel

An iron frying pan, 15in
(38cm) wide.   **£8-10**   *RE*

Two enamel mugs, 4 and
4½in (10 and 11cm) high.
£8-10 each   *CHA*

An enamel bathroom
mug holder, 10in (25cm)
high.   **£8-10**   *CHA*

Kitchen Equipment

Two enamel milk cans, 9in (23cm) high.
£10-12 *CHA*

A Victorian cutlery cleaner, with rubber rollers and end buff, 8in (20cm) high. **£40-45** *SCO*

A vegetable grater, 15in (38cm) high.
£15-18 *SCO*

Cross Reference
Scales & Balances

A pair of sweet scales and weights, c1909.
£40-45 *SCO*

An Empire Jubilee Model cream maker, with instructions and recipes, c1930, 8½in (20cm) high.
£25-30 *PC*

Egg separators.
Tin. **£1-5**
Ceramic.
£8-10 each *AL*

Two sugar thermometers, 10 and 11½in (25 and 28cm) long.
£8-10 each *MCA*

A soda syphon, 1960s, 11½in (29cm) high.
£10-15 *CAB*

A Victorian Proctor's Patent vegetable mincer and shredder, 14½in (37cm) high.
£20-25 *ROS*

A sulphur dipped match holder, c1780, 6in (15cm) high.
£30-35 *SAD*

Knives

A knife box with a selection of knives, 15in (38cm) long.
£50-55 *CHA*

Two steel bread knives, with carved ivory handles.
Top. **£120-130**
Bottom. **£50-60** *BS*

A mangel knife, 16in (41cm) long.
£19-20 *SCO*

A selection of steel bread knives, with carved sycamore handles, late 19th/early 20thC.
£20-60 each *BS*

Moulds

Three butter prints, c1860, 4 to 5in (10 to 13cm) diam. **£90-100 each** *HOW*

A hand carved mould, 6in (15cm) diam.
£38-40 *SCO*

A bunch of grapes mould, 8½in (21cm) high.
£40-50 *CHA*

An ice cream mould, 11in (28cm) high.
£45-50 *SCO*

Two copper jelly moulds, one of oval castle form, the other cylindrical with overlapping money pattern around the rim, 4 and 5in (10 and 12.5cm) high. **£200-210** *L*

Two German enamel cake moulds, 10in (25cm).
£8-10 each
CHA

A sponged mould,
c1840-60.
£40-50 *CHA*

An Edwardian glass jelly
mould, 6in (15cm) high. **£20-25** *PC*

A selection of hand carved confectionery moulds,
8½ to 18in (21 to 46cm). **£40-65 each** *SCO*

A selection of
chocolate
moulds.
£1-10 each
CHA

Utensils

A Victorian basting ladle, 16in (41cm) long.
£15-18 *SCO*

A chopping bowl and chopper set, 8½in (21cm) diam.
£85-90 *SCO*

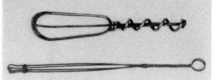

A Devonshire tedder chopper, 12in (31cm) long. **£15-18** *SCO*

An early suet chopper, 9in (23cm) long.
£42-48 *SCO*

A hand carved yew wood spoon, c1800, 9in (23cm) long. **£45-50** *HOW*

A brass toasting fork, 19in (48cm) long.
£35-40 *SCO*

A Victorian dough whisk, 12in (31cm) long, and a dough break, 10in (25cm) long.
£10-25 each *SCO*

Lighting

A set of Lucas chrome lamps, c1930, 9½in (24cm) wide.
£100-125 *RE*

> **Cross Reference**
> Automobilia

A miner's lamp, c1900, 9in (23cm) high.
£85-110 *RE*

A gas lamp, c1920, 33in (84cm) long.
£20-30 *RE*

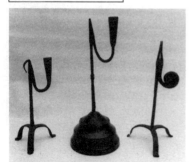

Three wrought iron rush nips, English, 18thC.
£120-150 *KEY*

> **Cross Reference**
> Candlesticks

A pair of early Victorian glass wall lights converted to electricity.
£700-1,000 *ASH*

A Lucas brass car inspection lamp, c1923, 10½in (26cm) long.
£65-70 *BS*

A brass and galvanised ship's lamp, 19in (48cm) high. **£30-50** *RE*

A war-time gas lamp, 11in (28cm) high.
£45-50 *ROS*

Cross Reference
Bicycle Lighting

A miner's lamp, 11in (28cm) high.
£40-45 *WIN*

A gas lamp, c1920, 10½in (26cm) high to bend.
£20-30 *RE*

A pair of ship's companionway lamps, c1920
£90-110 *COB*

A brass clip-on desk lamp, 13in (33cm).
£60-70 *ML*

A Victorian brass spring loaded student's lamp, with hooded metal reflector, 12in (30.5cm) high.
£90-120 *ML*

An Edwardian brass hall lantern, 14in (35.5cm) high. **£30-40** *ARC*

An Art Deco china cat lamp, with hand made silk shade, 15½in (40cm) high.
£160-180 *ML*

A brass hanging gas lamp with stained and cut glass panels, late Victorian, 8 by 22in (20 by 56cm).
£250-300 *ASH*

> **Cross Reference**
> Ceramic Cats
> Railways

A chrome lamp, 1930s, 20½in (52cm) high.
£40-50 *HEW*

A French brass light.
£260-280 *ASH*

A gas lamp, c1920, 33in (83.5cm).
£20-30 *RE*

A Victorian silver gilt carriage lamp, with a monogram and fitted with a vesta case, engraved with retailer's name Clark, 20 Old Bond Street, maker's initials J.B. & A.J., London 1883, 6in (15cm) high.
£1,000-1,250 *CSK*

French glass hanging light, c1920, 6in high.
£35-40 *ML*

Locks

For a further selection of locks and keys please see Miller's Collectables Price Guide Volume III, pp300-304.

An early brass night latch lock, 19thC, 3in (9cm) high.
£80-100 *BS*

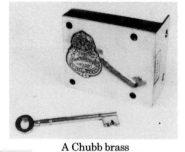

A Chubb brass strongroom door lock and key in working order, 19thC, 4 by 3in (10 by 9cm).
£50-60 *BS*

An Edwardian copper Pullman lamp, with milk glass shade, 19½in (49cm) high. **£80-100** *ML*

An original lock with key in working order, 19thC, 4in (10cm) square.
£30-40 *BS*

Luggage

A Louis Vuitton double hinged trunk, covered in early chequered material, lined with white cotton with 4 compartments, 2 with lids, original LV labels No. 29447, 26½in (67cm) wide.
£1,100-1,250   *ONS*

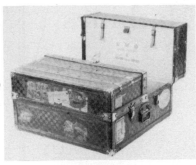

A painted tin trunk with brass fittings, early 19thC, 30in (76cm) wide.
£60-75   *CHA*

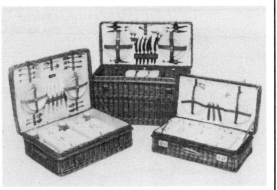

l. A Harrod's retailed Coracle wicker picnic basket filled with blue plastic Bandalasta fittings, apparently unused;
£350-375
c. a Harrod's retailed Coracle wicker hamper with Bandalasta fittings, wicker divisions for a dozen bottles, apparently unused;
£440-460
r. and a wicker picnic case with plastic fittings by Bandalasta.
£40-50   *LAY*

Although also slightly bigger, it is worth noting the extra value a Harrod's label makes!

A leather rent collector's bag, 16in (41cm).
£45-50   *ROS*

A Louis Vuitton ladies trunk, lined with white cotton and labelled LV Paris, London No. 762284, with 2 trays, the top one with 2 compartments with lids, 36in (91cm) wide.
£1,050-1,200   *ONS*

Formerly the property of Mary Duchess of Roxburghe, with Floors Castle Duke of Roxburghe label.

MAKE THE MOST OF MILLERS
Condition is absolutely vital when assessing the value of any item. Damaged pieces appreciate much less than perfect examples. However, a rare, desirable piece may command a high price even when damaged.

A black leather dressing case by Drew & Sons, with silver topped bottles, ivory brushes, paper knife, leather wallets containing manicure set, lined with green satin, initialled MEB, 13½in (34cm) wide.
£110-130   *ONS*

A green leather dressing case, with shagreen clothes brush, vanity mirror and ivory comb, with brass fittings and foul weather cover, 17½in (45cm) wide.
£130-150   *ONS*

Machines

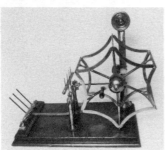

A brass wool winder,
with mahogany base,
28in (71cm) long.
£300-400 *ARC*

Three Bryans wooden
cased glass fronted
coin-operated arcade
machines,
l. **£450-550**
c. **£300-400**
r. **£150-250** *BWe*

A butter churn, c1900.
£120-150 *RE*

An iron chestnut roaster. **£70-80** *ARC*

A New Crown Jewel
mangle, by Jas. Mutch of
Aberdeen, 63in (160cm) high.
£90-120 *Bon*

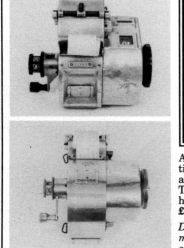

A Gibson pre-production
ticket issuing machine,
as used by London
Transport, 6½in (16cm)
high.
£500-700 *PC*

*Decimalised production
models sell for £40-70
each.*

The Red Star washing
machine, by Beatty Bros.
Limited, the circular
washing tub with 3 iron
hoops, the hinged cover
with crank handle and
cast iron spur cog
mechanism, turning the
washing head with
4 pegs, one missing,
horizontally mounted
cast iron mangle,
embossed The Star
Wringer, the whole
apparatus on 4 feet,
49½in (125cm) high,
together with 6 clothes
pegs. **£80-120** *Bon*

METALWARE
Brass

A group of brass hand bells, c1915, 3 to 4in (8 to 10cm) high.
£10-15 each   *CSA*

Cross Reference
Bells

A Victorian brass toddy kettle, 9½in (24cm) wide.
£75-100   *PSA*

A brass fly pin box, c1920, 4in (10cm) long.
£20-30   *PSA*

A brass letter rack, 8in (20cm) long.
£25-30   *ROS*

Door Furniture

A brass spill vase, 4½in (11cm) high.
£12-18
ROS

A selection of door handles and knockers.
£18-20 each   *CHA*

A brass letter box, 8½in (21cm) long.
£12-15   *ROS*

A brass letter box, damaged, 12in (31cm) long.
£8-12   *ROS*

A brass bell, 4in (10cm) high.
£18-20   *ROS*

A Victorian brass letter box, 8in (20cm) long.   **£25-30**   *ROS*

A brass letter box, 9in (23cm) long.
£18-20   *ROS*

Bronze

A bronze Japanese tigress, 19thC, 12in (31cm) long. **£200-230** *PSA*

An Oriental bronze elephant, c1900, 4in (10cm) long. **£150-170** *GMC*

Austrian Bronzes

Two Austrian cold painted bronze pheasants on an onyx dish, c1910, 4½in (11cm) high. **£110-130** *GMC*

An Austrian bronze horse and foal, the horse with paint removed, c1890, 6½in (16cm) long. **£320-350** Foal, c1900, 2½in (6cm) long. **£90-120** *GMC*

An Austrian cold painted bronze bird on a marble base, marked Geschutzt on tail, c1900, 5in (13cm) high. **£120-150** *GMC*

Two Austrian cold painted bronze budgerigars on an onyx dish, c1910, 4½in (11cm) high. **£110-130** *GMC*

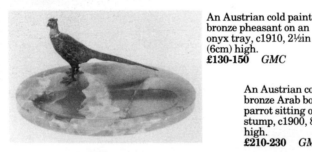

An Austrian cold painted bronze pheasant on an onyx tray, c1910, 2½in (6cm) high. **£130-150** *GMC*

An Austrian cold painted bronze Arab boy, with parrot sitting on a tree stump, c1900, 8in (20cm) high. **£210-230** *GMC*

An Austrian cold painted bronze guinea fowl, c1890, 4in (10cm) long. **£125-135** Eagle, c1900, 3½in (9cm) long. **£60-80** *GMC*

Cross Reference
Toys
Bears

Three Austrian bronze bears and a badger, the badger marked Geschutzt on base, all c1890, each 3in (8cm) long. **£80-100 each** *GMC*

A selection of Austrian bronze cats, the 3 largest all cold painted, c1900, ½ to 3in (2 to 8cm) high. **£30-120 each** *GMC*

Two miniature Vienna cold painted bronze horses, one with saddle, stamped Geschutzt on bridle, c1900, 1 and 2in (3 and 5cm) long. **£40-60 each** *GMC*

Two Austrian bronze Old English bulldogs, the larger cold painted, the smaller with paint removed, c1890, 2 and 3in (5 and 8cm) long. Large **£120-140**   Small **£50-70**   *GMC*

An Austrian cold painted bronze deer with fawns and a lion, c1900, 3 and 3½in (8 and 9cm) long.   **£90-110 each**   *GMC*

Three Austrian bronze cold painted terriers, c1900, 1½ to 3½in (4 to 9cm) high. Small **£50-60** Large **£80-90 each**   *GMC*

A selection of Austrian bronze pug dogs, c1910, ½ to 1½in (2 to 4cm) high. **£30-90 each** *GMC*

A selection of Austrian cold painted bronze items, the dancing girl marked Bergmann Franz, and the dandy gentleman with serial number on base, c1900, 1½ to 3½in (4 to 9cm) high.
£70-95 each   *GMC*

An Austrian bronze pup, marked Geschutzt on tail and Deposée on base, Victorian import mark, c1880, 5in (13cm) long.   **£300-350**   *GMC*

Copper

A Victorian coffee pot, 9in (23cm) high.
£120-140   *PSA*

A kettle, 9½in (24cm) high.
£50-55   *ROS*

Flatware

A pair of Victorian silver plate fish servers, c1850, 13in (33cm) long.
£50-60   *ROS*

A set of 6 early George V silver gilt and guilloche enamel coffee spoons, the spoon backs decorated in colours in the Royal Worcester style with a still life of fruit, enamel handles, damaged, London import marks for 1924, cased.
£100-150   *HSS*

Pewter

A jug/tankard, c1800, 6in (15cm) high.
£135-145   *HOW*

A charger, c1770, 13½in (34cm) diam.
£140-150   *HOW*

A tankard with holes in the handle and 'puzzle' features, c1800, 4½in (11cm) high.
£125-135   *HOW*

A pair of candlesticks, c1845, 9½in (24cm) high.
£115-125   *HOW*

Cross Reference
Candlesticks

A pair of knife rests, shaped as panthers, 4in (10cm).
£20-30 *PSA*

An engraved napkin ring, 19thC, 1in (3cm).
£5-10 *PSA*

A Continental figure of a man, 5in (13cm) high. **£30-40** *LIL*

A trophy tankard, c1911, 5½in (14cm) high.
£30-40 *PSA*

An early ½ gill measure, 2in (5cm) high.
£20-25 *PSA*

A Victorian pint pot, 5in (13cm) high.
£30-40 *PSA*

A jug/tankard, c1800, 5in (13cm) high.
£155-165 *HOW*

A ½ pint measure, 3in (8cm) high.
£30-35 *PSA*

Art Nouveau Pewter

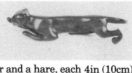

Knife rests shaped as a panther and a hare, each 4in (10cm).
£15-25 each *PSA*

A W.M.F. figural vase, designed by Albert Mauer, with stamped marks to base, 20½in (52cm) high.
£900-1,200 *P*

An Art Nouveau type vase, 5in (13cm) high.
£20-30 *PSA*

DID YOU KNOW?
Miller's Collectables Price Guide is designed to build up, year by year, into the most comprehensive reference system available.

A plate by Richard King, London, c1725, 8in (20cm) diam.
£45-55 *PSA*

An entrée dish with blue and green enamelling, marked Connell 33 Cheapside 02203, 10½in (26cm) wide. **£50-60** *ROW*

A Liberty & Co. Tudric rose bowl, impressed 6 Made in England Tudric Pewter 011. **£140-200** *P*

A blotter, with pewter inset, 10 by 8in (25 by 20cm). **£30-40** *PSA*

Silver

A pill box, Birmingham 1902, 1½in (4cm) diam. **£65-80** *PSA*

A Germanic wolf's head stirrup cup, with an open landscape, import marks for London 1925, 6in (15cm) high, 213gr. **£370-450** *HSS*

A pin tray, Birmingham 1903, 4in (10cm) long. **£35-45** *PSA*

An Edwardian Vesta case, by H. Matthews, London 1903, 32gr. **£140-200** *HSS*

Card Cases

An early Victorian visiting card case, by Nathaniel Mills, Birmingham 1840, 4 by 3in (10 by 8cm), 66gr. **£210-250** *HSS*

A Victorian card case, with views of Windsor Castle and Abbotsford House, by Joseph Willmore, Birmingham 1842, 4 by 3in (10 by 8cm). **£660-750** *P(S)*

An Edwardian visiting card case, by Chrisford & Norris, Birmingham 1904, 4 by 3in (10 by 8cm). **£170-200** *HSS*

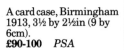

A card case, Birmingham 1913, 3½ by 2½in (9 by 6cm). **£90-100** *PSA*

A Victorian card case, decorated in high relief with a view of Newstead Abbey, Nottinghamshire, the home of Lord Byron, by Nathaniel Mills, Birmingham, dated 1837. **£820-900** *HSS*

Children's Items

A selection of Dutch silver miniature furniture, settee 2½in (6cm) wide.
£70-90   *PSA*

Cross Reference
Dolls House Furniture

A rattle, Birmingham 1936, 3in (8cm).
£50-60   *PSA*

A silver and bone rattle, 3in (8cm) long.
£25-35   *PSA*

Two silver and bone rattles, l. Birmingham, 1947. r. Birmingham, 1935.
£40-50 each
PSA

Two silver covered prayer books, Birmingham 1903, 2 by 2in (5 by 5cm).   **£50-80 each**   *PSA*

A pair of glove stretchers, Birmingham 1908, 7½in (19cm) long.   **£25-40**   *ROS*

Dressing Table Accessories

A composite Edwardian Art Nouveau three-piece dressing table set, Birmingham, c1903, various makers.
£230-300   *HSS*

An early George V dressing table box, Chester 1911, 4½in (11cm) square.
£340-400   *HSS*

Pin Cushions

A late George V six-piece dressing table set, comprising: 2 hair brushes, 2 clothes brushes and a comb, Birmingham 1929, in a satin and velvet lined case.
£200-250   *HSS*

A George V novelty pin cushion, in the form of a silver elephant pulling a two-wheeled polished sea shell cart, Birmingham 1928, 4in (10cm) long.
£160-200   *HSS*

Tableware

Four silver novelty pin cushions: An Edwardian long horned bull, Birmingham 1906, 3in (7cm) long.
£180-200
An early George V, boot, Birmingham 1912, 5in (12cm) long.
£150-200
A pair of Edwardian French court shoes, by H. Matthews, Birmingham 1906, 3in (8cm) long.
£260-300 *HSS*

> **Cross Reference**
> Sewing

A Shelley Harmony cake stand, c1935, 8in (20cm) diam.
£18-20
CSA

A composite set of 6 napkin rings, with maker's mark HG & S, Birmingham, c1936, 96gr.
£125-150 *HSS*

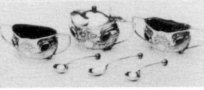

A Victorian silver hot water jug.
£230-300 *HCH*

An Edwardian three-piece condiment set.
£100-150 *HSS*

A George I style plain pear-shaped hot milk jug, by Wakeley & Wheeler, 8oz.
£100-150 *C(S)*

> **Cross Reference**
> Tea Making

A Dutch silver miniature cow creamer, the loop tail forming the handle and the hinged cover stamped with a pendant husk, with maker's mark B.H.M., London import mark 1906, 107gr, 4in (10cm) long.
£500-600 *HSS*

A late Victorian wafer holder of scallop shell form, opening to reveal pierced hinged grilles, with rustic cast stand and overhead handle, 10in (25cm) high.
£190-250 *HSS*

A George III baluster mug, with scroll handle, by Thomas Rush, London 1740, 8oz, 4in (10cm).
£320-350 *P(S)*

A Regency style tea kettle, stand and lamp, with engraved Greek key pattern borders, by Garrard & Co., 1913, 22oz. **£280-350** *C(S)*

A Victorian fluted pear-shaped hot water jug, with ebonised scroll handle, London mark 1892, 10½in (26cm), 19oz.
£300-400 *AG*

A Mappin & Webb salver, with piecrust rim, on hoof feet, Sheffield 1932, 8in (20cm) diam, 8oz.
£140-160 *P(O)*

A plain baluster milk jug, with moulded rim foot, by Hamilton & Inches, Edinburgh 1901, 14oz.
£220-300 *C(S)*

A George IV circular wirework swing-handled cake basket, the rim cast with foliage, with honeycomb wirework body, central crested foliate reserve on reed and ribbon collet foot, by R. Gainsford, Sheffield 1821, 14oz.
£550-650 *P(O)*

A Liberty & Co. Tudric biscuit barrel and lid, designed by Archibald Knox, impressed 9 Made in England, Tudric, 0194.
£260-300 *P*

Vinaigrettes

A George III bag vinaigrette, with wrigglework engraved decoration, the silver gilt grille pierced with a cornucopia and flowers, by John Shaw, Birmingham 1817.
£160-200 *Bon*

A George III vinaigrette, with engraved scalework to cover, prick engraved sides and suspensory loop to side, the gilt grille with lozenge piercing, Birmingham 1793.
£100-150 *Bon*

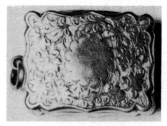

A Victorian silver vinaigrette, leaf engraved with suspensory loop, gilt interior with leaf engraved hinged grille, Birmingham 1893.
£120-150 *Bon*

A Georgian vinaigrette, with reeded sides and applied foliate border, the cover with foliate engraving around oval cartouche.
£85-100 *Bon*

A George IV silver gilt vinaigrette, with concave reeded sides and engine turned to base, foliate pierced grille, by Thomas Shaw, Birmingham 1826.
£220-300 *Bon*

A William IV vinaigrette, by Thomas Shaw, Birmingham 1831.
£140-200 *Bon*

A William IV vinaigrette, with engraved basketwork cover, and foliate engraving to base, scroll pierced silver gilt grille, by Thomas Shaw, Birmingham 1834. **£60-100** *Bon*

A George III Trafalgar commemorative silver vinaigrette, with prick engraved base, the hinged cover engraved with a portrait of Nelson and the motto 'England Expects Every Man to Do His Duty', the gilt interior with a hinged grille, stamped and pierced with the 'Victory' and chased with Trafalgar Oct.21.1805.
£820-900 *Bon*

A George IV vinaigrette, engine turned to sides, cover and base, with foliate pierced silver gilt grille, by John Betteridge, Birmingham 1825. **£100-150** *Bon*

A George III silver gilt vinaigrette, the cover, sides and base with engraved lozenge design, the cover with vacant rectangular cartouche, suspensory loop to side, foliate pierced grille, by John Shaw, Birmingham 1813.
£140-200 *Bon*

A George III bag vinaigrette, with foliate pierced silver gilt grille, by John Shaw, Birmingham 1790.
£150-200 *Bon*

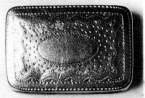

A George III vinaigrette, with rounded rectangular prick engraved cover, sides and base, lattice pierced grille, by Joseph Wilmore, Birmingham 1806. **£40-60** *Bon*

A silver and agate vinaigrette, the reeded sides with moss agate panel inset to cover, engine turned to base, pierced foliate grille, by Nathaniel Mills, Birmingham 1833.
£180-200 *Bon*

Silver Plate

A George IV vinaigrette, foliate engraved to cover against a cross hatched background, foliate engraved sides and base, with oval pierced and engraved silver gilt grille, by Ledsam, Vale and Wheeler, Birmingham 1825.
£120-200 *Bon*

A pair of Sheffield plate chambersticks, the tulip shaped sockets with detachable copper sconces, 7in (17cm) wide.
£150-250 *HSS*

Cross Reference
Kitchenalia
Candlesticks

A pair of candlesticks, with detachable sconces, by WWH & Co., 12in (30.5cm) high.
£160-180 *GH*

A two-handled florally
engraved tray, by
Mappin & Webb, 27in
(69cm).
£130-150   *GH*

Toast Racks

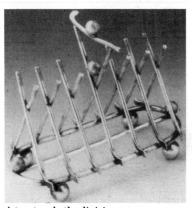

A late Victorian toast rack, the
arched uprights on a wrythen fluted
shell base, supported on 4 bun feet,
Sheffield 1900, 5in (13cm) long,
103gr.   **£70-100**   *HSS*

An orange squeezer,
12½in (32cm) high.
£60-80   *BEV*

A Dixon's silver plated
toast rack, 7in (18cm)
wide.   **£55-65**   *BEV*

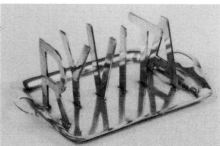

A Sheffield silver
plated toast rack,
spelling 'Ryvita',
7½in (19cm)
wide.
£55-65   *BEV*

A toast rack, the divisions
modelled as crossed golf
clubs, with golf club and
ball handle, a golf ball at
each end, on plain ball
feet.   **£200-250**   *AG*

Art Nouveau
Metalware

A Newlyn School copper tray,
decorated in relief around a
central plateau, 15in (38cm)
wide.   **£130-150**   *P*

An Arts and Crafts silver
casket decorated with
applied strapwork
hinges, escutcheon and
corner pieces, maker's
mark W & Co.
Birmingham 1903, 5in
(12cm) wide.
£120-160   *P*

A pair of copper and brass
candlesticks, by W. A. S.
Benson, 10in (25cm) high.
£400-450   *NCA*

An Arts and Crafts
hanging cupboard set
with bronze panels by
Esther Moore, in black
stained beech, 27in
(68cm) wide.
£250-350   *P*

*Esther Moore exhibited
widely between 1890 and
1911 and was influenced
by the work of Gilbert.*

A Newlyn School copper
photo frame, 12in
(30.5cm) high.   **£350-380**   *NCA*

A pewter figural inkwell
in the manner of a
Martin Brothers
grotesque bird, with a
blue ceramic well, 4in
(10.5cm) high.
£140-160   *P*

Cross Reference
Inkstands

A W.M.F. pewter dish, 14in (36cm).
£200-300   *ASA*

A copper firescreen with
beaton iron surround.
£110-130   *NCA*

A pewter mirror, probably Osiris,
c1900.   **£600-800**   *DID*

A silver repoussé picture frame,
decorated in relief with
kingfishers and water plants,
stamped maker's marks W.N
and Chester hallmarks for 1904
Patent 9616, on wood back
panel, 12½in (32cm).
£1,500-2,000   *C*

A Goberg iron and brass
candlestick, 12in
(30.5cm) high.
£150-180   *NCA*

A Tudric pewter muffin dish and cover,
9½in (24cm) diam.   **£250-400**   *CSK*

A silver gilt
jug, by
George
Angel,
London
1878.
**£1,700-
2,000**   *DID*

MILITARIA
Badges

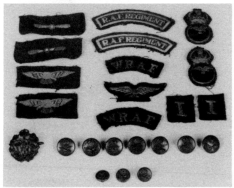

A Canada badge.
£4-6 *ROS*

A Leicestershire
Regiment Hindoostan
badge.
£5-10 *ROS*

A collection of W.R.A.F. uniform badges and
buttons. **£1-5 each** *RE*

An On War Service badge,
1915. **£8-10** *ROS*

A Machine Gun Corps badge.
£10-12 *ROS*

A Royal Artillery Ubique badge.
£5-6 *ROS*

Brass Cap Badges

An Inniskillen badge.
£5 10 *ROS*

An Australian Commonwealth
Military Forces badge.
£8-10 *ROS*

Regimental Brooches

The 10th Royal Hussars,
gold and enamel brooch.
£440-460 *S*

The King's Royal
Rifle Corps badge,
in fitted case.
£200-250 *S*

Helmet Plates

A post 1902 officer's silvered helmet plate of the Royal West Kent Regiment 1st Vol. Batt., maker's label on reverse, Hobson & Sons, 13 & 5 Lexington St., London W.
£100-120 *WAL*

A post 1902 officer's gilt helmet plate of the East Surrey Regiment.
£120-150 *WAL*

Shoulder Belt Plates

A brass plate of the 3rd Nottinghamshire Local Militia.
£90-100 *CSK*

An officer's gilt and white metal plate of the 30th Bengal Native Infantry.
£440-460 *CSK*

A post 1902 officer's gilt and silver plated rectangular plate of The King's Own Scottish Borderers.
£210-220 *WAL*

Belt Clasps

An officer's plate of The Royal Regiment of Artillery, worn 1823-33.
£350-375 *WAL*

An officer's oval plate of the Manx Volunteers, engraved with crown and motto.
£310-320 *WAL*

An Indian Army officer's gilt and silver special pattern waist belt clasp of the 6th Regiment.
£310-320 *WAL*

A Victorian Dragoon Guards officer's gilt and silver plated waistbelt plate, with VR cypher and motto.
£100-120 *WAL*

Edged Weapons
Bayonets & Knives

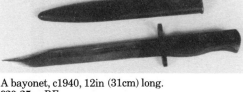

A bayonet, c1940, 12in (31cm) long.
£20-25 *RE*

An Edwardian bowie knife, stamped Wingfield Rowbotham & Co., Sheffield, clipped back blade 6in (15cm). **£50-60** *WAL*

A late Victorian Graham Knife, stamped crowned VR, W. Thornhill & Co., London, clipped back blade 5in (12.5cm) long. **£100-120** *WAL*

A bush knife with military stamp, c1940, 16in (40.5cm) long.
£50-55 *RE*

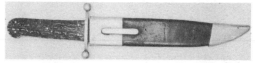

A bowie knife, by J. Rodgers & Sons, Sheffield, clipped backed blade, 7½in (19cm). **£150-200** *WAL*

A Weimar Republic police dress bayonet, crosspiece and locket stamped P.Fr 221, by Eickhorn, with plated blade, 17in (43cm) long. **£250-275** *WAL*

Daggers

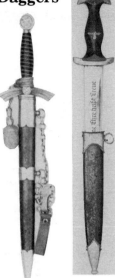

A Nazi M1933 SS dagger, etched at forte with 'RZM' and 'M 7/37 RZM 1051/38'.
£320-350 *WAL*

Dirks

A Nazi 1st pattern Luftwaffe officer's dagger.
£250-300 *WAL*

A Nazi SA dagger, by Gebr. Becker.
£120-150 *WAL*

A Nazi 1933 SS dagger, with German silver hilt mounts, by Robert Klaas.
£350-400 *WAL*

An officer's gilt mounted dirk, of the Seaforth Highlanders, by R. & H. B. Kirkwood, with plain notched back fullered blade, 12in (31cm), in case.
£750-800 *CSK*

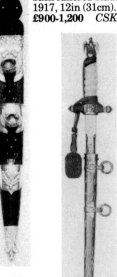

An officer's silver mounted dirk, of the Seaforth Highlanders, plain plated notched back fullered blade, 1917, 12in (31cm).
£900-1,200 *CSK*

A Nazi Naval officer's dirk, by Eickhorn.
£160-200 *WAL*

Oriental & Tribal

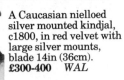

A Caucasian nielloed silver mounted kindjal, c1800, in red velvet with large silver mounts, blade 14in (36cm).
£300-400 *WAL*

A Caucasian kindjal, with tapering double edged blade of flattened diamond section, late 19thC.
£600-700 *CSK*

A silver mounted ivory hilted Sumbawa execution kris, dated AH1172 (=1758 AD), with pattern welded blade 22½in (57cm).
£200-250 *WAL*

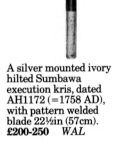

A Sumatran kris, with five-wave pattern welded blade, ivory hilt, wooden scabbard inset with a tortoiseshell panel, 20in (51cm).
£300-400 *CSK*

A Persian Qjar all steel dagger, 19thC, 11in (28cm) blade.
£150-200 *WAL*

A Chinese enamelled silver mounted dagger with Indian moghul jade hilted khanjar hilt, straight SE blade 13in (33cm), 19thC.
£850-950 *WAL*

A Malayan dagger bade bade, with hippopotamus tusk hilt and mounts, 19thC, 14in (36cm), with wooden sheath.
£80-100 *WAL*

A Ceylonese dagger pia kaetta, 18thC, 12in (31cm).
£280-350 *WAL*

A Malayan silver mounted dagger bade bade, the silver hilt and wooden sheath with carved black horn, 19thC, fullered blade 10in (25cm).
£75-85 *WAL*

Swords

An American Revolutionary War period cutlass, the 26½in (67cm) blade struck with running wolf mark.
£250-350 *WAL*

A French silver hilted smallsword, struck with 3 silver marks, c1745, 29in (74cm) blade.
£470-550 *C*

An English basket hilted backsword, with straight single edged blade, with double edged tip, with black leather scabbard and steel chape, 35in (89cm).
£400-500 *WAL*

An officer's half basket hilted backsword, c1780, fitted with earlier blade 32½in (82cm), and woven copper wire bound sharkskin covered grip.
£400-500 *WAL*

An English silver hilted smallsword, blade worn, late 18thC, 31½in (80cm) blade.
£500-600 *S*

An English silver mounted hunting hanger, with agate grip, blade worn and grip with flaws, mid-18thC.
£720-800 *S*

A Scottish basket hilted broadsword with fluted bun shaped pommel, scabbard incomplete and tip of blade missing, c1755, 35in (89cm) blade.
£350-500 *C*

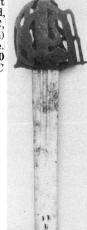

A Scottish ribbon hilt broadsword, late 17thC, 31in (79cm) blade.
£850-900 *C*

A cup tilt rapier, English or French, damaged, c1638, 42½in (107cm) blade.
£800-1,200 *CSK*

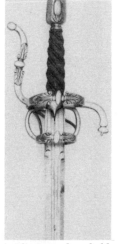

A silver hilted smallsword, late 18th/early 19thC, some repair and blade worn, 32½in (82cm) blade.
£550-650 *S*

A riding sword, probably German, early 17thC, 39½in (100cm) blade.
£1,400-1,600 *CSK*

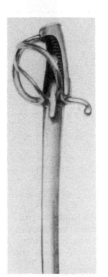

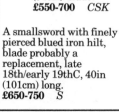

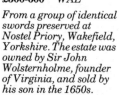

A French AN XI Light Cavalry trooper's sabre, stamped 'A.R.', with brass triple bar hilt, plain brass mounts, curved blade 34½in (87cm).
£300-350 *WAL*

A smallsword with finely pierced blued iron hilt, blade probably a replacement, late 18th/early 19thC, 40in (101cm) long.
£650-750 *S*

An English basket hilted broadsword, early 17thC, 37in (94cm) blade.
£550-700 *CSK*

A Cromwellian basket hilted backsword, with straight single edged blade 32½in (82cm).
£500-600 *WAL*

From a group of identical swords preserved at Nostel Priory, Wakefield, Yorkshire. The estate was owned by Sir John Wolsternholme, founder of Virginia, and sold by his son in the 1650s.

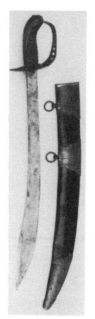

A US Society sword, with straight plated blade, by W. A. Raymond New York, with plated scabbard.
£65-100 *WAL*

An officer's basket hilted sword, of the 2nd Volunteer Battalion the Royal Highlanders, in metal scabbard.
£300-350 *C(S)*

An early 19thC cutlass, with wide heavy curved blade, the locket engraved Webb, Manufacturer, 57 Piccadilly, London.
£350-450 *CSK*

The firm of Charles Webb is listed in May and Annis as being at that address 1804-20.

An officer's 1822 type Mameluke full dress sword, of the 9th Lancers, by Prosser, Manufacturers to the King, London, c1830.
£850-950 *CSK*

A Victorian Infantry officer's sword, pattern of 1822, in brass scabbard inscribed Dudley.
£110-150 *C(S)*

An officer's spadroon, c1790.
£200-300 *WAL*

Oriental

A swept hilt German rapier, deeply struck in the fullers 'In Te Domine Speravi' on both sides, with maker's marks, pitted with age and wear, c1610.
£550-650 *WAL*

A Georgian 1821 pattern Heavy Cavalry officer's un-dress sword, in its steel scabbard.
£160-250 *WAL*

A Mameluke sabre, in original purple velvet covered wooden scabbard, 19thC, 29in (74cm) blade.
£400-500 *CSK*

A gold mounted Persian shamshir, 18th/19thC, 32½in (82cm) blade.
£700-800 *CSK*

Captured by the vendor's grandfather at the battle of Tel-El-Kebir, 1882.

Headddress

A Nazi Waffen SS steel helmet, field grey green finish, both transfer shield badges, leather lining and chinstrap.
£350-400   *WAL*

A Nazi Waffen SS officer's peaked cap.
£150-200   *WAL*

An Imperial German Bavarian Infantry Other Ranks Reservist's pickelhaube, with brass helmet plate, brass mounts, leather lining and chinstrap, both cockades, inside of neck guard, dated 1905.
£160-200   *WAL*

A Cromwellian lobster tailed helmet 'pot', with original leather lined borders.
£850-950   *WAL*

An ARP helmet, c1940.
£10-12   *RE*

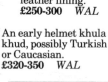

An Imperial German Prussian Guard Artillery Other Ranks pickelhaube, white metal helmet plate, leather backed chinscales and mounts, small ball mount, both cockades, leather lining.
£250-300   *WAL*

A WWI tank driver's face mask, leather covered and chamois lined.
£110-150   *WAL*

An early helmet khula khud, possibly Turkish or Caucasian.
£320-350   *WAL*

An Imperial German Wurttemberg Infantry N.C.O.'s pickelhaube, with brass helmet plate and mounts, both cockades, leather backed brass chinscales, leather and silk lining, with old ink written label inscribed 'XIII Armeecorp Inf. Regt. No. 124 Unteroffizier Eigentumhelm'.
£250-300   *WAL*

An Imperial German Prussian Infantryman's pickelhaube, with brass helmet plate and mounts, leather lining and chinstrap, both cockades, some damage and restoration.
£150-200   *WAL*

Medals

East and West Africa medal, 1 bar Gambia 1894, A. L. Rood, AB, HMS Raleigh.
£90-100 *WAL*

Naval General Service 1793, 2 clasps, Trafalgar, Martinique, Geo. White, Master's Mate, original riband.
£1,200-1,500 *S*

The roll confirms George White as a Master's Mate aboard H.M.S. Dreadnought for Trafalgar, and as an Acting Lieutenant aboard H.M.S. Captain for Martinique.

A Naval General Service medal, 1793, 2 clasps, Martinique, The Potomac 17 Aug. 1814, Edwd. Collier, Midshipman, original riband.
£1,900-2,500 *S*

The roll confirms Edward Collier as a Midshipman aboard H.M.S. Belleisle for Martinique, and as a Master's Mate aboard H.M.S. Euryalus for The Potomac.

A C.M.G. pair of medals to Colonel C. A. Bayley, 31st Foot, comprising The Most Distinguished Order of St. Michael and St. George Companion's breast badge, in gold and enamels, with usual swivel ring suspension and riband buckle, c1830, and the Military General Service, 1793, 3 clasps, Egypt Talavera, Albuhera, Lieut. & Adjt. 31st Foot & D.A.A.G.
£1,800-2,500 *S*

Colonel Charles Andrew Bayley, C.M.G., served in the Egypt Campaign with the 25th Foot and afterwards in the Peninsular from 1808 until 1812, as Adjutant of the 31st Foot, being present at the affair of Alberche and the Battle of Albuhera while acting in this capacity.

An Indian Mutiny 1857, 2 bars Defence of Lucknow, Lucknow, D. Lamond, 78th Highlanders.
£250-300 *WAL*

The 78th were part of Sir Henry Havelock's 1st Relief force.

An Order of the Slovakian Cross Grand Cross neck badge, WWII Nazi Puppet State.
£800-900 *CEN*

A WWII group Distinguished Flying Cross, to a Bomber Pilot with named Cadet Forces Medal, ERII.
£500-600   *CEN*

A 'Suez' D.S.M. Group to Able Seaman R. B. Loader, Royal Navy, Distinguished Service Medal, Eliz.II (A.B.), Naval General Service, 1915, Eliz.II, 1 clasp, Near East, D.S.M., A.B., R.N. and Royal Naval Reserve L.S. medal, Eliz.II L.P.A., R.N.R.
£2,750-3,000   *S*

Able Seaman Loader was a Bofors Gunner aboard the frigate H.M.S. Crane, attacked in error by Israeli Air Force. Able Seaman Loader continued to fire at bombers by manual control after controls of the weapons were damaged.

A group of decorations and medals awarded to Flying Officer R. E. Gillman, R.A.F., WWII, comprising Distinguished Flying Cross, Distinguished Flying Medal, Campaign stars for 1939-45, Atlantic, with bar France & Germany, and Africa Defence and War Medals.
£1,450-2,000   *CSK*

A USA Grand Army of the Republic 1861-66 Veterans badge/medal, reverse with Patent dates May 4 1886, June 22 1886, edge impressed F 16C39.
£30-40   *WAL*

Two groups of WWI medals to brothers, one the Distinguished Conduct Medal, the other The Military Medal.
£450-550   *CEN*

A Military M.B.E. in case.
£45-50   *COB*

USSR Order of Friendship medal.
£300-400   *CEN*

Pistols

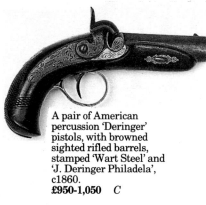

A flintlock pistol, signed lock with bevelled border, safety catch chipped, by Robert Wogdon, London, London proof marks, c1780, 15½in (39cm).
£1,100-1,500 *CSK*

A pair of American percussion 'Deringer' pistols, with browned sighted rifled barrels, stamped 'Wart Steel' and 'J. Deringer Philadela', c1860.
£950-1,050 *C*

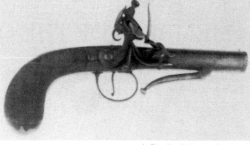

A single trigger over-and- under percussion pocket pistol, by Joseph Egg, London, c1825.
£2,500-3,000 *C*

A flintlock boxlock pistol, with folding rest, by Alexr. Wilson, London.
£450-550 *C(S)*

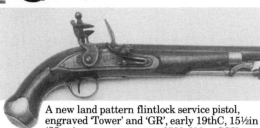

A 16 bore flintlock holster pistol by Rimes, with Tower private proofs and engraved 'London', c1760, 13in (33cm) overall, barrel 7½in (19cm).
£350-450 *WAL*

A pair of French percussion boxlock pocket pistols, signed Gastinne Renette à Paris, c1850, 6½in (16cm).
£900-1,000 *C*

A new land pattern flintlock service pistol, engraved 'Tower' and 'GR', early 19thC, 15½in (39cm).
£500-600 *CSK*

A pair of percussion boxlock pocket pistols, with reblued twist octagonal barrels, engraved brass actions, engraved hammers, signed Horton, Salop, Birmingham proof marks, c1840, 6in (15cm).
£1,050-2,000 *C*

A 22 bore all steel Scottish flintlock belt pistol, by T. Murdoch, c1760, 11½in (29cm) and 7in (18cm) barrel.
£3,000-3,500 *WAL*

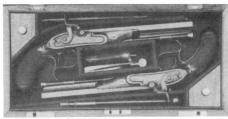

A pair of percussion
duelling pistols,
converted from flintlock,
with browned octagonal
barrels, signed Lambert,
London, Birmingham
proof marks, c1850,
14½in (37cm).
£1,200-1,500   *C*

A pair of percussion
target pistols, with
browned twist octagonal
sighted barrels, by
Samuel Nock, Regent
Circus, Piccadilly,
London, No. 7971, c1850,
16in (41cm).
£3,000-3,500   *C*

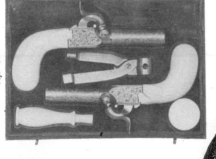

A pair of Belgian boxlock
percussion pocket pistols,
with etched twist turn off
barrels, and ivory butts,
cracked, Liège proof,
mid-19thC, 6in (15cm),
in original fitted case.
£1,400-1,600   *C*

A pair of German small
percussion pistols, with
octagonal rifled barrels,
engraved back action
locks signed in gold and
with pivoting safety
stops, engraved German
silver mounts, by
Christoph Schilling in
Suhl, No. 4162, c1860,
5in (13cm).
£1,750-1,850   *C*

A Bohemian small
percussion pistol, with
rebrowned octagonal
rifled sighted barrel,
German silver
escutcheon, by A. V.
Lebeda of Prague, c1850,
6in (15cm).
£950-1,000   *C*

A pair of silver mounted percussion
duelling pistols, converted from
flintlock, by Wilson, Minories, London,
London silver hallmarks for 1792,
maker's mark of Moses Brent, 15in
(38cm).   **£3,300-3,500**   *C*

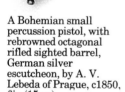

A pair of 50 bore
percussion boxlock
pocket pistols, with
Birmingham proofs and
number '42' and
'Mortimor, London',
lightly pitted overall, one
barrel scored, 6in (15cm)
overall, turn off barrels
2in (5cm).
£200-300   *WAL*

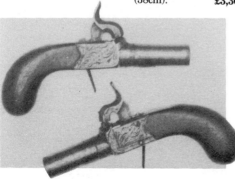

A pair of 46 bore brass
framed percussion
boxlock pocket pistols,
c1840, with Birmingham
proofs, 6in (15cm)
overall, turn off barrels
1½in (4cm).
£370-500   *WAL*

A presentation Westley Richards patent 36 bore 5-shot double action percussion revolver, No. 96, engraved 'Mr H.C. Williamson, Czarina Yacht', dated 1854, 12½in (32cm).
£1,200-1,500   *C*

This revolver incorporates British Patent No. 14,027 of 20 March 1852 and No. 993 of 3 May 1854. It appears that only about 300 revolvers of this type were produced.

A Colt 1849 model pocket percussion revolver, No. L269209, with full accessories including Dixon Colts pocket flask, London proof marks, in original lined and fitted oak case, 9½in (24cm).
£1,750-2,000   *C*

A gold decorated 54 bore Beaumont-Adams 5-shot double action percussion revolver, No. 23,145R and B7497, barrel engraved 'London Armoury', London proof marks, 12in (31cm).
£1,500-2,000   *C*

A 5-shot .54 bore percussion revolver, by Irving Wallace, in fitted case with accessories.
£950-1,000   *CEN*

A 5-shot .80 bore percussion revolver, by Lees of Perth, in fitted case with accessories.
£800-900   *CEN*

An Adams patent 54 bore 5-shot double action percussion revolver, No. 32,45R and B16,741, London Armoury Company mark and London proof marks, 12in (31cm).
£1,500-2,000   *C*

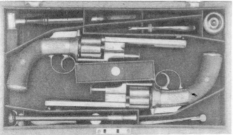

A pair of 6-shot percussion Transitional revolvers, by G. Wellborne, Doncaster, Birmingham proof marks, mid-19thC, 13in (33cm).
£1,750-2,000   *C*

A Beaumont-Adams patent 54 bore 5-shot double action percussion revolver, in original lined and fitted oak case, accessories including Dixon flask, London proof marks, 12in (31cm).
£1,000-1,500   *C*

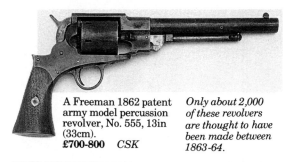

A Freeman 1862 patent army model percussion revolver, No. 555, 13in (33cm). **£700-800** *CSK*

Only about 2,000 of these revolvers are thought to have been made between 1863-64.

A Nazi 9mm Walther P38 semi-automatic pistol, No. 3936b, 8½in (21cm) overall. **£200-250** *WAL*

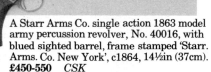

A .20 Bedford & Walker air pistol, nickel plated brass barrel stamped 'Pat Jan 18, July 18, '76. Pat in Eng', c1880, 13½in (34cm). **£80-150** *WAL*

A Starr Arms Co. single action 1863 model army percussion revolver, No. 40016, with blued sighted barrel, frame stamped 'Starr. Arms. Co. New York', c1864, 14½in (37cm). **£450-550** *CSK*

A Continental flintlock tinder lighter, probably Italian or Dutch, 1740, 6in (15cm). **£400-450** *WAL*

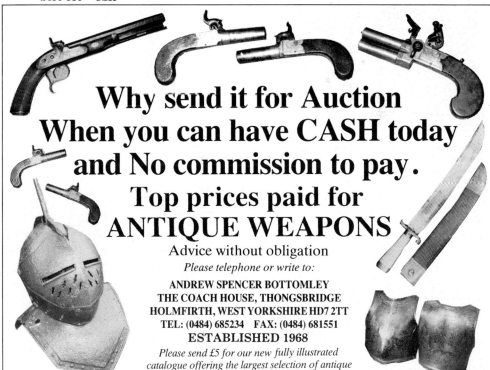

Powder Flasks

A French brass mounted
horn powder flask,
R1168, some damage.
£75-150   *WAL*

A further selection of powder flasks is
featured in previous editions of Miller's
Collectables Price Guides, available
from Millers Publications.

Uniforms

The elaborate scarlet full
dress tunic of a Nepalese
General, marked
General Sir Tez Shum
Sher JBR and dated 21st
March 1930.
£180-250   *CSK*

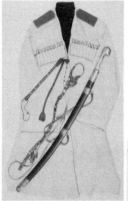

The shashqua, belts,
tunic, whip and
cartouches surrendered
by a Cossack Officer to
Commander
McCullough, Royal
Navy, in 1917, minor
moth damage to coat.
£2,000-2,500   *WAL*

A pair of WWII RAF
ex-ace bomber pilot's
boots, 13½in (34cm).
£45-50   *ROS*

A family group of items
relating to the Rifle
Brigade, an officer's
Astrakhan busby,
complete with caplines,
brass plate engraved
L. Stopford Sackville,
Esq., The Rifle Brigade,
pouch and pouchbelt,
Major's full dress tunic
and roll-collar mess
jacket, mess waistcoat
and braided patrol
jacket, by Sandilands &
Son, an earlier full dress
tunic of Rifle Brigade
Field Officer's pattern
and Ashantee War
Medal 1873-74, with
clasp COOMASSIE
inscribed LIEUT. L.R.S.
SACKVILLE 2nd BN.
RIFLE BRIGADE, and
other items of uniform.
£1,500-2,000   *CSK*

An early Scottish
all brass plaid
brooch, axle
of pin cracked,
4in (10cm) diam.
£120-150   *WAL*

A Cromwellian trooper's
half armour, lobster
tailed helmet with triple
bar face guard, leather
waistbelt, black painted
protective finish overall,
mounted on a wooden
stand, some restoration.
£1,100-1,300   *WAL*

A WWII U.S. Air Force
uniform.
£85-100   *ACL*

Rifles &
Muskets

A .52 model 1819 Hall's patent US breech loading flintlock rifle, stamped J.H. Hall H. Ferry U.S. 1837, 53in (135cm).
£800-900 *WAL*

A 14-bore double barrelled German percussion sporting gun, by F. Fakler of Aichach, c1850, 48in (122cm) overall.
£450-550 *WAL*

A double barrelled 14-bore percussion sporting gun, with rebrowned twist barrels 29in (74cm), engraved on top rib 'Egg, London', 45in (114cm) overall.
£200-250 *WAL*

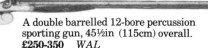

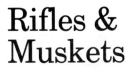

A double barrelled 12-bore percussion sporting gun, 45½in (115cm) overall.
£250-350 *WAL*

A 10-bore double barrelled German percussion sporting gun, by F. Fakler of Aichach, c1850, 47in (119cm) overall.
£450-550 *WAL*

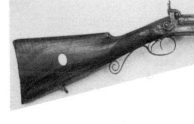

A Continental 16-bore double barrelled percussion sporting gun, with silver escutcheon engraved 'This Gun Belonged To Baron Charles De Rothschild Used About 1850', signed Weber & Schulteis in Frankfurt, Liége proof, mid-19thC, 32in (81cm) barrels.
£550-600 *CSK*

A double barrelled 18-bore percussion sporting gun, 47½in (120cm) overall.
£160-200 *WAL*

An English flintlock breech loading repeating gun, the Lorenzoni principle, signature possibly that of Robert Smyth Fecit, late 17thC, 29in (74cm).
£900-1,000 *CSK*

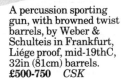

A percussion sporting gun, with browned twist barrels, by Weber & Schulteis in Frankfurt, Liége proof, mid-19thC, 32in (81cm) barrels.
£500-750 *CSK*

A Lovell's 1839 pattern 10 bore military percussion musket, 49½in (126cm), barrel 33in (84cm), some damage and restoration.
£250-300 *WAL*

An early 19thC 80 bore air rifle, 46½in (118cm), slender twist barrel 31in (79cm), ramrod pipes tubed to take replacement steel ramrod.
£1,350-2,000 *WAL*

A 10-bore Volunteer Brown Bess flintlock musket, by Ketland & Co., with Tower private proofs, 58in (147cm) overall.
£450-550 *WAL*

Trench-Art

A WWI souvenir brass paper knife, 7in (18cm) long.
£10-12 *ROS*

Four silver menu holders, by Henry Steward-Brown, London 1891, in the form of the antelope of the Warwickshire Regiment, 3in (8cm) high.
£175-250 *CSK*

A pair of bronze figures, one of the Scots Greys, the other a French Cuirassier.
£600-650 *CSK*

A well modelled bronze figure of a French officer, in late 19thC uniform, 20in (51cm) high.
£600-800 *CSK*

A silver inkwell, in the form of a miniature fire brigade helmet of Merryweather pattern, London 1932, 4in (10cm) high. **£450-550** *CSK*

General Militaria

A Victorian print, Military Quadrille, printed in polychrome, 15 by 12in (38 by 31cm).
£18-25 *MA*

A recruiting poster, 1915.
£60-70 *COB*

A marquetry portrait of Lord Mountbatten, from a sketch by Roth of the Evening News, 9 by 6in (23 by 15cm).
£35-45 *PSA*

A collection of material relating to the 10th Prince of Wales's Own Royal Hussars, including a waist belt and Sabretache, c1820, and 2 prints.
£1,300-1,500 *S*

A heavy iron folding campaign armchair, with swept upholstered seat and padded armrests, locking pins missing, 27 by 49in (69 by 125cm) when folded flat.
£150-250 *CSK*

Despite its weight this chair was taken to the Crimea by an officer of the 11th Hussars, Coleraine Robert Vansittart 1833-86, Cornet 1852, Lieut. 1853, Captain 1855, retired 1858. For his Crimean War service he received the medal and 3 clasps and the Turkish medal.

A 19thC sportsman's combination tool, with dog whistle, 12-bore cartridge extractor stamped 12, 4in (10cm) overall.
£110-150 *WAL*

An embroidered regimental badge and allied flags, 1914-18.   **£30-35** *COB*

A lacquered brass bar type percussion cap dispenser by F. Joyce, stamped 'F. Joyce- London-24', 5in (13cm) overall.
£120-150 *WAL*

General Sir Edward Kerrison, in the manner of Sir Thomas Lawrence, an oil on canvas, c1840, 27 by 22in (69 by 56cm).
£900-1,000 *CSK*

The distinguished Commander of light cavalry is more generally depicted in Hussar dress and is one of few British soldiers to have had the rare uniform of a General Officer of Hussars. He received the GCH in 1831 and KCB in 1840.

Stanley L. Wood, A Matabele at Bay, signed and dated oil on canvas, 1897, 43½ by 34in (110 by 86cm).
£1,100-1,500 *CSK*

The British South Africa Company had come into conflict with the Matabele in 1893 but this picture may well show an incident in the subsequent Matabele Uprising of March-October 1896.

An S.O.E. agent's suitcase wireless receiver/transmitter, Transceiver No. 3 Mark II, known also as B2, with earphones and tap key, the millboard suitcase, 16½ by 12½in (42 by 32cm).
£1,000-1,500 *CSK*

This model, in use from 1943 onwards, had the advantage of almost instantaneous conversion from mains to battery power to avoid a tell-tale break in transmission if the mains were cut by security forces.

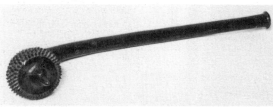

A Polynesian ritual club, 32in (81cm) long.
£150-160 *HUN*

An Italian fascist banner of red, white and green silk, 23in (59cm) square.
£200-250 *CSK*

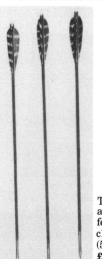

Three Indian arrows, some feathers replaced, c1800, 21in (53cm) long.
£14-20 each *ARB*

Three embroidered crimson silk 'Company Colours', known also as 'Camp Flags' and carried by markers, of the Grenadier Guards, a Victorian flag of the 5th Company, a post 1901 flag of the 16th Company and a Victorian flag of the 26th Company.
£700-800 *CSK*

316

A Canadian soldier's match box cover from WWI, brass, 2½in (6cm) high. **£10-12** *ROS*

The Rifle Manual and Firing, by J. Jones, plates 1 to 12, lacking plates 3 and 13, hand coloured etchings, printed by R. Ryan and J. Brettell published by R. Ryan and T. Smith, London 1804, with margins, unframed, London 1804, 7 by 8½in (18 by 22cm) and smaller. **£550-650** *CSK*

A tapering ebony baton, inscribed upper end, Comando von Herr Hinrich Müller, Obrist Lieutent. des Regiments St. Nicolay, 25in (64cm) long. **£420-500** *CSK*

This style of baton is inspired by the simple classical wooden baton traditionally carried by field commanders in an earlier era. In certain regions of Germany batons seem to have been carried until very early in the 19thC by some officers commanding regiments. The title of this regiment 'St. Nicolay' may possibly refer to Sankt Nicolay, a suburb of Hamburg. In local units of urban militia, officers were elected: Müller may have commanded such a unit.

A regimental guidon of the 18th Light Dragoons (Hussars), bearing the number 3, 3rd Squadron, 23 by 35in (59 by 89cm), framed and double glazed. **£1,750-2,200** *CSK*

Embroidered ornamentation as a trumpet banner of the Royal Arms as used up to 1801, 18 by 21in (46 by 53cm). **£350-500** *CSK*

A 19thC sportsman's game counter, engraved 'Hares' and 'Rabbits' accordingly, 1½in (3.5cm) diam. **£200-250** *WAL*

Four Indian decorated arrows, c1800. **£20-30 each** *ARB*

FURTHER READING
Badges of the British Army 1820-1960, F. Wilkinson, Arms & Armour Press.
Campaign Medals of the British Army 1815-1972, R. W. Gould, Arms & Armour Press.
Sword, Lance & Bayonet, Charles Ffoulkes & E. C. Hopkinson, Arco Publishing Co., 1967.
Military Fashion, John Mollo Barry & Jenkins.
Collecting Metal Shoulder Titles, R. A. Westlake, Frederick Warne, 1980.
Weapons of the British Soldier, Col. H. C. B. Rogers, Sphere Books Ltd., 1972.
Swords of the British Army, Brian Robson, Arms & Armour Press.

Miniatures

Two miniature
pen knives, 1½in
(3.3cm) long and
with corkscrew,
2in (5cm) long.
£4-8 each *ROS*

For a larger selection of Miniature
Collectables see Miller's Collectables
Price Guide Vol III, pp325-331
available from Millers Publications.

Money Banks
& Money Boxes

A George VI Coronation
Post Office Savings Bank
money box, 4 by 3in
(10 by 7.5cm).
£20-30 *HAL*

A WWI money box, 6in
(15cm) high.
£10-15 *HAL*

A small Portobello
money box, modelled as a
two-storey house
coloured in raspberry,
blue and green, c1840,
3½in (9cm) high.
£100-150 *LR*

Two tin savings banks:
l. 1950s, r. 1920s, 5in
(13cm) high.
When the money reaches
the target, the drawer
opens.
£15-20 *HAL*

A Punch and Judy
money box, c1950, 4½in
(11cm) high.
£30-40 *HAL*

A leap-frog bank, by
Shepard Hardware Co.,
damaged, 5in (12.5cm)
high.
£4,400-5,000 *CNY*

A horse race money box
with flanged base, by
J. & E. Stevens, designed
by John D. Hall, no label.
£7,000-7,500 *CNY*

A large Prattware money box
modelled as a Gothic cottage, in
typical Prattware colours, c1790,
6in (15cm) high. **£500-550** *LR*

A tin money box in the style of the Queen Mother's dolls house, 3½in (8.5cm) high.
£20-25 *DOL*

A Prattware cottage money box, painted in Yorkshire palate of beige, blue and green, c1810, 5in (12.5cm) high.
£350-400 *LR*

A Cupola bank, by J. & E. Stevens, designed by Diedrich Diekman, some damage, 7in (18cm) high.
£4,800-5,200 *CNY*

'I Always Did 'Spize a Mule', an American money box, c1879, 10in (25cm).
£250-300 *HAL*

A George V Coronation money box, 1911, 7½in (19cm) high.
£45-55 *HAL*

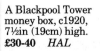

An American owl money box, 19thC, 6in (15cm) high.
£250-300 *HAL*

A Blackpool Tower money box, c1920, 7½in (19cm) high.
£30-40 *HAL*

A plastic television
savings box, c1960s.
£7-12 *COB*

A boy robbing a bird's
nest money box, by
J. & E. Stevens, designed
by Charles A. Bailey, 6in
(15cm) long.
£11,000-12,000 *CNY*

A Creedmoor money box,
USA, 19thC, 9½in
(49cm) wide.
£275-325 *HAL*

A butting buffalo money
box, by Kyser & Rex Co.,
7½in (19cm) long.
£3,000-3,500 *CNY*

A boy scout camp money
box, by J. & E. Stevens,
designed by Charles A.
Bailey, trap missing,
10in (25cm) long.
£10,000-11,000 *CNY*

An eagle and eaglets
money box, c1883, 6in
(15cm) wide.
£300-350 *HAL*

A magician bank, by
J. & E. Stevens, designed
by Charles A. Bailey, no
trap, 8in (20cm) high.
£4,000-4,500 *CNY*

A clown on globe
money box, by J. &
E. Stevens,
designed by James
H. Bowen, 9in
(23cm) high.
£1,100-1,500 *CNY*

Dinah, an English
money box, early 1920s,
6½in (16cm) high.
£120-180 *HAL*

A Black Sambo money
box, c1900.
£60-70 *HAL*

A Panorama money box,
by J. & E. Stevens,
designed by James
Butler, some wear, 6½in
(16cm) high.
£2,000-3,000 *CNY*

A picture gallery bank,
by Shepard Hardware
Co., some wear, 8½in
(21cm) high.
£4,800-5,200 *CNY*

A lighthouse money box, re-painted, 10½in (26cm) long.
£1,100-1,500 *CNY*

A mammy and child money box, by Kyser & Rex, some damage, 9in (23cm) high.
£6,400-6,800 *CNY*

A goat, frog and old man money box, by Mechanical Novelty Works, replacements, 7½in (19cm) long.
£2,500-3,000 *CNY*

A hen and chick money box, by J. & E. Stevens, designed by Charles A. Bailey, incomplete, 10in (25cm) long.
£4,000-4,500 *CNY*

A circus money bank, by Shepard Hardware, repaired, 9in (22.5cm) diam.
£13,000-14,000 *CNY*

A Peg-Leg beggar money box, by Judd Mfg. Co., possibly re-painted, 5½in (14cm) high.
£3,000-3,500 *CNY*

A North Pole Bank, by J. & E. Stevens, c1910, 6½in (16.5cm) long.
£3,200-3,500 *CNY*

A Bull Dog Bank, American, c1880, 7½in (19cm) high.
£350-400 *HAL*

A confectionery bank, by Kyser and Rex, incomplete, 8½in (21cm) high.
£5,000-5,500 *CNY*

A Jonah and the Whale money box, by Shephard Hardware Co., some damage, 10in (25cm) long.   **£1,200-1,500** *CNY*

A Mason's mechanical bank, by Shepard Hardware Co, c1887, 7½in (19cm) long.
£1,200-1,500 *CNY*

A group of ceramic banks, American and Mexican, c1890.
£100-150 *CNY*

A palace cast iron bank, Moore, by Ives, 8in (20cm) high.
£1,100-1,500 *CNY*

A tank and cannon
money box, English,
c1918, 10in (25cm) wide.
£250-280 *HAL*

A lion and monkey
money box, American,
c1883, 9½in (24cm) high.
£300-350 *HAL*

A cast iron house money
box, American, 19thC,
5½in (14cm) high.
£40-50 *HAL*

A William Tell money box, American,
c1885, 10½in (26.5cm) wide.
£250-300 *HAL*

A Hall's Excelsior Bank,
c1869, 5½in (14cm) high.
£150-200 *HAL*

Cash Registers

A National brass £.s.d.
cash register, 17in
(43.5cm) high.
£200-250 *ARC*

A frog money box, American, c1882,
8in (20cm) wide. **£250-300** *HAL*

A money box depicting a
mule entering a barn,
c1880, 8½in (21.5cm)
wide.
£200-250 *HAL*

A National cash register,
American, c1890, 18in
(46cm) high.
£100-150 *ARC*

An Uncle Sam money
box, by Shepard
Hardware Co., some
damage, 11½in (29cm)
high.
£1,000-1,500 *CNY*

Stump Speaker money
bank, by Shepard
Hardware, paint worn
and repairs, 9½in (24cm)
high.
£950-1,000 *CNY*

A National cash register,
1896, 17in (43.5cm) high.
£200-250 *ARC*

Mechanical Music

A 26-key portable reed barrel organ, with eight-air barrel in varnished case with fretwork front panel, 19in (48cm) wide.
£1,300-1,500 *CSK*

A musical box, by Nicole Frères, No. 42303, playing 12 airs, in rosewood veneered case, 22in (56cm) wide. **£1,320-1,500** *CSK*

A Polyphon with single comb, top wind motor and walnut case, with monochrome print in lid, 11in (28cm) wide.
£450-500 *CSK*

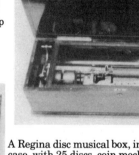

A Regina disc musical box, in an oak case, with 25 discs, coin mechanism removed, 16in (41cm) wide.
£2,600-3,000 *CSK*

A Longue Marche interchangeable cylinder musical box, with Sublime Harmony combs, patent plates for Longue Marche and Sublime Harmony, transfer label of Jesse S. Nimkey, Ludgate Hill, in an amboyna veneered case, c1875, 41in (104cm) wide.
£1,500-2,000 *CSK*

A musical box, by B. H. Abrahams, No. 5745, playing 30 airs, with nickel plated movement, zither attachment, 26in (66cm) wide.
£600-650 *CSK*

A key-wind musical box, No. 12225, playing 24 airs, 23½in (60cm) wide.
£1,500-2,000 *CSK*

A single comb Polyphon Excelsior, No. 7438, in quarter veneered walnut case, colour print inside, with 12 zinc discs, some damage, 16in (41cm) wide. **£1,100-1,500** *CSK*

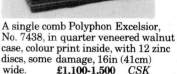

A Polyphon with double combs, in a walnut case, with 13 discs, dampers detached, 15½in (39.5cm) wide. **£650-700** *CSK*

A penny-in-the-slot singing bird in cage, probably by Bontems, the single bird with moving tail, head and beak, in domed brass cage, on giltwood base, 20in (51cm) high. **£1,600-2,000** *CSK*

A Harpe Harmony Piccolo zither musical box, playing 10 operatic and other airs, with tune indicator, tune selector, tune sheet, speed control and zither attachment, in rosewood case, some damage, 26½in (67cm) wide. **£2,800-3,200** *CSK*

A Comet disc musical box, German, the centre drive movement playing on single comb contained in walnut veneered case with top wind motor, lid cracked, with 18 metal discs, c1900, 13in (33cm) wide. **£500-550** *S*

A musical box, playing 8 airs, in ebonised case, with a French clock movement striking on bell and releasing musical tune on the hour, with Bremond tune sheet, some damage, 26in (66cm) wide. **£1,600-2,000** *CSK*

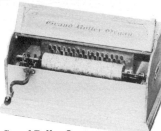

A Grand Roller Organ, with 32-key action in light oak case, with six 13in (33cm) 'cobs'. **£1,600-2,000** *CSK*

A Britannia upright disc musical box, with single comb movement, in walnut 'smoker's cabinet', with 5 discs, 30½in (77.5cm) wide. **£1,000-1,500** *CSK*

A Symphonion disc musical box, German, the driven disc playing on 2 combs, in veneered oak case, with a collection of discs, some damage, c1900, 60in (152cm) high. **£2,700-3,300** *S*

A musical box, playing 8 patriotic and other airs accompanied by 16-key organ, in crossbanded rosewood veneered case, with tune sheet and inlaid lid, 23in (59cm) wide. **£1,700-2,300** *CSK*

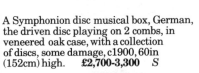

A musical box, by J. H. Heller, No. 6282, playing 6 airs with tune sheet and rosewood grained case, 16in (41cm) wide. **£650-1,000** *CSK*

An Orchestral musical box, No. 1759, by S. Troll Fils, Geneva, playing 8 airs accompanied by drum, castanets, 20-note organ and 6 engraved bells, in grained burr walnut case, parts lacking, 29in (74cm) wide.
£3,800-4,200   *CSK*

A singing bird box, in shaped enamel and silver gilt case, the bird with moving tail, wings and metal beak, 5in (12cm) wide.   **£2,000-2,500**   *CSK*

Gramophones

A Decca gramophone, French, c1920, 11in (28cm) square.   **£90-120**   *Hol*

An Edison Standard phonograph, model A, c1906, 25in (64cm) high.
£525-550   *Hol*

An Edison Gem phonograph, with lid, c1903, 18in (46cm) high.
£375-400   *Hol*

An Edison Bell Puck phonograph, c1901, 14in (36cm) wide.
£350-400   *Hol*

An Industria Induphone 138, c1923, 13in (33cm) wide.   **£300-350**   *Hol*

A Chardin Puck phonograph, French, c1902, 14in (36cm) wide.
£400-450   *Hol*

A Columbia QQ phonograph, with lid, c1903, 15in (38cm) long.
£350-400   *Hol*

A Thorens Cameraphone, c1920, 11in (28cm) wide.
£160-200   *Hol*

A Graphophone Type AB
with floating reproducer,
in oak case, lacks horn.
£450-500   *CSK*

An Edison Standard
phonograph, Model B,
No. 325930, now with
combination pulley,
Model O reproducer with
turn-over stylus bar and
19in (48cm) black
octagonal horn, and
106 wax cylinders.
£465-485   *CSK*

A Lioret Le Merveilleux
phonograph, with
floating card and
Celluloid reproducer and
one cylinder, in maroon
leather covered carton,
lacks drive pulley, 7½in
(19cm) high.
£1,400-1,600   *CSK*

A GECoPhone Type BC
2001 three-valve
receiver, in 'smoker's
cabinet' walnut case with
door enclosing control
panel and battery
compartment below,
dealers trade plaque and
BBC transfer, a
GECoPhone cone
speaker on hexagonal
'lamp stand', in maker's
case, and 2 headphones.
£460-480   *CSK*

A Mikiphone pocket gramophone,
with Mikiphone soundbox, black
composition resonator, and circular
nickel plated casing, in maker's
presentation carton with instruction
booklet, lacks needle tin and
cracked resonator. **£460-480**   *CSK*

An HMV model 193
re-entrant tone chamber
gramophone, No.
1930000104, with 5A
soundbox, oak case,
1930, 44½in (113cm)
high.
£4,000-4,500   *CSK*

A Pathé Democrat phonograph, 18½in
(47cm) high.   **£375-400**   *Hol*

A Type BS coin operated graphophone,
with coin mechanism, floating
reproducer and connector, in oak case,
flexible parts lacking.
£700-1,000   *CSK*

FURTHER READING
The Illustrated History of Talking Machines, by
Daniel Marty, Edita.
Collecting Phonographs and Gramophones, by
Christopher Proudfoot, Christie's.

A Standard Model A disc
talking machine, with
Columbia pattern tone
arm, small flower horn,
oak case and replacement
turntable.
£330-360   *CSK*

A double spring Monarch gramophone, by Gramophone & Typewriter Ltd, in oak case with bolt-brake, 10in (25.5cm) turntable, goose neck tone-arm, early bevel-drive motor with vertical governor, G & T transfer and brass witch's hat horn, c1904, 22½in (57cm) long. **£750-1,000** *CSK*

Like many of the first tone-arm models this has the back bracket mounted off centre to conceal the holes drilled for a travelling arm support. The soundbox now fitted is a later His Master's Voice Exhibition.

An HMV Model 5 horn gramophone with double spring motor, 10in (25.5cm) turntable, HMV Exhibition soundbox, oak case and green Morning Glory horn, c1915. **£900-1,000** *CSK*

An Algraphone console cabinet gramophone, No. M.135, Serial No. 387, in mahogany case, with serpentine record compartments, the mechanism with Motophon electric motor and Graham turntable, Sonat soundbox, Gramolith tone-arm with automatic stop, lacks horn, 61in (55cm) wide. **£500-600** *CSK*

A table Polyphon, with single comb movement, speed regulator, top-wind motor, colour print and inlaid lid, with one disc and transfer of William Whiteley, Westbourne Grove, 11in (28cm). **£660-700** *CSK*

An HMV Model 10 automatic gramophone, with 5A soundbox, re-entrant tone chamber and electric motor driving turntable and record selector mechanism, in oak case of Jacobean design with panel doors enclosing fretwork grille, with maker's instruction leaflet, 1930, 41in (104cm) high. **£1,600-2,000** *CSK*

The Model 10 appears never to have been included in a Gramophone Company catalogue. The instruction book included with this example has a printer's code for November 1929. According to an internal report of March 1929, the model was due to be introduced on September 1st of that year, with a manufacturing schedule of 2,500 for the first year. Presumably this was never achieved, and both the Automatic 1/2 and 10 were replaced by the all-electric W12 and W15 earlier than had been expected in 1929.

An E. M. Ginn Expert Junior gramophone, with Expert four-spring soundbox, electric motor and painted papier mâché horn, 24in (61.5cm) diam. **£1,400-1,800** *CSK*

An HMV Monarch gramophone with double spring motor, in oak case, 10in (25.5cm) turntable, goose neck tone arm and fluted oak horn, 1910, no soundbox. **£1,200-1,500** *CSK*

An EMG Mark 10a hand made gramophone, with EMG four-spring soundbox, electric motor, originally clockwork, in crossbanded oak veneered case and painted papier mâché horn, c1930, 28½in (72.5cm) diam. **£2,400-2,800** *CSK*

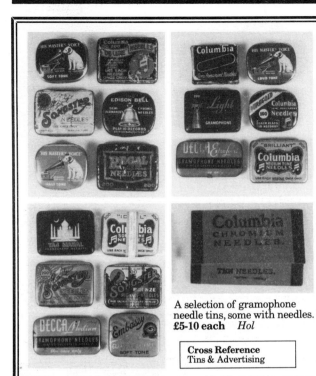

A selection of gramophone needle tins, some with needles.
£5-10 each   *Hol*

Cross Reference
Tins & Advertising

His Master's Voice fibre needle cutter, 4in (10cm) wide.
£25-30   *Hol*

A Gramophone fibre needle sharpener, originally 7s 4d, 5in (12.5cm) wide.
£25-30   *Hol*

Two 45rpm postcard records of Stairway of Love, featuring Clovelly, and Glorious Devon featuring Brixham, 1960s.   **£6-8 each**   *Hol*

A Columbia record cleaner, 3in (7.5cm) diam.
£12-15   *Hol*

A 'His Master's Voice' Speed Tester, 2½in (6.5cm) long.
£25-30   *Hol*

A selection of picture discs used for advertising, c1930.
£15-20 each   *HEW*

A Fisher Price music box record player, c1970, 8in (20cm) high.
£12-15 *Hol*

A painted papier mâché model of Nipper, 13½in (35cm) high.
£900-1,000 *CSK*

A Palais Royale musical stand, formed as a harp with dolphin top rail, the brass base with mother-of-pearl top containing a musical movement with sectional comb, signed Alibert 4941, playing 2 airs, 7in (18.5cm) wide.
£1,600-2,000 *CSK*

A selection of picture discs used for advertising, c1930.
£15-20 each *HEW*

A selection of phonograph cylinders, 4½ to 5in (11 to 12.5cm) high.
£5-10 each *Hol*

A reproduction Edison advertisement, 15 by 9in (38 by 22.5cm).
£18-20 *Hol*

A selection of gramophone needles in tins.
£4-6 each *ROS*

A set of dictaphone cylinders, 7in (17.5cm) high. **£65-70** *Hol*

A Mastertone children's gramophone, c1920, 17½in (44.5cm) high.
£275-300 *Hol*

Musical Instruments

A B-flat clarinet, branded René Duval to the bell, in case, with 3 mouth pieces.
£50-60 *CSK*

A silver plated alto saxophone, engraved Henri Selmer 4, Place Dancourt, Paris, No. 16900, in fitted case bearing maker's label.
£500-600 *CSK*

A silver plated alto saxophone by Paul Cavour, Paris, and engraved Invicta Model, in case.
£200-300 *CSK*

A Simple System rosewood oboe d'amore, branded Gold Medal 1878. G. Mahillon London & Brussels, lacking crook, in case, c1880, sounding length 23½in (59.7cm).
£450-550 *CSK*

An eight-keyed ebony and ivory mounted clarinet, each section branded A. Snazel, Colchester, c1840, sounding length 23in (58.5cm).
£150-200 *CSK*

Ambrose Snazel, 1832-50. Dealers at Culver Street, Colchester.

A clarinet, each section branded Hawkes & Son Denman Street, Piccadilly Circus, London, uncased, early 20thC.
£10-15 *CSK*

An alto saxophone, engraved Henri Selmer Paris, in case, and some Big Band ephemera relating to the history of the instrument.
£700-800 *CSK*

An ebony oboe, branded A. Santoni, Paris, in case, and a nickel plated Boehm system flute engraved René Duval, No. 74355, in case, sounding length 24in (61cm).
£180-200 *CSK*

An alto saxophone by Martin, in a matt and polished silver finish, engraved Martin Elkhart Ind. to the bell and numbered 80890, Low Pitch, in case.
£275-325 *CSK*

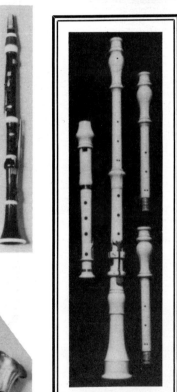

l. A one-keyed ivory flageolet by F. Tabard, gold square padded key and gold mounts, c1830. **£1,800-2,000**

c. A two-keyed ivory oboe by J. Panormo, with silver gilt octagonal padded keys, and 3 corps de réchange lengths.
£3,300-3,500 *C*

An Italian mandolin, inlaid with tortoiseshell and mother-of-pearl, labelled Michele Maratea, Napoli 1897, in case.
£60-100 *CSK*

An Italian mandolin, inlaid with mother-of-pearl and tortoiseshell with central butterfly motif and labelled Stridente, Napoli, in fitted case.
£100-120 *CSK*

An Italian viola, labelled Barbieri Bruno Liutaio in Mantova/anno 1960 n. 56, the scroll plain, the varnish of a golden orange colour, length of back, 16in (41cm).
£1,800-2,000 *C*

A viola d'amore, unlabelled, the pegbox of a later date surmounted with a carved human head, set for 7 playing and 7 sympathetic strings, the varnish of a golden brown colour, 14½in (37cm) string length, in case.
£900-1,000 *C*

A Triola mechanical zither, with hand operated roll mechanism and 6 rolls, 22in (56cm) wide. **£850-1,000** *CSK*

A mahogany, walnut and mother-of-pearl inlaid five-string tenor banjo, branded The Barnes & Mullins 3A Catalogue No. 1498.
£120-150 *CSK*

A piano accordion, in pearlised plastic, German, 1930s.
£60-75 *PC*

A piano accordion, with case.
£70-80 *ROS*

A flat backed mandolin banjo, in a case bearing the maker's label Arthur O. Windsor, Musical Instrument Manufacturer, 95 Newhall Street, Birmingham, length of back 11in (28cm).
£130-150 *CSK*

MAKE THE MOST OF MILLERS
Price ranges in this book reflect what one should expect to *pay* for a similar example. When selling, however, one should expect to receive a lower figure. This will fluctuate according to a dealer's stock, saleability at a particular time, etc. It is always advisable, when selling, to approach a reputable specialist dealer or an auction house which has specialist sales.

Oriental

A pair of Kutani vases, 1920s, 2in (5cm) high.
£35-45 *BOW*

An ivory netsuke of 2 seated boys playing go, the details stained black, signed Ryo, 2in (5cm) wide. **£550-600** *CSK*

An ivory netsuke of a recumbent open mouthed karashishi, stained black, age cracks, 2in (5cm) long.
£300-400 *CSK*

A Japanese Banko ware bisque porcelain saki pot, depicting a boy playing with a tiger, impressed mark, late 19thC, Meiji period, 3in (7.5cm) high.
£35-45 *BOW*

A wood netsuke of a dancing actor, signed Kiyonobu, 18thC, 3in (9cm) high.
£100-150 *CSK*

A stained ivory netsuke of a monkey, seated on the back of a horse, stained black, 1in (2.5cm) long.
£200-250 *CSK*

A stag antler netsuke, carved and pierced with a long tailed bird, reverse with rockwork, worn, 2in (5cm) high.
£300-350 *CSK*

Netsuke

A stained ivory netsuke of a coiled snake resting on top of a human skull, 1½in (3.5cm) long.
£300-400 *CSK*

A Narikado horn netsuke kakihan, with a cloisonné cockerel with green, white, black and yellow plumage, signed on a gilt metal tablet, 18thC, 2in (5cm) wide.
£780-850 *CSK*

A stained ivory netsuke of a namazu, with open mouth and swollen abdomen, age cracks, 2in (5cm) long.
£400-450 *CSK*

Japanese Satsuma ware

A pair of vases, signed in red, c1920, Taisho period, 10in (25cm) high.
£140-180 *BOW*

A vase, gold seal mark, c1920, Taisho-Showa period, 8in (20cm) high.
£80-100 *HOW*

A dish, mid-19thC, Edo period, 7½in (19cm) diam. **£35-45** *BOW*

A vase, c1880, Meiji period, 7in (17.5cm) high. **£70-90** *BOW*

A vase, signed Denzan, gold and black mark, c1900, Meiji period, 6½in (16.5cm) high. **£120-140** *BOW*

A vase, mid-19thC, Edo period, 14in (35.5cm) high. **£120-140** *BOW*

A pair of lozenge shaped vases, brown seal mark of Nihon, c1920, Taisho period, 2½in (6cm) high. **£50-60** *BOW*

A vase, c1930, Showa period, 10½in (26.5cm) high £65-85 *BOW*

A saki bottle with scenes from Japanese opera, damaged, mid-19thC, Edo period, 6in (15cm) high. **£50-60** *BOW*

A pair of vases, signed in gold Denzan with a round shimazu mon of Satsuma Province, c1915, Taisho period, 8in (20cm) high. **£180-220** *BOW*

A vase, signed Dai Nihon Satsuma Yaki with shimazu mon in red, late 19thC, Meiji period, 6½in (16.5cm) high. **£70-80** *BOW*

A pair of unusual vases with gods, demons and animals moulded in relief, c1920, Taisho period, 8in (20cm) high.
£380-420 *BOW*

A koro, c1920, Taisho period, 4in (10cm) high.
£75-85 *BOW*

A koro (incense burner), with Disciples of Buddha pattern, gold and brown seal mark, c1915, Tokyo School, 5in (12.5cm) high.
£150-175 *BOW*

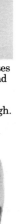

A Tokyo style bowl, Disciples of Buddha, Taisho period, c1915, 4½in (11.5cm) wide.
£50-60 *BOW*

A basket, c1930, Showa period, 7in (17.5cm) high.
£30-40 *BOW*

A vase, signed Kyoto Yaxi, seal mark, c1910, Taisho period, 5½in (13cm) high.
£65-85 *BOW*

A saki flask, with a scene from a Japanese opera, mid-19thC, Edo period, 6in (15cm) high.
£70-85 *BOW*

A Rakan figure, a Disciple of Buddha holding a bowl, enamelled in gosu blue, brown and black, early/mid-19thC, Edo period, 9in (23cm) high.
£100-120 *BOW*

Oriental Snuff Bottles

A rock crystal snuff bottle, c1850.
£700-800 *S(HK)*

A pair of Tokyo style vases, with Disciples of the Buddha, seal mark in red Chochuzan, c1915, Taisho period, 8in (20cm) high.
£280-320 *BOW*

> **Cross Reference**
> Ceramics

A marbled lacquer snuff
bottle and dish, c1850.
£1,000-2,000   *S(HK)*

A glass snuff bottle and
dish, c1800.
£1,200-2,200   *S(HK)*

A glass overlay snuff
bottle, 18thC.
£2,500-3,000   *S(HK)*

A bamboo snuff bottle
and dish, c1850.
£3,000-4,000   *S(HK)*

A 'peanut' agate snuff
bottle, c1825.
£2,500-3,500   *S(HK)*

A walrus ivory snuff
bottle and dish, c1850.
£2,300-3,300   *S(HK)*

A miniature ivory snuff
bottle, c1800, 1in (3cm)
high.
£1,400-2,400   *S(HK)*

A moulded porcelain
snuff bottle, with
immortals crossing
a sea, levitating
and watching,
mark and period
of Jiaqing.
£300-400   *S(S)*

A porcelain snuff bottle,
with six-character seal
mark of Qianlong in
iron-red on base, c1850.
£850-950   *S(HK)*

A cloisonné enamel snuff
bottle, Qianlong period.
£2,500-3,500   *S(HK)*

A porcelain snuff bottle,
seal mark and period of
Qianlong.
£5,000-6,000   *S(HK)*

A glass snuff bottle
by Bi Rongjiu,
signed and dated
Autumn 1898.
£1,100-2,100   *S(HK)*

A chalcedony snuff
bottle, c1850.
£700-800   *S(HK)*

A miniature glass snuff bottle, c1850, 1½in (3.5cm) high.
£1,000-2,000 *S(HK)*

A porcelain snuff bottle and dish, Daoguang period, three-character mark an yu tang on bottle, shende tang zhi on foot of dish.
£1,800-2,800 *S(HK)*

A cinnabar lacquer snuff bottle, carved with 4 figures in a landscape.
£250-350 *S(S)*

An amber snuff bottle, c1800.
£2,000-3,000 *S(HK)*

A moulded porcelain snuff bottle, reticulated with dragon and phoenix and covered in a coral enamel imitating cinnabar lacquer, mark and period of Jiaqing.
£325-375 *S(S)*

A pair of blue and white miniature snuff bottles, c1850, 1in (3cm) high.
£1,800-2,800 *S(HK)*

A lacquered wood snuff bottle, c1850.
£1,400-2,000 *S(HK)*

A miniature pewter snuff bottle, c1850, 1½in (3.5cm) high.
£500-700 *S(HK)*

A jade snuff bottle, Qianlong period.
£1,300-2,300 *S(HK)*

A carved glass snuff bottle, c1800.
£1,100-2,100 *S(HK)*

A 'thumbprint' agate snuff bottle, the random pattern well centred on each side, c1755.
£300-350 *S(S)*

A Peking glass snuff bottle, each side carved in low relief with a peach, c1800.
£360-400 *S(S)*

A carved ivory snuff bottle, worked with numerous figures in and before pavilions, stained.
£350-400 *S(S)*

Cross Reference
Colour Section

Paint Boxes

A prize colour box, by Newman,
London, c1875, 9in (22.5cm) long.
£150-200 *JAS*

A paint box, by Driver &
Shaw, c1770, 15in (38cm)
long. **£2,000-2,800** *JAS*

A draughtsman's colour
box, paints broken,
c1900, 10in (25cm) wide.
£50-100 *JAS*

A mahogany paint box,
by Reeves & Son,
original water pot, c1855.
£580-700 *JAS*

A paint box, by Reeves,
c1781, 9in (22.5cm) long.
£450-500 *JAS*

A reward box, by Reeves
& Son, c1878, 8½in
(21cm) long.
£475-550 *JAS*

A mahogany caddy box, by
Reeves & Son, containing brushes,
c1881, 9in (22.5cm) wide.
£350-440 *JAS*

A draughtsman's set by
Winsor & Newton,
c1882, 10in (25cm) wide.
£350-500 *JAS*

A mahogany paint box,
by Winsor & Newton
Ltd., original water pot,
c1910, 9in (22.5cm) wide.
£565-700 *JAS*

A paint box, by
C. Raynhams, c1770, 7in
(17.5cm) long.
£480-500 *JAS*

A student's paint box, by
Reeves, c1900.
£50-95 *JAS*

A reward box, by Charles
Roberson, c1856, 9in
(22.5cm) wide.
£185-200 *JAS*

A mahogany Landseer paint box, by
Reeves, c1890, 9in (22.5cm) wide.
£190-200 *JAS*

An empty paint box,
c1881, 8in (20cm) wide.
£40-50 *JAS*

A colour box, by James
Newman, early 19thC,
9in (22.5cm) wide.
£250-350 *JAS*

A colour box, by
James Newman,
London, c1785,
9in (22.5cm)
wide.
£550-800 *JAS*

A paint box, by Winsor &
Newton, original water
pot, crayons, etc., c1870,
9in (22.5cm) wide.
£360-550 *JAS*

A mahogany caddy box,
by Newman, original
palettes in top, c1840,
10in (25cm) wide.
£480-550 *JAS*

A mahogany paint box,
by Reeves & Son,
c1851, 9in (22.5cm)
wide.
£285-300
JAS

A colour box, by James
Newman, original water
pot, some paints missing,
c1781, 9in (22.5cm) wide.
£400-450 *JAS*

A Reeves pocket
paint box,
c1900, 6 by
4½in (15 by
11cm).
£90-100 *JAS*

A Victorian magazine
case of drawing
instruments, by A. G.
Thornton, with
G. Rowney paints, c1869,
15 by 8in (38 by 20cm).
£750-850 *JAS*

A Reeves box of watercolours in poor condition, c1880, 7 by 4in (18 by 10cm).
£25-30 *JAS*

A George Rowney colour box, c1880, 7½ by 4in (19 by 10cm).
£30-40 *JAS*

A paint box, without lid, with famous Griffin or Sea Lion design, c1870, 4 by 1½in (10 by 4cm).
£50-65 *JAS*

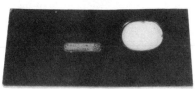

A travelling pocket paint palette, by Roberson & Co., Long Acre, London, c1855, 7½ by 3½in (19 by 9cm).
£70-80 *JAS*

A Reeves olive wood thumb hole easel box, c1895, 12 by 8in (31 by 20cm).
£280-400 *JAS*

A Lechertier Barbe & Co., box of colours, with green leather tooled lid, c1878, 11 by 6in (28 by 15cm).
£480-550 *JAS*

A Winsor & Newton quarter pan paint box, mid-19thC.
£85-100 *JAS*

The Claude Hayes artist's palette, by Reeves & Son Ltd., c1910, 11½ by 9in (29 by 23cm).
£120-150 *JAS*

A Reeves & Son watercolour pocket paint box, with original japanned finish, 5in (13cm) high.
£65-75 *BS*

A Winsor & Newton, quarter pan paint box, c1880, 3 by 2in (8 by 5cm).
£70-100 *JAS*

A Victorian colour box, by Reeves, c1880, 6 by 3in (15 by 8cm).
£15-20 *JAS*

Palettes

Two Victorian mahogany palettes by
J. W. Love, Glasgow, 8½ by 5in (21 by
13cm). **£40-50**
9½ by 7½in (24 by 19cm).
£65-75 *JAS*

A late Victorian slide-out
thumb hole oil palette, 12 by
14½in (31 by 37cm).
£120-150 *JAS*

A Victorian Winsor &
Newton, oil colour box,
9½ by 6½in (24 by 16cm).
£160-200 *JAS*

A Reade Brothers artist's
oil colour box, c1820,
16 by 10½in (41 by
26cm).
£435-520 *JAS*

Two Victorian Rowney
porcelain palettes,
originally from paint
boxes.
£100-110 each *JAS*

An unmarked oil colour
box, 15 by 11½in (38 by
29cm).
£120-150 *JAS*

A Reeves travelling
thumb hole palette box,
c1895, 9 by 6in (23 by 15cm).
£190-220 *JAS*

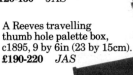

Two Victorian porcelain palettes, large by
Rowney, 7½in (19cm) long.
£100-110
Small, French palette, 5½in (14cm) long.
£95-100 *JAS*

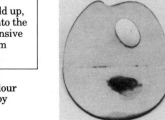

DID YOU KNOW?
Miller's Collectables
Price Guide is
designed to build up,
year by year, into the
most comprehensive
reference system
available.

A chamois
leather covered
travelling
palette for
chalks, c1855,
8in (20cm) long.
£35-45 *JAS*

An unmarked oil colour
box, 14 by 10in (36 by
25cm).
£120-150 *JAS*

Accessories

Two jars of pigments, 'Smalt Dumont' and 'Oxide Ed. Green Chrome', 19thC, 7½in (19cm) high.
£140-160 each *PC*

A selection of tubes of Newman's paints, 3in (8cm) long. **10p-£1 each** *PC*

A black ceramic pestle for grinding pigment, c1880, 4in (10cm) diam.
£45-50 *JAS*

A silver miniature palette, in original case, presented as an award, c1815, 2in (5cm) long.
£600-650 *JAS*

A selection of various 18th and 19thC bottles, 3½ to 4in (9 to 10cm) high.
50p-£1 each *PC*

A brass and leather graining roller, c1815, 4in (10cm) diam.
£95-150 *JAS*

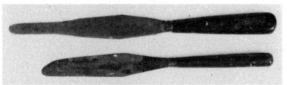

Two C. Roberson palette knives, c1865, 7½ and 9½in (19 and 24cm) long.
£30-50 *JAS*

A selection of 18th and 19thC bottles, 3 to 6½in (8 to 16cm). **£1-7 each** *PC*

A block of sanguine chalk, 19thC.
£70-100 *JAS*

Artist's turpentine tins, 3½in (9cm) high.
£12-15 each *JAS*

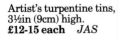

A selection of oil brushes, 14in (36cm) long.
50p-£1 each *PC*

Pigment scoops, with original lapis lazuli and gamboge pigments, c1780.
£50-100 each   *PC*

A nest of ceramic paint saucers, mid-19thC.
£30-35 each   *JAS*

A handkerchief box, 7½in (19cm) sq.
£30-40   *FOB*

A patterned corner unit, 11in (28cm) high.
£55-65   *FOB*

A George IV shaped tray, painted with a flower spray and heightened with gilt, 31in (79cm).
£625-700   *P(O)*

A papier mâché bowl.
£30-40   *FOB*

Papier Mâché

Papier Mâché was often used as a substitute for wood, being cheaper and easier to work. Highly decorative examples exist of many types of useful household furnishings, from small jewellery boxes to tables and even chairs. Elaborate and fine quality decoration is desired by collectors, along with a restrained use of mother-of-pearl inlay, with flowers and birds being especially popular. Trays and drinks coasters are also keenly sought. Damage, and badly repaired damage, can have a disastrous effect on value.

A chinoiserie pattern corner display unit, c1886, 12in (31cm) high.
£75-85   *FOB*

A pair of patterned spill vases, 5in (13cm) high.
£45-50   *FOB*

A daisy patterned plate, c1885, 9in (23cm) diam.
£35-45   *FOB*

A chinoiserie patterned spill vase, c1880, 5in (13cm) high.
£30-35   *FOB*

Two floral patterned powder boxes, 2½ and 3in (6 and 8cm) high. **£30-40 each** *FOB*

A papier mâché and mother-of-pearl platter, handles missing, 10in (25cm) diam. **£40-50** *FOB*

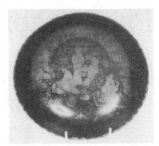

A chinoiserie patterned bowl, c1880, 9in (23cm) diam. **£55-65** *FOB*

Two chinoiserie patterned powder boxes, 2½ and 3in (6 and 8cm) high. **£30-40 each** *FOB*

A crumb tray and brush, 12in (31cm) wide. **£50-60** *FOB*

A French magazine rack, 11½in (29cm) high. **£30-40** *FOB*

A biscuit box, 3in (7.5cm) high. **£25-35** *FOB*

A Victorian glove box, 12in (31cm) long. **£15-20** *SCO*

A glove box, 12in (31cm) long. **£35-40** *FOB*

Patch Boxes

During the 18thC it was extremely fashionable both in England and France to wear beauty spots or patches. These were kept in highly decorated, usually circular, boxes made from precious metals and enamels.

These beauty patches were also used to cover pox marks and scars.

A Staffordshire enamel patch box, the hinged cover inscribed 'I give to receive what will not deceive', around a pendant husk swagged urn with lilac enamel sides and base, some damage, early 19thC. **£70-80** *HSS*

A further selection of patch boxes is featured in previous editions of Miller's Collectables Price Guides, available from Millers Publications.

Photographs

A collection of photographs by various photographers, comprising 17 morocco bound albums, 8 complete with clasps, 1850s and later.
£270-400 *CSK*

A collection of photographs by F. Hollyer, R. Carlyle, E. Gottheil, Brady and others, costume, theatrical, family portraits and mixed travel, 1850s and later.
£310-350 *CSK*

A collection of 16 moroccan leather albums, 13 complete with clasps, 1850s and later.
£310-350 *CSK*

An Edwardian photograph.
£12-15 *COB*

A brass framed photograph by Mrs Dexters, of Lynn, 1860, 3½ by 4½in (9 by 11cm).
£20-30 *MA*

> **Cross Reference**
> Automobilia

A seated nude, 6th plate daguerreotype, in American style embossed paper covered case, c1850.
£650-800 *S*

John Thomson, 'The Crawlers', Woodburytype print, mounted on paper with ruled border in red, modern window mount, c1876, 4½ by 4in (10 by 11cm).
£95-110 *CSK*

A leather wallet photograph frame, 4 by 3in (10 by 8cm).
£30-35 *RE*

Heinz Hajek-Halke, double exposure nude and street scene, c1927, printed later, silver print, titled, signed, dated and inscribed on reverse in ink 'Reprint in original format Heinz Hajek and stamped in ink 'HHH Inventar', 16 by 12in (40 by 30cm).
£720-750 *S*

Edward S. Curtis, 3 orotones, including 'Canon De Chelley-Navaho', 'The Lone Chieftain' and 'The Vanishing Race'.
£4,800-5,500 *S(NY)*

Alexander Gardner, 'A sharpshooter's last sleep, Gettysburg, Pennsylvania', albumen print, on the two-toned sketchbook mount printed with the photographer's credit, copyright and Washington D.C., studio address, title, number 40 and date, matted, 1863, printed c1866, 7 by 9in (17.5 by 23cm).
£2,000-2,500 *S(NY)*

A Victorian tinted photograph in a case, 3 by 4in (8 by 10cm).
£30-40 *PSA*

Eadweard Muybridge, 18 plates from the photographer's Animal Locomotion, including men, women, men on horseback and animals, collotypes, each printed on two-toned folio leaves, 1887.
£1,300-1,500 *S(NY)*

Lewis Morris Rutherfurd, 3 lunar studies, albumen prints, each blind stamped lower left, 'Photo by L.M. Rutherfurd, enl. by A. Brothers', mounted, c1870, each 13½ by 10½in (34 by 26cm).
£900-1,000 *S(NY)*

Henri Cartier-Bresson, a silver print of Marilyn Monroe on the set of The Misfits, 1959, and a portrait of Marilyn Monroe with Arthur Miller, 1950s, the reverse stamped in ink with Fox Photos Ltd credit.
£450-500 *S*

George Hurrell, Jane Russell, 1940s, silver print, mounted on card, 14 by 10½in (36 by 26cm).
£200-400 *S*

Timothy O'Sullivan, 'Grand Canyon, Colorado River, Near Paria Creek, Looking West', albumen print, on the two-toned Wheeler Survey mount, framed, 1872, 11 by 8in (28 by 20cm).
£2,000-2,500 *S(NY)*

A collection of photographs by Scowen & Co., Zangaki and H. Arnoux, of Ceylon and the Near East, 58 albumen prints, 9½ by 7in (24 by 18cm) and 8½ by 11in (21 by 28cm) in an album, 1880s. **£275-300** *CSK*

Robert Frank, 'London 1951', silver print, signed and titled in ink in the margin, the reverse stamped in ink 'Robert Frank archive copyright inscribed all rights reserved' and and dated in ink 'Robert Frank 1980', 11 by 14in (28 by 35cm). **£3,800-4,500** *S*

Milton Greene,
2 photographs of Marilyn
Monroe, each signed and
dated by the
photographer in ink and
with the photographer's
authenticity and
copyright stamps on the
reverse, 1971 and 1978,
each 16 by 20in (41 by
51cm). **£720-800** *S(NY)*

André Kertész, Eiffel
Tower, Paris, 1926,
gelatin silver print,
printed later, signed,
titled and dated in pencil
on the verso, framed,
8 by 10in (20 by 25cm).
£1,000-2,000 *CNY*

W. Grancel Fitz,
Baseball, gelatin silver
print, 1930s, stamped on
the verso, 10½ by 11½in
(26 by 29cm).
£1,100-1,200 *CNY*

Ansel Adams, 'Mt
McKinley and Wonder
Lake, Mt McKinley
National Park, Alaska',
c1947, printed in 1980,
15½ by 19in (39 by
48cm).
£3,500-4,000 *S(NY)*

Philippe Halsman,
3 photographs of Marilyn
Monroe, including the
portrait used for the
cover of Life magazine
1952, signed by the
photographer in pencil
and each with the
photographer's copyright
stamp on the reverse,
matted, 1950s, printed
later, various sizes.
£1,500-2,000 *S(NY)*

Cecil Beaton, self
portrait, silver print,
inscribed on reverse in
ink 'I like this one C.B.',
stamped in ink with
photographer's credit
'Beaton' sitting date
'Jan 8 1951'.
£500-600 *S*

*A hand coloured version
of this image was used for
the back of the paper
wrapper of Cecil Beaton,
Photobiography, London,
1951.*

William Henry Jackson,
'The Portal, entrance to
the San Juan', albumen
print, on a two-toned
mount, printed with the
title and sub title,
'Denver and Rio Grande
Railway–The Scenic
Line of America', matted,
1880s, 22 by 17in (56 by
43cm).
£1,900-2,000 *S(NY)*

Weegee, Murder Scene,
the photographer's
'A. Fellig' credit and date
stamps on the reverse,
matted, framed, 1937,
7½ by 10in (19 by 25cm).
£500-600 *S(NY)*

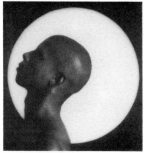

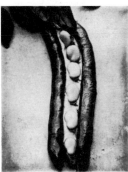

Robert Mapplethorpe, 'André', signed, dated and numbered '1/10' by the photographer in ink in the margin, backed with card, signed by the photographer and titled, dated and numbered in an unidentified hand in ink and with the photographer's copyright stamp on the reverse, matted, framed, 1984, No. 1 in an edition of 10, 15in (38cm) square. **£4,500-5,500** *S(NY)*

Bill Brandt, Abstract Nudes, 2 photographs, each signed by the photographer in ink in the margin, 1958 and 1977, printed later, each 13½ by 11½in (34 by 29cm). **£1,000-1,500** *S(NY)*

Ansel Adams, 'Merced River Cliffs, Autumn, Yosemite Valley, California', c1939, printed in 1980, 15½ by 19½in (39 by 49cm). **£2,000-2,500** *S(NY)*

Charles Jones, 'Bean Longpod', silver gelatin print, titled and monogrammed 'C.J.' in pencil on reverse, c1900, 8 by 10in (20 by 25cm). **£700-900** *S*

Weegee, Mona Lisa Distortions, a series of 13 photographs of the Mona Lisa smoking pot, one signed and one titled 'POT' by the photographer in ink in the margin, 12 with gouache over painting on the image, 12 with the circular 'Weegee' stamp and one with the photographer's 451 West 47th Street, New York City studio stamp on the reverse, 1960s, each 8½ by 7in (21 by 18cm). **£2,300-3,000** *S(NY)*

Robert Mapplethorpe, 'Ken Moody', signed by the photographer and titled, dated and numbered '1/10' in an unidentified hand in ink and with the photographer's copyright stamp on the reverse, matted, framed, 1984, No. 1 in an edition of 10, 15in (38cm) square. **£4,500-5,500** *S(NY)*

DID YOU KNOW?

Miller's Collectables Price Guide is designed to build up, year by year, into the most comprehensive reference system available.

David Bailey, 'Isle of Skye 82', silver print, signed and dated in margin 'D. Bailey 82', flush mounted on card, signed on reverse in ink and stamped in ink with photographer's credit, completed in ink with title and confirming an edition of 25 printed in 1982 by the photographer, 12 by 16in (30 by 41cm). **£200-300** *S*

Robert Frank, 'Rodeo New York City', c1955, silver print, flush mounted on board, the reverse with 4 Museum of Modern Art, New York exhibition loan labels, one signed in ink 'R. Frank' and stamped in ink with Robert Frank Archive credit, 13½ by 8½in (34 by 21cm). **£9,000-10,500** *S*

Photograph Frames

A photograph frame decorated with roses, 8 by 6in (20 by 15cm).
£55-65   *BG*

A brass photograph frame, c1900, 3½ by 2½in (9 by 6cm).
£20-30   *FOB*

A silver and paste photograph frame, 2 by 1½in (5 by 4cm).
£25-35   *FOB*

A Victorian porcelain photograph frame, 5½in (14cm) square.
£45-55   *BG*

A photograph frame decorated with daisies, 6in (15cm) square.
£45-55   *BG*

A photograph frame decorated with heather, 8 by 6in (20 by 15cm).
£55-65   *BG*

An Art Nouveau photograph frame, Birmingham 1910, 7in (18cm) high.
£200-300   *ROS*

A brass photograph frame, c1900, 4 by 3½in (10 by 9cm).
£30-40   *FOB*

A Continental porcelain photograph frame, c1890, 6½in (16cm) high.
£40-50   *FOB*

A photograph frame from Great Yarmouth, 6½ by 5in (16 by 13cm).
£45-55   *BG*

A Victorian rosewood oval picture frame, 4½in (11cm) high.
£25-35   *FOB*

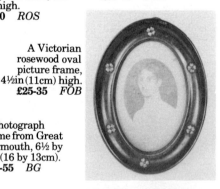

A ceramic photograph frame, with green border decorated with roses, 8 by 5in (20 by 13cm).
£55-65   *BG*

A photograph frame decorated with roses, 6½ by 5in (16 by 13cm).
£45-55   *BG*

A pair of French 'Poker Work' frames, painted in green and orange, with Art Nouveau prints of girls dancing, c1910.
£250-270 *HOW*

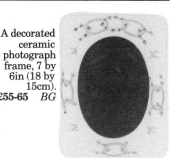

A decorated ceramic photograph frame, 7 by 6in (18 by 15cm).
£55-65 *BG*

A ceramic photograph frame decorated with roses, 10 by 8in (25 by 20cm).
£65-70 *BG*

A photograph frame with poppies, 6in (15cm) square. **£45-55** *BG*

An Art Nouveau painted picture frame, 9in (23cm) high.
£40-45 *HEW*

An Art Nouveau metal photograph frame, c1900.
£40-45 *COB*

Playing Cards

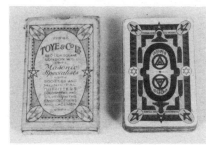

A pack of Masonic cards, with box, c1950.
£5-7 *COL*

Three packs of advertising playing cards, Persil, Walpamur and Bryant & May, 1970s.
£2-5 each *COL*

'Jeu des Nouveaux Cris de Paris', a deck of 32 hand coloured engraved cards, in original pictorial box, c1880. **£450-500** *CSK*

Four packs of advertising playing cards, Castella, Woodbine, Kingsway and Bachelor, 1950-70. **£2.50-4 each** *COL*

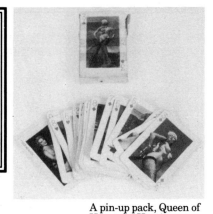

A pin-up pack, Queen of Hearts by Harrison Marks, c1950. **£6-8** *COL*

Three packs of miniature playing cards for children, patience cards in wrapper, unused, 1930, others 1950. **£2-4 each** *COL*

Police

Police helmet plates. **£8-12 each**
Isle of Man plate. **£5-7** *COB*

A further selection of Police items is featured in previous editions of Miller's Collectables Price Guides, available from Millers Publications.

Portrait Miniatures & Silhouettes

An 18thC miniature of General Holwell, the reverse with a lock of hair, 2in (5cm) high. **£610-650** *CSK*

J. T. Holwell, Lt. Governor of Calcutta, one of the 23 who survived out of 146 confined in the Black Hole by the Nabob A.D. 1756, was born A.D. 1700, died 1798.

A pair of bronzed silhouettes of William and Elizabeth Mabson, by the Hubard Gallery, impressed marks, in ebonised frames, 10½in (27cm). **£350-450** *S(S)*

A miniature of a lady, enamel, in a fitted red leather circular case, school of Jean-François Soiron, 2½in (6cm) diam. **£440-500** *CSK*

An Officer of the Twentieth Foot Regiment, with forward-combed brown hair, wearing scarlet jacket, gilt epaulettes and white cross-belt, English School, c1835, in papier mâché frame, 3in (8cm).
£350-400 *S(S)*

A lady, Austrian School c1840, with gilt metal frame, 2½in (7cm) high.
£250-300 *C*

A lady called Mrs Allen, wearing a pink ribboned white dress, by Maria Isabella Pitt, signed on reverse, 1850, cracked, in gilt frame, 5in (13cm).
£210-300 *S(S)*

A silhouette portrait of a gentleman, in a papier mâché frame, c1815, 4½ by 4in (11 by 10cm).
£85-95 *HOW*

An Officer, wearing scarlet jacket, silver epaulettes, white cross-belt with badge of the 16th Bengal Infantry Regiment, yellow collar, by Frederick Buck, c1815, in gilt frame, 2½in (7cm).
£400-450 *S(S)*

A gentleman, in blue coat edged in gold, gilt wood frame, attributed to Samuel Finney, 2in (5cm) high.
£90-120 *CSK*

An Italian portrait miniature, octagonal on bloodstone, the gentleman wearing traditional dress with white collar, 17thC.
£360-400 *Bon*

A lady, oil on copper, the reverse with signature Rocco Borri, Italian School, c1700, in carved gilt wood frame, 3½in (9cm) high.
£350-400 *CSK*

Two children of the Hastings family, by William Egley 1798-1870, Lord Henry and Lady Constance, signed on reverse with the address 75 Connaught Terrace and dated 1844 and 1845, 2in (5cm) high. **£800-1,000** *C*

A pair of bronzed silhouettes of John and Mary Mabson, by the Hubard Gallery, impressed mark, in ebonised frames, 10½in (27cm).
£470-550 *S(S)*

A silhouette of a gentleman by John Miers, with verre églomisé border and turned ebonised frame, the reverse with Miers trade label No. 11, creased and small tears, c1795.
£650-700 *S(S)*

A miniature of a lady, wearing a white dress, in a carved ivory frame, 19thC.
£280-350 *Bon*

An enamel portrait of Admiral Barrington, with the inscription 'Admiral Barrington 1722 Seat Painter', in gilt metal frame.
£400-500 *Bon*

A silhouette portrait of a gentleman, in a papier mâché frame, c1820, 5½ by 5in (14 by 13cm).
£80-90 *HOW*

An oval miniature of a gentleman wearing the Order of the Garter, a yellow jacket with white ruff and a blue cloak, in white metal frame, 5½in (14cm). **£400-500** *Bon*

A silhouette and drawn-in ink portrait of a gentleman, commemorating his death, in a papier mâché frame, c1815, 4½ by 4in (11 by 10cm).
£110-150 *HOW*

School of Cosway, Mr H. Wood, in gold cased oval pendant frame, c1790, 2½in (6cm) high.
£600-700 *CSK*

A silhouette cut-out portrait of a young girl, in a papier mâché frame, c1820, 4½ by 4in (11 by 10cm).
£90-100 *HOW*

Cross Reference
Papier Mâché

Madame Sophie, in yellow dress, in gilt metal easel frame with paste border, after Jean-Marc Nattier, 2in (5cm) high.
£275-300 *CSK*

Madame Sophie, 1734-82, was the daughter of Louis XV of France.

Major General Sir Charles Bruce K.C.B., in scarlet and green uniform with gold epaulettes, by William Wood, inscribed on the reverse, 3in (8cm) high, in fitted red leather case.
£2,000-2,500 *CSK*

An Austrian Officer, wearing blue jacket and sash, silver epaulettes and scarlet cloak, watercolour on card, c1815, in gilt frame, 5½in (14cm).
£350-400 *S(S)*

A lady, wearing a white dress with a mauve ribbon, English School, c1800, in gilt frame with hair reverse, 2½in (7cm).
£500-550 *S(S)*

A Continental cigarette case, with coat-of-arms engraved on front, and hidden compartment inside revealing a naked beauty, import marks for Birmingham 1909, 3½in (9cm) wide.
£770-850 *CSK*

Postcards

Reproduction postcards are currently very popular, both as usable cards to send and as modern collectables for the future. Prices vary from 50p upwards. The original cards will be about £2-5 each, depending of course on condition.

The 'teddy' postcards are charming enough to be collectable at any time.

A card. **50p-£5** *ChL*

Two Hearts That Beat As One.
50p-£5 *ChL*

A teddy fishing.
50p-£5 *ChL*

A birthday card.
50p-£5 *ChL*

Four cards showing a teddy bear in different situations.
50p-£5 *ChL*

A card.
50p-£5 *ChL*

A Christmas card.
50p-£5 *ChL*

Best Christmas Wishes.
50p-£5 *ChL*

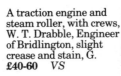

A traction engine and
steam roller, with crews,
W. T. Drabble, Engineer
of Bridlington, slight
crease and stain, G.
£40-60 *VS*

A steam lorry with
election posters,
Canterbury.
£150-200 *VS*

Sutton-on-Trent floods, 1912.
£20-30 *VS*

A traction engine smash,
Tiverton, Devon,
Sept. 1st 1907, VG.
£70-90 *VS*

A horse drawn removal
van, Joseph Whittle,
Bolton, VG.
£25-35 *VS*

Steam cleansing vehicle, Bootle Corporation, EX
to MT.   **£40-60** *VS*

Accident to a Steam Roller at Chislehurst,
November 12, 1912, slight corner crease, G.
£70-100 *VS*

Steam lorry, slight album corner marks, VG.
£40-60 *VS*

Steam lorry, Sheldon & Co., of Osney Mills, Oxford, outside A. W. Neames, Baker, of Towersey, some scuffing, G to VG.
£40-60 *VS*

Horse drawn delivery wagon, Worksop, slight album corner marks, VG. **£30-50** *VS*

Steam roller with road laying gang, published Gravesend 1910, sent by driver, very slight creasing, G. **£38-52** *VS*

Steam lorries, plain back, slight album corner marks, G.
£20-30 *VS*

Steam traction lorry, by Worthing Portrait Co., very slight fading, VG.
£50-70 *VS*

Oldham Corporation Cleansing Department
lorries, EX to MT.
£40-60 *VS*

Floods at Maidenhead, published by Bill Series,
album corner marks, G to VG.
£40-60 *VS*

Steam roller and caravan, by Bantock, VG to EX.
£40-60 *VS*

A gypsy encampment at East Wyckham, slight
fading, G.   **£25-35** *VS*

Country Districts Supplies, Maidstone, some staining
to reverse and minor creasing, G.
£30-40 *VS*

Sinking a well,
Stanerwick,
Wiltshire, note
on reverse
'1st well –
3,500,000
million gals a
day', G.
£20-30 *VS*

International
Stores,
Reading,
by May, VG.
£20-35 *VS*

Marston's Pale Ale,
advertisement, some
foxing and knocks, G.
£16-22 *VS*

Spanish Civil War,
propaganda poster card,
slight corner rounding, G.
£65-85 *VS*

With Captain Scott at
the South Pole, Fry's
advertisement, VG to
EX.
£25-35 *VS*

Shop Front, Star
Provisions, by J. Thomas
of Swansea, G to VG.
£15-20 *VS*

A selection of 1920s nudes.
£1-3 each *FOB*

Shop fronts, W. Smellie, VG.
£15-20 *VS*

A Perfect Breakfast Table, Fry's advert, slight foxing to reverse, G.
£16-22 *VS*

Footballers in Training, Oxo advert, sepia, G to VG.
£25-50 *VS*

A tram at Cambourne, Cornwall, slight creasing and fading, G.
£20-30 *VS*

Trial tram trip, Hastings, Sussex, July 1905, G.
£25-35 *VS*

An advertisement for Font-Romeu, entitled Golf in the High Mountains, by Naudy, with advertisement for the Grand Hotel to reverse, French, G to VG.
£25-45 *VS*

Delivery van, very slight corner crease, G.
£30-40 *VS*

Children opening cupboard full of Fry's, very slight album corner marks, VG.
£18-25 *VS*

Delivery van, Halifax Corporation, slight corner crease, G to VG.
£25-35 *VS*

Delivery lorry, E. Duckney of Halifax, VG to EX. **£25-35** *VS*

The Titanic leaving Southampton, VG.
£50-80 *VS*

MAKE THE MOST OF MILLER'S
Condition is absolutely vital when assessing the value of any item. Damaged pieces appreciate much less than perfect examples. However, a rare, desirable piece may command a high price even when damaged.

Posy Holders

A Victorian posy holder, with wirework bowl and looped handle, white metal vine leaves, applied with 5 hanging bunches of grapes, with chain and finger loop attached, 5in (13cm).
£460-500 *CSK*

An Ekco AD65 brown Bakelite radio, 1934.
£750-850 *RC*

An Ekco AD76 brown Bakelite radio, 1935.
£750-850 *RC*

A late Victorian cornet shaped posy holder, with chain finger loop and pin attached, George Unite, Birmingham 1897, 5in (13cm).
£420-500 *CSK*

A McMichael radiogram, in good working order, 18½in (47cm) wide.
£75-85 *ROS*

A Philco radio, 1931, 16in (41cm) high.
£225-275 *Hol*

A further selection of posy holders is featured in previous editions of Miller's Collectables Price Guides, available from Millers Publications.

Radios

A G.E.C. AC37 brown Bakelite radio, 1936.
£350-450 *RC*

A Canadian DeForest-Crosley set, motor tuned, 1938. **£850-950** *RC*

A Mullard MB3 battery receiver, 1934.
£350-450 *RC*

A Philips 634C
superinductance
receiver, 1933.
£850-950 *RC*

An Art Deco Pye walnut
radio, with rising sun
design.
£250-300 *GIL*

A Bush radio DAC 90,
c1950, 12in (31cm) wide.
£55-65 *Hol*

A Ekco AC76 brown
Bakelite cased radio, in
working order, designed
by Wells Coates and
produced c1934, 16in
(41cm) high.
£300-400 *C(S)*

A Philco 444 black
Bakelite people's set,
1936.
£750-850 *RC*

A Regentone A353 radio,
1950.
£200-300 *RC*

An Emor Globe
AC100, in
chrome, 1946.
£1,200-1,700 *RC*

An R.G.D. 1046 luxury
radiogram, 1947.
£900-2,000 *RC*

A Ferranti 145 brown
Bakelite set, 1945.
£450-550 *RC*

A Trans-Oceanic Zenith
radio, American, late
1940s, 17in (43cm) wide.
£90-120 *AAM*

A Ferranti 146
brown Bakelite
set, 1946.
£350-450 *RC*

A Motorola
portable valve
radio, 1950s,
9½ by 13in
(24 by 33cm).
£200-250
AAM

A Ducastel Ondine radio set, with mirror dial, French, 1950s.
£250-350 *RC*

A Marconi T19A set, 1948.
£350-450 *RC*

An MIR MIS4 Soviet table radio, unrestored, 1950. **£350-400** *RC*

Railways

A London, Brighton & South Coast Railway copper station lamp top, c1910.
£300-400 *SRA*

A selection of various railway lamps.
£20-40 each *ONS*

A British Rail ganger's horn, c1940s, 15in (38cm) long.
£20-30 *Hol*

Signs

A North British Railway cast iron sign, c1910.
£200-300 *SRA*

A Great North of Scotland Railway enamel advertising sign, c1910.
£200-300 *SRA*

Makers' Plates

A selection of plates, 1913-36,
GNR. **£480-520**
LNER. **£1,200-1,500**
ONS

A works plate, 1901.
£600-800 *SRA*

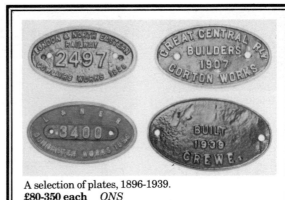

A selection of plates, 1896-1939.
£80-350 each *ONS*

A selection of plates,
1895-1918.
£200-800 each *ONS*

Models

A gauge 1 electric model
of the Pennsylvania Rail
Road Class GG1
locomotive, No. 4889,
built for Marketing
Corporation of America,
30in (76.2cm) long.
£3,500-4,500 *CSK*

*This model is new and is
complete with warranty
card and limited Edition
Certificate 1/90.*

A gauge 1 two rail
electric model of the New
York Central Rail Road
4–6–4 locomotive and
tender, Commodore
Vanderbilt, built by
Aster for Fulgurex,
No. 099, new, in original
packing and box, with
instructions, 37in (94cm)
long.
£2,500-3,000 *CSK*

DID YOU KNOW?
Miller's Collectables
Price Guide is
designed to build up,
year by year, into the
most comprehensive
reference system
available.

Three Bassett-
Lowke gauge 1
engines.
£1,000-1,500 each
SRA

Cross Reference
Toys

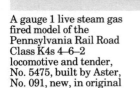

A gauge 1 live steam gas
fired model of the
Pennsylvania Rail Road
Class K4s 4–6–2
locomotive and tender,
No. 5475, built by Aster,
No. 091, new, in original
packing and box, with
instructions, 32½in
(82.5cm).
£4,000-4,500 *CSK*

A gauge 1 live steam gas
fired model of the
L.S.W.R. Adams Radial
4–4–2 side tank
locomotive No. 520, with
copper boiler, in L.S.W.R.
livery, 15½in (39.5cm)
long.
£650-850 *CSK*

A 3½in (8.5cm) gauge model of L.N.E.R. 4–6–2 locomotive and tender, No. 113, Hielan Lassie, built by Earsdon, 16½in (42.5cm) long.
£1,400-2,000 *CSK*

A 5in (12.5cm) gauge model of an 0–6–0 side tank locomotive, built to the designs of Butch by E. Lofthouse, finished in black, 28in (71cm) long.
£1,400-1,800 *CSK*

This model has not been steamed.

Name Plates

A train headboard, Cornish Riviera Express, 1950.
£1,500-2,000 *SRA*

An L.M.S. Royal Scot Class nameplate, 1930.
£6,000-7,000 *SRA*

A Great Western Railway nameplate, c1930.
£5,000-6,000 *SRA*

An L.M.S. Jubilee Class nameplate and badge. **£16,500-17,000** *SRA*

A Great Western Railway nameplate, 1930.
£3,000-4,000 *SRA*

A Southern Railway Schools Class nameplate, c1930.
£4,000-5,000 *SRA*

An L.N.E.R. brass nameplate, c1930.
£4,000-5,000 *SRA*

A British Railways
station totem sign, 1950.
£100-300 *SRA*

An L.N.E.R. brass nameplate, c1930.
£5,000-7,000 *SRA*

The Royal Scot headboard, c1950.
£750-1,000 *SRA*

Numbers

A Great Western Railway locomotive cabside
numberplate. **£1,000-1,500** *SRA*

A G.W.R. cast brass cabside 4077, original
paintwork, unrestored from 4–6–0 express
Chepstow Castle, built 1923 withdrawn August
1962, with BR receipt, purchased April 1963 for
7s 1d. **£3,000-3,500** *ONS*

A G.W.R. cast iron
numberplate 6374 from
4300 Class, built 1921
withdrawn 1962.
£350-450 *ONS*

Tableware

A selection of metal tableware, mainly G.W.R.
£30-60 each *ONS*

A selection of
toast racks.
£60-160 *ONS*

l. A L.N.E.R.
spirit stove oval
dish, 12in
(30.5cm).
£170-220
r. A Glasgow &
S.W. soup tureen
and cover.
£90-110 *ONS*

A selection of railway company tankards.
£30-75 each *ONS*

A Caledonian Railway
cake stand. **£220-250**
A Highland Railway
bowl. **£350-400**
A G.W.R. cake stand.
£35-50 *ONS*

l. A London Midland & Scottish dish with pierced drainer, 12in (30.5cm) diam.
£30-50

r. A Great Central Railway vegetable dish, with detachable handle, marked Dewsbury and coat-of-arms.
£150-200   *ONS*

Michael, The Broads, published by L.N.E.R./ L.M.S., 1937.
£950-1,100   *ONS*

Railway Posters

You May Have A Friend Here, He Is In Your Usual Train, published by Railway Executive Committee.
£35-55   *ONS*

Cross Reference
Posters

Charles Pears, Southend on Sea, published by L.M.S./L.N.E.R.
£300-350   *ONS*

Great North of Scotland Railway, Moray Firth Coast, The Scottish Riviera, c1910.   **£200-300**   *SRA*

R. C. Leighton, For Your Holidays Come To The Canadian Pacific Rockies.
£130-180   *ONS*

Clear Road Ahead, Monmouth Castle, on linen.
£320-380   *ONS*

Terence Cuneo, Forging Ahead, published by B.R., damaged.
£50-100   *ONS*

W. E. Leadley, Marlborough For Downs and Forest, published by G.W.R.
£150-200
ONS

Leslie Carr, All Clear For The Guns on British Railways.
£150-200   *ONS*

Lander, North Wales, lithograph in colours, printed by Waterlow & Sons Ltd., backed on linen, 40 by 50in (101.5 by 127cm).
£180-200   *CSK*

Great Western Railway, c1910.
£300-400   *SRA*

Rock & Pop

A presentation plaque offering The Jackson Five the key to Newark, New Jersey, and a scrap album filled with press cuttings inscribed on spine The Jackson 5, February 1976, Victor Music Corporation, Philippines.
£160-200 *CSK*

Sam Cooke, Dion and others, early concert poster from The Vets Memorial Auditorium, printed by Globe Posters, Baltimore, mounted on original billboard, 35½ by 22in (90.5 by 56cm). **£825-925** *CSK*

An English souvenir concert programme, signed on reverse by Buddy Holly, Jerry Allison and Joe Mauldin, 1958.
£990-1,100 *CSK*

An early concert poster Buddy Holly And The Crickets at the Philharmonic Hope Hall, Street, Liverpool, Thursday, 20th March, 1958, 25 by 18in (64 by 46cm), framed.
£770-800 *CSK*

A cotton advertising banner, with The Cream in red and blue plastic lettering, late 1960s.
£825-900 *CSK*

A black denim tour jacket embroidered in multi colours with 'Madonna 87', autographed, 1987, with letter of authenticity.
£2,200-2,700 *S(NY)*

Madonna wore this jacket during her 1987 Club Life tour.

A presentation gold disc for the album Kissing to be Clever by Culture Club, French, reverse signed and inscribed by Boy George, 1983.
£500-600 *S*

An illustrated souvenir tour programme Rolling Stones, 1966, signed inside by all 5 members of the group, and 4 others including Keith Moon and John Entwistle on back cover.
£500-550 *CSK*

A promotional postcard signed by Buddy Holly, Joe Mauldin and Jerry Allison, with a black and yellow patterned silk handkerchief worn by Holly in the 1950s, 22 by 17½in (56 by 44.5cm).
£950-1,000 *CSK*
A pair of slate grey suede shoes with maker's name Thom McAn stamped inside, worn by Holly during the late 1950s.
£460-500 *CSK*

Various artists, a bill poster for Idols On Parade! The Rock'n'Trad Spectacular, at the Gaumont, Cardiff, Friday, March 10, 30 by 40in (76 by 101.5cm).
£175-200 *CSK*

A signed photograph of Eric Clapton, 1990, 8 by 8in (20 by 20cm), and a signed publicity postcard.
£165-200 *CSK*

A Remo Weather King bass drum skin, signed Angus Young, AC/DC and Malcolm Young, 21in (53cm) diam.
£200-250 *CSK*

The Beach Boys and Albert Hammond, a presentation gold disc inscribed Presented to Carl Wilson to commemorate the sale of more than 500,000 copies of the Capitol Records Inc. long playing record album Best of the Beach Boys, Vol 2, 21 by 17in (53 by 43cm), framed.
£825-925 *CSK*

Two souvenir concert programmes, Louis Armstrong's British Tour, 1956, signed on back cover, and The Fabulous Platters, 1960, signed by the group on the front cover.
£260-300 *CSK*

A Remo Weather King drum skin, signed and inscribed 'Thanks for your help! Cheers Phil Collins', 14in (35.5cm) diam.
£280-320 *CSK*

An advertising poster for James Brown, 1960s.
£440-500 *S*

A Western style two-piece cream leather suit, with hand written label inside Made By Mike McGregor for Roy Orbison, and an affidavit stating that it was made for and worn by Roy Orbison.
£825-925 *CSK*

Two early Doors concert posters, finished in purple and orange with black and white lettering, 1967, 21 by 27in (53 by 69cm), and another Doors poster, 13 by 18½in (33 by 47cm).
£1,000-1,500 *S(NY)*

Three rare promotional posters for God Save The Cambridge Rapist, Jack The Ripper, and Myra Hindley, printed, each signed by Jamie Reid, mounted on card, 23½ by 18in (60 by 46cm).
£500-550 *CSK*
The Sex Pistols promotional handbill sticker for No Future, signed by artist Jamie Reid, framed, with 4 badges.
£70-100 *CSK*

A bail bond signed by Jim Morrison, and 7 other documents relating to the case, 1969, 29 by 24in (74 by 61cm).
£9,000-9,500   *S(NY)*

On March 1, 1969, The Doors performed a concert in Miami. Afterwards, Jim Morrison was arrested for the reasons indicated on the bail bond.

A Rolling Stones tour poster, for 8th October 1965 at the ABC, Stockton-on-Tees, fold creases, minor tears at edges.
£550-600   *S*

Buddy Holly's Birth Certificate, the official Texas Department of Health Bureau of Vital Statistics Certificate of Birth for Charles Hardin Holly, complete with all information, signed by the Deputy, Annie L. Crow.
£650-700   *S(NY)*

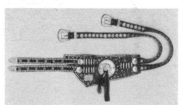

Michael Jackson's belt, black leather with double buckles.
£3,500-4,000   *S*

Worn by the singer on the Bad tour and the 'Librarian Girl' photographic session.

A Super Chromonica by M. Hohner, played by Buddy Holly in 1950s, with original case, c1956.
£2,250-2,500   *S(NY)*

A collection of early Kate Bush lyrics and tapes, 1970s.
£2,800-3,000   *S*

A group of documents concerning the Rolling Stones' appearance at the London Palladium, 1st August 1965, fold creases, tears and 2 small holes.
£1,650-1,850   *S*

This was the only time the Stones ever played at the Palladium and they actually hired it for the occasion and booked all the support acts: the Walker Brothers were eventually replaced by the Moody Blues.

A Bruce Springsteen autographed album cover Born to Run, and an album of 40 black and white photographs.
£450-500   *S(NY)*

Four Janis Joplin posters and concert tickets, including a black and white poster of Janis Joplin in the nude, signed lower right by the photographer, all matted and framed. **£550-650** *S(NY)*

A pair of Elton John's glasses and a signed album, The Very Best Of Elton John.
£600-700   *S*

Donated by Elton John to Models 1 to raise money for the Save The Children Bangladesh Fund.

Instruments

Keith Moon's Premier part-drum kit, chrome finish, comprising bass drum with group logo, 22in (56cm), 2 floor tom toms, 16in (40.5cm), 2 hanging tom toms, 14in (35.5cm), 2 brass drum spurs, and one tom tom post.
£8,800-9,000 *S*

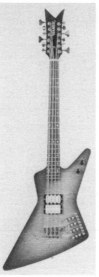

John Entwistle's Hamer Explorer 12 string bass guitar, 48in (122cm), in flight case.
£800-1,200 *CSK*

A Phil Lynott/Thin Lizzy Fender Precision bass guitar, Serial No. S904076, c1978.
£1,300-1,500
CSK

Jon Bon Jovi's Kalamazoo Oriole acoustic guitar, Serial No. 971 F27, signed, 41in (104cm) long, in case.
£400-600 *CSK*

Marc Bolan's tambourine, signed and inscribed 'Love Marc Bolan XX', with T. Rex sticker, 7½in (18.5cm) diam.
£350-400 *CSK*

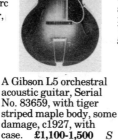

A full size Spanish classical acoustic guitar, signed by Bob Dylan, inscribed 'To Simon, Best Wishes, 10.12.86'.
£700-750 *CSK*

A Gibson L5 orchestral acoustic guitar, Serial No. 83659, with tiger striped maple body, some damage, c1927, with case. **£1,100-1,500** *S*

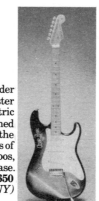

The Rolling Stones Fender Squire II Stratocaster, No. S946037, white guitar, signed by Keith Richards, Mick Jagger, and Ron Wood.
£2,500-3,000 *S(NY)*

A Fender Stratocaster 73646 electric guitar, signed by the members of Los Lobos, with case.
£580-650
S(NY)

Benny Goodman's Selmer Signet soloist clarinet, Serial No. 27300, in original case, and letter of authenticity from Benny Goodman.
£2,500-3,000 *S(NY)*

Cross Reference
Musical Instruments

Beatles

A souvenir concert programme for The Beatles/Mary Wells tour, signed on cover by each member and inscribed 'To Dennis' by Paul McCartney, 1964.
£900-1,000   *CSK*

A machine print publicity photograph of The Beatles, signed by each member of the group and inscribed 'To Tony all the best! Paul McCartney (The Beatles)', 1964, 7 by 5in (17.5 by 12.5cm).
£600-700   *CSK*

A presentation gold disc, Help!, mounted above a reduction of the cover and a plaque bearing the R.I.A.A. Certified Sales Award, 21 by 17in (53 by 43cm), framed.
£1,500-2,000   *CSK*

An inner sleeve, signed and inscribed by John Lennon and Yoko Ono, 16 by 28in (41 by 71cm).   **£650-750**   *CSK*

Two albums, Unfinished Music No. 1: Two Virgins, Apple Records, signed and inscribed on the cover, 1968, and The Beatles, Apple Records, signed and inscribed, 1968.
£1,100-1,500   *CSK*

Beatles autographed black and white book photograph, inscribed, c1964.
£1,300-1,400   *S(NY)*

A brass nameplate engraved with black lettering, Apple, 9 by 12in (22.5 by 30.5cm).
£450-500   *CSK*

John and Cynthia Lennon's address book, given to Brian Epstein, completed between 1967 and early 1970s.
£3,800-4,200   *CSK*

A printed menu for the 'B.O.A.C. . . . Beatles Bahamas Special', signed on cover by John Lennon 3 times and by Paul McCartney, George Harrison and Ringo Starr, 1965.
£800-1,000   *CSK*

A single sided acetate Emidisc of Lucy In The Sky With Diamonds, dated 14.3.67, and various albums and singles.
£660-700   *CSK*

A baking tray, signed on base by John and Yoko, 1969, 5in (12.5cm) diam.
£330-350 *CSK*

The signatures were obtained in Amsterdam during John and Yoko's Bed-In for Peace, 25-31 March 1969.

A single, Instant Karma, by John and Yoko Ono, Apple Records, signed and inscribed on the original printed sleeve, 1970.   **£350-400**   *CSK*

An album cover, Revolver, Capitol Records, signed by each member of the group and inscribed 'To Sheila', 1966.
£1,500-2,000   *CSK*

Autographs obtained during The Beatles 1966 US tour.

A presentation gold disc, Yellow Submarine, 21 by 17in (53.5 by 43cm), framed.
£2,000-2,500   *CSK*

Two signed machine print photographs from a 1970 calendar, 9 by 9in (22.5 by 22.5cm).
£770-800   *CSK*

A presentation platinum disc, Sgt. Pepper's Lonely Hearts Club Band, 21 by 17in (53 by 43cm), framed.
£2,600-3,000   *CSK*

A short birth certificate with John Lennon's details, issued 1960.
£1,700-2,000   *CSK*

A souvenir concert programme for The Beatles/Roy Orbison tour, signed by 4 Beatles, and 4 others, 1963; and 2 publicity photographs.
£880-1,000   *CSK*

Back cover only of album A Hard Day's Night, signed by The Beatles.
£950-1,100   *S*

John Lennon and Yoko Ono's handwritten notes to Derek Taylor, 1969.
£1,300-1,400   *S(NY)*

Please Please Me by The
Beatles, signed on back
cover, 1963.
£1,400-1,500 *S*

A signed and inscribed
copy of P.S. I Love
You/Love Me Do, 1962.
£1,200-1,500 *S*

A signed second edition
of In His Own Write by
John Lennon, some
damage, 1964.
£700-800 *S*

A contract, letter and poster relating
to The Beatles concert at
Abergavenny, 1963.
£1,600-1,650 *S*

A signed ticket for the
EMI reception,
November 18th, 1963,
signed by The Beatles,
4½ by 6in (11.5 by 15cm).
£800-850 *S*

A Buckingham Palace card signed by The
Beatles, 4 by 5in (9.5 by 12cm), framed and
glazed.
£1,200-1,500 *S*

A signed first edition of
The True Story of The
Beatles, some damage,
1964.
£400-450 *S*

A photograph and menu
card, signed by The
Beatles, 1965, 10 by 8in
(25.5 by 20.5cm).
£800-900 *S*

A 3-D postcard to Julian
Lennon, inscribed in
different colours by John
Lennon, 1970.
£2,000-2,200 *S(NY)*

A presentation gold disc, Imagine, by John Lennon and Plastic Ono Band, 21 by 17in (53 by 43cm), framed.
£2,800-3,000 *CSK*

An album cover of Beatles VI, signed by The Beatles.
£1,600-1,650 *S*

John Lennon's sunglasses, green tinted non-prescription circular glasses with silver rims, in original worn purple velvet lined case, c1967.
£1,900-2,000 *S(NY)*

A sleeve for the single I Saw Her Standing there, American, signed by all members of the group, c1964
£2,200-2,500 *S*

Beatles autographs on paper, each one on a separate piece of paper, framed with the album cover of Sgt. Pepper's Lonely Hearts Club Band, 22 by 30in (55.5 by 76cm).
£800-900 *S(NY)*

John Lennon autograph, signed 'To Joel John Lennon, '69', and a signed itinerary by Paul and Linda McCartney for their 1989-90 World tour, frame size 14 by 18in (35.5 by 45.5cm).
£1,000-1,100 *S(NY)*

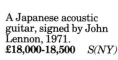

A presentation gold disc, Let It Be, mounted above a plaque bearing the R.I.A.A. Certified Sales Award and inscribed, 17 by 13in (43 by 33cm), framed.
£900-1,100 *CSK*

Beatles Mersey Beat Award, with custom metal plaque engraved 'Mersey Beat Award No. 1, The Beatles 1963', 21 by 12in (53 by 30.5cm).
£1,300-1,500 *S(NY)*

A Japanese acoustic guitar, signed by John Lennon, 1971.
£18,000-18,500 *S(NY)*

MAKE THE MOST OF MILLERS
Price ranges in this book reflect what one should expect to *pay* for a similar example. When selling, however, one should expect to receive a lower figure. This will fluctuate according to a dealer's stock, saleability at a particular time, etc. It is always advisable, when selling, to approach a reputable specialist dealer or an auction house which has specialist sales.

Jimi Hendrix

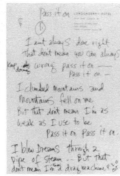

Twenty-five unpublished black and white photographs of The Jimi Hendrix Experience, at the Royal Albert Hall, 1969, and 5 more.
£2,600-3,000 *S*

Jimi Hendrix handwritten lyrics for the song Pass It On, on Londonderry Hotel stationery, 1970.
£1,300-1,500 *S(NY)*

Jimi Hendrix Are You Experienced Cover Art, 1967, 33 by 22in (84 by 55.5cm).
£2,100-2,500 *S(NY)*

Jimi Hendrix's Electric Lady Mixing Console, 96 by 48in (243.5 by 122cm).
£4,200-5,000 *S(NY)*

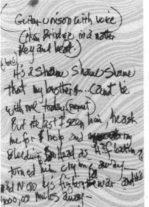

Jimi Hendrix handwritten signed lyrics for Room Full of Mirrors, 1968-70.
£20,700-21,500 *S(NY)*

A platinum album award for Are You Experienced?, presented to Warner Bros. Records to commemorate the sale of more than 1 million copies, framed, 20 by 16in (50.5 by 41cm).
£1,700-1,800 *S(NY)*

Bobby Lee Co. guitar strap, 1970.
£2,800-3,000 *S(NY)*

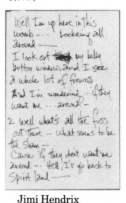

Jimi Hendrix handwritten lyrics for Belly Button Window, 1970.
£8,500-9,000 *S(NY)*

A black suede headband with copper coloured flowered pattern, and suede ties, c1969.
£1,200-1,300 *S(NY)*

A Marshall MKII JTM 45 100 watt Super Amplifier, top Serial No. 7451, 66 valve, c1967.
£600-700 *CSK*

Jimi Hendrix's brooch, with a blue metal ashtray from an airline.
£350-450 *S(NY)*

Jimi Hendrix's scarf, c1969.
£2,300-2,800 *S(NY)*

Jimi Hendrix handwritten
lyrics for Calling All Devil's
Children, on 2 sheets,
12 by 8in (30 by 21cm).
£1,800-2,000 *S*

A portrait photograph by Jim Marshall,
1967, printed 1989, taken at the sound
check for the Monterey Pop Festival, 17th
June 1967, 11 by 16in (28 by 40.5cm).
£500-550 *CSK*

A piece of paper signed
and inscribed by Jimi
Hendrix, 5 by 8in (12.5
by 20cm).
£700-800 *CSK*

Jimi Hendrix
handwritten lyrics for
Come On Down, c1968.
£1,400-1,600 *S(NY)*

Jimi Hendrix's first
single, Hey Joe, Polydor
Records, signed and
inscribed on label 'Stay
Kool, Dig the sounds
Jimi Hendrix', 1966,
with his second single,
Purple Haze, Track
Records, signed and
inscribed on sleeve, 1967.
£950-1,500 *CSK*

A presentation gold disc,
Electric Ladyland, 21 by
17in (53 by 43cm),
framed.
£600-700 *CSK*

Jimi Hendrix's belt buckle and guitar
strings, with an unused set of Fender
Spanish guitar strings in original
plastic case, c1970.
£1,000-1,200 *S(NY)*

A typescript contract/
notice of agreement
between A. Schroeder
Music Publishing Co.
Ltd. and the Performing
Right Society Ltd.,
concerning the division
of fees payable by the
Society, May 12th, 1967.
£1,100-1,500 *CSK*

A page
from an
autograph
book.
£800-900
CSK

375

Elvis Presley

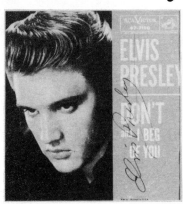

Two autographed 45 rpm record sleeves, framed, 11 by 11in (28 by 28cm).
£640-675   *S(NY)*

A signed and inscribed photograph, c1976, 10 by 7in (25 by 17.5cm), a signed scrap of paper, 11 by 7in (28 by 17.5cm), and 5 Presley family autographs.
£450-500   *CSK*

An EP, Elvis Sails, RCA, signed by Presley on original cover.
£400-450   *CSK*

An exhibition gold disc for the RCA Victor single King Creole, 14½ by 10½in (37 by 26.5cm), framed.
£400-500   *CSK*

A handwritten letter from Elvis Presley to an English fan, 1960, envelope damaged.
£600-650   *S*

Black silk pyjamas monogrammed with EP in red, c1972.
£900-1,000   *S(NY)*

A cream cotton decorated 'Silver Concho' stage jumpsuit, and a framed photograph of Elvis wearing it on stage, 1970, framed, 21 by 18in (53 by 46cm).
£9,500-10,000   *S(NY)*

Two autographed movie posters, 41 by 27in (104 by 69cm).
£450-500   *S(NY)*

A white puffed sleeve shirt, and a photograph of Elvis wearing it on stage, c1972.
£900-1,000   *S(NY)*

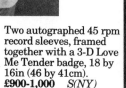

Two autographed 45 rpm record sleeves, framed together with a 3-D Love Me Tender badge, 18 by 16in (46 by 41cm).
£900-1,000   *S(NY)*

A handwritten note, framed, with photograph of Elvis and a plaque, 1976, 23 by 19in (59 by 48cm).
£7,700-8,000 *S(NY)*

A yellow silk autographed stage scarf, 40 by 40in (101.5 by 101.5cm).
£500-600 *S(NY)*

Two autographed souvenir menus from Las Vegas Hilton, framed, 12 by 15½in (30.5 by 39cm), framed.
£500-600 *S(NY)*

A boxer's robe of cream satin bound with emerald green satin, from the United Artists film Kid Galahad 1962, and a letter of authenticity confirming the provenance. **£5,200-5,500** *CSK*

An Edwardian style shirt, and a photograph of Elvis wearing it on stage, 1972, 9 by 12in (22.5 by 30.5cm).
£2,200-2,500 *S(NY)*

A presentation gold disc, Burning Love, 17 by 13in (43 by 33cm), framed.
£800-1,000 *CSK*

A decorated cream stage cape with gold lamé lining, worn on stage during summer 1972.
£4,800-5,000 *S(NY)*
A white cotton stage cape with black satin lining, 1971, with photograph of Elvis Presley wearing it on stage.
£7,500-8,500 *S(NY)*

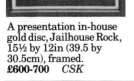

A presentation in-house gold disc, Jailhouse Rock, 15½ by 12in (39.5 by 30.5cm), framed.
£600-700 *CSK*

A gold record for Suspicious Minds, presented to Chips Moman, the producer, framed, 13 by 17in (33 by 43cm).
£580-600 *S(NY)*

Film & TV Memorabilia

A revised final shooting script of Casablanca, dated June 1, 1942, 160 pages, bound in original orange paper covers.
£2,500-3,000 *C(NY)*

A black rubber cowl for Batman, and yellow and black bat insignia, 1989.
£500-600 *C(NY)*

A leather covered make-up box, decorated with plaque inscribed Mae West, 14in (36cm) long.
£900-1,000 *S(NY)*

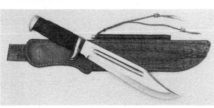

A hunting knife from Crocodile Dundee, the steel blade stamped J. Bowring, 15in (38cm) long, 1986, with certificate of authenticity and magazine article.
£2,800-3,200 *S*

A wooden model of the Bates' house in Psycho, 36in (91.5cm) high.
£600-700 *S*

This was used for advertising and promotional purposes.

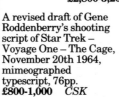

A revised draft of Gene Roddenberry's shooting script of Star Trek – Voyage One – The Cage, November 20th 1964, mimeographed typescript, 76pp.
£800-1,000 *CSK*

A pair of Dame Edna Everage's glasses, red frames marked Dame Edna's Famous Face Furniture Anglo American Eyewear, and a signed black and white publicity photograph.
£700-800 *S*

Donated by Barry Humphries to Models 1 to raise money for the Save The Children Bangladesh Fund.

A signed film still from Star Trek III, The Search for Spock, and a signed and inscribed Star Trek Three Year Calendar, 1976-78, 9 by 12in (22.5 by 31cm). **£190-220** *CSK*

A costume from Robocop II, with letter of provenance.
£1,700-1,800 *S*

Two dresses and a pair of white leather shoes for The Great Gatsby, 1976. **£580-680** *C(NY)*

This film received an Academy Award for costume design.

A beaded gown designed by Edith Head for Carroll Baker in Harlow, 1965. **£700-800** *C(NY)*

Doctor Who

The costume worn by Lynda Bellingham as The Inquisitor, the Gallifreyan High Court Judge of the tribunal of the Time Lords, includes dress, tunic, sash, skullcap and shoes. **£280-300** *Bon*

An outfit designed by Edith Head for Jane Fonda in Barefoot In The Park, 1967, severely faded. **£70-100** *C(NY)*

The costume worn by a Sontaran, enemy of the Doctor, who attempts to steal the Time Lords' key to time travel, includes 2 jackets, neckpiece and trousers. **£200-300** *Bon*

DID YOU KNOW?
Miller's Collectables Price Guide is designed to build up, year by year, into the most comprehensive reference system available.

Nabil Shaban as Sil, a Mentor, a reptilian monster financier on the planet Thoros-Betar, wearing a costume including body, neck and head. **£450-500** *Bon*

The white coat and trousers worn by Ingrid Pitt as Solow, the scientist inside Sea Base Four, an undersea military base on Earth in 2084. **£80-100** *Bon*

The costume worn by David Banks as the Cyber Leader, leader of the Cybermen, inhabitants of the planet Mondas, with invulnerable silver plastic bodies, includes silver suit, chest pack, helmet, boots, gloves and broken Cybergun. **£1,300-1,500** *Bon*

The costume including helmet and body armour, shoulder piece, leggings, hands and feet, worn by Christopher Farries as Sauvix, leader of the Sea Devils, reptilian relations of the Silurians on Earth during the Eocene period. **£260-300** *Bon*

Scales & Balances

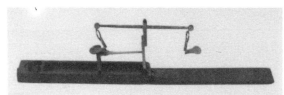

A cased set of steel balance scales, c1820.
£45-55 *HOW*

A cased set of brass balance scales for sovereigns, 19thC, 11in (28cm) wide.
£90-100 *HOW*

> A further selection of Scales and Balances is featured in previous editions of Miller's Collectables Price Guides, available from Millers Publications.

Scientific Instruments

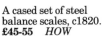

A pair of Asprey's silver plate and mother-of-pearl opera glasses, 11½in (29cm) long.
£120-150 *ROS*

A French brass graphometer, signed 'Soleil à Paris, Passage Treydeau', with associated oak carrying case, interior inscribed in pencil with numerous personal and place names, 18thC, 11in (28cm) wide.
£500-800 *C*

A demonstration static electricity machine, c1920, 15in (38cm) wide.
£100-120 *DHO*

A drawing set, by Pallant, late 19thC, 14½in (37cm) long.
£60-80 *DHO*

An Italian brass scale rule, unsigned, with shaped end, 18thC, 8½in (21cm) long.
£550-650 *C*

A demonstration paddle wheel, with engraved brass plaque 'Newcastle 1848, J.D. Weatherley Esq. Mayor, N.G. Lambert, Esq., J. Archbold, Esq. – Aldermen –, mid-19thC, 14in (36cm) wide.
£800-900 *C*

A brass Wheatstone pattern heliochronometer, 19thC, 8in (20cm) high.
£1,000-1,500 *C*

380

A brass simple tellurion, signed W.J. Shaw Maker, with mahogany base and glass dome, 19thC, 9in (23cm) high. **£2,000-2,500** *C*

The gearing and fine work of this instrument resembles that of a clock maker rather than an instrument maker, and is likely to be John Shaw of Sheffield, who had correspondence with the Board of Longitude concerning improvements to chronometers in 1827.

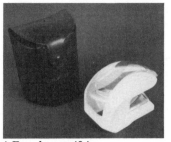

A French magnifying glass and case. **£5-7** *ROS*

A magnetic dip, for determining the angle of magnetism at any one point, 8in (20cm) high. **£120-150** *DHO*

Compasses

A brass dip circle, signed on the base 'Robinson, 38 Devonshire Street, Portland Place, London', 19thC, 12in (30cm) high. **£600-800** *C*

A fishskin drawing etui with bone sectors, proportional rule and brass instruments, with trade label in lid by Blunt, c1810, 6½in (16cm) long. **£180-220** *DHO*

A Victorian multi-purpose folding gadget/compass/microscope/binoculars and signalling mirror, 3in (8cm) long. **£15-25** *MA*

A traveller's brass compass and sundial, finely engraved, possibly German, late 18thC, 2in (5cm) diam. **£250-280** *DHO*

A wrist compass, c1916. **£10-12** *COB*

A brass compass, c1900. **£45-60** *COB*

A brass table compass, signed Brüder Voigtlaender in Wien No. 857, 19thC, 5in (13cm) diam. **£100-150** *CSK*

A late 18thC gimbaled compass, with azimuth sights for taking bearings, in fitted mahogany box, 12in (31cm) square. **£400-500** *DHO*

Medical Instruments

A lacquered brass and glass breast pump, by Einsle, 16 St Martin's Lane, London, in mahogany case, 19thC, 5in (13cm) wide. **£250-300**   *CSK*

A lacquered brass Tate-type vacuum pump, unsigned, late 19thC, 19in (48cm) high. **£500-600**   *CSK*

An early 19thC trepanning set, 7½in (19cm) wide. **£650-700**   *CSK*

A Maw pattern enema pump, with ivory plunger handle and articulated nozzle, in leather case, 10½in (26cm) long. **£250-300**   *CSK*

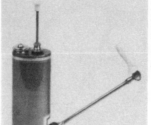

An enema pump, in fitted box, c1880, 10½in (26cm) long. **£60-80**   *DHO*

A French Victorian brass enema, 9in (23cm) high. **£60-80**   *DHO*

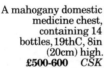

A fishskin box with brass fittings, for medical instruments, 18thC, 7in (18cm) high. **£70-80**   *DHO*

A mahogany domestic medicine chest, containing 14 bottles, 19thC, 8in (20cm) high. **£500-600**   *CSK*

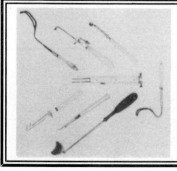

Eight dental instruments, including tooth saw frame, an electric cautery, mechanical forceps, spring tweezers, cheek retractor, 2 tongue retractors and tooth holder each with ivory or ebony handles, various makers, 19thC. **£700-1,000**   *CSK*

A satinwood and ebony strung mahogany domestic medicine chest, containing 16 bottles, 19thC, 9in (23cm) high. **£800-900**   *CSK*

Cross Reference
Boxes

Microscopes

A brass compound monocular microscope, signed on the folding tripod base Imperial Compound Microscope Archromatic by Carpenter & Westley 21 Regent St, London, 19thC. **£700-1,000** *CSK*

A binocular microscope, by H. Crouch, with accessories and fitted mahogany case, c1870, 15in (38cm) high. **£450-500** *DHO*

A compound monocular microscope, signed BAKER 244 High Holborn, London, with sub-stage condenser and mirror, 19thC, 15in (38cm) high. **£300-400** *CSK*

A selection of micro photographs, by J. B. Dancer, c1880. **£8-12 each** *DHO*

A solar microscope, used to project on to a wall for demonstrations, with accessories and fitted box, c1800, 11½in (29cm) wide. **£600-700** *DHO*

A Dutch brass monocular microscope unsigned, in a pyramid shaped mahogany case, late 18thC, 16½in (42cm) high, and a set of handwritten instructions, inscribed Rectory Bolton 1788. **£500-600** *CSK*

A black enamelled and lacquered brass compound monocular microscope, by W. Watson and Sons (van Huerck Model) No. 333, with accessories, in mahogany case, 16in (40cm) high. **£1,000-1,500** *CSK*

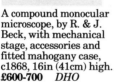

A botanical microscope, unsigned, with accessories, in tooled leather case, early 19thC, 5in (13cm) wide. **£250-300** *CSK*

A compound monocular microscope, by R. & J. Beck, with mechanical stage, accessories and fitted mahogany case, c1868, 16in (41cm) high. **£600-700** *DHO*

A Cary type microscope, by West, complete with accessories, in mahogany box, c1830, box 7½in (19cm) wide. **£380-420** *DHO*

A polarising microscope, by T. W. Watson, with fitted mahogany case and accessories, c1870. **£800-900** *DHO*

An achromatic microscope, by Carpenter & Wesley, with fitted mahogany case, c1850, 19½in (49cm) high. **£1,000-1,200** *DHO*

A Wilson screw barrel microscope, with accessories, in fitted fishskin box, c1740, box 3 by 5in (8 by 13cm). **£550-650** *DHO*

A Victorian student's microscope, 7in (18cm) wide. **£40-50** *DHO*

An R. & J. Beck compound microscope, with 2 mahogany fitted cases, which fit into a third case, c1870, 21in (53cm) high. **£1,500-2,000** *DHO*

A Victorian student's microscope, with slightly larger separate objectives, a live box and slides, all covered in fine quality paper, 8in (20cm) wide.
£70-80 *DHO*

A brass compound monocular microscope, signed BAKER 244 High Holborn, London, in a mahogany cabinet, 19thC, 21in (53cm) high.
£600-700 *CSK*

A Culpeper type microscope, in a lacquered case, by W. & S. Jones, complete with drawer of accessories, c1790, 13in (33cm) high. **£700-800** *DHO*

A brass compound binocular microscope, signed on the base J. Casartelli, Optician, Manchester, in mahogany case, 19in (48cm) high, 19thC.
£1,200-1,500 *CSK*

A compound monocular microscope, by Baker, in original condition, with mahogany case, c1870, 14in (36cm) high.
£350-400 *DHO*

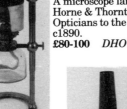

A simple microscope, in fitted simulated fishskin case, early 19thC, 4in (10cm) wide.
£350-450 *CSK*

A microscope lamp, by Horne & Thornthwaite, Opticians to the Queen, c1890.
£80-100 *DHO*

A microscope lamp, by W. Watson, used in conjunction with a microscope in low light conditions, 13in (33cm) high.
£100-120 *DHO*

A compound Cary type microscope by Dixey, when assembled screws in to the top of the box, with bone slides and accessories, c1840, box 6in (15cm) wide. **£240-280** *DHO*

A compound monocular microscope, with bull's-eye live box and slides, mahogany case and fittings, c1840.
£150-180 *DHO*

Navigation Instruments

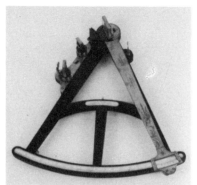

A lacquered brass box sextant, signed Allan, London, issued by the Hon. the Commissioners of the Board of Longitude, in fitted mahogany case, 19thC, 4in (10cm) wide.
£500-600   *CSK*

A sextant by Berge, late Ramsden, c1800.
£1,200-1,400   *DHO*

A ship's octant, with engraved arm, made by Gregory & Wright, London, for Archibald Williamson, engraved, in a mahogany shaped box, 1784, 17in (43cm) high.   **£800-1,000**   *DHO*

A Cary sextant, with gold and platinum seals and vernier, complete with accessories, in mahogany box, c1800, box 11½in (29cm) wide.
£900-1,000   *DHO*

An ebony and lacquered brass octant, by G. Christian, Strand, Liverpool, with trade label for J. Steel & Co., in shaped oak carrying case, early 19thC, 10in (25cm) radius.
£400-500   *C*

A brass surveying pocket sextant, in leather case, c1875, 6in (15cm) long, folds down to 3in (8cm).
£180-220   *DHO*

Cross Reference
Shipping

An octant, signed by Henry Hughes & Son, in shaped mahogany box, c1830, 13in (33cm) high.
£300-350   *DHO*

A brass three-ring sextant, by H. M. Emmanuel & Son, by appointment to the Queen, with 5 sighting tubes and filter, in mahogany box.
£300-350   *DHO*

A ship's 28-second sand glass, used in conjunction with the ship's log for determining speed, on a turned wood stand with 4 shaped pillars, c1830, 5½in (14cm) high.
£100-120   *DHO*

A brass sextant bell frame, by Heath & Co, with 3 tubes and filters, last certificate examination 1930, c1890, box 11in (28cm) wide.
£300-420   *DHO*

Spectacles

A silver framed lorgnette with marcasite decoration, and 5 others.
£250-300 *CSK*

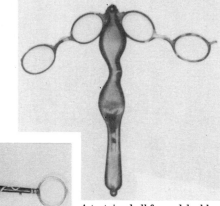

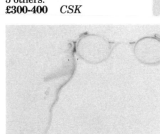

A silver framed lorgnette, in leather covered case, 4in (10cm) long, and 5 others.
£300-400 *CSK*

A pair of silver gilt and tortoiseshell lorgnettes, in fitted case.
£260-300 *Bon*

A tortoiseshell framed double lorgnette, the handle 7in (18cm) long and 5 others.
£300-350 *CSK*

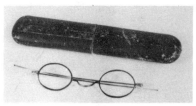

A framed lorgnette, the shaped mother-of-pearl guards with suspension ring, and 5 others.
£250-300 *CSK*

A pair of early Victorian spectacles, with case, 7in (18cm) long.
£25-30 *ROS*

Two pairs of Chinese folding sides spectacles, one in ray skin case, the other in woven case.
£170-200 *CSK*

A pair of 'Martins Margins' iron framed spectacles with loop ends, one horn rim cracked, 18thC. **£350-400** *CSK*

Surveying Levels

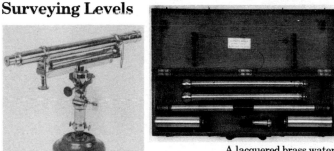

A brass surveying level, unsigned, with walnut display stand, 18thC, 19in (48cm) long.
£350-400 *C*

A lacquered brass water level, unsigned, in oak case, the lid with trade label for G. Straus, 4 Rue Pont d'Ile, Liege, 22in (56cm) wide.
£250-350 *CSK*

Two pairs of Chinese folding sides spectacles, both in shagreen cases, 6 and 7in (15 and 18cm) long. **£250-300** *CSK*

A lacquered brass surveying level, signed on the horizontal plate G. Adams London, with associated mahogany and brass tripod, late 18thC, 13½in (34cm) long. **£2,000-3,000** *CSK*

Theodolites

A lacquered brass double telescope surveying level, signed on the silvered dial Pistor and Martins BERLIN, No. 604, in oak case, 19thC, 10in (25cm) high. **£3,500-4,500** *CSK*

An Italian brass surveying level, signed on the limb LA FILOTECNICA Ing. A. Salmoiraghi & C. MILANO No. 17934, in fitted carrying case, 19thC, 13in (33cm) wide. **£350-450** *CSK*

A French brass centesimal theodolite, signed Secretan Paris No. 10808, late 19thC, 14in (36cm) long. **£400-500** *CSK*

A brass theodolite by OTTO FENNELL SÖHNE CASSELL No. 19813, on three-screw tripod mounting. **£250-350** *CSK*

An oxidised and lacquered brass transit theodolite, signed on the silvered compass dial Stanley, Gt. Turnstile, Holborn, LONDON No. 8363, on tripod mounting, in mahogany case, late 19thC, 13½in (34cm) wide. **£750-800** *CSK*

A brass theodolite, signed on the silvered compass THOMPSON & CO Optician, Liverpool, with maker's trade label, in mahogany case, 19thC, 12½in (32cm) wide. **£500-600** *CSK*

A theodolite by T. Cooke, with full vernier and 5 degree compass, c1900, 13½in (34cm) high. **£550-650** *DHO*

An American brass theodolite, signed on the horizontal plate B. Pike & Son N. York, on staff mounting, in mahogany case, early 19thC, 11in (28cm) wide. **£750-850** *CSK*

A mining dial, by Gardiner, Glasgow, c1830, 10in (25cm) high. **£200-250** *DHO*

A brass surveyor's theodolite, by Thompson of Liverpool, with half vernier and full compass, in mahogany box, c1850, 16in (41cm) wide.
£550-650 *DHO*

An oxidised and lacquered brass theodolite, signed on the silvered compass dial T. Street Commercial Rd., Lambeth, LONDON, in mahogany carrying case, late 19thC, 16½in (42cm) wide.
£550-600 *CSK*

A good quality circumferentor, late 18thC, 9½in (24cm) high.
£500-550 *DHO*

A brass and bronze theodolite, by Mackenzie, half vernier and full compass, c1830, 16½in (42cm) wide.
£800-1,000 *DHO*

Telescopes

A Victorian telescope, in pinewood box, with tripod, c1870, 26½in (67cm) wide.
£380-450 *DHO*

A telescope and original tripod, in rosewood case, 5in (13cm) wide.
£200-250 *DHO*

A brass miniature refracting telescope, unsigned, but Dollond pattern, late 18thC, 4in (10cm) long.
£320-400 *C*

A Dollond telescope, with original library tripod, celestial and terrestrial eyepieces, in fitted mahogany box, 54in (137cm) long.
£1,100-1,300 *DHO*

A lacquered brass 2in (5cm) reflecting telescope, signed on the eyepiece tube Ramsden London, 18thC, 14in (36cm) long.
£1,500-1,800 *CSK*

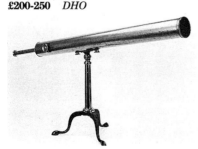

A brass 3in (8cm) refracting telescope, unsigned, with carrying case, late 19thC, 40½in (102cm) long. **£420-500** *C*

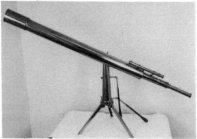

A Ross telescope, with horizontal and vertical gearing mechanism, with lenses and original box, c1850, 62in (157cm) long.
£1,200-1,400   *DHO*

A French brass 3in (8cm) refracting telescope, signed Mon de L'Ingr CHEVALLIER, Optician Place de Pont Neuf, 15, Paris, with associated mahogany tripod, 19thC, 39in (99cm) long.
£800-1,200   *CSK*

A bronzed iron and lacquered brass starfinder telescope, by Horne & Thornthwaite London, mid-19thC, 14in (36cm) high.
£720-800   *C*

A Gregorian reflecting telescope by W. S. Jones, with original speculum mirror, late 18thC, 17in (43cm) long.
£600-800   *DHO*

A mid-Victorian hand held telescope by Dollond, two-drawer, 32in (81cm) when extended.
£140-160   *DHO*

A French telescope, 9in (23cm) when extended, unusual in that this telescope splits in the barrel.
£80-100   *DHO*

A brass 3in (8cm) refracting telescope, signed on the body tube L. Casella, Maker to the Admiralty and Ordnance, London, and some mirror accessories, late 19thC, 60½in (153cm) long.
£1,500-2,000   *CSK*

A polished brass 4in (10cm) refracting telescope, signed on the back plate Clarkson London, and a carrying case, late 19thC.
£2,000-3,000   *CSK*

Weather

A Deco chrome and Bakelite barometer, thermometer and hygrometer, 7in (18cm) high.
£75-100   *PC*

A Deco Bakelite thermodial, with chrome trim, 4½in (11cm) high.
£20-25   *PC*

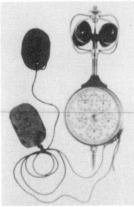

An American Deco Bakelite and chrome barometer, 5 by 7½in (13 by 19cm).
£60-70 *PC*

A windspeed meter, by Davis of Derby, late 19thC, 5in (13cm) high.
£150-180 *DHO*

A anemometer, signed Lenoir & Forster, Wien, No. 391, in green japanned case, 7in (18cm) long.
£350-500 *CSK*

FURTHER READING

The Divided Circle, J. A. Bennett, Phaidon, Christie's.

The Great Age Of The Microscope, G. L. E. Turner, Adam Hilger.

History Of The Telescope, King, Dover Press.

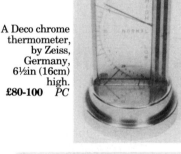

A Deco chrome thermometer, by Zeiss, Germany, 6½in (16cm) high.
£80-100 *PC*

A sunshine recorder, 20°C, by Negretti & Zambra, 6½in (16cm) high.
£50-60 *DHO*

A mahogany stick barometer, the bone plates signed Knight & Sons, Foster Lane, London, the case with plain cistern cover and mounted with a mercury thermometer, 36in (92cm).
£800-1,000 *S*

A modern Negretti and Zambra barograph, contained in a light oak case, 16in (41cm).
£350-450 *DEN*

A rosewood stick barometer with flat moulded pediment, the ivory scales inscribed T. & R. Willats, 98 Cheapside, London, with vernier, knob lacking, above cased thermometer, with turned cistern cover, 37in (94cm).
£600-700 *CSK*

A mid-18thC sundial, by Benjamin Cole, 13in (33cm) diam.
£300-400 *DHO*

Scripophily

Great Britain

A Claridges Hotels share certificate, depicts cruise ship and train, very decorative in orange/yellow/black, dated 1921. **£60-70**   *SCR*

Bray Waddington & Company, £50 share certificate, manufacturer of rolling stock acquired by Leeds Forge, which subsequently became part of Metro-Cammell, black on pink, dated 1865.   **£15-20**   *SCR*

Littleport Public Hall Co. Ltd., share certificate in black/white, with red paper seal, dated 1890.
£10-14   *SCR*

The Amalgamated and Pneumatic Tyre Co. Ltd., early tyre company with Dunlop connection, 2 types of certificate: share certificate, black/white, dated 1898, Debenture, black/white wheel designs, dated 1899.   **£10-14 each**
Pair. **£18-22**   *SCR*

A. C. de Murrieta & Co, debenture certificate, engraved by Bradbury Wilkinson, issued in 1891:
£100 debenture, signed by Lord Sudely and A. de Murrieta, blue/white, 2,500 originally issued.
£18-22
£500 debenture, signed by Lord Sudely and C. de Murrieta, green/white, 500 originally issued.
£25-35
£1,000 debenture, signed by C. Murrieta and J. de Murrieta, red/white, 500 originally issued.
£30-40
Set of three.
£70-80   *SCR*

Towards the end of the 19thC the 4 Murrieta brothers were enormously wealthy financiers. C. de Murrieta & Co. Ltd. was a quasi merchant bank and was involved in many suspect transactions. The company only lasted a short time, collapsing in the wake of the 1890 Barings crisis.

A National Provincial Bank Ltd. share certificate, an agreement in 1963 between the National Provincial, the District and the Westminster Banks resulted in the formation of today's National Westminster Bank, this certificate depicts the original bank's headquarters, green/beige, 1960s.
£5-10   *SCR*

European

A S.A. Vieille Cure De Cenon share certificate in liqueur company, showing a large bottle with chateau backdrop, 2 types:
Action de Frs. 2500, red, dated 1952.
£8-12
Action de Jouissance, blue, dated 1929.
£28-32   SCR

A Companhia De Navegacao share certificate, depicting harbour scene with Gothic style surround, multicoloured, issued in Ponta Delgada, Portugal 1920.   **£90-100   SCR**

A Compania Madrilena Almacenes Generales bearer share, a storage and transportation company, blue/brown/gold, dated 1906.   **£20-30   SCR**

A Compagnie Maritime De La Seine founders' share, which depicts views of the London Thames River and Parisian Seine, light/dark brown, c1899.
£20-30   SCR

A La Carbonera Metalurgica Espanola share certificate, an early Spanish coal and iron ore mining company located at Montsech, the company also constructed a railway from Lerida to the mines, on thick paper with vignette of railway and mine, brown/black, dated 1873.
£20-30 *SCR*

A Compania General De Coches De Lujo share certificate, with large vignette of coach and horses, beige/blue/red, dated Madrid 1909.
£120-130 *SCR*

An Italian & Austrian Railway Company share certificate, in English and Italian, printed on pink paper.
£50-60 *SCR*

The company was incorporated in 1845 to construct a line from Verona to Ancona. Brunel was to be the engineer. It would appear that for some reason the line was never built.

A Lombardy-Venetian Railway bond for 200 Austrian guilders, with surround of vignettes of train, ship and produce, issued in Vienna 1883.
£45-55 *SCR*

A Kreuger & Toll share certificate 3 types:
1 bearer share, green.
5 bearer shares, brown.
£14-16 each
10 bearer shares, red.
£18-22 *SCR*

A famous Swedish company which dominated the world match industry and became powerful enough to be a provider of funds to European states. Greatest fame arose from involvement in major accusations of fraud and its eventual collapse. Kreuger committed suicide but doubts of the fraud still persist today, late 1920s.

USA

A Wagner Palace Car Company share certificate, an early deluxe carriage company, vignettes of loco and grand buildings, brown/black, c1888.
£20-30 *SCR*

The European & American Steam Shipping Co. share certificate, black/white, ordinary share of £9, dated 1857. **£20-30** *SCR*

The San Cebrian Railway & Collieries Co. Ltd. share certificate, Waterlow printed, a British financed Spanish railway and coal mine, black/white, dated 1885.
£16-20 *SCR*

Atlantic & Pacific
Railroad Company
$1,000 bond, with
vignette of Indians and
surveyors overlooking
river scene, brown/black
with coupons, dated 1880.
£25-35 *SCR*

A Michigan Central
Railroad $1,000 bond,
this railroad dominated
both passenger and
freight business between
Chicago and the Atlantic
seaboard, red/black,
dated 1909. **£18-22**

A Vandalia Railroad
share certificate, with
loco flanked by warrior
and 'Peace', brown/black,
c1915.
£16-20 *SCR*

*The company was a
consolidation of several
smaller lines.*

A New York Central &
Hudson Railroad
Company $1,000 bond,
formed by the
amalgamation of several
lines this became one of
the major railroads with
a mileage in excess of
3,750, vignette of a train
and sailship at dockside,
green/black, dated 1898.
£20-30 *SCR*

A Baltimore Shipbuilding & Dry
Dock Company stock certificate,
with vignette of dry dock, small
capitalisation and therefore considered
scarce, green/black, c1905. **£60-70** *SCR*

A New Jersey & Seashore
Railroad Company share
certificate, with vignette
of the loco 'America', the
main business of the line
was passenger traffic
between Philadelphia
and the South New
Jersey Shore resorts,
green, c1938.
£14-16 *SCR*

Worldwide

A New England
Consolidated
Oil Co. share
certificate, with
vignette of oil
derricks and
gold seal,
registered in
South Dakota,
black/white,
dated 1901.
£18-22 *SCR*

A Plantation Jules Van
Lancker bearer share in
a Congolese plantation
company, depicting
natives working on farm,
red, dated 1927. **£10-14** *SCR*

An S.A. Mines De Plomb & De Zinc Du Djebel Oudiba (Tunisia) bearer share certificate, a North African mining company with a view of sand dunes with village to one side seen through Moroccan arch, brown/green, dated 1924.
£12-16 *SCR*

An El Banco Chileno Garantizador De Valores unissued bond, small format with vignette of lion and allegorical scenes, green/black, c1900. **£12-18** *SCR*

A 'La Nacional' Compania Mexicana De petroleo SA bearer share certificate for early Mexican oil company, with vignette of oil field and terminal with Mexican eagle at the top and affixed revenue stamps, brown, dated 1916. **£10-14** *SCR*

An Electric Light & Power Supply Company share certificate, dramatically designed in early Egyptian power company, depicts cars, ships, sphinx, etc., brown/black, c1923.
£70-80 *SCR*

A Cia. Agricola Y Colonizadora De Tobasco Y Chiapas SA bearer share certificate, in an agricultural company located in the southern Mexico states of Chiapas and Tobasco, with large vignette of plantation/river scene, olive/black, dated 1912.
£10-14 *SCR*

A Rio Plata Mining Company Arizona, share certificate, with vignette of miners flanked by US and Mexican eagles, green/black, c1910.
£8-12 *SCR*

A La Rose Mines share certificate, a company incorporated in Ontario, with a vignette of miners working below ground, brown/black, c1922.
£10-14 *SCR*

A Co. Gen. De Tobacos De Filipinas share certificate, the company still exists and its shares have kept the same design, these are the early issue of 1882 and are in excellent condition, brown/white.
£80-90 *SCR*

Serviette Rings

Initialled ivory serviette rings, with silver letters.
£8-10 each   *ROS*

A further selection of serviette rings is featured in previous editions of Miller's Collectables Price Guides, available from Millers Publications.

Sewing

A mahogany gulls wing knitting sheath, 8in (20cm) long.
£35-40   *PSA*

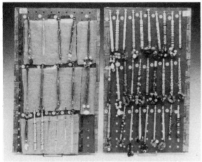

A collection of 250 lace bobbins, including 6 modern silver bobbins, 3 with Royal commemorative inscriptions, a group of 33 bone bobbins with carved, stained and wired decoration, 4 glass bobbins and a large quantity of wood bobbins, with card index.
£900-1,000   *Bea*

A lace making barrel, with drawer at the back and bobbins, 13in (33cm) long.
£50-55   *RE*

For a further selection of sewing collectables please refer to Miller's Collectables Price Guide Volume III, pp386-391.

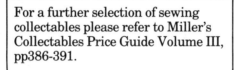

A bone lucet for making cords, early 19thC, 3in (8cm).
£6-8   *CA*

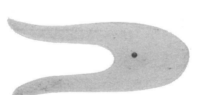

A patent darning mushroom with coiled spring, early 20thC.
£10-14   *CA*

A plastic darner, with thread, needle etc. inside, 1940s.
£6-8   *CA*

A blue plastic holder for knitting wool ball, c1950.
£10-14   *CA*

A rosewood sewing companion, with reel holder, pin cushion and thimble rest, 19thC, 4½in (11cm).
£75 100   *P(O)*

Three shuttles for factory looms, 19in (48cm) long.
£8-12 each   *RE*

Shipping

Two naval ashtrays.
£5-6 each *COB*

A spoon For the
Destruction of US
Battleship Maine, 1898.
£25-30 *COB*

A Royal Naval
ashtray, 1978.
£2-3 *COB*

A Royal Navy copper
ashtray.
£4-5 *COB*

A Copeland tureen lid
from Royal Yacht, c1905.
£100-200 *COB*

A selection of ship's
matchbooks.
£1-2 each *COB*

A wooden jigsaw
puzzle,
c1930.
£30-35 *COB*

A pack of playing
cards, 1950s.
£4-5 *COB*

Cross Reference
Playing Cards

An oil
painting
of the
Lusitania
by Simon
Fisher.
£130-150
COB

Shipping Co. playing cards. **£5-7 each** *COB*

A pen and ink drawing
by H. Wylie, c1910.
£60-65 *COB*

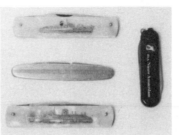

A moulded plastic scale
model of the Queen
Elizabeth ocean liner, in
a glass and mahogany
display case, 21½in
(55cm) long.
£30-40 *TAV*

Hamburg-Amerika
Linie, an advertisement
on glass of the Quadruple
Screw and Turbine
Express Steamer
Emperator The Largest
Vessel in the World, with
inset barometer and
hydrometer, 24 by 16½in
(61 by 42cm).
£400-450 *ONS*

A selection of shipping
companies' penknives.
£3-15 each *COB*

Shipping company
souvenir spoons.
£5-6 each *COB*

| Cross Reference |
| Posters |

An oil painting of the Queen Elizabeth on
the Solent by H. Gurnell, c1950, 30 by
40in (76 by 101.5cm). **£100-120** *COB*

A silver R.N. Division
badge.
£25-30 *COB*

A formal photograph of officers lost on the Titanic, on the bridge, Capt. E. J. Smith & Dr O'Loughlin, First Officer W. M. Murdoch & Purser McIlroy and 2 others, taken by A. J. F. Bond, Bodmin, 8 by 6in (20 by 15cm). **£350-400** *ONS*

A poster by M. H. Poulton, New Zealand For The World's Best Sport.
£230-250 *ONS*

A poster by Bernard Gribble, Canadian Pacific Spans The World, Most Convenient Route to Canada-USA-Japan-China, New Zealand & Australia.
£350-400 *ONS*

Shipping Postcards

Titanic

An informal group photograph of officers from the Titanic, of H. G. Lowe, H. J. Pitman, C. H. Lightoller, and J. Groves Boxhall, by Lafayette, London, signed by each, on card, annotated by Pitman, 4½ by 6in (11 by 15cm).
£1,100-1,200 *ONS*

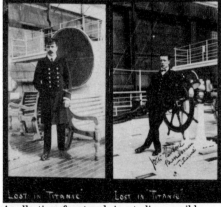

A collection of postcard size studies, possibly taken on board the Titanic.
£350-400 *ONS*

Postcards featuring reproductions of famous posters are becoming increasingly collectable. One of the most popular at present is the classic series of shipping posters, a selection of which are featured here.
£8-10 the set *MAP*

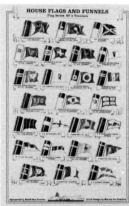

A selection of flags and funnels postcards sold in a series of 8, illustrating different companies' flags from the turn of the century.
£2-3 set of 8   *MAP*

A set of 32 U.S.A. Cunard postcards, printed to commemorate the 150th Anniversary of the oldest trans-Atlantic passenger line.
£12-15   *MAP*

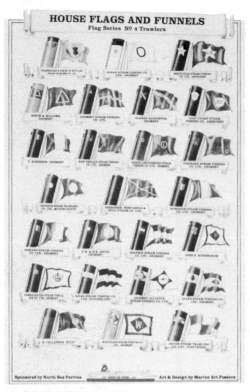

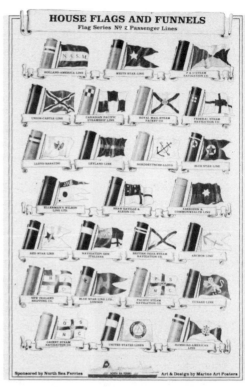

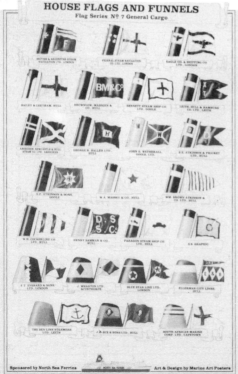

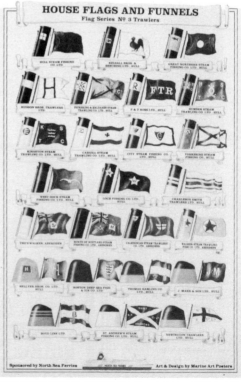

Signs, Advertising & Packaging

An American thermometer, c1960, 13in (33cm) high. **£15-20**   *AAM*

An enamel advertising sign, slight repainting, 42in (106.5cm) wide. **£300-350**   *S*

A George V metal plaque from a telegraph pole, 8 by 6in (20 by 15cm). **£25-30**   *PC*

A 30mph limit sign, c1930, 22in (56cm) high. **£50-60**   *PC*

A bronze framed underground sign, late 1930s, 54in (137cm) wide. **£120-150**   *PC*

A Craven 'A' clock, 13in (33cm) square. **£100-150**   *RE*

A chromo lithographic display poster. **£150-200**   *K*

An enamel sign, early 20thC. **£50-90**   *K*

Crisp Packets

This collection of crisp and other snack cellophane packets from the 1970s probably has no value at all at present. However, it is worth remembering that many areas of collectables featured in our books probably started off completely valueless – watch this space!

Smoking

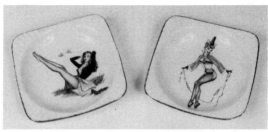

A pair of Wade ashtrays,
c1950, 4in (10cm) square.
£10-15   *BEV*

An album of matchbooks,
c1930, 10 by 11in (25 by
28cm).
£45-50   *AAM*

A selection of German
porcelain pipe bowls,
painted with pictures of
young ladies, 5 to 6in
(12.5 to 15cm) long.
£210-230 each   *P(S)*

An Art Deco ashtray, 3in
(7.5cm) diam.   **£20-30**   *PC*

Two armchair pipe racks, c1930, 2½in (6.5cm) high.
£8-12 each   *MA*

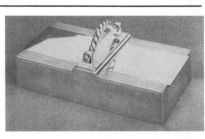

Cigarette Smoking

A smoker's box in the
form of a coal truck,
South Western Railway,
11in (28cm) long.
£250-300   *RP*

A cigarette box, stamped
with French hallmarks
and Cartier Paris S9121,
c1944, 10½in (26cm)
long.   **£2,700-3,000**   *C*

A cheroot holder and
case, 3in (7.5cm).
£15-20   *ROS*

A coin operated bar cigarette box,
c1940, 12in (30.5cm) high.   **£60-70**   *Hol*

A match striker. **£20-30** *HEW*

A German gilt lined cigarette case, with secret compartment revealing a seated semi-naked maiden, import marks for London, 3½in (9cm). **£1,200-1,500** *CSK*

A cigarette case, c1930, 4in (10cm) wide. **£12-15** *CAC*

An erotic cigarette holder, with ivory stem carved as a naked lady, 4in (10cm) long. **£160-180** *Bon*

Lighters

A gun shaped petrol lighter, c1950, 4in (10cm) long. **£12-15** *Hol*

. A cigarette machine, taking silver threepenny bits, 11½in (29cm) high. **£70-80** *ROS*

A fur covered lighter, by Luxe. **£8-10** *COL*

A circular petrol lighter, by Thorens, c1930. **£25-30** *Hol*

Two Zippo lighters, c1980. **£10-12 each** *COL*

A cannon petrol lighter, 1970. **£10-15** *COL*

A selection of Zippo lighters, c1950-70. **£10-12 each** *COB*

For a further selection of Match Strikers please refer to previous editions of Miller's Collectables, available from Millers Publications.

Snuff Boxes

An oval enamel snuff box, 2in (5cm) wide.
£140-160 *CSK*

A gorilla snuff box, 18thC, 3in (7.5cm) long. **£300-500** *R de R*

A rosewood and brass snuff box, 2in (5cm) wide.
£15-18 *ROS*

A Scandinavian carved shoe snuff box, 2½in (6.5cm) wide.
£80-90 *PSA*

A French enamel snuff box, 19thC, 3in (7.5cm) wide.
£170-200 *CSK*

A Continental enamel snuff box, 3½in (8.5cm) wide.
£100-120 *CSK*

A Samson enamel rectangular snuff box, 19thC, 3½in (8.5cm) wide.
£150-200 *CSK*

A boot snuff box without a lid, early 19thC, 3½in (8.5cm) wide.
£30-35 *PSA*

A Samson enamel snuff box, painted with a maritime scene, and the sides with flowers, 19thC, 3in (7.5cm).
£300-350 *CSK*

A Continental horn snuff box, inlaid with three-colour gold and silver flowers, late 18th/early 19thC, 2½in (6cm) wide.
£380-400 *CSK*

Two Edwardian snuff
boxes in lacquered
rosewood.
£40-50 each   *BEV*

A Victorian snuff box, by
Edward Edwards, engine
turned to cover and base,
the cover with crest and
motto, London 1843.
£180-200   *Bon*

A Samson enamel
rectangular snuff box,
painted with British and
French ships, with a
portrait bust of Lord
Nelson inside the lid,
3½in (8.5cm) wide.
£275-300   *CSK*

A German papier mâché
snuff box cover, early
19thC, with later base,
3½in (9cm) diam.
£330-360   *CSK*

A snuff box by Nathaniel
Mills, with chased floral
scroll thumbpiece,
Birmingham 1833, 2½in
(6.5cm) wide.
£170-200   *Bon*

A George III snuff box, by
Cocks and Betteridge,
foliate engraved, flat
hinged cover,
Birmingham 1811.
£120-150   *Bon*

A George III snuff box, by
Samuel Pemberton, with
shaped bar thumbpiece
to convex cover,
Birmingham 1810.
£200-250   *Bon*

A George III snuff box by
Joseph Willmore, the flat
hinged cover with bar
thumbpiece and
engraved
commemorative
inscription, Birmingham
1817.
£65-75   *Bon*

A William IV snuff box,
with engine turned cover
and base, applied foliate
bar thumbpiece,
Birmingham, c1830.
£110-150   *Bon*

An oval enamel snuff
box, with views of
Beachy Head, Pevensey
and Hastings Castle, 2in
(5cm) wide.
£350-400   *CSK*

A George III snuff box by
John Shaw, with banded
engine turning to cover,
commemorative
inscription to interior,
Birmingham 1817.
£80-100   *Bon*

SPORT

A poster of the Harlem
Globetrotters Show,
£1-2 *COL*

A pair of snow shoes.
£60-100 *MSh*

Three colour reproductions of Johnnie
Walker advertisements, Fishing 1820,
Cricket 1820, and Golfing 1820,
after Tom Browne, in common mount,
17½ by 30½in (44 by 77.5cm).
£160-180 *CSK*

Baseball

Frontispiece and 41 hand coloured plates from Mingaud
(M) The Noble Game of Billiards, translated by John
Thurston, 1830. **£500-550** *CSK*

A pen, ink and watercolour
of Jack Johnson v James J.
Jeffries, Heavy Weight
World Title Fight, 1912, by
J. Swetman, in circular
mount, 16in (40.5cm) diam
£130-150 *CSK*

An uncut sheet of R327 issued by National
Chicle Gum Co., blank on reverse prints, printer's
proof marks at edges, framed, mint, 9 by 9½in
(22.5 by 24cm). **£15,000-15,500** *S(NY)*

A pair of French tin
decoy partridges, with
replacement feet, 10½in
(26.5cm) high.
£225-250 *CHA*

A Goudey uncut sheet
with No. 106 Lajoie, of
25 cards, uncut, 1934,
framed, 14 by 11½in
(36 by 29cm).
£47,000-50,000 *S(NY)*

*Lajoie was printed in
1934 and mailed with a
letter of explanation to
anyone who wrote to the
company asking about
the missing card in 1933,
consequently it is
extremely rare, let alone
on an uncut sheet; the
sheet is a final production
sheet with backs and in
full colour. Only 5 copies
are known to exist of this
sheet.*

Cross Reference
Baseball – Colour Section

A chromolithograph of
Kent, Lord Harris, by
Spy, 1881.
£350-400   *CSK*

A collection of Phantom
World Series Press Pins
from 1938, the first
Phantom World Series
Press Pin at Pittsburgh,
to 1988, 57 different
teams, various formats.
£10,500-11,000   *S(NY)*

Cricket

A watercolour on ivory,
A Boy with Bat, by
Brenda Francklyn,
signed and dated 1911,
5½ by 4in (14 by 10cm).
£300-350   *CSK*

A coloured engraving,
after William Drummond
& Charles J. Basbe, of
The Cricket Match
between Sussex & Kent
at Brighton, by G. H.
Phillips, published by
E. Gambart & Co.,
London, and W. H.
Mason, Brighton, 1849,
26½ by 37½in (67 by
95cm), and the
companion lithographic
Key Plate.
£300-400   *CSK*

A watercolour,
A Boy with Bat,
English School,
19thC, 9 by 7in
(22.5 by 18cm).
£370-400   *CSK*

A chromolithograph of
'Ranji', K. S. Ranjitsinhji,
framed, 1897.
£130-150   *CSK*

A photograph of the Philadelphians
at the Brighton Match, July 21st,
22nd, 1884, with team list on
mount, framed and glazed, 9 by
11in (22.5 by 28cm).
£200-220   *CSK*

Golf

A box of Colonel blue-ring paper tees, original box. **£660-700** *C(S)*

A dimple patterned Gutty golf ball, used by Harry Vardon in the Open Championship, 1899, on silver base, inscribed 'This ball played the first nine holes', with silver plaque inscribed 'Open Championship played Sandwich, June 6th and 7th 1899, won by H. Vardon', 3in (7.5cm) high.
£3,500-4,000 *C(S)*

Three copies of Golfing Magazine, August 1902, June 1903 and October 1912. **£160-200** *C(S)*

A golf poker, 16in (41cm) high. **£20-30** *HEW*

A gilt bronze model of a golfer, stamped Argentor-Wein, on onyx base, 12in (30.5cm) high.
£520-600 *C(S)*

A complete set of resin tee plaques, for the ladies' tees of the Princes Course, Gleneagles.
£750-850 *C(S)*

A brass Gutty golf ball mould for a mesh patterned golf ball, by John White & Co., Edinburgh, No. 946, Patent No. 11917, and a cast iron bench press. **£3,500-4,000** *C(S)*

A mahogany and stained beechwood ballot box, fitted with 2 drawers, c1900, 13in (33cm).
£4,500-5,000 *C(S)*

By repute, this ballot box was removed from North Berwick Golf Club.

The Princes Course, Gleneagles, was a 9 hole course designed by the head greenkeeper, George Alexander, and constructed in the summer of 1928. It was extended in 1974 to 18 holes.

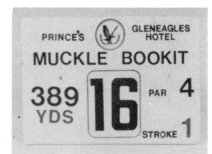

A complete set of resin tee plaques, for the gentlemen's tees of the Princes Course, Gleneagles. **£1,750-2,000** *C(S)*

A blue painted metal ball box, advertising Dunlop Golf Balls, 9in (23cm) wide. **£500-600** *C(S)*

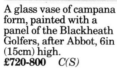

A glass vase of campana form, painted with a panel of the Blackheath Golfers, after Abbot, 6in (15cm) high. **£720-800** *C(S)*

A Doulton Lambeth stoneware jug, decorated with 3 raised panels, damaged, 7in (18cm) high. **£250-300** *C(S)*

A silver and enamel medal, inscribed 'Ladies Medal Tarbrax and District Golf Club, 1924', in fitted case. **£1,000-2,000** *C(S)*

A papier mâché figure of The Penfold Golfer, 20in (51cm) high. **£550-600** *C(S)*

A papier mâché figure of The Dunlop Caddy, the head modelled as a dimpled golf ball, 15½in (39cm) high. **£360-400** *C(S)*

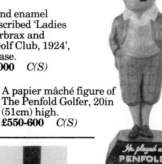

Golf Clubs

A Browns patent tinned rake mashie, with pierced rounded face, the sole stamped Browns Patent and VL & D, N.Y. **£3,500-4,000** *C(S)*

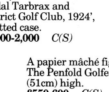

A Dalrymples patent bronze cross headed club, probably manufactured by Hutchison of North Berwick, c1890. **£2,700-3,000** *C(S)*

An unusual mid-iron, with curved face and sole, c1890. **£1,250-1,500** *C(S)*

A mammoth niblick, the head stamped Saville rustless iron LB 78 Jermyn Street, London SW, c1910, face 3½in (9cm) deep. **£600-650** *C(S)*

A Cardinal giant niblick by Bishop & Henry, retailed by Murray, Pitlochry. **£770-850** *C(S)*

413

A scared head long nosed playclub, the head stamped Harous, the sole with bone inset, shaft repaired.
£1,500-2,000 *C(S)*

A scared head Transitional driver, the head stamped A. Patrick, the toe damaged, c1880, and another driver.
£350-450 *C(S)*

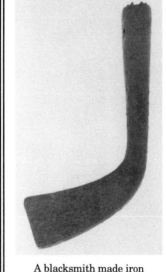

A blacksmith made iron club head, with cut-off nose and curved sole, 5in (13cm) hosel, late 17th/early 18thC.
£44,000-45,000 *C(S)*

A Sprague patented aluminium headed putter, with unusual adjustable ball socket, stamped S. Sprague and Co., Boston.
£950-1,000 *C(S)*

A patented putter, with metal head and wooden inset, c1910.
£880-950 *C(S)*

A long nosed scared head baffing spoon by McEwan, stamped McEwan with owner's initials CDC and JHCL, c1850.
£6,600-7,000 *C(S)*

A Mills patent aluminium headed mallet putter, Patent No. 42186.
£900-950 *C(S)*

An Auchterlonie patent putter.
£120-150 *C(S)*

An unusul steel headed roller putter, the cylindrical head fitted with 4 ball bearing filled rollers.
£360-400 *C(S)*

A long nosed scared head short spoon, by Auchterlonie of St. Andrews, a smooth faced mashie and a socket head wooden putter.
£880-1,000 *C(S)*

A patented convex faced putter, the Helerwhit Patent No. 247116, the shaft stamped Made in Scotland.
£350-400 *C(S)*

A scared head long nosed brassie, the head stamped J. McRobie, the sole with horn inset and brass plate, c1885. **£850-950** *C(S)*

A smooth faced lofter by J. McRobie, the head stamped L. J. McRobie. **£420-500** *C(S)*

A pottery plaque with a portrait of J. Quinn, Celtic F.C., 10in (25cm) high. **£180-200** *C(S)*

A Scotland International No. 15 jersey, bearing embroidered badge inscribed 'F.I.F.A. World Cup, Argentina 1978'. **£220-300** *C(S)*

This jersey is purportedly the one worn by Archie Gemmill during the Scotland-Holland game. Scotland won this game 3–1, Gemmill firstly converting a penalty and then going on to score one of the classic goals of the tournament.

Football

A football shaped teapot, c1930, 6½in (16cm) high. **£100-150** *HEW*

A 9ct gold and enamel Scottish Football League medal, the reverse inscribed 'Winners – League Cup – Rangers F.C., 1977-78 season'. **£420-500** *C(S)*

A 9ct gold and enamel Scottish Football Association medal, the reverse inscribed 'Winners, Scottish Cup', 1963-64. **£460-550** *C(S)*

A 9ct gold and enamel Scottish Football League Championship medal, the reverse inscribed 'First Division, Season 1971-72, Celtic F.C.'. **£400-450** *C(S)*

A football trophy, on onyx pedestal, with silver plaque inscribed 'Presented by Scottish Football Association, To Commemorate the Winning of the British International Trophy, in its First Year, 1935-36, D. McCulloch, Brentford F.C.', base chipped, 5½in (14cm) high. **£200-250** *C(S)*

A 15ct gold and red enamel Southern Football League medal, the reverse inscribed 'Northampton Town F.C., J. Manning, 1908-9', in original fitted case.
£300-350 *C(S)*

A Britannia pottery figure of Wee MacGregor, dressed as a Rangers F.C. player, holding a football in his right hand, inscribed 'A. Bennet', 14½in (37cm) high.
£385-450 *C(S)*

A. Bennet played for both Celtic and Rangers, between 1904-13.

A 9ct gold and enamel Glasgow Charity Cup medal, inscribed 'Charity Cup, won by Celtic F.C., J. McMenemy, 1935-36'.
£300-350 *C(S)*

Celtic defeated Rangers 4–2 in this match.

A Britannia pottery figure of Wee MacGregor, dressed as a Celtic F.C. player, his right foot resting on a football, on circular base, 14in (36cm) high.
£250-300 *C(S)*

Two commemorative postal covers, celebrating John Greig, Rangers F.C., Testimonial Match, Sunday April 16th 1978, -v- Scotland Select, fully autographed by both teams, framed and glazed.
£150-200 *C(S)*

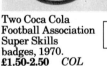

Two Coca Cola Football Association Super Skills badges, 1970.
£1.50-2.50 *COL*

Cross Reference
Coca Cola

A Newcastle United F.C. team photograph, season 1909-10, framed and glazed.
£165-200 *C(S)*

A Scotland International football jersey, with button-up neck and white cotton collar, bearing embroidered cloth badge, S.V.E., 1930/31.
£720-750 *C(S)*

This jersey was worn by J. McGrory, Celtic F.C. Scotland defeated England 2–0 at Hampden, both teams sharing the Home International Championship on 4 points.

Football Programmes

Bradford -v- Wrexham,
November 24th 1969.
£1-2 *COL*

Manchester United -v-
Leeds United, March
23rd 1970, semi-final
replay.
£1-3 *COL*

An F.A. Challenge Cup
Competition, 1920-21,
Final Tie programme,
Tottenham Hotspur -v-
Wolverhampton
Wanderers, 23/4/21, at
Stamford Bridge.
£550-600 *C(S)*

*Spurs defeated Wolves
1–0 in front of a crowd of
72,000.*

Burnley -v-
Southampton,
October
13th 1965.
50p-£1 *COL*

Arsenal -v- Liverpool,
January 8 1966.
£1-2 *COL*

Arsenal -v-
Sparta,
October
2nd 1946.
£2-4 *COL*

Queen's
Park
Rangers
-v- Oldham
Athletic,
April 19th
1965.
50p-£1
COL

Workington -v-
Doncaster August 21st
1971.
£1-2 *COL*

England -v- Austria,
November 28th 1951.
£2-4 *COL*

Tea Making

One of the most popular areas we featured in last year's Miller's Collectables Price Guide, Volume III, was Coffee Making. We showed an extremely varied and interesting collection highlighting the great variety of items that can be collected under a common theme. This year with thanks to our contributor, we have repeated the exercise taking Tea Making as the theme.

A Chinese tea jar, 19thC.
£80-100 *TBC*

A wooden chest opening to depict a hearth, the kettle is a single cup tea strainer on a chain in American silver, c1850, the fire tongs are sugar nips and the shovel a sugar or caddy spoon.
£400-450 *TBC*

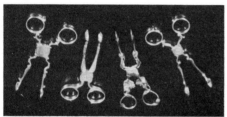

A collection of English sugar nips, late 18thC.
£70-200 each *TBC*

Afternoon Tea, a Royal Doulton group, 1935-82.
£200-250 *TBC*

Cat merchants and tea dealers at Tong Chow, drawn by T. Allom and engraved by T. A. Prior, mid-19thC.
£200-300 *TBC*

A tea drinking scene and British field sports, late 20thC.
£100-150 *TBC*

A selection of English sugar tongs, 18th/19thC.
£15-150 each *TBC*

A print of monkeys gathering tea, published by R. Ackermann, 1821.
£100-150 *TBC*

A Continental tea party group, late 20thC.
£200-250 *TBC*

A tea party at Bagnigge Wells, from a print after George Morland, in original 18thC frame.
£300-350 *TBC*

Three silver Georgian tea canisters, by Samuel Taylor, London 1750.
£8,500-9,000 *TBC*

A ceramic tea jar, with French silver base cover and lid, c1850.
£1,650-2,000 *TBC*

A moustache cup and saucer, early 20thC.
£60-100 *TBC*

A brass and tortoiseshell steam engine form tea casket, the front opens to reveal a sliding compartment for tea, another below for spoons, the tender houses the sugar box, mid-19thC, 14½in (37cm) long.
£3,500-4,000 *TBC*

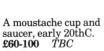

A Chinese tea jar, made for the Asian market, 19thC. **£140-200** *TBC*

A Chinese porcelain tea jar, mid-19thC. **£100-150** *TBC*

A Swiss Edwardian tea locomotive, made as a gift to a Spanish Consul, 1902. **£2,500-3,000** *PC*

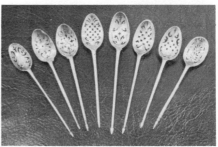

A pair of silver rococo tea canisters, Samuel Taylor, London 1750.
£2,800-3,500 *TBC*

A selection of English silver mote spoons, 17thC.
£100-150 *TBC*

Teapots

A silver bead edge teapot, with bright cut decoration and pear wood handle, by Hester Bateman, London 1783. **£2,000-2,500** *TBC*

A can shaped silver teapot, by Hester Bateman, 1783. **£2,000-2,500** *TBC*

A Japanese tea kettle with silver gilt decoration, c1880, 6in (15cm) high. **£1,750-2,000** *TBC*

A Belleek Chinese style tea urn, First Period, c1865. **£8,000-10,000** *PC*

A Chinese blue and white teapot, recovered from under the South China Seas by Capt. Michael Hatcher in 1983, c1645. **£600-700** *TBC*

l. A Raku tea masters bowl, in glazed black with grey waisted body, 19thC. **£350-400**
r. A Tetsubin cast iron tea kettle, mid-19thC. **£500-600** *TBC*

A Copeland teapot with pewter lid, 19thC, 5½in (14cm) high. **£70-85** *PSA*

A bullet shaped teapot, by Edward Pocock, London 1729. **£5,500-6,000** *TBC*

A Chinese silver teapot, Sui Hsing, of the Hsien Feng Dynasty, 1850s. **£600-800** *TBC*

A Davenport teapot and stand, c1820.
£150-200   *TBC*

An Art Nouveau mauve, green and ochre metal teapot, with plated lid, 5½in (14cm) high.
£75-80   *HEW*

A 'famille verte' miniature teapot, Kangxi period, c1662.
£450-500   *TBC*

A Christopher Dresser electro plated teapot and stand, late 19thC.
£2,500-3,000   *TBC*

An enamelled Yixing teapot and warmer, decorated in overglaze blue, 19thC.
£230-300   *TBC*

A Doulton teapot and stand with poem, 'This is the house that Jack built', 1920s.
£150-200   *TBC*

A Chinese teapot, with a silver lid, c1790.
£1,000-1,500   *TBC*

A lacquered tea kettle, mid-20thC.
£2,000-2,500   *TBC*

A Staffordshire teapot with stand, early 20thC.
£60-100   *TBC*

A Bauhaus silver and ebony teapot, with tea strainer, by Marianne Brandt, c1924, 3in (8cm).
£120,000-125,000   *PC*

A Chinese teapot, with silver spout and wooden handle on silver mounts, c1750.   **£1,000-2,000**   *TBC*

Tea Caddies

A late Victorian tea caddy and cover in the Georgian style, London 1892, 430gr.
£380-450 *HSS*

A George IV penwork two-division tea caddy, with crimson stained interior and a floral spray on the underside of the top, c1820, 9½in (24cm).
£360-400 *S(S)*

A Tea company promotional caddy, early 20thC.
£100-150 *TBC*

A George IV maple tea caddy, with rosewood mouldings and segmented medallion of exotic veneers, c1830, 14½in (37cm) wide.
£500-550 *S(S)*

A Regency burr yew wood tea caddy, with maker's label.
£250-300 *SWO*

A George III mahogany tea caddy, inlaid with cherry wood and sycamore, interior with label Made by John Scott, Woodhall, County of Cumberland, 1800, 10½in (26cm) wide.
£400-450 *S(S)*

A satinwood and polychrome painted tea caddy, 11in (28cm) wide.
£400-450 *C*

An ivory, tortoiseshell veneered and pewter strung two-division tea caddy, on silvered ball feet, early 19thC, 7in (18cm) wide.
£300-350 *C*

A George III mahogany, chequer strung and boxwood outlined tea caddy, with canted angles, with 2 lidded compartments, 7½in (19cm) wide.
£400-500 *CSK*

The Wedgwood 'Lazy Susan', c1880.
£600-700   *TBC*

Tea Urns

A Sheffield plated urn, early 19thC.
£1,500-2,000   *TBC*

A brass Russian samovar, early 20thC.
£1,000-1,500
TBC

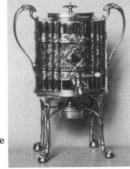

An Art Nouveau silver plated domestic urn, late 19thC.
£400-450   *TBC*

An Art Nouveau Reed and Barton silver plated urn, late 19thC.
£450-500   *TBC*

Teapot Stands

A copper plated commercial tea maker, mid-20thC.
£400-500   *TBC*

A selection of teapot stands dating from 1800 to 1950.
£25-150 each   *TBC*

Telephones

A sign, 1930s, 23in (59cm) wide.
£60-100 *RE*

A Type 162 telephone with bell set 25, c1929.
£100-125 *PC*

A chest telephone, used by telephone girls in the 1930s.
£25-35 *ROS*

An early candlestick telephone, with steering wheel dial, c1915.
£150-250 *SM*

A wall telephone with brass fittings, 17½in (44cm) high.
£150-200 *RE*

An Ericsson intercommunication telephone, 1930s.
£60-100 *SM*

A KTAS Ericsson skeleton magneto, c1900.
£300-600 *SM*

An original telephone with handle and BT connection, 1940s.   **£95-100** *ROS*

An American 300 telephone, early 1950s.
£75-85 *PC*

A Bell Telephone Mfg.Co., Antwerp, metal desk set, 1930s.
£50-95 *SM*

An 'A' and 'B' coin box, unused since decimalisation in early 1970s.
£350-425   *BHE*

A No. K6 telephone kiosk, c1935.
Unrestored **£400-450**
Restored
£1,000-1,450   *BHE*

A National Telephone Co. enamelled iron kiosk sign, c1905.
£30-80   *SM*

A Standard Telephones & Cables, London, Bakelite intercommunication telephone, 1930s.
£80-100   *SM*

A No. 232 kiosk telephone, c1935.
£150-200   *BHE*

FURTHER READING
Britains Public Payphones, M. Goss, British Telecom, 1984.
Introduction to Telephony & Telegraphy, E. J. Jolley, Pitman, 1968.

A copper telephone, with brass hinged carrying handle and Bakelite hand piece.
£60-70   *HCC*

A Fyns Kommunale black painted metal telephone with wind up bell.
£90-110   *HCC*

An early Post Office candlestick telephone, with solid back transmitter and number label, c1915.
£95-200   *SM*

TEXTILES
Costume
Ladieswear

A georgette dress with machine embroidery, black and cream, 1920s, 40in (102cm) long. **£100-120**   *CLA*

A black chiffon evening dress with red beaded trim, 1920s, 45in (114cm) long. **£175-200**   *ACL*

A fancy dress costume, made for a ballerina, depicting horses and the first motor cars 'The Road to Ruin', c1916. **£550-600**   *ACL*

A fine cotton dress, with beaded decoration, washable, 1920s, 41in (104cm) long. **£320-350**   *ACL*

Black crêpe cocktail dress with lace appliqué, 1939-40, plastic zip, 44in (111.5cm) long. **£65-75**   *ACL*

A beaded and diamanté trimmed silk crepe dress, 1920s, 43in (109cm) long. **£280-300**   *ACL*

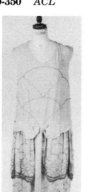

A cream silk crepe evening dress, trimmed with beads, 1920s. **£150-180**   *ACL*

A silk velvet evening dress, with beading and satin insert, 1920s, 42in (107cm) long. **£110-125**   *ACL*

A cut velvet and chiffon evening dress, c1916, 55½in (140cm) long. **£125-135**   *CLA*

A cotton evening dress with glass beaded trim, 1920s, 41in (104cm) long. **£350-380**   *ACL*

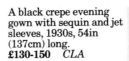

A black crepe evening gown with sequin and jet sleeves, 1930s, 54in (137cm) long.
£130-150   *CLA*

A silk crepe de chine evening dress and bolero, c1940.
£85-95   *CLA*

A patterned velvet and silk coat, c1915, 58in (147cm) long.
£175-200   *ACL*

A black silk satin evening dress, with bead trimming, c1918, 46in (117cm) long.
£180-200   *ACL*

A working dress, as worn by a seamstress or factory worker, c1915, 51in (130cm) long.
£40-45   *ACL*

A cream silk tennis dress/shorts with a long cream silk scarf with tennis racquet motifs, c1920, scarf 96in (244cm) long.
£40-50
Dress, 36in (92cm) long.
£70-80   *CLA*

A silk brocade patterned evening coat with scalloped edges, c1930, 55in (140cm) long.
£140-150
CLA

A black crepe evening dress with bias cut diamanté trim, 1930s, 58in (147cm) long.
£150-180   *CLA*

A black crepe evening gown with glass lozenge decoration, 1930s, 56in (142cm) long.
£100-120   *CLA*

A black crepe evening gown with bolero, paisley patterned top, 1930s, 60in (152cm) long.   **£95-120**   *CLA*

A silk velvet evening coat, c1926.
£130-140 *CLA*

A cream and gold figured brocade ball gown, 1950s.
£65-75 *CLA*

A Norman Hartnell pink silk grosgrain coat with black plastic decoration, c1950, 38in (97cm) long.
£75-80 *CLA*

A figured silk New Look dress lined in silk, 1950s, 45½in (115cm) long.
£55-60 *CLA*

A black taffeta dress with white painted spots, 1950s, 46in (117cm) long.
£40-50 *CLA*

A navy and white wool dress, unworn, fully lined with Liberty design, dress shields and leather flower, c1938, 43in (109cm) long.
£55-60 *CLA*

A herringbone tweed belted Utility suit, with Utility mark, c1940, 46in (117cm) long.
£60-70 *CLA*

A Victorian style child's coat, hat and muff, coat made from a paisley wool shawl, possibly made later, 42in (107cm) long.
£230-250 *ACL*

A grosgrain coat, 1950s, 43in (109cm) long. **£50-60** *CLA*

A brown worsted Utility suit, with Utility mark, 1940s, 42in (107cm) long.
£60-70 *CLA*

A grosgrain watermarked taffeta and satin short evening dress, 1950s. **£45-50** *CLA*

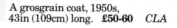

Ladies Underwear & Nightwear

Cami-knickers in peach georgette with cream lace appliqué, c1930.
£35-45 *ACL*

A silk and lace bed jacket, 1920s, 25in (64cm) long.
£65-75 *CLA*

A leather corset, laces at the front and half way down the back, possibly Victorian, 26in (66cm) long.
£100-120 *CLA*

A petticoat in hand embroidered pure silk crepe de chine, c1930.
£30-35 *CLA*

A chiffon house gown, 1970s.
£50-60 *ACL*

A pair of Victorian cotton lawn knickerbockers, trimmed with broderie anglais.
£70-85 *ACL*

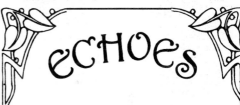

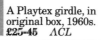

An Edwardian corset.
£50-75 *ACL*

A Playtex girdle, in original box, 1960s.
£25-45 *ACL*

Ladies Hats

A black Marabou hat,
c1900.
£85-100   *CLA*

An original Edwardian
cap, worn by Jean Marsh
in Upstairs Downstairs.
£75-100   *ACL*

Cross Reference
Film & TV Memorabilia

A late 1930s hat and bag.
£35-50   *CLA*

An Edwardian ostrich
feather hat.
£85-110   *ACL*

A silk Christian Dior
turban, c1930.
£100-140   *CLA*

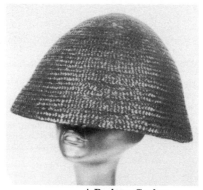

A Barbara Goalen
beehive hat in navy
straw, 1950s.
£40-50   *CLA*

An original jockey cap,
1920s.
£85-100   *CLA*

A wine velvet
hat, c1930.
£35-50   *CLA*

A velvet and straw hat,
c1928.
£35-40   *CLA*

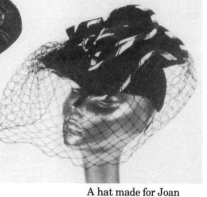

A hat made for Joan
Collins for Private Lives,
black and white, 1930s
style.
£300-350   *ACL*

A reproduction Victorian
hat box, 13in (33cm)
diam.
£20-25 *BGA*

A silver chain purse,
1941, 3 by 2in (8 by 5cm).
£30-40 *PSA*

A Victorian beaded bag,
6½in (16cm) wide.
£10-20 *FOB*

Ladies Handbags

A red Bakelite bag, 1960s.
£30-45 *CLA*

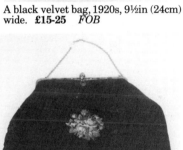

A black velvet bag, 1920s, 9½in (24cm)
wide. **£15-25** *FOB*

An Edwardian hand embroidered black
velvet bag, 8 by 11in (20 by
28cm).   **£30-40** *FOB*

An evening bag, with
crescent shaped top with
ram and devil type knop,
possibly Oriental, 9in
(23cm) high.
£15-20 *DOL*

An evening bag, 1960s,
5½ by 7½in (14 by 19cm).
£30-45 *CLA*

Cross Reference
Textiles
Costume

A gold evening bag,
1950s. **£40-55** *CLA*

A silver mesh purse,
3½ by 4in (9 by 10cm).
£40-50 *PSA*

Two sovereign purses, with beads on silk, c1830, 3in (7.5cm) diam.
£20-45 each *TOR*

A drawstring purse with rose design, c1810, 3½in (8.5cm) high.
£30-95 *TOR*

An ormolu top beaded on silk purse, 4in (10cm) high.
£30-95 *TOR*

A pocket purse, silk with white beads, 8½in (21cm) high.
£45-95 *TOR*

An English silk purse with hallmarked silver top, marked 1794.
£50-150 *TOR*

A Victorian beaded drawstring bag, 6in (15cm) long.
£50-70 *LB*

An embroidered evening bag with 'The Three Monkeys' clasp, 1930s, 8in (20cm) wide.
£10-15 *LB*

A beaded drawstring reticule with rose design, 7in (17.5cm) high.
£45-95 *TOR*

A purse with silver gilt top, with spider web pattern in silver and silk thread, 3½in (8.5cm) high.
£50-150 *TOR*

A silk and bead purse with ormolu top, with church design, c1810, 3½in (8.5cm) high. **£25-75** *TOR*

A purse with ormolu top, with beads on silk, c1810, 4in (10cm) diam. **£25-75** *TOR*

A miser's purse with silk beads and steel fittings, dated 1849, 11in (28cm) long.
£40-130 *TOR*

A silk and bead ormolu top purse with flowers and vase design, c1810. **£25-75** *TOR*

A beaded bag with rose design, c1920, 9in (22.5cm) wide. **£140-160** *LB*

A double ended miser's purse with beaded patterns on silk, 13in (33cm) long.
£50-150 *TOR*

A beaded drawstring reticule, c1820, 6in (15cm) high.
£45-95 *TOR*

A silk miser's purse with ormolu beads and fittings, c1830, 10in (25cm) long.
£25-95 *TOR*

A beaded miser's purse with steel fittings, 8½in (21cm) long.
£40-190 *TOR*

A beaded bag, with
frame inlaid with jet, 6in
(15cm) long. **£40-50** *LB*

A silk velvet purse with
steel fittings, c1800, 4in
(10cm) high.
£30-75 *TOR*

A mesh bag with clasp
and chain handle,
damaged, 9in (22.5cm)
long. **£50-60** *LB*

Lace

A Maltese silk
handkerchief with lace
border.
£18-25 *LB*

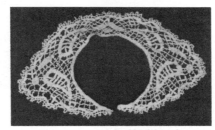

A Bedfordshire lace
collar.
£12-15 *LB*

An Edwardian lace
handkerchief bag, lined
with silk, 9in (22.5cm)
long.
£25-35 *LB*

A machine lace collar,
4in (10cm) deep.
£15-20 *LB*

An Irish lace collar,
c1910.
£25-30 *LB*

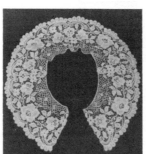

A machine lace ecru
collar.
£12-15 *LB*

A Maltese ecru lace
collar.
£15-20 *LB*

Linen

A linen table cloth with drawn thread and inserted lace.
£25-30 *ROS*

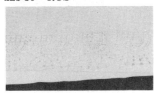

A linen pillow case, with crochet edge.
£25-30 *ROS*

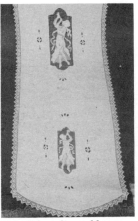

An Edwardian table runner, 42in (106.5cm) long. **£25-35** *LB*

A cotton lawn handkerchief with lace trimming.
£3-10 *LB*

A set of 6 hand embroidered linen napkins. **£18-25** *LB*

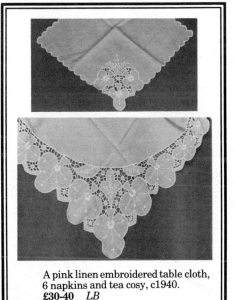

A pink linen embroidered table cloth, 6 napkins and tea cosy, c1940.
£30-40 *LB*

A cream crochet topped nightdress case with silk ribbon, c1910, 20in (51cm) wide. **£20-30** *LB*

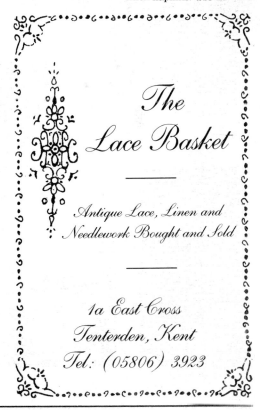

Menswear

A frock coat, c1900, 43in (109cm) long.
£100-125
Waistcoat.
£70-85   *ACL*

A Burton's double breasted worsted Utility suit.
£45-70   *ACL*

A man's Fair Isle sweater, c1920.
£70-80   *ACL*

A demob suit, large size.
£60-80   *ACL*

A black and cream silk crepe dressing gown, Noel Coward style, 1930s.
£180-240   *ACL*

A boater, late 1930s.
£20-30   *ACL*

A black velvet naval dress suit, complete with hat and shoes.
£350-400   *ACL*

A trilby hat, 1920s.
£40-60   *ACL*

A panama, 1950s.
£20-25   *ACL*

Gentlemen's Hats

A gentleman's smoking cap.
£25-30   *LB*

A check cap and scarf, 1930s.
£20-25 each   *ACL*

Patchwork

A patchwork cushion made from old fabric, 12in (31cm) square. **£30-35** *ROS*

Quilts & Blankets

A top hat, scarf, braces and cane, 1920s.
Hat. **£140-180**
Scarf. **£30-45**
Braces. **£20-35**
Cane. **£85-100** *ACL*

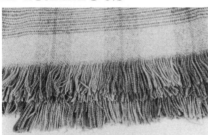

A Welsh grey and terracotta handwoven wool blanket. **£45-50** *CHA*

A Welsh patchwork quilt, c1900, 77in (195.5cm) wide. **£150-200** *FOR*

A quilt stitched in traditional Welsh style, c1880. **£150-200** *FOR*

A Welsh brown check handwoven wool blanket. **£35-40** *CHA*

437

Samplers

A wool sampler, dated
1879, some damage,
15½in (39cm) long.
£35-40 *LB*

A needlework sampler
by Maria Sinfield, dated
1820, some damage, 15in
(38cm) long.
£400-450 *C(S)*

A needlework sampler
by Alice Buckley, dated
1841, 19in (49cm) long.
£250-300 *Bon*

Tiles

Tins

Six Poole pottery tiles
from the Waterbirds
series, designed by
Harold Stabler,
impressed marks, 6in
(15cm) square.
£110-200 *CSK*

A collection of Poole pottery tiles, 5in
(13cm) square.   **£400-500** *CSK*

A decorative tin, 11½in
(29cm) high.
£20-25 *CHA*

> **Cross Reference**
> Ceramics

> **Cross Reference**
> Signs & Advertising

A dried milk
tin, 7in
(18cm) high.
£1-3 *RE*

A violet powder tin, 3in
(8cm) high.
£3-5 *RE*

A pair of I.C.I. tins, 9½in
(24cm) high.
£35-45 *CHA*

An American Can Co. money
box, Chicago Exhibition 1934,
3½in (9cm) high.
£18-20 *AAM*

> **Cross Reference**
> Money Boxes

Toiletries

A Thorne's toffee tin,
c1920, 5½in (14cm) wide.
£5-6 *HEW*

A gilt powder compact,
with watch and perfume,
3½in (9cm).
£125-135 *CLH*

A Continental powder
compact with gilt and
mirrored interior, the
base engine turned, the
sides with guilloche
enamelled bands, the
front painted with a
scene from Gilbert and
Sullivan's 'HMS
Pinafore', London 1927.
£140-150 *CSK*

A powder compact with Egyptian
motif, 1920s, 1½in (4cm).
£55-65 *CLH*

An Avon aftershave
bottle, in the shape of a
Harley Davidson
motorcycle, c1960, 7½in
(19cm) wide.
£5-6 *AAM*

An Edwardian silver gilt and tortoiseshell
travelling dressing set,
by Asprey. **£400-500** *HSS*

A French turquoise and
pearl inlaid eleven-piece
dressing table set,
largest toilet jar 9in
(23cm).
£1,800-2,000 *CNY*

TOYS
Animals

A straw filled donkey, with squeaker and glass eyes, c1930, 7in (18cm) high.
£18-20   *PSA*

A set of Schuco clockwork Walt Disney Three Little Pigs, comprising a drummer No. 789390, a flautist No. 789389 and a violinist No. 789388, each stamped Schuco, c1934.
£1,000-1,500   *S*

A French flock covered carton Boston terrier, with chain pull growl, 18in (46cm) long.
£400-450   *CSK*

A Linemar battery operated walking elephant, c1950, 10in (25cm) wide.
£90-110   *ChL*

A nightdress case, c1940, 17in (43cm) wide.
£8-12   *ChL*

A German Hermann monkey, with teddy pin, 1930s.
£35-75   *ChL*

A squeaky Felix, c1930, 14in (36cm) high.
£45-65   *ChL*

A Steiff pull along dog, on wooden wheels, pale yellow plush, Steiff button in ear and pull ring 'barker', 18 by 16in (46 by 41cm).
£150-200   *WW*

Three Steiff animals, c1930-60, 4 to 7in (10 by 18cm) high.   **£20-60 each**   *ChL*

A French springing tiger automaton, with clockwork movement, hide worn, whiskers sparse, early 20thC, 13½in (34cm) long.
£400-600 *S*

A French clockwork dog, c1880, 8½in (21cm) wide.
£230-270 *ChL*

A dog with muzzle, c1865, 8in (20cm) wide.
£100-140 *ChL*

A fur covered clockwork nodding goat, possibly by Roullet & Decamps, 16½in (42cm) high.
£420-450 *C(S)*

A Pelham Puppet, Minnie Mouse, 11in (28cm) high.
£35-45 *ChL*

A Celluloid goat with nodding head, c1920, 10in (25cm) wide. **£20-25** *CA*

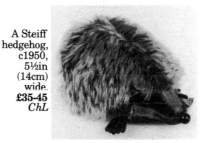

A Steiff hedgehog, c1950, 5½in (14cm) wide.
£35-45 *ChL*

A straw filled zebra, c1950, 8in (20cm) wide.
£10-12 *PSA*

A Japanese battery operated monkey with a drum, c1960, 10½in (26cm) high.
£50-70 *ChL*

A Steiff dog on wheels, with pin in ear, c1880, 11in (28cm) wide.
£200-300 *ChL*

A Steiff straw stuffed dog on wheels, original terracotta felt, has acquired a knitted coat, glass eyes, metal axles and cast wheels.
£70-80
In good condition. **£350-450** *CHA*

Automatons

A French Lambert automaton of a lady combing her hair, head stamped in red Déposé Tête Jumeau 6, clockwork movement causing her to raise comb and mirror to reflect her face, c1890, 23in (59cm) high. **£2,000-3,000** *S*

A French musical automaton of a conjurer, probably by Renou, with Jumeau head impressed 1, standing at a table lifting an oval box revealing coloured balls, moving her head, stop-start and keywind musical mechanism, damaged, c1900, 16in (41cm) high.
£1,700-2,000 *S*

A monkey automaton.
£250-350 *GIL*

Bébé Niche, a clockwork musical automaton, as the music plays the girl turns, nods her head from side to side while lifting the flap of the basket from which a yapping dog appears, probably by Lambert, catalogue No. 35, damaged, 21½in (54cm) high.
£2,700-3,000 *CSK*

A bisque headed clockwork automaton, with original bedding, as the music plays she sits up, opens her eyes, rocks the baby and lies down again, restored, 13½in (34cm) long.
£1,000-1,500 *CSK*

> **Cross Reference**
> Dolls

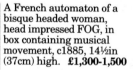

A French automaton of a bisque headed woman, head impressed FOG, in box containing musical movement, c1885, 14½in (37cm) high. **£1,300-1,500** *S*

Disney

A French musical Punchinelle automaton, manivelle musical mechanism, the composition headed Punch in original costume moves his arms and legs as if dancing when the winding handle is turned, late 19thC, 10½in (26cm).
£1,000-1,500 *S*

A bisque headed clockwork musical automaton, a standing man who as the music plays, turns his head and raises a cigarette holder to his lips while waving a handkerchief in his left hand, by Lambert, early 20thC, 24in (61cm) high.
£3,500-4,000 *CSK*

Two early Japanese bisque figures of Mickey Mouse, each stamped Japan, 6½in (16cm) high.
£350-400 *CNY*

A Linemar battery operated Mickey Mouse drummer, c1955, with original box, 11in (28cm).
£550-650 *CNY*

A pair of early Charlotte Clark Mickey and Minnie cloth dolls, each stamped Copyright Walt Disney Productions, 18½ and 17½in (47 and 44cm) high.
£1,300-1,500 *CNY*

An early Japanese Celluloid Mickey whirligig, 9½in (24cm) high.
£1,500-2,000 *CNY*

A sheet of Disney window stickers, 1980s.
£2-3 *COB*

An early Japanese Celluloid and tinplate Mickey and Minnie Mouse Playland, 10½in (26cm).
£2,000-2,500 *CNY*

A boxed Seiberling set of Snow White and the Seven Dwarfs, c1937, 5 to 9in (13 to 23cm) high. **£650-750** *CNY*

A Mickey Mouse Waddle Book, New York 1934.
£5,500-6,000 *CNY*

This is one of the very few existing Waddle Books unused and complete.

An Emerson Mickey Mouse wooden radio, with serial No. and designed to operate on AC and DC current, c1935, 7in (18cm) wide.
£1,600-2,000 *CNY*

Two dwarfs by Leonardo, English factory, 1930, 7in (18cm) high.
£40-50 each *HEW*

An Emerson wooden Mickey Mouse radio, c1933, 7in (18cm) wide.
£1,600-2,000 *CNY*

Figures & Arks

A painted wooden Noah's ark, early 20thC, 37in (94cm) long. **£250-300** *Bon*

A German painted wooden Noah's ark, including 4 papier mâché and wood figures, and approximately 84 animals, some damage, mid-19thC, 21in (53cm). **£850-1,000** *S*

A German flat lead garden scene, possibly Heinreichsen, including approximately 115 painted items, mid-19thC. **£700-750** *S*

A collection of 15 painted lead anthropomorphic animals, by Britains, some damage. **£65-75** *HSS*

A Heyde lead elephant hunting scene, comprising 19 items, minor paint loss, late 19thC. **£400-500** *S*

A painted wood and composition menagerie, c1870, Sonneberg, in original box inscribed in pencil, and with paper shop label on the base reading Cordeux Clifton. **£2,000-2,500** *CSK*

A straw work model Noah's ark, the back with slide, 19thC. **£320-350** *AG*

Games

A set of German printed cloth skittles, 3 tabby cats, 3 pug dogs and 3 geisha girls, together with a wooden ball, some damage, 7 and 9in (18 and 23cm) high.
£750-1,000 *S*

Three English chess sets, comprising an ivory set, possibly from the workshop of Charles Hastilow, 19thC.
£480-550 *S*

A complete set of 28 ivorine dominoes, 8 by 5in (20 by 13cm).
£30-40 *PSA*

A Whist/ Bridge marker, 4 by 2in (10 by 5cm).
£6-8 *ROS*

Ombro Cinema, a clockwork musical shadow theatre, with Charlie Chaplin and George Roby, in original box with spare scroll, published by Saussine Paris, c1910.
£320-400 *CSK*

A French speaking picture book, in boxed cover, c1910, 12 by 9½in (31 by 24cm).
£650-750 *S*

An English ivory chess set, red stained and natural, kings and queens with petalled tops, contained in an Indian painted and gilt wood box, minor chipping, late 19thC, 3½in (9cm).
£320-400 *S*

A Burmese carved ivory chess set, Macao, king as Carlos I of Portugal, queen as Marie Amelia, opposition as Oriental figures, rooks with flags, 19thC, king 5in (13cm).
£1,250-2,000 *S*

> **Cross Reference**
> Playing Cards

445

Horses & Fairground Animals

A German painted wooden horse and sleigh, mid-19thC, 13in (33cm) high, sleigh 16½in (42cm) long.
£250-350   *S*

An American carved wood horse, 55in (140cm).
£1,100-1,500   *CNY*

A brown cloth covered rocking horse, late 19thC, 39in (99cm) long.
£60-70   *CHA*

A brown cloth covered rocking horse, mid-19thC, 40in (102cm) long.
£180-250   *CHA*

An American carved wood horse, 55in (140cm) long.
£5,200-5,500   *CNY*

A painted hessian horse, was probably originally on wheels, early 19thC, 26in (66cm) long.
£50-100   *CHA*

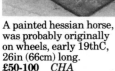

A Victorian pull along horse on wheels, c1890, 9½in (24cm) high.
£120-140   *PSA*

An American carved and painted pine dapple grey rocking horse, with leather bridle and brass rosettes, real horse hair mane and tail, yellow glass eyes, leather ears, saddle and fringed saddle blanket, on shaped rockers with black outlining and decorated platform, late 19thC, 61in (155cm) long.
£1,620-2,000   *S(NY)*

A Victorian skin covered horse, 18½in (47cm) high.
£200-500   *ChL*

A French carved wood donkey with nodding head, by Gustave Bayol of Angers, in natural wood with a metal maker's plaque, c1885, 49in (125cm) long.
£3,700-4,000   *CNY*

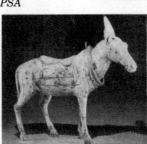

A French horse trotting toy, jockey
costume frail, hide on horse sparse,
late 19thC, 14½in (37cm) long.
£200-400 *S*

A wooden horse, c1930,
10in (25cm) high.
£70-80 *ChL*

A carved wood horse,
52in (132cm) long.
£1,850-2,500 *CNY*

A light brown ram, with deeply
carved horns and fur, carved
saddle and dog's head at cantle,
and a blanket, 39in (99cm)
high. **£5,000-5,500** *CNY*

A brown ram, with deeply carved
horns and fur, damaged, 41in (104cm) high.
£2,700-3,000
CNY

A white cloth covered
rocking horse, early
20thC, 40in (102cm) long.
£40-60 *CHA*

A multi-coloured giraffe,
with carved saddle,
blanket and looped tail,
59in (149cm) high.
£6,000-7,000 *CNY*

A French carved wooden
horse, by Henri Bayol,
52in (132cm) long.
£3,500-4,000 *CNY*

A Victorian wooden horse and cart, horse
9½in (24cm) long, the cart 18in (46cm) long.
£250-300 *DOL*

Scale Models

A 2in (5cm) scale model of a Burrel road traction engine, named Goliath, with coal fired boiler. **£3,500-4,000** *AH*

A Pocher display model of a 1931 8c-2300 Alfa Romeo racing car, plastic and metal, with detailed interior and dashboard, spoked wheels with sprung suspension and detailed chassis, 20in (51cm) long.
£140-160 *WAL*

A GRP scale model of an inshore power boat, with detailed cockpit and engine, 36in (92cm) long.
£45-55 *TAV*

Steam Engines

Two hardwood gypsy caravans, with detailed and fitted interiors, 20½in (50cm) and 22in (56cm) long.
£80-100 *TAV*

A Märklin vertical steam engine, with whistle, sight glass, burner and accessories, paint worn.
£65-85 *WAL*

A Carette hot air engine and accessories, c1910, 17in (44cm) wide.
£800-1,000 *S*

A German stationary steam plant, c1930, 12½in (32cm) wide. **£240-260** *S*

A Mamod toy steam tractor.
£140-160 *JL*

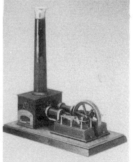

A Bing hot air engine, c1920, 15in (38cm) wide.
£500-600 *S*

Space Toys & Robots

A boxed Japanese tinplate keywind Atomic Robot Man, c1950, box damaged, 5in (12.5cm) high.
£500-550 *CNY*

A selection of space games and amusements, c1960. **£300-350** *S*

A Horikawa battery operated tinplate and plastic Dino Robot, worn, 12in (31.5cm) high, with original box.
£380-420 *S*

A Yonezawa battery operated tin and plastic Cragstan's Mr Robot, unboxed, c1960, 11½in (29cm) high.
£480-520 *S*

A Nomura mechanised Robbie robot, unboxed c1955, 13in (33cm) high.
£300-400 *S*

A battery operated robot, c1960, 9in (22.5cm) high.
£60-80 *ChL*

A Dan Dare No. 1 Space Ship Builder set, by A. & M. Bartram, with instructions, in original box, with a jigsaw puzzle, a Chad Valley Space Ship Construction Game, in original boxes, and a birthday card from Dan Dare and Digby.
£550-650 *CSK*

Teddy Bears

An English golden plush teddy bear, squeaker inoperative, c1930, 9½in (24cm) high. **£160-180** *CSK*

A Steiff Excelsior filled blond plush teddy bear, once the Mascot for Gainsborough Rugby Club, growler inoperative, early 20thC. **£1,200-1,500** *HSS*

A German cinnamon plush teddy bear, some stuffing missing, early 20thC, 26in (66cm) high. **£700-750** *HSS*

A Steiff white plush teddy bear, with button in ear, worn, pads replaced, c1920, 27in (69cm) long. **£850-950** *S*

A pair of Steiff blonde plush teddy bears, one with button removed, worn, 10in (25cm) high. **£500-600** *S*

A silver plush Steiff bear, button removed, early 20thC, 16in (32cm) high. **£500-600** *S*

A plush teddy bear, English, c1950, 14in (36cm) high. **£45-50** *PSA*

Bears

l. A teddy bear covered in pale beige mohair, with plastic eyes, hump, marked with Steiff button to left ear, paw pads replaced, 13in (33cm) high.
£130-150 *C(S)*

r. A Petsy bear of dual coloured auburn plush, with replacement clear button eyes, hump, marked with Steiff button to left ear, pads replaced, 24in (61cm) high.
£770-1,000

A European carved bear at the piano, in original box, 3in (7.5cm) high.
£30-60 *SP*

A Steiff teddy bear, c1980.
£35-40
Dressed in 1930s clothes.
£18-20 *COB*

A Sheriff bear, 1930s.
£50-60 *COB*

A carved bear box, sold as a tourist item, 4in (10cm) high.
£20-30 *SP*

Tinplate Toys

A Marx wind up Amos 'n' Andy tinplate taxicab, in original lithographed box, 8in (20cm) wide.
£780-850   *CNY*

An Ernst Plank diver, early 20thC, 7½in (19cm) high.
£250-275   *HAL*

A hand painted ladybird, c1910, 7in (17.5cm) long.
£200-220   *HAL*

A Lehmann Wild West Bucking Bronco with clockwork mechanism, G.R. Patent Engl Patent, patented USA 25th Jan. 1927, in original box, 8in (20cm) high.
£480-520   *HSS*

A set of 3 Chad Valley circus vehicles, c1940, in original box, 7in (17.5cm) long.
£400-500   *HAL*

A Louis Marx pair of Amos 'n' Andy tinplate walkers, in original lithographed box, c1930, 12in (30.5cm) high.
£1,500-1,750   *CNY*

A Lehmann Paddy and the Pig, 6in wide.
£500-600   *HAL*

A German Tramway Co. tinplate horsedrawn bus, with advertising, late 19thC, 12½in (32cm) long.
£600-700   *HAL*

Aircraft

A Fleischmann tinplate Dornier DO-X waterplane, with clockwork motor, paint chipped, with newspaper clippings describing the aircraft on which the toy was modelled, mid-1920s.
£3,000-3,500 *S*

The Dornier DO-X first flew in 1929, and at that time was the largest aircraft in the world. Only 3 examples of the full sized aircraft were built, and they were never used in regular commercial service.

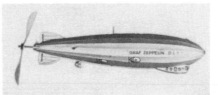

An English roundabout, c1950, 6in (15cm) high.
£30-35 *HAL*

A tinplate keywind Graf Zeppelin DLZ 127, with large working rear propellor, c1925, 11in (28cm) long.
£270-350 *CNY*

> **Cross Reference**
> Aeronautica

A Schuco tinplate keywind Lufthansa four-engine passenger airplane, with 2 visible pilots, c1952, 19in (48cm) long.
£700-750 *CNY*

A Lehmann tinplate and paper Ikarus airplane, paper wings, finished in red and yellow, c1912, 10½in (26cm) long.
£3,000-3,500 *CNY*

Motor Cars

A Tipp & Co tinplate keywind German Army bomber monoplane, c1938, 14½in (37cm) long. **£900-1,000** *CNY*

A Carter Paterson van, by Wells, c1920, 7in (18.5cm) long. **£500-600** *HAL*

A Bing tinplate clockwork limousine, with nickel plated headlamps, 14in (35cm) long.
£1,700-2,000 *Bon*

A plastic and tin Brimtoy Pocketoy, c1950.
£25-35 *HAL*

A Karl Bub tinplate car, c1920, 11½in (29cm) long. **£800-900** *HAL*

A Hess racing car with
flywheel mechanism,
8½in (21cm) long.
£700-800   *HAL*

A Tipp & Co. car, c1920,
15½in (39.5cm) long.
£1,000-1,200   *HAL*

A Burnett Ubilder racing
car, c1930, 11in (28cm)
long.
£200-250   *HAL*

A Karl Bub tinplate car, c1914.
£1,000-1,200   *HAL*

A Bandit Chase plastic
and tin car and motor
bike, English, c1950.
£45-55   *HAL*

A Bing steelplate Royal
Mail van, c1929,
repainted, 22in (57cm)
long.
£1,750-1,850   *CNY*

A Gunthermann tinplate
clockwork four-seater
tonnneau, and 4 hand
painted military
passengers, playworn,
c1908, 8in (19.5cm) long.
£4,500-5,000   *S*

A Gunthermann Captain
Campbell's Blue Bird
tinplate clockwork speed
record car, lacking
driver, in original box,
20in (50.5cm) long.
£1,100-1,500   *C(S)*

A Hessmobil tinplate
open lorry No. 1040,
incomplete, c1920, 10in
(26cm) long.
£280-300   *S*

A German G & K van,
c1920, 5½in (13.5cm)
long.
£600-700   *HAL*

A Lines Bros. Triang
Magic Sports Car
No. MT4, with clockwork
motor, bright metal
radiator and electric
headlamps, solid rubber
tyres, in original box,
16½in (41.5cm) long.
£900-1,100   *C(S)*

A Wells fire engine,
British, c1930, 6½in
(16.5cm) long.
£150-175   *HAL*

A Japanese Trademark
tinplate four-seater
vintage car, with
lithographed detail and
lever action spring
driven motor, Patent
No. 27579, 5½in (14cm)
long.
£55-60   *HSS*

A German lithographed
tinplate four-seat open
tourer, damaged, c1910,
8in (20cm) long.
£550-600   *CSK*

Ships

A Bing tinplate keywind
ocean liner with 4 stacks,
some repainting, c1920,
14½in (36.5cm) long.
£1,000-1,500   *CNY*

A Bing battleship, c1908,
19in (48cm) long.
£3,000-4,000   *HAL*

A Fleischmann liner,
c1930, 18in (45.5cm)
long.
£800-900   *HAL*

A Bing tinplate
clockwork motorboat,
c1910, some damage,
11in (28cm) long.
£200-250   *WAL*

Toys

A pair of gollies, dressed in 1930s printed satin garments, worn, c1900, 15in (38cm) high.
£400-500 *S*

A tumbling clown toy, 15½in (39.5cm) wide.
£55-65 *CHA*

A six-faced soft toy, blonde and green plush, straw filled, possibly American, worn and repaired, c1910, 22in (56cm) high.
£220-250 *S*

A wooden clapper board toy, c1920, toy 13in (33cm) high.
£55-65 *Hol*

A golly by Chad Valley, 18in (46cm) high.
£20-30 *ChL*

A German miniature tin bucket, 3½in (8.5cm) high. **£10-15** *ChL*

An egg tossing clockwork chef, c1950, 10in (25cm) high.
£20-25 *PSA*

A tin beach bucket, c1950, 7in (17.5cm) high.
£10-15 *ChL*

A tin beach bucket, c1950, 7in (17.5cm) high.
£10-15 *ChL*

Toy Soldiers

The Royal Horse Artillery, Britains set No. 316, comprising: field gun and limber in olive green and 7 horses, in original box, minor paint chipping, box worn.
£1,800-2,000 *WAL*

A Heyde boxed set of Roman procession figures, comprising: 2-horse chariot, 2 standards, 4 mounted warriors, 10 foot warriors, 2 trumpeters, lady with child, lion, warrior with hound, German, slight damage.
£50-60 *WAL*

Britains French Zouaves, No. 142, 8 charging with rifles, in original box with liner, slight damage.
£85-100 *WAL*

A Britains 155mm American gun, No. 2064, complete with loader rounds, and trail spades, in original box, minor damage.
£85-100   *WAL*

Britains French sailors, running officer with sword and 7 sailors running with rifles, in associated Britain's box, minor wear.
£190-210   *WAL*

Britains Infanterie de Ligne, No. 192, 8 marching at the slope, in original box with liner and tissue, damaged.   **£110-120**   *WAL*

A Britains 18in Howitzer, mounted for field service, No. 2107, in olive green, in original box with instruction sheet, box with minor damage.   **£75-85**   *WAL*

A Britains model tank, Royal Tank Corps No. 1203, in olive green, with driver and machine gunner, original box, minor wear.
£160-180   *WAL*

A four-wheeled mobile searchlight, No. 1718, painted in dark blue, complete with stabilisers, adjustment handle and bulb, minor damage.
£55-65   *WAL*

Eleven mounted Bedouin Arabs by Britains, paintwork and restoration to animals' limbs.   **£150-200**   *HSS*

A Britains Royal Engineers General Service limbered wagon, No. 1330, in review order, wagon and limber in olive green, with 2 horses, minor damage, in original box.
£230-250   *WAL*

Britains Togoland warriors, No. 202, 8 standing firing with bows, in original box with liner, damaged.
£50-60   *WAL*

Trains

A live steam model 4–4–2 locomotive with 6 wheeled tender, in maroon and black, 49in (124cm) long overall. **£500-600** *WAL*

A North Eastern fish van, c1930, 5in (13cm) wide. **£40-50** *HAL*

Bassett-Lowke

An O gauge clockwork Duke of York 4–4–0 locomotive and tender, in maroon livery, with box. **£200-300** *Bon*

A wooden monorail suspension railway, with lithographed tinplate coaches modelled after the Schwebebahn at Wuppertal, Germany, by J. Spear & Sohne, original wooden box, c1910. **£500-525** *CSK*

A further selection of Bassett-Lowke trains is featured in previous editions of Miller's Collectables Price Guides, available from Millers Publications.

Bing

An O gauge electric train set, comprising an 0–4–0 engine and tender number 0-35, in original box, c1920.
£300-350 *HSS*

A gauge II 4–4–0 steam locomotive, No. 593 cab, with pressure gauge and safety whistle, remnants of LSWR green livery, in poor condition, c1903, 14in (36cm) long.
£650-1,000 *S*

A live steam tank engine, c1912, 8½in (21cm) long. **£300-350** *HAL*

A pullman carriage, c1920, 12in (31cm) long.
£75-100 *HAL*

A Bing for Bassett-Lowke CR railway tank locomotive, 10½in (26cm) long. **£700-750** *HAL*

Hornby

A dublo super detail restaurant car, c1960, with box, 9½in (24cm) long.
£90-100 *HAL*

An O gauge 4–6–2 electric locomotive 'Princess Elizabeth', numbered 6201, in L.M.S. maroon, slight paint wear, in original presentation box.
£2,000-2,500 *S*

An electric No. 2 special Southern 4–4–2 locomotive, 1930s, 7in (18cm) long.
£280-320 *HAL*

No. 1 special tank clockwork locomotive, 1930s, 7in (18cm) long. **£175-200** *HAL*

A pre-war dublo electric tender locomotive, Sir Nigel Gresley, No. 4498, L.N.E.R., in original box.
£110-150
A pre-war dublo clockwork DL7 tank locomotive, No. 6917, L.M.S., in original box.
£720-750 *C(S)*

A dublo suburban coach, 1950s, 7in (18cm) long. **£5-10** *HAL*

An E320 4–4–2 locomotive and tender, Lord Nelson, electric motor, finished in L.N.E.R. green with black/white lining, tender missing.
£270-350 *AH*

Lionel

A No. 2 special 4–4–0 locomotive and tender, 3 rail electric, finished in L.N.E.R. green with white lining, tender missing. **£1,200-1,500** *AH*

A GG1 engine, No. 2360, green with 5 stripes, marked Pennsylvania, excellent condition.
£500-600 *JL*

AA Alco diesel engines, marked Rock Island, in good condition.
£200-250 *JL*

A Hudson 4–6–4 steam engine, No. 773, with tender 2426W, marked Lionel Lines, excellent condition, with original box for engine.
£850-1,000 *JL*

Trackside

A Lionel industrial water tower, No. 193, with black superstructure, and 2 American Flyer water towers, one with original box.
£80-120 *JL*

A Hornby dublo wooden engine shed, c1930, 12½in (32cm) wide. **£150-200** *HAL*

Vehicles

An army ambulance, No. 1512, pre-war, in olive green, with driver and wounded man on stretcher, minor paint chipping, original box. **£300-350** *WAL*

A Ranlite Austin toy car in green and black Bakelite, c1930, damaged 10in (25.5cm) long. **£550-600** *S*

A No. 3 Scalextric model motor racing set, with electric tinplate racing cars, 4 rubber drivers, track, transformer, fences, original box, guarantee and instructions, c1958. **£400-425** *CSK*

A selection of Britains vehicles:
l. Bluebird, slight damage to top of body, boxed.
£65-75
c. A British Army beetle lorry, No. 1877, boxed.
£55-65
r. A miniature barrage balloon, comprising a winch lorry and silver balloon, No. 1855, with instructions.
£100-120 *AH*

A Britains motor Machine Gun Corps set No. 1793, in olive green, khaki and brown, original box, pre-war. **£200-225** *WAL*

A British Tourist Association brass bus, 4½in (11cm) long. **£4-5** *PC*

> **Cross Reference**
> Toy Soldiers

An army lorry, with tipping loadbed, No. 1334, in olive green, with driver, minor paint chipping, in original box, pre-war, worn. **£170-200** *WAL*

Noddy and his car, c1950, 4in (10cm) long. **£70-80** *HAL*

A mechanical transport and Air Force equipment 18-wheeled underslung lorry, with optional winch, No. 1642, in olive green, pre-war, with original box, minor damage. **£525-550** *WAL*

A Tri-ang steel plate London Green Line single deck bus, in original box, c1965, 23in (58.5cm) long. **£320-350** *CNY*

Corgi

A Corgi RAC Radio
Rescue Land Rover,
boxed, 3½in (8.5cm) long.
£50-60 *HAL*

A Corgi Batmobile, boxed, c1960,
5½in (14cm) wide.
£80-120 *HAL*

A Corgi Simon Snorkel fire
engine, boxed, c1960, 11½in
(29.5cm) long. **£20-25** *HAL*

A Corgi Riviera Gift Set with
boat, skier and trailer, c1960,
10in (25cm) wide. **£40-60** *HAL*

A Corgi James Bond DB5
car, boxed, c1960, 5in
(12.5cm) wide.
£60-80 *HAL*

A Corgi safari set,
boxed, c1960,
6in (15cm) long.
£70-85 *HAL*

A Corgi Yellow
Submarine,
boxed,
c1960, 6½in
(16cm) wide.
£180-200 *HAL*

A Corgi
Sting Ray,
boxed,
c1960, 3½in
(8.5cm)
long.
£15-20
HAL

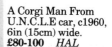

A selection of Corgi and Dinky toys, in poor condition.   **£1-4 each**   *HAL*

A Corgi James Bond Aston Martin, boxed, c1965.
£4-5   *PC*

A Corgi Man From U.N.C.L.E car, c1960, 6in (15cm) wide.
£80-100   *HAL*

Dinky

A Dinky jeep, boxed, c1950, 3in (7.5cm) long.
£25-30   *HAL*

A Dinky Police Range Rover, boxed, c1970, 4in (10cm) long.
£15-20   *HAL*

A Dinky fire engine, 1970s, 6in (15cm) long.
£10-20   *HAL*

A Dinky AEC fire engine, unboxed, c1970, 5in (12.5cm) long.
£10-20   *HAL*

A Scout car, boxed, c1950, 3in (7.5cm) long.
£10-20   *HAL*

A Massey Harris tractor, c1950, boxed, 3½in (8.5cm) long.
£30-50   *HAL*

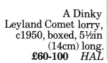

A Dinky Leyland Comet lorry, c1950, boxed, 5½in (14cm) long.
£60-100   *HAL*

A Lyons Swiss Rolls van,
boxed, 5in (12.5cm) long.
£350-500 *HAL*

A Captain Scarlet Spectrum
Pursuit Vehicle, boxed, c1960,
6½in (16cm) long.
£60-100 *HAL*

A VW Beetle, boxed,
c1950, 3½in (8.5cm) long.
£30-50 *HAL*

A Dinky Express Horse
Box Hire Service lorry,
boxed, c1950, 6½in
(16.3cm) long.
£60-100 *HAL*

A gun tractor, boxed,
c1950, 5in (14cm) long.
£50-85 *HAL*

A Thunderbird 2, boxed,
c1960, 6½in (16cm) long.
£100-150 *HAL*

A Newmarket Racehorse Transport Services
lorry, boxed, c1950, 7in (18cm) long.
£200-300 *HAL*

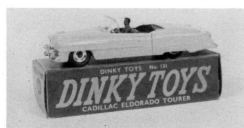

A Cadillac Eldorado
Tourer, boxed, c1950, 5in
(12.5cm) long.
£50-100 *HAL*

Three racing cars, c1930,
4in (10cm) long.
£30-60 each *HAL*

A passenger car gift set, c1950, boxed.
£600-750 *HAL*

Three advertising vans, c1930, 3in (7.5cm) long.
£100-250 each *HAL*

An E-type Jaguar, boxed, 1988.
£4-5 *PC* *This is new.*

A dark blue trojan Beefy
Oxo van. **£170-200** *WAL*

A Nash Rambler Fire Chief's car,
boxed, c1950, 4in (10cm) long.
£30-50 *HAL*

AA hut, motorcycle patrol and guides,
No. 44, boxed. **£250-300** *C(S)*

A selection of Austin vans, boxed, c1950, 3½in (8.5cm) long.
£80-100 *HAL*

A Dinky Jensen FF (Ferguson Formula),
c1960, 4½in (11.5cm) long.
£15-25 *HAL*

Minic

A petrol tank lorry, clockwork
motor requires attention, some
age wear, in original box.
£45-55 *WAL*

A police traffic control
car, with 2 policemen,
loud speaker, and
clockwork motor, some
age wear, in original box.
£70-80 *WAL*

A fire engine, complete with bell,
bucket and ladder, some age
wear, in associated box.
£90-100 *WAL*

Matchbox

Three Matchbox Superfast cars, boxed, c1970. **£3-5 each**
Unboxed **50p-£1 each** *HAL*

A Matchbox gift set of military vehicles, boxed, c1960.
£80-100 *HAL*

Three Matchbox vehicles, c1950, 1½ to 2½in (3 to 7cm) long.
£5-25 each *HAL*

Models of Yesteryear by Lesney, 1960s, boxed, 4 to 5in (10 to 13cm) wide. **£7-15 each** *HAL*

A Packard, Models of Yesteryear, by Lesney, boxed, 3in (7.5cm) long.
£7-15 *HAL*

Collectors Old Toy Shop Halifax

Urgently wish to buy for top international prices all kinds of old toys: particularly unusual toy money boxes, mechanical tin-plate novelties, cars, ships and transport toys. Dinky and diecast toys, train sets and locomotives or what have you.

We are regular buyers at all toy auction sales and we are sure our offers will pleasantly surprise you.
Regular dealer contacts encouraged.
Tell me what's coming up in your local saleroom. Excellent commissions for information.

**JOHN AND SIMON HALEY
89 Northgate, Halifax, Yorkshire**
Tel: (0422) 822148

A Matchbox truck, boxed, c1960, 2in (5cm) long.
£4-5 *HAL*

A steamroller, Models of Yesteryear, by Lesney, boxed, c1960, 3in (7.5cm) long.
£50-60 *HAL*

Treen

A wooden cash drawer, 8½ by 12in (21 by 31cm). **£20-30** *ARC*

A Victorian hand carved boot, c1850, 4in (10cm) long. **£30-50** *HOW*

A Mauchline ware box, 3in (8cm) high. **£15-18** *ROS*

A 19thC mahogany miniature cradle, raised on 2 rockers, 24in (61cm). **£350-450** *P(O)*

A 17thC carved hardwood spice box, the swivel cover with central star motif, 11in (28cm). **£250-350** *P(O)*

A wooden needle case with needles, 3½in (9cm). **£7-8** *SCO*

Tunbridge Ware

A stickware caddy spoon, 3½in (9cm) long. **£200-250** *STR*

A sealing wax outfit, label in the base reads T. Barton, 3½in (9cm) diam. **£450-500** *STR*

A rosewood stationery casket, with paper lined compartmented interior, 8½in **£350-400** *HSS*

Waxed Plaques

Osborne Plaques were produced in Faversham, Kent, between 1899 and 1965. They are three dimensional representations of buildings, historical events and personalities made in great detail from plaster of Paris and then finished in wax.

The business producing these plaques was founded by Arthur Osborne, when he returned from America in 1898. The finish attained was trade named Ivorex and every piece was hand-made, hand-finished and painted. By the start of World War II there had been about 440 different designs and, at its peak of production, about 45,000 pieces could be produced in a year.

They are not too well known at present and this could be a very good time to start a collection.

The Old Curiosity Shop, 8½ by 6in (21 by 15cm). **£35-40** *JMC*

The Cenotaph, 8 by 3in (20 by 8cm). **£20-25** *JMC*

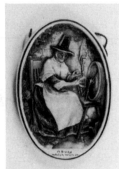

A Busy Welsh Woman, 5in (13cm). **£20-22** *JMC*

Blarney Castle, 10 by 8in (25 by 20cm). **£45-50** *JMC*

An Irish cottage interior, 9 by 6in (23 by 15cm). **£30-35** *JMC*

The Old Whaler, 9 by 6in (23 by 15cm). **£20-25** *JMC*

The Grave of the Unknown Warrior, Westminster Abbey, 6 by 3in (15 by 8cm). **£20-25** *JMC*

An Irish Jaunting Car, 4 by 5in (10 by 13cm). **£15-20** *JMC*

Irish Transport, and
Irish Transport free
standing, both 5 by 4in
(13 by 10cm).
£15-25 each   JMC

A Shakespeare's House
calendar, not complete,
4 by 2½in (10 by 6cm).
£12-15   JMC

Holyrood Palace and Arthur's
Seat, Edinburgh, 3 by 4½in
(8 by 11cm).   £20-25   JMC

Princes Street,
Edinburgh, 7½ by 11½in
(19 by 29cm).
£45-50   JMC

A Friendly Call,
9 by 6in
(23 by 15cm).
£20-25   JMC

The Home of
Charles Dickens,
Gadshill,
Rochester, 8½
by 6in
(21 by 15cm).
£30-35   JMC

Tower of London, framed
but not glazed, 12 by
16in (31 by 41cm).
£90-100   JMC

The Western Towers,
Canterbury Cathedral,
in original frame, 11 by
9in (28 by 23cm).
£60-70   JMC

Westminster Abbey, 3 by
4½in (8 by 11cm).
£15-20   JMC

Llanberis Pass, 10 by 8in
(25 by 20cm).   £45-50   JMC

The West Gate, Canterbury, 6 by 8in (15 by 20cm). **£40-45** *JMC*

Windsor Castle in original frame, glazed, 12 by 16½in (31 by 42cm). **£90-100** *JMC*

An Irish Cottage, one free standing, 4 by 5in (10 by 13cm) and 6 by 9in (15 by 23cm). **£20-30 each** *JMC*

The Angelus, 6 by 9in (15 by 23cm). **£20-25** *JMC*

Windsor Castle, 7 by 11in (18 by 28cm). **£35-40** *JMC*

Ann Hathaway's Cottage, 6 by 9in (15 by 23cm). **£25-30** *JMC*

St. Ives Harbour and Sea Gulls, 9 by 6in (23 by 15cm). **£30-35** *JMC*

The Man with Toothache, Wells Cathedral, 3 by 4½in (8 by 11cm). **£40-45** *JMC*

The Tower of London, 7½ by 11½in (19 by 29cm).
£45-50 *JMC*

Edinburgh Castle and National Gallery, 3 by 4½in (8 by 11cm) and 7 by 11in (18 by 28cm).
£20-45 each *JMC*

West Gate Canterbury, in original frame, 9 by 11in (23 by 28cm).
£60-70 *JMC*

Canterbury Cathedral, 3 by 4½in (8 by 11cm).
£15-20 *JMC*

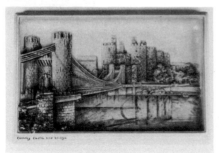

The Old Folk's Home, 6 by 9in (15 by 23cm).
£20-25 *JMC*

MAKE THE MOST OF MILLERS
Price ranges in this book reflect what one should expect to *pay* for a similar example. When selling, however, one should expect to receive a lower figure. This will fluctuate according to a dealer's stock, saleability at a particular time, etc. It is always advisable, when selling, to approach a reputable specialist dealer or an auction house which has specialist sales.

Conway Castle and Bridge, 7 by 11in (18 by 28cm).
£30-35 *JMC*

Shakespeare's House, 6 by 9in (15 by 23cm).
£25-30 *JMC*

Watches

A white metal keyless
pocket watch by Cyma,
with Hebrew characters,
second hand missing,
5cm diam.
£220-300   *C*

A white metal keyless
open face Mickey Mouse
pocket watch, by
Ingersoll, 5cm diam.
£450-500   *C*

> **Cross Reference**
> Disney

A gentleman's 9ct
white gold
keyless-wind Rolex
Imperial Prince
open faced dress
watch, import
mark Glasgow,
1931.
£550-600   *S(S)*

A German 14ct gold
hunter pocket watch,
A. Lange & Son.
£350-400   *HCH*

A silver purse watch, with black and
blue enamel decor by Tavannes,
with silvered dial, signed movement
under snap-on back jewelled to the
third, 4.7 x 3.3cm.
£350-450   *CSK*

A Rolex silver half
hunter pocket watch,
marked W & D,
No. 807844, early
20thC, 3.5cm diam.
£750-850   *C*

An 18ct gold
key-wind open
faced fob watch,
Chester, 1861.
£200-300   *S(S)*

Watch Holders

A gentleman's 18ct gold
cased key-wind open
faced pocket watch,
London, 1820.
£350-450   *S(S)*

An elephant watch stand,
11in (28cm) high.
£750-850   *SBA*

A walnut stand with
silver watch, 6½in
(16cm) high.
£130-200   *SBA*

Wristwatches

A gold calendar chronograph wristwatch, by Gubelin, 1½in (4cm) diam.
£2,000-2,500   *C*

A gentleman's steel Tudor Oyster date automatic chronotime, the dial with 3 subsidiary dials, date aperture and scale bezel, the winding crown and twin chronograph crowns with screw down action, on maker's steel bracelet.
£375-450   *CSK*

A lady's platinum and diamond wristwatch with diamond shoulders and diamond graduated line bracelet.
£900-1,200   *CSK*

A gold and enamel lady's bracelet watch, with presentation case, 19thC, 3cm diam.
£2,200-2,500   *C*

A pink gold chronograph wristwatch, by Universal, Geneve, Uni-Compax, the movement jewelled to the centre with 17 jewels, 3.7cm diam.
£700-800   *C*

An early gold single button chronograph wristwatch, by Le Roy, with white enamel dial, outer tachymetric scales, subsidiary dials for running seconds and elapsed minutes, sweep centre seconds operated by a single button, the case with snap-on back, the polished movement calibre 167 jewelled to the centre, 3.5cm diam.
£1,800-2,000   *C*

A Movado gentleman's gold automatic wristwatch, 3cm diam.
£320-400   *C*

A gentleman's Continental wristwatch, the dial with dart markers and subsidiary seconds signed Certina, the stepped case with sculptured lugs, on leather strap.
£275-350   *CSK*

A Royama gold and diamond set calendar wristwatch, in D-shaped case, with presentation box.
£900-1,000   *C*

A gentleman's platinum wristwatch, by Hamilton, model Rutledge, with 19 jewels, No. J19726.
£500-700   *C*

A gentleman's gilt/steel quartz wristwatch, by Ebel, with gold bezel, the brushed gilt dial with raised baton numerals, the case with gold winder, the back secured by 4 screws, No. 181902, with flexible tapered steel bracelet and clasp.
£250-300 *C*

Cartier

A gold tank wristwatch, the white enamel dial with Roman numerals, the signed back secured by 4 screws in the band, No. 780866106, the signed movement jewelled to the centre, with black leather strap and signed gold deployant clasp.
£1,500-2,000 *C*

A gentleman's gold wristwatch, with stepped bezel, the white enamel dial with Roman numerals, signed back, No. 2510318, 2.2cm diam.
£1,250-1,500 *C*

A gentleman's steel Panthere automatic calendar wristwatch, square.
£550-700 *C*

Jaeger-le Coultre

A stainless steel Reverso wristwatch, No. 24749, 15 jewels.
£1,100-1,500 *C*

A gentleman's gold driver's watch, in case with D-shaped lugs, with maker's brown suede strap and gilt buckle.
£450-600 *C*

Longines

A gold wristwatch, in curvex tonneau case, jewelled to the third, 1920s.
£660-800 *C*

A gentleman's gold wristwatch, the signed movement jewelled, with bimetallic balance and micrometer regulation.
£450-500 *C*

A stainless steel Reverso wristwatch, No. 34138.
£1,500-2,000 *C*

A gold wristwatch, the movement with monometallic balance, micrometer regulation.
£250-300 *C*

Omega

A pink gold three-part case wristwatch, with domed glass, subsidiary seconds square, maker's mark, the signed movement jewelled to the third.
£1,750-2,000 *C*

A gentleman's stainless steel novelty wristwatch, with case.
£320-450 *CSK*

A gentleman's 18ct gold Constellation wristwatch, the dial with baton markers, date aperture and sweep centre seconds, lettered Automatic Chronometer, Officially Certified, with integral mesh bracelet, in maker's case.
£700-800 *CSK*

Patek Philippe

A gold wristwatch, in turtle case with wire lugs, No. 192969, numbered inside dust ring 287460, frosted gilt bar movement with bimetallic balance jewelled to the third and numbered 192969, c1918, with original numbered presentation case.
£6,500-7,000 *C*

A stainless steel Nautilus waterproof calendar wristwatch, with date aperture, PPC flexible steel bracelet and deployant clasp, in original cork presentation case, 3.8cm square.
£2,750-3,000 *C*

A lady's gold wristwatch, No. 429122 ref. 3457, the signed movement jewelled to the centre and numbered 854205, 1950s, 1in (3cm) diam.
£1,500-2,000 *C*

Rolex

A lady's gold Rolex Oyster Perpetual bubble back wristwatch, made for Brock & Co, the case with screw-down winder and screwed back numbered 4486, signed movement, brown leather strap and gilt buckle.
£1,500-1,750 *C*

A silver Rolex Prince Observatory wristwatch, in waisted case, snap-on back with RWC Ltd mark and numbered 77064 971, signed observatory movement with 15 jewels, adjusted to 6 positions and for all climates, numbered 7216.
£2,750-3,500 *C*

A gold/steel Rolex Oyster Chronometer wristwatch, in tonneau case with pink gold milled bezel, screwed back with RWC mark, numbered 30904.
£1,000-1,500 *C*

A steel and white gold Oyster Perpetual Datejust Chronometer wristwatch, model Turnograph, with steel flexible bracelet and deployant clasp.
£850-1,000 *C*

A steel and gold chronograph wristwatch, the silvered dial with outer telemetric scale, the snap-on back with maker's mark, numbered 039664 2508, the signed movement jewelled to the centre, 1930s, 3cm diam.
£3,500-4,000 *C*

Vacheron Constantin

A gold wristwatch, with 17 jewels and 5 adjustments, bimetallic balance, numbered 405414, in unsigned tonneau case.
£1,200-1,500   *C*

A gentleman's gold Prince Quarter Century Club wristwatch, the duo-dial signed Eaton with subsidiary seconds, snap-on back numbered 268899 1862, signed Extra Prima observatory movement with 15 jewels, timed to 6 positions, numbered 73710, with original mottled brown Rolex Prince presentation case.
£4,000-4,500   *C*

A lady's 18ct gold Oyster Perpetual Datejust Chronometer wristwatch, with screwed back, numbered 6900, the signed movement numbered 979760, with flexible gold bracelet and deployant clasp.
£2,500-3,000   *C*

A gentleman's Continental square wristwatch, the case with domed shoulders, on leather straps.
£450-600   *CSK*

A gold Oyster Perpetual Chronometer bubble back wristwatch, screwed back with maker's mark, numbered 5015, signed movement numbered N82001, 3cm diam.
£2,000-2,500   *C*

A silver wristwatch, the snap-on back with maker's mark, W & D stamp, numbered 6664, the signed movement with 15 jewels.
£600-650   *C*

A gentleman's gold wristwatch, in oval case, the snap-on back with maker's mark, numbered 523596 39007, the signed movement jewelled to the centre adjusted to heat, cold, isochronism and to 5 positions, numbered 690922, with maker's brown leather strap and gold buckle.
£750-850   *C*

A gilt/steel Standard convex wristwatch, the snap-on back with maker's mark, the movement jewelled to the centre with 17 jewels.
£650-750   *C*

A gentleman's gold Oyster Perpetual Chronometer bubble back wristwatch, screwed back with maker's mark and number 3127, signed movement numbered N15352.
£3,500-4,000   *C*

Swatch Watches

Swatch Watches

Since Swatch Watches were founded in 1983 they have produced over 80 million watches featuring 600 different designs.

Every year two new Swatch Watch collections are designed and produced, with the previous collections ceasing production. Artists and designers from all over the world are employed. The special edition Swatch Watches are usually made in quantities of less than 10,000, and the limited edition Art watches usually less than 500.

A selection of scubas, Medusa, Hyppocampus, Happy Fish, Blue Moon and Barrier Reef, 1991. **£70-100 each** *C*

Encantador PWB157, Pop Collection, winter 1990, Christmas Special. **£95-120** *C*

Blue Leaves LR109 and Beaujolais GN104 from the Metamorphosis Series Winter 1989. **£150-200** *C*

Swatch Art Collection – Fondation Maeght 1988, Pol Bury GZ110, limited edition of 5,000. **£460-500** *C*

A Blanc de Blanc PWBW104, special edition white from Haute Couture Series, Pop Swatch Collection 1990. **£100-150** *C*

Swatch Art Collection, Rorrim 5 GZ107 – Tadanori Yokoo 1987, with original packaging and Japanese ink brush, limited edition of 5,000. **£1,000-1,500** *C*

Olympia Specials,
Olympia Logo GZ400,
1984 – gentleman's,
limited edition.
£300-400 *C*

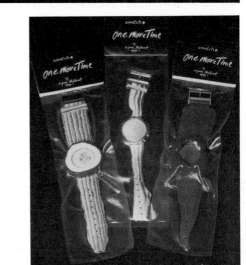

The Swatchetables Collection, 1991, designed
by Alfred Hofkunst, Cucumber, Red Pepper,
and Bacon and Egg, limited edition of 9,999
of each model. **£400-500 each** *C*

Mozart GZ114 – Special
Series Christmas in
Vienna 1989, limited
edition of 7,500.
£550-600 *C*

Limelight, re-edition
1987, Sir and Lady
Limelight GB106/LB110,
limited edition, with
Calafatti bracelets.
£370-500 *C*

Mimmo Paladino GX113
No. 021/100 Art
Collection 1989, limited
edition of 120.
£13,500-14,000 *C*

*This model won first
prize for the 'Draw your
Swatch Competition',
120 pieces were made
and presented to world
celebrities in politics,
commerce, show business,
the arts and sport.*

Coco Noir PWBB,
142-Special edition black
from Haute Couture
Series, Collection 1990.
£170-200 *C*

Olympia Specials,
Olympia II GZ402, 1990
– gentleman's, limited
edition.
£330-400 *C*
Olympia Specials,
Olympia II LZ102, 1990
– ladies, limited edition.
£220-300 *C*

Hollywood Dream
GZ116 – Special Series
1990, limited edition of
9,999.
£600-700 *C*

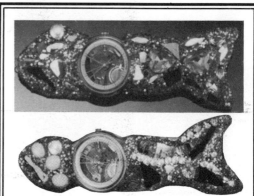

Two versions of Jelly
Fish, 1985, created by
Andrew Logan, limited
edition of 30.
£2,500-3,500 each *C*

*This model was
commissioned by Swatch
for the 1985 Alternative
Miss World Contest.
Each piece is unique and
signed by the artist. They
were given exclusively to
notable guests at the
event.*

Swatch Art Collection –
Fondation Maeght, 1988,
Pierre Alechinsky
GZ401, limited edition of
5,000.
£460-500 *C*

A chronometer special
series, Turbine GK125,
movement No. 125,
testing completed on
23.4.90, limited edition of
1,000 with original box
and certificate stating
this watch is a quartz
crystal chronometer.
£400-600 *C*

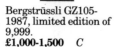

Bergstrüssli GZ105-
1987, limited edition of
9,999.
£1,000-1,500 *C*

Sir Limelight GB106,
Limelight Re-edition
1986 with Marmorata
bracelet, limited edition.
£350-400 *C*

A chronometer special
series, BMX GP104,
movement No. 1153,
testing completed on
3.5.90, limited edition of
1,000, with original box
and certificate describing
this watch as a quartz
crystal chronometer.
£450-600 *C*

Keith Haring Art Collection, modèle avec Personnages GZ100, Mille Pattes GZ103, Serpent GZ102, Blanc sur Noir GZ104.
£1,800-2,000 each   *C*

Keith Haring was already known as a graffiti artist when in 1985 he was asked to design a special for Swatch USA, this model Modèle à Personnages was followed by three more in autumn 1985. Each was produced in a limited edition of 9,999. The artist died recently in New York.

A chronometer special series, Jelly Fish GK124, movement No. 184, testing completed on 1.5.90, limited edition of 2,000, in original box and certificate stating this watch is a quartz crystal chronometer.
£850-950   *C*

Sir and Lady Limelight GB106/LB110, 1985, limited edition.
£550-600   *C*

These are the first of the 'Precious' series, with small diamonds, synthetic rubies, emeralds and sapphires.

Kiki Picasso Art Collection 1985, limited edition of 140.
£18,000-20,000   *C*

Swatch Art Collection – Fondation Maeght 1988, Valeri Adami GZ111, limited edition of 5,000.
£460-500   *C*

An Orgy prototype, designed by Keith Haring and signed by the artist, only 2 of this prototype known.
£6,000-6,500   *C*

Writing

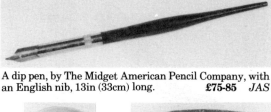

A dip pen, by The Midget American Pencil Company, with an English nib, 13in (33cm) long. **£75-85** *JAS*

A George VI post box from a sub post office in Ludlow, 29in (74cm) high.
£200-250 *PC*

A Victorian post box, usually attached to telegraph poles, 20in (51cm) high.
£150-200 *PC*

A Victorian bronze pen wipe, c1890, 3in (7.5cm) high.
£185-200 *JAS*

A French ivory desk seal, 19thC, 3½in (9cm) long.
£400-450 *Bon*

A Victorian notebook with shell motif, 2½in (6cm) wide.
£38-40 *PSA*

A Lambert typewriter, No. 3494, with blue and gilt lines and oak case with transfer, inkpad replaced, by Lambert Typewriter Co., New York.
£500-600 *CSK*

A bookmark, embroidered on paper, mounted on a silk ribbon, 19thC.
£8-10 *PSA*

A giant novelty pencil, by Miles & Everett, 14in (36cm).
£65-75 *JAS*

A Salter Visible Standard typewriter with four-row Universal keyboard in plated frame and red and gilt lined japanned body, with japanned carrying case.
£1,200-1,600 *CSK*

An Underwood typewriter, 20in (51cm) wide.
£12-15 *ROS*

Inkstands

A Victorian snail inkwell, 5½in (14cm) wide.
£285-300 *JAS*

A Chamberlain's Worcester porcelain inkwell, inscribed with crown over Chamberlain's Worcester in brown, slight discolouration, 1½in (4cm) high.
£600-700 *HSS*

An inkstand, with mother-of-pearl and Paris porcelain wells, made for the Paris Exhibition, 9in (22.5cm) wide.
£180-200 *CHA*

A Georgian style plated inkstand.
£115-120 *Sim*

A mother-of-pearl shell inkwell, 6in (15cm) wide.
£20-25 *ROS*

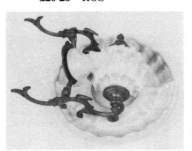

A French pink lustre ceramic snail inkwell, early 19thC, 6in (15cm) wide.
£350-375 *JAS*

A plastic desk stand, c1930, 11½in (29cm) wide.
£50-60 *PC*

Paper Clips

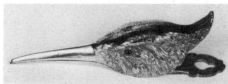

A ptarmigan paper clip.
£100-125 *RdeR*

A fish paper clip, 19thC, 4in (10cm) long.
£100-150 *RdeR*

DID YOU KNOW?
Miller's Collectables Price Guide is designed to build up, year by year, into the most comprehensive reference system available.

An Indian paper clip.
£50-75 *RdeR*

Fountain Pens

The Waterman Pen Prophet, in contemporary blue bindings with gilt tooling, 1922-30, 3 volumes.
£1,900-2,000 *Bon*

A white metal filigree safety pen, marked Zodiac Suo, with 18ct nib, and 3 others.
£95-100 *Bon*

A novelty soldier pen with wing-flow nib, unmarked.
£50-60 *Bon*

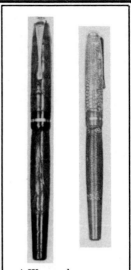

A Wyvern brown crocodile 101 pen with warranted nib, and a grey lizard 101 with Wyvern nib, c1948.
£80-100 *Bon*

A lacquered Namiki lever filled pen, with Maki-E design on the barrel, and Asprey Namiki No. 6 nib, c1920.
£2,400-2,600 *CSK*

A Moore mottled red and black non-leakable No. 2 pen, with American Fountain Pen Co. nib, c1903.
£75-85 *Bon*

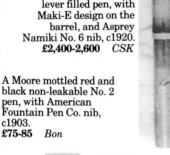

A silver and marble visible All American pen, with piston filler and All American nib, by Conklin, c1930.
£110-150 *Bon*

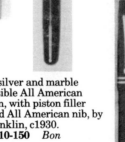

A silver pearl oversize Vacumatic pen, with black section and two-colour Vacumatic nib, c1934.
£140-150 *Bon*

A Dunhill-Namiki chased black hard rubber lever filler pen, with medium Dunhill-Namiki No. 3 nib, c1930.
£200-250 *Bon*

A Swan advertising display board for The New Leverless pen, sold at 21/–, holding 6 pens, green and red lizard skin, mottled green and black, mottled blue, and black, c1933.
£280-300 *CSK*

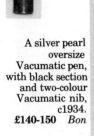

Two John Dunhill Two Pen double barrelled pens, each with 2 nibs, alternated by safety pen mechanism, black plastic, with 2 cap bands and Dunhill ball clips, one missing 1 nib.
£200-300 each *CSK*

De La Rue

A gold marble lever-filler pen, with 33 nib and a silver/visible 5600-34 with No. 3 nib, c1930.
£70-90 *Bon*

A gold plated ¾-length pen, with over/underfed nib, c1915, and a gold plated Onoto Dainty lever-filler.
£75-95 *Bon*

A silver green/visible Magna 1873-98 pen, with 14ct gold De La Rue band two-colour No. 7 nib, c1937.
£160-180 *Bon*

A black Onoto Magna 1873-78, with two-colour No. 7 nib, c1938, and an Onoto 79 with two-colour No. 5 nib.
£75-95 *Bon*

Mabie Todd

A black Swan leverless 2060 pen, with No. 6 Eternal nib, c1948, and a Swan Minor, a metal pocket and a box.
£90-100 *Bon*

A red/gold/green L205/ 62, with No. 2 nib, c1933, a leverless pen with No. 6 nib, and a leverless pen with No. 4 nib.
£80-100 *Bon*

A black L330-60 leverless pen, with No. 3 nib, c1935.
£55-75 *Bon*

Parker

A red Lucky Curve Senior pen, c1926, and a black Lucky Curve Senior, c1928.
£120-150 *Bon*

A black 51 Custom pen and pencil set, with presentation box, and a boxed Sheaffer set.
£75-95 *Bon*

A red Lucky Curve Senior pen, with Duofold pen nib, c1926, and a Duofold pencil, c1927.
£120-150 *Bon*

A Lapis Junior Duofold, with Duofold nib, c1931.
£85-95 *Bon*

A jade Lucky Curve Deluxe ladies pen and pencil set, with Duofold pen nib and leather Parker Pouch, c1927.
£180-200 *Bon*

A red hard rubber Lucky Curve Senior pen, with large format imprint, c1929, and a black/pearl Duofold Deluxe Junior, with Deluxe nib, c1931.
£110-130 *Bon*

A jade Lucky Curve Senior pen and pencil set, with single cap band and Lucky Curve nib, c1927.
£180-200 *Bon*

Sheaffer

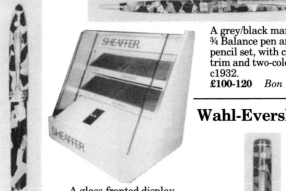

A grey/black marble ¾ Balance pen and pencil set, with chrome trim and two-colour nib, c1932.
£100-120 *Bon*

Wahl-Eversharp

A true blue Lucky Curve Junior pen, with Parker pen nib, c1927, and 2 pencils.
£140-160 *Bon*

A glass-fronted display cabinet, with built-in light, 28½in (72cm) wide.
£300-350 *Bon*

A black/pearl Lifetime Balance pen, with replacement 5-30 nib, c1929.
£30-50 *Bon*

A red lucky Curve Senior pen, with twin cap bands and Duofold nib, c1927.
£90-100 *Bon*

A P.F.M. IV Demonstrator pen and ball-point set, c1959.
£420-450 *Bon*

A mother-of-pearl inlaid Slender Balance pen, lever-filled with 33 nib, c1934, and 3 others.
£75-85 *Bon*

A black and pearl Gold Seal pen, with signature nib, c1928.
£150-200 *Bon*

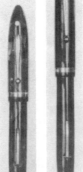

A jet Lifetime Senior pen, with Lifetime nib, c1923.
£110-120 *Bon*

A 9ct gold 61 Barley pen and pencil, both with presentation boxes, 1978 and 1977.
£380-400 *Bon*

A black jack-knife lady's safety pen, with Duofold nib, and 2 others, 1918-27.
£90-110 *Bon*

A black/green Lifetime Balance pen, with Lifetime nib, c1930.
£110-120 *Bon*

A black/pearl gold-seal Personal Point, with Art Deco cap band, rollerball clip and interchangeable Gold Seal Manifold nib, c1929.
£240-260 *Bon*

Waterman

A silver-ray ink-view pen, with brown nib, c1936, and 4 other items. **£70-100** *Bon*

A rare black hard rubber 12P pump filler pen, with No. 2 nib, c1903. **£380-400** *Bon*

A 9ct Line and Dot pen, with NW2 nib, London 1925. **£130-150** *Bon*

A 0558 gold plated basket weave filigree overlaid pen, with No. 8 nib, damaged, c1925. **£2,800-3,000** *Bon*

A gold plated 155/45 Safety pen, with No. 5 nib, damaged, and 5 other items. **£200-220** *Bon*

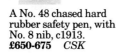

A No. 48 chased hard rubber safety pen, with No. 8 nib, c1913. **£650-675** *CSK*

A jade Lady Patricia pen, with later No. 2 nib, and one other, c1930. **£100-120** *Bon*

A white metal filigree overlay 452 basket weave pen, with No. 2 nib, c1925. **£140-160** *Bon*

A 42 Safety pen, a 12S and a 13 eye dropper with twin chased bands, nibs worn. **£90-100** *Bon*

A large ribbed pen, with orange ends and emblem nib, c1940. **£140-160** *Bon*

An Onyx Patrician pen, with Patrician nib, c1929. **£200-250** *Bon*

A No. 7 Red Ripple pen, with red cap band and nib, damaged, and 2 others, c1929. **£70-90** *Bon*

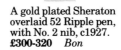

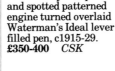

A gold plated Sheraton overlaid 52 Ripple pen, with No. 2 nib, c1927. **£300-320** *Bon*

A 9ct barleycorn panel and spotted patterned engine turned overlaid Waterman's Ideal lever filled pen, c1915-29. **£350-400** *CSK*

An Ink-view Demonstrator pen, with Waterman nib, c1939. **£180-200** *Bon*

FURTHER READING

Collecting Writing Instruments, Dietmar Geyer, Millbank Books, Schiffer Publishing Ltd.
Fountain Pens & Pencils: The Golden Age of Writing Instruments, George Fischler and Stuart Schneider, Millbank Books, Schiffer Publishing Ltd.

DIRECTORY OF SPECIALISTS

This directory is in no way complete. If you wish to be included in next year's directory or if you have a change of address or telephone number, please could you inform us by December 31st 1992. Entries will be repeated in subsequent editions unless we are requested otherwise. Finally we would advise readers to make contact by telephone before a visit, therefore avoiding a wasted journey, which nowadays is both time consuming and expensive.

AERONAUTICA

London
Alfie's Antique Market,
13-25 Church Street, London,
NW8
Tel: 071-723 6066

Adrian Forman,
Aeronautical Gallery, Gallery
120, Grays Antique Market,
58 Davies Street, W1
Tel: 071-629 6599

Hampshire
Cobwebs,
78 Northam Road, Southampton
Tel: (0703) 227458

AUTOMOBILIA

London
AAA Stand,
Alfie's Antique Market, 13-25
Church Street, London NW8
Tel: 071-724 5650

Brian R. Verrall & Co,
20 Tooting Bec Road, London,
SW17
Tel: 081-672 1144

Kent
Falstaff Antiques Motor
Museum,
63-67 High Street, Rolvenden,
Nr. Cranbrook
Tel: (0580) 241234

Gloucestershire
Cotswold Motor Museum,
The Old Mill, Bourton on the
Water
Tel: (0451) 21255

Hampshire
Cobwebs,
78 Northam Road, Southampton
Tel: (0703) 227458

Lincolnshire
The Complete Automobilist
Dept 1, The Old Rectory,
Greatford, Nr. Stamford
Tel: (077 836) 312

West Midlands
Walton & Hipkiss,
111 Worcester Road, Hagley,
Stourbridge
Tel: (0562) 885555/886688

South Yorkshire
Bardwell Antiques,
919 Abbeydale Road, Sheffield
Tel: (0742) 584669

ART DECO

London
Beverley & Beth,
30 Church Street, Marylebone
NW8
Tel: 071-262 1576

Decodence (Bakelite) (Gad
Sassower),
Shop 13, The Mall, Camden
Passage, N1
Tel: 071-354 4473

Cheshire
Nantwich Art Deco and
Decorative Arts,
87 Welsh Row, Nantwich
Tel: (0270) 624876

Kent
Rowena Blackford at Penny
Lampard's,
Antique Centre, 31 High Street,
Headcorn
Tel: (0622) 890682/861360

Hampshire
Gazelles,
31 Northam Road, Southampton
Tel: (0703) 235291

Lancashire
A.S. Antiques,
26 Broad Street, Pendleton,
Salford
Tel: 061-737 5938

Wiltshire
Clem Harwood,
The Old Bakery, Keevil,
Nr. Trowbridge
Tel: (0380) 870463

Scotland
Millars,
9-11 Castle Street,
Kirkcudbright
Tel: (0557) 30236

BAROMETERS

London
Patrick Capon,
350 Upper Street, Islington, N1
Tel: 071-354 0487/081-467 5722

Barometer Fair, at
Cartographia Ltd,
Pied Bull Yard, Bury Place,
Bloomsbury, WC1
Tel: 071-404 4521/4050

Avon
Barometer Shop,
3 Lower Park Row, Bristol
Tel: (0272) 272565

Cheshire
Derek Rayment Antiques,
Orchard House, Barton Road,
Barton, Nr Malpas
Tel: (0829) 270429

Essex
It's About Time,
863 London Road,
Westcliff-on-Sea
Tel: (0702) 72574

Hereford & Worcs
Barometer Shop,
New Street, Leominster
Tel: (0568) 3652

Somerset
Bernard G. House
(Mitre Antiques),
Market Place, Wells
Tel: (0749) 72607

Wiltshire
P. A. Oxley,
The Old Rectory, Cherhill,
Nr. Calne
Tel: (0249) 816227

BAXTER PRINTS

Cambridgeshire
Cambridge Fine Art Ltd,
Priest House, 33 Church Street,
Little Shelford
Tel: (0223) 842866/843537

Leicestershire
Charnwood Antiques,
Coalville, Leicester
Tel: (0530) 38530

BOTTLES

London
Rob Gee,
Flea Market, Camden Passage,
London, N1
Tel: 071-226 6627

Georgian Village – 1st Floor,
Islington Green, London, N1
Tel: 071-226 1571/5393

Isle of Wight
Kollectarama,
Old Railway Station,
Horringford, Arreton
Tel: (0983) 865306

Staffordshire
Gordon The 'Ole Bottleman,
25 Stapenhill Road, Burton-on-
Trent
Tel: (0283) 67213

South Yorkshire
British Bottle Review,
2 Strafford Avenue, Elsecar,
Nr. Barnsley
Tel: (0226) 745156/(0709)
879303

BOXES

London
Barham Antiques,
83 Portobello Road, London,
W11
Tel: 071-727 3845

Avon
Gloria Gibson,
2 Beaufort West, London Road,
Bath BA1 6QB
Tel: (0225) 446646

Berkshire
Boxes From Derek McIntosh,
10 Wickham Road, Stockcross,
Newbury
Tel: (0488) 38295

Mostly Boxes,
92 & 52B High Street, Eton,
Windsor
Tel: (0753) 858470

Yorkshire
Danby Antiques,
65 Heworth Road, York
Tel: (0904) 415280

BUCKLES

London
Moderne,
Stand 5, Georgian Village,
Camden Passage, N1

Avon
Jessie's Button Box,
Great Western Antique Centre,
Bartlett Street, Bath
Tel: (0272) 299065

BUTTONS
London
The Button Queen,
19 Marylebone Lane, W1
Tel: 071-935 1505

Monica Jaertelius, The Mall,
Camden Passage, N1
Tel: 081-546 2807

Dorset
The Old Button Shop,
Lytchett Minster
Tel: (0202) 622169

Herefordshire
The Button Museum,
Kyrle Street, Ross-on-Wye
Tel: (0989) 66089

BUTTON HOOKS
London
David Hogg,
S.141 Grays Antique Market,
58 Davies Street, W1
Tel: 071-493 0208

Noelle Antiques,
S.26 Chelsea Antiques Market,
253 Kings Road, SW3
Tel: 071-352 5581

Kent
The Variety Box,
16 Chapel Place, Tunbridge
Wells
Tel: (0892) 31868/21589

North Wales
Paul Gibbs,
25 Castle Street, Conwy
Tel: (0492) 593429

CAMERAS
London
Jessops,
65 Great Russell Street, WC1
Tel: 071-831 3640

Vintage Cameras Ltd,
254 & 256 Kirkdale, Sydenham,
SE26
Tel: 081-778 5416/5841

London & Essex
Cliff Latford Photography,
G006, Alfie's Antique Market,
13-25 Church Street, London,
NW8
and Colchester, Essex
Tel: 071-724 5650/
(0206) 564474

Hertfordshire
P. Coombs,
87 Gills Hill Lane, Radlett
Tel: (0923) 856949

Warwickshire
Fred Topping,
Warwick Antique Centre,
20 High Street, Warwick
Tel: (0926) 499078

West Yorkshire
The Camera House,
Oakworth Hall, Colne Road,
Oakworth
Tel: (0535) 642333

CARD CASES
London
Eureka Antiques,
105 Portobello Road, W11
(Saturdays)

Grays Antique Market,
58 Davies Street, W1
Tel: 071-629 7034

Avon
Carr Linford,
10-11 Walcot Buildings, London
Road, Bath
Tel: (0225) 317516

Cheshire
Eureka Antiques,
7A Church Brow, Bowdon
Tel: 061-926 9722

Shropshire
F. C. Manser & Son Ltd,
53 Wyle Cop, Shrewsbury
Tel: (0743) 51120

CERAMICS
Art Deco
London
A.J. Partners (Shelley),
S.133/114, Alfies Antique
Market, 13-25 Church Street,
NW8
Tel: 071-258 3602

Beverley,
30 Church Street, Marylebone,
NW8
Tel: 071-262 1576

Dimech,
248 Camden High Street,
London, NW1
Tel: 071-485 8072

Jag
Unit 6, Kensington Church
Street Antiques Centre, 58-60
Kensington Church Street, W8
Tel: 071-938 4404

New Century,
Art Pottery, 69 Kensington
Church Street, W8
Tel: 071-376 2810

Past & Present,
York Arcade, Unit 5, Camden
Passage, N1
Tel: 071-833 2640

Patrician Antiques,
1st Floor Georgian Village,
Camden Passage, N1
Tel: 071-359 4560/071-435 3159

Rotation Antiques,
Pierrepont Row Fleamarket,
Camden Passage, London, N1
Tel: 071-226 8211

John White,
Alfie's Antique Market, 13-25
Church Street, NW8
Tel: 071-723 0449

Essex
A. Waine,
Tweedale, Rye Mill Lane,
Feering, Colchester

Hampshire
The Art Deco China Centre,
62 Murray Road, Horndean
Tel: (0705) 597440

Gazelles,
31 Northam Road, Southampton
Tel: (0703) 235291

Kent
Manor Antiques (Radford Ware)
2A High Street, Westerham
Tel: (0959) 564810

Norfolk
Neville Pundole,
1 White House Lane,
Attelborough
Tel: (0953) 454106

Shropshire
Antiques on the Square,
2 Sandford Court, Church
Stretton
Tel: (0694) 724111

Wales
Paul Gibbs Antiques,
25 Castle Street, Conwy
Tel: (0492) 593429

Warkwickshire
Rich Designs,
Sheep Street Antique Centre,
Stratford-upon-Avon
Tel: (0789) 772111

Art Deco Ceramics,
The Ocsbury, 10 Mill Street,
Warwick
Tel: (0926) 498068

Jazz,
Civic Hall, Rother Street,
Stratford-on-Avon
Tel: (0789) 298362

East Yorkshire
Tim Barnett,
Carlton Gallery, 60A Middle
Street, Driffield
Tel: (0482) 443954

Expressions,
17 Princess Street, Shrewsbury
Tel: (0743) 51731

Surrey
Church Street Antiques,
15 Church Street, Godalming
Tel: (0483) 860894

East Sussex
Le Jazz Hot,
14 Prince Albert Street,
Brighton
Tel: (0273) 206091

Tyne & Wear
Ian Sharp Antiques (Maling
Ware),
23 Front Street, Tynemouth
Tel: 091-296 0656

Wiltshire
Clem Harwood,
The Old Bakery, Keevil,
Nr. Trowbridge
Tel: (0380) 870463

West Yorkshire
Muir Hewitt,
Halifax Antiques Centre,
Queens Road/Gibbet Street,
Halifax
Tel: (0442) 366657/366657

Scotland
Millars,
9/11 Castle Street,
Kirkcudbright
Tel: (0557) 30236

Doulton
London
Britannia,
Stand 101, Grays Antique
Market, 58 Davies Street, W1
Tel: 071-629 6772

The Collector,
Alfie's Antique Market,
13-25 Church Street, NW8
Tel: 081-883 0024/071-706 4586

Doug Pinchin,
Dixons Antique Centre,
471 Upper Richmond Road
West, East Sheen, SW14
Tel: 081-878 6788/081-948 1029

Leicester
Janice Williamson,
9 Coverdale Road, Meadows
Wiston, Leicester
Tel: (0533) 812926

Norfolk
Yesteryear Antiques,
24D Magdalen Street, Norwich
Tel: (0603) 622908

Commemorative
London
Britannia,
Stand 101, Grays Antique
Market, 58 Davies Street, W1
Tel: 071-629 6772

British Commemoratives,
1st Floor, Georgian Village,
Camden Passage, N1
Tel: 071-359 4560

Surrey
Church Street Antiques,
15 Church Street, Godalming
Tel: (0483) 860894

East Sussex
Leonard Russell,
21 Kings Avenue, Mount
Pleasant, Newhaven
Tel: (0273) 515153

Warwickshire
Midlands Goss &
Commemoratives,
Warwick Antique Centre,
22 High Street, Warwick
Tel: (0926) 495704

Goss & Crested China

London
British Commemoratives,
1st Floor, Georgian Village,
Camden Passage, N1
Tel: 071-359 4560

Hampshire
Goss & Crested China Ltd,
62 Murray Road, Horndean
Tel: (0705) 597440

Kent
The Variety Box,
16 Chapel Place, Tunbridge
Wells
Tel: (0892) 31868/21589

Warwickshire
Midlands Goss &
Commemoratives,
Warwick Antique Centre,
22 High Street, Warwick
Tel: (0926) 495704

East Yorkshire
The Crested China Company,
Station House, Driffield
Tel: (0377) 47042

Staffordshire
London
Gerald Clark Antiques,
1 High Street, Mill Hill Village,
NW7
Tel: 081-906 0342

Jacqueline Oosthuizen,
1st Floor, Georgian Village,
Camden Passage, N1
Tel: 071-226 5393/071-352 5581
and
23 Cale Street, Chelsea, SW3
Tel: 071-352 6071

Jonathan Horne,
66B & C Kensington Church
Street, W8
Tel: 071-221 5658

Kent
Beaubush House Antiques,
95 High Street, Sandgate,
Folkestone
Tel: (0303) 49099

Lancashire
Roy W. Bunn Antiques,
34-36 Church Street,
Barnuldswick, Colne
Tel: (0282) 813703

Suffolk
Crafers Antiques,
The Hill, Wickham Market
Tel: (0728) 747347

West Sussex
Ray & Diane Ginns,
PO Box 129,
East Grinstead
Tel: (0342) 326041

Torquay Pottery
London
Jacqueline Oosthuizen,
1st Floor, Georgian Village,
Camden Passage, N1
Tel: 071-226 5393/071-359 4560
and
23 Cale Street, Chelsea SW3
Tel: 071-352 6071

Pot Lids
London
Rob Gee,
Flea Market, Camden Passage,
N1
Tel: 071-226 6627

East Sussex
Ron Beech,
Brambledean Road, Portslade,
Brighton
Tel: (0273) 423355

Warwickshire
Burman Antiques,
5A Chapel Street, Stratford-on-
Avon
Tel: (0789) 293917

Pottery
London
Robert Young Antiques,
68 Battersea Bridge Road, SW11
Tel: 071-228 7847

Valerie Howard,
131E Kensington Church
Street, London, W8
Tel: 071-792 9702

Nicolaus Boston,
Kensington Church Street
Antiques Centre, 58-60
Kensington Church Street, W8
Tel: 071-376 0425

Avon
Robert & Carol Pugh,
2 Beaufort Mews, St. Saviours
Road, Larkhall, Bath
Tel: (0225) 314713

Andrew Dando,
4 Wood Street, Bath
Tel: (0225) 422702

Hampshire
Millers of Chelsea Ltd,
Netherbrook House,
Christchurch Road, Ringwood
Tel: (0425) 472062

Kent
Angela Page Antiques,
Tunbridge Wells
Tel: (0892) 22217

Norfolk
The Kensington Pottery,
Winstanley Cats, 1 Grammar
School Road, North Walsham
Tel: (0692) 402962

Wales
Islwyn Watkins,
1 High Street/29 Market Street,
Knighton, Powys
Tel: (0547) 520145/528940

Howards Antiques,
10 Alexandra Road,
Aberystwyth, Dyfed
Tel: (0970) 624973

Warwickshire
Janice Paull,
125 Warwick Road, Kenilworth
Tel: (0926) 55253

Yorkshire
In Retrospect,
2 Pavement, Pocklinton, York
Tel: (0759) 304894

Victorian Ceramics
London
Sue Norman,
Stand L4 Antiquarius,
135 Kings Road, London, SW3
Tel: 071-352 7217

Avon
Scott's,
Bartlett Street Antiques
Centre, Bartlett Street, Bath
Tel: (0225) 625335

Buckinghamshire
Gillian A. Neale,
The Old Post Office, Wendover
Tel: (0296) 625335

Cumbria
Ceramic Restorers,
Domino Restorations,
129 Craig Walk, Windermere
Tel: (05394) 45751

Gloucestershire
Acorn Antiques,
Sheep Street, Stow-on-the-Wold
Tel: (0451) 831519

Nottinghamshire
Breck Antiques,
726 Mansfield Road,
Nottingham
Tel: (0602) 605263

Tyne & Wear
Ian Sharp Antiques (Sunderland
Lustre),
23 Front Street, Tynemouth
Tel: 091-296 0656

Warwickshire
Bow Cottage Antiques,
Stratford Antique Arcade,
Sheep Street, Stratford-on-Avon
Tel: (0789) 297249

COLLECTABLES
Kent
Collectables,
335 High Street, Rochester
Tel: (0634) 828767

Roses,
60 King Street, Sandwich
Tel: (0304) 615303

Gloucestershire
The Trumpet,
West End, Minchinhampton,
Nr. Stroud
Tel: (0453) 883027

Shropshire
Tiffany Antiques,
Unit 3, Shrewsbury Antique
Centre, 15 Princess Howe, The
Square, Shrewsbury
Tel: (0270) 257425
and
Unit 15, Shrewsbury Antique
Market, Frankwell Quay
Warehouse, Shrewsbury
Tel: (0270) 257425

East Sussex
Rin Tin Tin,
34 North Road, Brighton
Tel: (0273) 672424/733689

The Collectors Market,
The Enterprise Centre, Station
Parade, Eastbourne
Tel: (0323) 32690

West Sussex
Bygones, Collectors Shop,
123 South Street, Lancing
Tel: (0903) 750051/763470

CORKSCREWS
London
David,
141 Grays Antique Market,
Davies Street, W1
Tel: 071-493 0208

Patricia Harbottle,
Geoffrey Vann Arcade,
107 Portobello Road, W11
(Saturdays)
Tel: 071-731 1972

Bedfordshire
Christopher Sykes Antiques,
The Old Parsonage, Woburn
Tel: (0525) 290259

Cumbria
Bacchus Antiques,
Longlands at Cartmel
Tel: (044 854) 475

East Sussex
Chateaubriand Antiques
Centre,
High Street, Burwash
Tel: (0435) 882535

DOLLS
London
Brenda Gerwat-Clark,
Alfie's Antique Market, 13-25
Church Street, London, NW8
Tel: 071-706 4699

Brenda Gerwat-Clark,
Alfie's Antique Market, 13-25
Church Street, London, NW8
Tel: 071-706 4699

Chelsea Lion Dolls,
Chenil Galleries, 181-183 Kings
Road, London, SW3
Tel: 071-351 9338

Childhood Memories,
Teapot Arcade, Portobello,
London, W11

The Doll Cupboard,
Portwine Galleries, Unit No. 17,
175 Portobello Road, London,
W11
Tel: 071-727 4681/(0378) 76848

Dollyland,
864 Green Lanes, Winchmore
Hill, London, N21
Tel: 081-360 1053

Pat Walker,
Georgian Village, Camden
Passage, N1
Tel: 071-359 4560/071-435 3159

Yesterday Child,
24 The Mall, Camden Passage,
N1
Tel: 071-354 1601/
(0908) 583403

Avon
Bath Dolls' Hospital and Teddy
Bear Clinic,
2 Grosvenor Place, London
Road, Bath
Tel: (0225) 319668

Bristol Dolls Hospital,
50-52 Alpha Road, Southville,
Bristol
Tel: (0272) 664368

The China Doll,
31 Walcot Street, Bath
Tel: (0225) 465849

Cheshire
Dollectable,
53 Lower Bridge Street, Chester
Tel: (0244) 44888/679195

Gloucestershire
Lillian Middleton's Antique
Dolls Shop,
Days Stable, Sheep Street,
Stow-on-the-Wold
Tel: (0451) 31542

Parkhouse Antiques,
Park Street, Stow-on-the-Wold
Tel: (0451) 30159

Hampshire
Toys Through Time,
Fareham
Tel: (0329) 288678

Past & Present Crafts,
19 Ditton Close, Stubbington
Tel: (0329) 661377

Hereford & Worcester
J. Currie,
Dolls Toys & Games, Antique
Centre, Blackwell Street,
Kidderminster
Tel: (0562) 829000

Hertfordshire
Carrousel,
59 High Street, Hemel
Hempstead
Tel: (0442) 219772/42518

Kent
Amelia Dolls,
Pantiles Spa Antiques, The
Pantiles, Tunbridge Wells
Tel: (0892) 541377/(0342)
713223

Hadlow Antiques,
No. 1 The Pantiles, Tunbridge
Wells
Tel: (0892) 29858

The Magpie's Nest,
14 Palace Street, Canterbury
Tel: (0227) 764883

Oxfordshire
Peter Strange, Restorer,
The Willows, Sutton, Oxford
Tel: (0865) 882020

Surrey
Dorking Dolls House Gallery,
23 West Street, Dorking
Tel: (0306) 885785

Victoriana Dolls,
Reigate
Tel: (0737) 249525

East Sussex
Dolls Hospital,
17 George Street, Hastings
Tel: (0424) 444117/422758

Sue Pearson,
13½ Prince Albert Street,
Brighton
Tel: (0273) 29247

West Sussex
Recollect Studios,
Dept M, The Old School, London
Road, Sayers Common
Tel: (0273) 833314

West Yorkshire
Sue Rouse,
The Dolls House,
Gladstone Buildings, Hope
Street, Hebden Bridge
Tel: (0422) 845606
Queensway City Centre

Scotland
Toys & Treasures,
Wendy B. Austin-Bishop,
65 High Street, Grantown on
Spey, Morayshire
Tel: (0479) 2449

DOLLS HOUSE FURNITURE

Avon
The China Doll,
31 Walcot Street, Bath
Tel: (0225) 465849

Essex
Blackwells of Hawkwell,
733 London Road,
Westcliff-on-Sea
Tel: (0702) 72248

Kent
The Magpie's Nest,
14 Palace Street, Canterbury
Tel: (0227) 764883

Dolls House Workshop,
54A London Road, Teynham
Tel: (0795) 522445

TEDDY BEARS

London
Heather's Teddys,
World Famous Arcade,
177 Portobello Road, London,
W11
Tel: 081-204 0106

Pam Hebbs,
5 The Annexe, Camden
Passage, Islington, N1

Past and Present Toys,
862 Green Lanes, Winchmore
Hill, London N21
Tel: 081-364 1370

Berkshire
Asquiths of Windsor,
10 George V Place, Thames
Avenue, Windsor
Tel: (0753) 854954/831200

Gloucestershire
Park House Antiques,
Park Street, Stow-on-the-Wold
Tel: (0451) 30159

Oxfordshire
Teddy Bears,
99 High Street, Witney
Tel: (0993) 702616

East Sussex
Sue Pearson,
13½ Prince Albert Street,
Brighton
Tel: (0273) 29247

West Midlands
Mr Morgan,
F11 Swincross Road, Old
Swinford, Stourbridge
Tel: (0384) 397033

West Yorkshire
Memory Lane,
69 Wakefield Road, Sowerby
Bridge
Tel: (0422) 833223

COCKTAIL/ DRINKING

London
Beverley,
30 Church Street, Marylebone,
NW8
Tel: 071-262 1576

EPHEMERA
Cigarette Cards

London
Murray Cards (International)
Ltd,
51 Watford Way, Hendon
Central, NW4
Tel: 081-202 5688

Avon
Winstone Stamp Company,
S.82 Great Western Antiques
Centre, Bartlett Street, Bath
Tel: (0225) 310388

Middlesex
Albert's Cigarette Card
Specialists,
113 London Road, Twickenham
Tel: 081-891 3067

Somerset
The London Cigarette Card Co
Ltd,
Sutton Road, Somerton
Tel: (0458) 73452

Suffolk
W. L. Hoad,
9 St Peter's Road, Kirkley,
Lowestoft
Tel: (0502) 587758

Comics

London
Gosh Comics,
39 Great Russell Street, WC1
Tel: 071-636 1011

Top Ten Comics,
9-12 St. Annes Court, Soho, W1
Tel: 071-734 7388

Stateside Comics plc,
125 East Barnet Road, EN4
Tel: 081-449 5535

Oxfordshire
Comics & Showcase,
19-20 St. Clements Street,
Oxford
Tel: (0865) 723680

Somerset
Yesterday's Paper,
40 South View, Holcombe
Rogus, Wellington
Tel: (0823) 672774

West Midlands
Nostalgia & Comics,
14-16 Smallbrook, Queensway
City Centre, Birmingham
Tel: 021-643 0143

Scotland
AKA Comics & Books,
33 Virginia Street, Glasgow
Tel: 041-552 8731

Wales
Forbidden Planet,
5 Duke Street, Cardiff
Tel: (0222) 228885

Greetings Cards

London
Pleasures of Past Times,
11 Cecil Court, Charing Cross
Road, WC2
Tel: 071-836 1142

Matchboxes

Kent
Kollectomania,
4 Catherine Street, Rochester
Tel: (0634) 45099

Postcards

London
Memories,
18 Bell Lane, Hendon, NW4
Tel: 081-203 1772/081-202 9080

Cheshire
Avalon,
1 City Walls, Northgate Street,
Chester
Tel: (0244) 318406

Derbyshire
Norman King,
24 Dinting Road, Glossop
Tel: (045 74) 2946

Essex
R.F. Postcards,
17 Hilary Crescent, Rayleigh
Tel: (0268) 743222

Gloucestershire
Specialised Postcard Auctions,
25 Gloucester Street,
Cirencester
Tel: (0285) 659057

Hampshire
Garnet Langton Auctions,
Burlington Arcade,
Bournemouth
Tel: (0202) 552352

Kent
Mike Sturge,
39 Union Street, Maidstone
Tel: (0622) 54702

West Midlands
George Sawyer,
11 Frayne Avenue,
Kingswinford
Tel: (0384) 273847

Norfolk
Bluebird Arts,
1 Mount Street, Cromer
Tel: (0263) 512384/78487

Northamptonshire
Shelron,
9 Brackley Road, Towcester
Tel: (0327) 50242

Nottinghamshire
Reflections of a Bygone Age,
15 Debdale Lane, Keyworth
Tel: (06077) 4079

T. Vennett Smith,
11 Nottingham Road, Gotham
Tel: (0602) 830541

East Sussex
John & Mary Bartholomew,
The Mint Arcade, 71 The Mint,
Rye
Tel: (0797) 225952

South Eastern Auctions,
39 High Street, Hastings
Tel: (0424) 434220

West Sussex
Bygones, Collectors Shop,
123 South Street, Lancing
Tel: (0903) 750051/763470

Wiltshire
David Wells,
Salisbury Antique & Collectors
Market, 37 Catherine Street,
Salisbury
Tel: (0425) 476899

Beer Mats

West Midlands
Roger Summers,
92 Nursery Road, Edgbaston,
Birmingham

Scripophily

London
The Scripophily Shop,
Britannia House, Grosvenor
Square, W1
Tel: 071-495 0580

Essex
G.K.R. Bonds Ltd.,
PO Box 1, Kelvedon
Tel: (0376) 71711

FANS

London
Yvonne,
K3 Chenil Galleries, 183 Kings
Road, Chelsea, SW3
Tel: 071-352 7384

Kent
The Variety Box,
16 Chapel Place, Tunbridge
Wells
Tel: (0892) 31868/21589

Shropshire
F. C. Manser & Son Ltd,
53-54 Wyle Cop, Shrewsbury
Tel: (0743) 51120

FISHING

London
Jess Miller,
PO Box 1461, London W6
Tel: 081-748 9314

Dorset
Yesterday's Tackle & Books,
42 Clingan Road, Southbourne
Tel: (0202) 476586

Hampshire
Evans & Partridge Auctioneers,
Agriculture House, High Street,
Stockbridge
Tel: (0264) 810702

Shropshire
Vintage Fishing Tackle Shop
and Angling Art Gallery,
103 Longden Coleham,
Shrewsbury
Tel: (0743) 69373

Scotland
Jamie Maxtone Graham,
Lyne Haugh, Lyne Station,
Peebles
Tel: (072 14) 304

Jess Miller,
PO Box 1, Birnam, Dunkeld,
Perthshire
Tel: (03502) 522

Wales
Brindley John Ayers,
45 St. Anne's Road, Hakin,
Milford Haven, Pembrokeshire
Tel: (06462) 78359

GOLFING

London
Sarah Baddiel,
The Book Gallery, B.12 Grays
Mews, 1-7 Davies Mews, W1
Tel: 071-408 1239/081-452 7243

King & Country,
Unit 46, Alfie's Antique
Market, 13-25 Church Street,
NW8
Tel: 071-724 3439

Oxfordshire
Manfred Schotten,
Crypt Antiques, 109 High
Street, Burford
Tel: (099 382) 2302

Warwickshire
Smith Street Antique Centre,
7 Smith Street, Warwick
Tel: (0926) 497864

GLASS – EARLY 18thC/19thC

London
Christine Bridge,
78 Castelnau, SW13
Tel: 081-741 5501

East Gates Antiques,
Stand G006, Alfies Antique
Market, 13-25 Church Street,
NW8
Tel: 071-724 5650

Pryce & Brise,
79 Moore Park Road, Fulham,
SW6
Tel: 081-736 1864

Mark J. West – Cobb Antiques,
39B High Street, Wimbledon
Village, SW19
Tel: 081-946 2811/081-540 7982

Avon
Somervale Antiques,
6 Radstock Road, Midsomer
Norton, Bath
Tel: (0761) 412686

Essex
East Gates Antiques,
91a East Hill, Colchester
Tel: (0206) 564474

Kent
Variety Box,
16 Chapel Place, Tunbridge
Wells
Tel: (0892) 31868/21589

GLASS – 20thC

London
Frank Andrews – Monart
and Vasart,
10 Vincent Road, London, N22
Tel: 081-881 0658 (Home)

Beverley – Cloud Glass, Jobling,
30 Church Street, NW8
Tel: 071-262 1576

The Scottish Connection,
Alfie's Antique Market,
13-25 Church Street, NW8
Tel: 071-723 6066

Stephen Watson – Powell,
Alfie's Antique Market,
13-25 Church Street, NW8
Tel: 071-723 0678

HAIRDRESSING/ HAT PINS

London
Ursula,
P16, 15 & 14 Antiquarius,
135 Kings Road, SW3
Tel: 071-352 2203

Hertfordshire
Ambeline Antiques,
By George Antique Centre,
St. Albans
Tel: (0727) 53032/081-445 8025

Kent
The Lace Basket,
1A East Cross, Tenterden
Tel: (05806) 3923

Variety Box,
16 Chapel Place, Tunbridge
Wells
Tel: (0892) 31868/21589

INKWELLS

London
Patrician,
1st Floor, Georgian Village,
Camden Passage, N1
Tel: 071-359 4560/071-435 3159

Berkshire
Mostly Boxes,
92 & 52B High Street, Eton,
Windsor
Tel: (0753) 858470

Kent
Ann Lingard,
Ropewalk Antiques, Rye
Tel: (0797) 223486

Worcestershire
BBM Jewellery & Coins,
(Mr W. V. Crook),
8-9 Lion Street, Kidderminster
Tel: (0562) 744118

JEWELLERY
Victorian/ Edwardian

Cheshire
Eureka Antiques,
7A Church Brow, Bowden
Tel: 061-926 9722/5629
and
Geoffrey Vanns Arcade,
105 Portobello Road, W11

Gloucestershire
Lynn Greenwold,
Digbeth Street,
Stow-on-the-Wold
Tel: (0451) 30398

Hertfordshire
Forget Me Not,
By George Antique Centre,
23 George Street, St. Albans
Tel: (0727) 53032/(0903) 261172

Kent
Old Saddlers Antiques,
Church Road, Goudhurst,
Cranbrook
Tel: (0580) 211458

Norfolk
Peter Howkins,
39, 40 and 135 King Street,
Great Yarmouth
Tel: (0493) 844639

Wiltshire
Coppins of Corsham Repairs,
1 Church Street, Corsham
Tel: (0249) 715404

Art Deco

London
Pierre De Fresne 'Beaux Bijoux',
Q 9/10 Antiquarius, 135 Kings
Road, SW3
Tel: 071-352 8882

Abstract,
Kensington Church Street
Antique Centre,
58-60 Kensington Church
Street, W8
Tel: 071-376 2652

JUKE BOXES

London
Anything American,
33-35 Duddenhill Lane, NW10
Tel: 081-451 0320

Dorset
The Chicago Sound Company,
Northmoor House, Colesbrook,
Gillingham
Tel: (0747) 824338

Surrey
Nostalgia Amusements,
22 Greenwood Close, Thames
Ditton
Tel: 081-398 2141

KITCHENALIA

London
David,
141 Grays Antique Market,
Davies Street, W1
Tel: 071-493 0208

Relic Antiques,
248 Camden High Street,
London, NW1
Tel: 071-485 8072

Berkshire
Below Stairs,
103 High Street, Hungerford
Tel: (0488) 682317

Lancashire
The Old Bakery,
36 Inglewhite Road, Longridge,
Nr. Preston
Tel: (0772) 785411

Kent
Penny Lampard,
28 High Street, Headcorn
Tel: (0622) 890682

Up Country,
Old Corn Stores, 68 St John's
Road, Tunbridge Wells
Tel: (0892) 23341

Shropshire
Scot Hay House Antiques,
7 Nantwich Road, Woore
Tel: (063 081) 7118

Tiffany Antiques,
Unit 15, Shrewsbury Antique
Market, Frankwell Quay
Warehouse, Shrewsbury
Tel (0743) 50916/(0270) 225425
and
Unit 5, Telford Antique Centre,
High Street, Wellington, Telford
Tel: (0952) 56450

Surrey
Wych House Antiques,
Wych Hill, Woking
Tel: (04862) 64636

East Sussex
Ann Lingard,
Rope Walk Antiques, Rye
Tel: (0797) 223486

West Midlands
The Doghouse,
309 Bloxwich Road, Walsall
Tel: (0922) 30829

LE BLOND PRINTS

Warwickshire
Janice Paull,
125 Warwick Road, Kenilworth
Tel: (0926) 55253

LOCKS & KEYS

Nottinghamshire
The Keyhole,
Dragonwyck, Far Back Lane,
Farnsfield, Newark
Tel: (0623) 882590

LUGGAGE

London
Stanhope Bowery,
Grays Antique Market, Davies
Street, W1
Tel: 071-629 6194

METALWARE

London
Christopher Bangs,
SW11
Tel: 071-223 5676

Jack Casimir Ltd,
The Brass Shop, 23 Pembridge
Road, W11
Tel: 071-727 8643

Avon
Nick Marchant,
13 Orwell Drive, Keynsham,
Bristol
Tel: (0272) 865182

Bedfordshire
Christopher Sykes,
The Old Parsonage, Woburn
Tel: (0525) 290259

Derbyshire
Spurrier-Smith Antiques,
28b, 39-41 Church Street,
Ashbourne
Tel: (0335) 43669/42198

Kent
Old Saddlers Antiques,
Church Road, Goudhurst,
Cranbrook
Tel: (0580) 211458

Oxfordshire
Key Antiques,
11 Horse Fair, Chipping Norton
Tel: (0608) 3777

MILITARIA
Medals

Hampshire
Charles Antiques,
101 The Hundred, Romsey
Tel: (0794) 512885

Scotland
Edinburgh Coin Shop,
2 Powarth Crescent, Edinburgh
Tel: 031-229 3007/2915

East Sussex
Wallis & Wallis,
West Street Auction Galleries,
Lewes
Tel: (0273) 480208

Arms & Armour

London
Michael German,
38B Kensington Church Street,
W8
Tel: 071-937 2771

West Yorks
Andrew Spencer Bottomley,
The Coach House,
Thongsbridge, Holmfirth
Tel: (0484) 685234

Arms & Militaria

London
Pieter G. K. Oosthuizen,
16 Britten Street, London, SW3
Tel: 071-352 1094/071-352 1493

Hampshire
Romsey Medal Centre,
5 Bell Street, Romsey
Tel: (0794) 512069

Kent
Keith & Veronica Reeves,
Burgate Antiques, 10c Burgate,
Canterbury
Tel: (0227) 456500/(0634)
375098

Surrey
West Street Antiques,
63 West Street, Dorking
Tel: (0306) 883487

East Sussex
V.A.G. & Co,
Possingworth Craft Centre,
Brownings Farm, Blackboys,
Uckfield
Tel: (0323) 507488

Wallis & Wallis,
West Street Auction Galleries,
Lewes
Tel: (0273) 480208

Warwickshire
Arbour Antiques Ltd,
Poet's Arbour, Sheep Street,
Stratford-upon-Avon
Tel: (0789) 293453

Central Antique Arms &
Militaria,
Smith Street Antique Centre,
7 Smith Street, Warwick
Tel: (0926) 497864

Scotland
Edinburgh Coin Shop,
2 Polwarth Crescent, Edinburgh
Tel: 031-229 2915/3007

RADIOS

London
The Originals,
Stand 37, Alfie's Antique
Market, 13-25 Church Street,
NW8
Tel. 071-724 3439

Devon
Jonathan Hill,
2-4 Brook Street, Bampton
Tel: (0398) 31310

Hereford & Worcs
Radiocraft,
56 Main Street, Sedgeberrow,
Nr Evesham
Tel: (0386) 881988

RAILWAYS

Avon
Winstone Stamp Co,
Great Western Antique Market,
Bartlett Street, Bath
Tel: (0225) 310388

West Midlands
Railwayana Collectors Journal,
7 Ascot Road, Moseley,
Birmingham

ORIENTAL

London
Ormonde Gallery,
156 Portobello Road, W11
Tel: 071-229 9800/(042482) 226

493

Dorset
Lionel Geneen Ltd,
781 Christchurch Road,
Boscombe, Bournemouth
Tel: (0202) 422961

East Sussex
Chateaubriand Antique Centre,
High Street, Burwash
Tel: (0435) 882535

Warwickshire
Simon Bowler,
Smith Street Antique Centre,
Warwick
Tel: (0926) 400554

Scotland
Koto Buki,
The Milestone, Balmedie,
Aberdeen
Tel: (0358) 42414

PAPIER MÂCHÉ
London
Rosemary Fobbister,
The Original Chelsea Antique
Market, Stand 28, 245-263
King's Road, London, SW3
Tel: 071-352 5581

Kent
Antiques & Interiors,
22 Ashford Road, Tenterden
Tel: (05806) 5422

PERFUME BOTTLES
London
Patrician Antiques,
1st Floor, Georgian Village,
Camden Passage, N1
Tel: 071-359 4560/071-435 3159

Trio (Theresa Clayton),
Grays Mews, 1-7 Davies Mews,
W1
Tel: 071-629 1184

Avon
Somervale Antiques,
6 Radstock Road, Midsomer
Norton, Bath
Tel: (0761) 412686

Kent
Kent Cottage Antiques,
39 High Street, Rolvenden,
Nr. Cranbrook
Tel: (0580) 241719

POLICE MEMORABILIA
London
David,
141 Grays Antique Market,
Davies Street, W1
Tel: 071-493 0208

Dorset
Mervyn A. Mitton,
161 The Albany, Manor Road,
Bournemouth
Tel: (0202) 293767

Yorkshire
National Railway Museum,
Leeman Road, York
Tel: (0904) 621261

Sheffield Railwayana Auctions,
43 Little Norton Lane, Sheffield
Tel: (0742) 745085/(0860)
921519

SCIENTIFIC & MEDICAL INSTRUMENTS
London
Derek Howard,
The Original, Chelsea Antique
Market, 245-253 Kings Road,
SW3
Tel: 071-352 4113

Reubens,
44 Honor Oak Park, Brockley,
SE23
Tel: 081-291 1786

David Weston Ltd,
44 Duke Street, St James's, SW1
Tel: 071-839 1051/2/3

Bedfordshire
Christopher Sykes,
The Old Parsonage, Woburn
Tel: (0525) 290259

Surrey
David Burns,
116 Chestnut Grove, New
Malden
Tel: 081-949 7356

SEWING
London
The Thimble Society of London,
The Bees, S134 Grays Antique
Market, 58 Davies Street, W1
Tel: 071-493 0560

Kent
The Variety Box,
16 Chapel Place, Tunbridge
Wells
Tel: (0892) 31868/21589

Suffolk
Crafers Antiques,
The Hill, Wickham Market
Tel: (0728) 747347

SHIPPING
Hampshire
Cobwebs,
78 Northam Road, Southampton
Tel: (0703) 227458

North Humberside
Marine Art Posters Services,
42 Ravenspur Road, Bilton, Hull
Tel: (0482) 874700/815115

SILVER
London
Donohoe,
L25/7 M10/12 Grays Mews,
1-7 Davies Mews, W1
Tel: 071-629 5633/081-455 5507

Goldsmith & Perris,
Stand 327, Alfie's Antique
Market, 13-25 Church Street,
NW8
Tel: 071-724 7051

The London Silver Vaults,
Chancery House, 53-65
Chancery Lane, WC2
Tel: 071-242 3844

Kent
The Variety Box,
16 Chapel Place, Tunbridge
Wells
Tel: (0892) 31868/21589

Oxfordshire
Thames Gallery,
Thameside, Henley-on-Thames
Tel: (0491) 572449

Shropshire
F. C. Manser & Son Ltd,
53-54 Wyle Cop, Shrewsbury
Tel: (0743) 51120

SPORT – FOOTBALL
London
Final Whistle,
50, 61-63 Alfie's Antique
Market, 13-25 Church Street,
London, NW8
Tel: 071-262 3423

TARTANWARE
London
Eureka Antiques,
Geoffrey Vanns Arcade,
105 Portobello Road, W11
(Saturdays)

Grays Antique Market,
58 Davies Street, W1
Tel: 071-629 7034

Cheshire
Eureka Antiques,
18 Northenden Road, Sale
Tel: 061-962 5629

TELEPHONES
Cheshire
Dé Jà Vu Antiques,
Hatters Row, Horsemarket
Street, Warrington
Tel: (0925) 232677

Devon
Bampton Telephone & General
Museum of Communication and
Domestic History,
4 Brook Street, Bampton

Lancashire
British Heritage Telephones,
11 Rhodes Drive, Unsworth,
Bury
Tel: 061-767 9259

Scotland
Now & Then Classic Telephones,
7/9 Crosscauseway, Edinburgh
Tel: 031-668 2927/
(0592) 890235

TEXTILES
Samplers
London
Sophia Blanchard,
Alfie's Antique Market, Church
Street, NW8
Tel: 071-723 5731

Matthew Adams Antiques,
69 Portobello Road, W11
Tel: 081-579 5560

Quilts, Patchwork, Costume
London
Academy Costumes Ltd (Hire
Only),
25 Murphy Street, London SE1
Tel: 071-620 0771

Classic Costumes Ltd,
Tel: 081-764 8858/
071-620 0771

Chenil Galleries,
Enigma Z2, Pamela Haywood
Z3, Persifage Z5, Forthergill
Crowley D11-12, 181-183 Kings
Road, Chelsea
Tel: 071-351 5353

Act One Hire Ltd,
2A Scampston Mews,
Cambridge Gardens, London,
W10
Tel: 081-960 1456/1494

The Antique Textile Company,
100 Portland Road, Holland
Park, W11
Tel: 071-221 7730

The Gallery of Antique Costume
& Textiles,
2 Church Street, Marylebone,
NW8
Tel: 071-723 9981

Lincolnshire
20th Century Frocks,
Lincolnshire Art Centre, Bridge
Street, Horncastle
Tel: (06582) 7794/(06588) 3638

West Yorkshire
Echoes,
650A Halifax Road, Eastwood,
Todmorden
Tel: (0706) 817505

Wales
Paul Williams,
Forge Antiques, Synod Inn,
Llandysul, Dyfed

Linen & Lace
London
Antiquarius,
135-141 Kings Road, SW3
Tel: 071-351 5353

Audrey Field,
Alfie's Antique Market,
13-25 Church Street, NW8
Tel: 071-723 6066

Devon
Honiton Lace Shop,
44 High Street, Honiton
Tel: (0404) 42416

Kent
Antiques & Interiors,
22 Ashford Road, Tenterden
Tel: (05806) 5462

The Lace Basket,
1A East Cross, Tenterden
Tel: (05806) 3923

East Sussex
Chateaubriand Antique Centre,
High Street, Burwash
Tel: (0435) 882535

TILES
London
Ilse Antiques,
30-32 The Vaults, The Georgian
Village, Islington, N1

East Sussex
Ann Lingard,
Rope Walk Antiques, Rye
Tel: (0797) 223486

The Old Mint House,
Pevensey
Tel: (0323) 762337

Wales
Paul Gibbs Antiques,
25 Castle Street, Conwy
Tel: (0492) 593429

Victorian Fireplaces
(Simon Priestley),
Ground Floor, Cardiff Antique
Centre, 69/71 St Mary Street,
Cardiff
Tel: (0222) 30970/226049

TINS & METAL SIGNS
London
Keith, Old Advertising,
Unit 14, 155A Northcote Road,
Battersea, SW11
Tel: 071-228 0741/6850

Avon
Michael & Jo Saffell,
3 Walcot Buildings, London
Road, Bath
Tel: (0225) 315857

Oxfordshire
R.A.T.S.,
Unit 16, Telford Road, Bicester
Tel: (0869) 242161/40842

East Sussex
Rin Tin Tin,
34 North Road, Brighton
Tel: (0273) 672424/
(0273) 733689 (Eves)

Wiltshire
Relic Antiques, Lea,
Malmesbury
Tel: (0666) 822332

TOYS
Mechanical
London
Chelsea Lion,
Chenil Galleries, 181-183
King's Road, London SW3
Tel: 071-351 9338

Stuart Cropper,
Grays Mews, 1-7 Davies Mews,
W1
Tel: 071-629 7034

Avon
Great Western Toys, Great
Western Antique Centre,
Bartlett Street, Bath

Hampshire
Nostalgia Toy Museum,
High Street, Godshill, Isle of
Wight
Tel: (0983) 526254

Vectis Model Acutions,
95/96 High Street, Cowes, Isle of
Wight
Tel: (0983) 292272

Lincolnshire
Junktion Old Railway Station,
New Bolingbroke, Boston
Tel: (0205) 480087

Diecast Models
London
Colin Baddiel,
Grays Mews, 1-7 Davies Mews,
W1
Tel: 071-408 1239/081-452 7243

Past Present Toys,
862 Green Lanes, Winchmore
Hill, London N21
Tel: 081-364 1370

Buckinghamshire
Cars Only,
4 Granville Square, Willen
Local Centre, Willen, Milton
Keynes
Tel: (0908) 690024

Cornwall
Model Garage (Redruth) Ltd,
Lanner Hill, Redruth
Tel: (0209) 215589/211311

Isle of Wight
Nostalgia Toy Museum,
High Street, Godshill
Tel: (0983) 730055

Norfolk
Trains & Olde Tyme Toys,
Aylsham Road, Norwich
Tel: (0603) 413585

Shropshire
Stretton Models,
12 Beaumont Road, Church
Stretton
Tel: (0694) 723737

East Sussex
Clockwork and Steam,
35 Western Street, Brighton
Tel: (0273) 203290

Wallis & Wallis,
West Street Auction Galleries,
Lewes
Tel: (0273) 480208

West Sussex
Trains,
67 London Road, Bognor Regis
Tel: (0243) 864727

Warwickshire
Time Machine,
Paul M. Kennelly, 198 Holbrook
Lane, Coventry
Tel: (0203) 663557

West Midlands
Moseley Railwayana Museum,
Birmingham
Tel: 021-449 9707

Wiltshire
David Wells,
Salisbury Antique & Collectors
Market, 37 Catherine Street,
Salisbury
Tel: (0425) 476899

Yorkshire
Andrew Clarke,
42 Pollard Lane, Bradford
Tel: (0274) 636042

John & Simon Haley,
89 Northgate, Halifax
Tel: (0422) 822148

Wales
Corgi Toys Ltd,
Kingsway, Swansea Industrial
Estate, Swansea
Tel: (0792) 586223

Money Boxes
Yorkshire
John Haley,
89 Northgate, Halifax
Tel: (0422) 822148

Games
London
Donay,
35 Camden Passage, N1
Tel: 071-359 1880

Rocking Horses
London
Judith Lassalle,
7 Pierrepont Arcade (Wed &
Sat), Camden Passage, London
N1
Tel: 071-607 7121

Cornwall
The Millcraft Rocking Horse Co,
Lower Trannack Mill, Coverack
Bridges, Helston
Tel: (0326) 573316

Lincolnshire
Legends Rocking Horses,
Yew Tree Farmhouse, Holme
Road, Kirton Holme, Boston
Tel: (020 579) 214

Shropshire
The Rocking Horse Workshop,
Ashfield House, The Foxholes,
Wem
Tel: (0939) 32335

Somerset
Margaret Spencer & Co,
Dept AD, Chard Road,
Crewkerne
Tel: (0460) 72362

Scotland
Whittingham Crafts Ltd,
8 Pentland Court, Saltire
Centre, Glenrothes, Fife
Tel: (0592) 630433

Wales
Stuart & Pam MacPherson,
A.P.E.S.,
Ty Isaf, Pont Y Gwyddel,
Llanfair T.H., Abergele, Clwyd
Tel: (074 579) 365

TREEN
London
Simon Castle,
38B Kensington Church Street,
W8
Tel: 081-892 2840

Wynyards Antiques,
5 Ladbroke Road, W11
Tel: 071-221 7936

Buckinghamshire
A. & E. Foster,
Little Heysham, Forge Road,
Naphill
Tel: (024 024) 2024

TUNBRIDGEWARE
Berkshire
Mostly Boxes,
52B High Street, Eton
Tel: (0753) 858470

Kent
Strawsons Antiques
33, 39 & 41 The Pantiles,
Tunbridge Wells
Tel: (0892) 30607

The Variety Box,
16 Chapel Place, Tunbridge
Wells
Tel: (0892) 31868/21589

East Sussex
Barclay Antiques,
7 Village Mews, Little Common,
Bexhill-on-Sea
Tel: (0797) 222734

WALKING STICKS
London
Cekay Antiques,
Grays Antique Market,
58 Davies Street, W1
Tel: 071-629 5130

Michael German,
38B Kensington Church Street,
W8
Tel: 071-937 2771

WATCHES
London
Pieces of Time, Grays Mews,
1-7 Davies Street, W1
Tel: 071-629 2422

WRITING
London
Jasmin Cameron,
Stand J6 Antiquarius,
131-141 Kings Road, SW3
Tel: 071-351 4154

CALENDAR OF FAIRS from April 1992

This calendar is in no way complete. If you wish your event to be included in next year's edition or if you have a change of address or telephone number, please could you inform us by December 1st 1992. Finally we would advise readers to make contact by telephone before a visit, therefore avoiding a wasted journey, which nowadays is both time consuming and expensive.

We suggest you consult your local newspaper for further information.

London

APRIL

Sun 5th
Kensington Hilton, 179-199
Holland Park Avenue, W11
Ralph & Patricia Harvey.
Tel: 071-624 5173

The Park Court Hotel,
Lancaster Gate, Bayswater, W2
K M Fairs.
Tel: 071-794 3551

Picketts Lock Leisure Centre,
Picketts Lock Lane, N9
Jax Fairs.
Tel: (0444) 400570

Rutlish School, Mostyn Road,
Off Kingston Road, Merton
Park, SW19
Margaret Browne Fairs.
Tel: 081-874 3622

Sun 12th
Dulwich College, SE1
Margaret Browne Fairs
Tel: 081-874 3622

Kensington Palace Hotel,
De Vere Gardens, Kensington
High Street, W8
Ralph & Patricia Harvey.
Tel: 071-624 5173

The Park Lane Hotel,
Piccadilly, W1
K M Fairs.
Tel: 071-794 3551

The Selfridge Hotel, Orchard
Street, W1
Adams Antiques Fairs.
Tel: 071-254 4054

Sun 19th
The Royal Garden Hotel,
Kensington High Street, W8
K M Fairs.
Tel: 071-794 3551

Fri 24th-26th
Chelsea Bracante Fair, Old
Town Hall, SW3
Bagatelle Fairs.
Tel: (0428) 685452

London Hilton on Park Lane,
22 Park Lane, W1
Ralph & Patricia Harvey.
Tel: 071-624 5173

The Park Lane Hotel,
Piccadilly, W1
K M Fairs.
Tel: 071-794 3551

Royal Horticultural Halls,
Vincent Square, Victoria, SW1
Adams Antiques Fairs.
Tel: 071-254 4054

Thurs 30th-May 3rd
Westminster Antiques Fair,
Horticultural Old Hall, SW1
Penman Antiques Fairs.
Tel: (0444) 482514

MAY

Fri 1st-2nd
Arms Fair, Ramada Inn, SW6
Tel: 071-405 7933

Sun 3rd
Kensington Hilton, Holland
Park Avenue, W11
Ralph & Patricia Harvey.
Tel: 071-624 5173

The Park Court Hotel,
Lancaster Gate, Bayswater, W2
K M Fairs.
Tel: 071-794 3551

Picketts Lock Leisure Centre,
Picketts Lock Lane, N9
Jax Fairs.
Tel: (0444) 400570

Rutlish School, Mostyn Road,
Off Kingston Road, Merton
Park, SW19
Margaret Browne Fairs.
Tel: 081-874 3622

Sun 10th
Dulwich College, SE21
Margaret Browne Fairs.
Tel: 081-874 3622

London Marriott Hotel,
Grosvenor Square, W1
Ralph and Patricia Harvey
Tel: 071-624 5173

The Park Lane Hotel,
Piccadilly, W1
K M Fairs.
Tel: 071-794 3551

Royal Horticultural Halls,
Vincent Square, Victoria, SW1
Adams Antiques Fairs.
Tel: 071-254 4054

Sun 17th
Kensington Palace Hotel, De
Vere Gardens, Kensington High
Street, W8
Ralph & Patricia Harvey.
Tel: 071-624 5173

The Park Lane Hotel,
Piccadilly, W1
K M Fairs.
Tel: 071-794 3551

The Selfridge Hotel, Orchard
Street, W1
Adams Antiques Fairs.
Tel: 071-254 4054

Tues 19th
The Wembley International,
Antique & Collectors Fair,
Wembley Exhibition Centre,
Wembley
International Antique &
Collectors Fair Co Ltd.
Tel: (0636) 702326

Sat 23rd
London Decorative Arts Fair,
Kensington Town Hall,
Hornton Street, off Kensington
High Street, W8
Bagatelle Fairs.
Tel: (0428) 685452

The Portman Inter-Continental,
22 Portman Square, W8
K M Fairs.
Tel: 071-794 3551

Fri 29th-31st
Chelsea Art Fair, Old Town
Hall, SW3
Bagatelle Fairs.
Tel: (0428) 685452

Sun 31st
London Hilton on Park Lane,
22 Park Lane, W1
Ralph & Patricia Harvey.
Tel: 071-624 5173

The Park Court Hotel,
Lancaster Gate, Bayswater, W2
K M Fairs.
Tel: 071-794 7001

JUNE

Thurs 4th-14th
Fine Art & Antiques Fair,
Olympia, W14
Philbeach Events Ltd.
Tel: 071-370 8211/8234

Sun 7th
Kensington Hilton, 179-199
Holland Park Avenue, W11
Ralph & Patricia Harvey.
Tel: 071-624 5173

The Park Lane Hotel,
Piccadilly, W1
K M Fairs
Tel: 071-794 3551

Picketts Lock Leisure Centre,
Picketts Lock Lane, N9
Jax Fairs.
Tel: (0444) 400570

Rutlish School, Mostyn Road, off
Kingston Road, Merton Park,
SW19
Margaret Browne.
Tel: 081-874 3622

Wed 10th-20th
Grosvenor House Antiques
Fair, Park Lane, W1
Evan Steadman
Communications Group.
Tel: (0799) 526699

Fri 12th-15th
International Ceramics Fair,
Park Lane Hotel, Piccadilly, W1
Brian Haughton.
Tel: 071-734 5491

Fri 12th-14th
London Ceramics Fair,
Cumberland Hotel, Marble Arch
Wakefield Ceramics Fair.
Tel: (0634) 723461

Sun 14th
Alexandra Palace Antique &
Collectors Fair, Wood Green,
N22
Pig & Whistle Promotions.
Tel: 081-883 7061

Brocante Antiques Fair,
Kensington Town Hall,
Hornton Street, off Kensington
High Street, W8
Bagatelle Fairs.
Tel: (0428) 685452

Dulwich College, SE21
Margaret Browne Fairs.
Tel: 081-874 3622

London Marriott Hotel,
Grosvenor Square, W1
Ralph & Patricia Harvey.
Tel: 071-624 5173

The Park Court Hotel,
Lancaster Gate, Bayswater, W2
K M Fairs.
Tel: 071-794 3551

Sun 21st
Kensington Palace Hotel,
De Vere Gardens, Kensington
High Street, W8
Ralph & Patricia Harvey.
Tel: 071-624 5173

London Hilton on Park Lane,
22 Park Lane, W1
K M Fairs.
Tel: 071-794 3551

The Park Lane Hotel,
Piccadilly, W1
K M Fairs.
Tel: 071-794 3551

The Portman Inter-Continental,
22 Portman Square, W1
K M Fairs.
Tel: 071-794 3551

Royal Horticultural Halls,
Vincent Square, Victoria, SW1
Adams Antiques Fairs.
Tel: 071-254 4054

JULY
Sun 5th
Kensington Hilton, Holland
Park Avenue, W11
Ralph & Patricia Harvey.
Tel: 071-624 5173

The Park Court Hotel,
Lancaster Gate, Bayswater, W2
K M Fairs.
Tel: 071-794 3551

Rutlish School, Mostyn Road, off
Kingston Road, Merton Park,
SW19
Margaret Browne Fairs.
Tel: 081-874 3622

The Selfridge Hotel, Orchard
Street, W1
Adams Antiques Fairs.
Tel: 071-254 4054

Sun 12
Dulwich College, SE21
Margaret Browne Fairs.
Tel: 081-874 3622

London Marriott Hotel,
Grosvenor Square, W1
Ralph & Patricia Harvey.
Tel: 071-624 5173

The Park Lane Hotel,
Piccadilly, W1
K M Fairs.
Tel: 071-794 3551

Royal Horticultural Halls,
Vincent Square, Victoria, W1
Adams Antiques Fairs.
Tel: 071-254 4054

Sun 19th
Kensington Palace Hotel, De
Vere Gardens, Kensington High
Street, W8
Ralph & Patricia Harvey.
Tel: 071-624 5173

The Park Court Hotel,
Lancaster Gate, Bayswater, W2
K M Fairs.
Tel: 071-794 3551

Sun 26th
The Park Lane Hotel,
Piccadilly, W1
K M Fairs.
Tel: 071-794 3551

Tues 28th
The Wembley International
Antique & Collectors Fair,
Wembley Exhibition Centre,
Wembley
International Antique &
Collectors Fair Co Ltd.
Tel: (0636) 702326

Avon
MAY
Tues 12th-16th
West of England Antiques Fair,
Assembly Rooms, Bath
Tel: (0249) 75306

JULY
Thurs 16th-18th
Ceramics Fair, Assembly
Rooms, Bath

Bedfordshire
APRIL
Sun 19th-20th
Fine Art & Antique Fair,
Mentmore Towers

Sun 26th
Putteridge Recreation Centre,
Putteridge Lane, Stopsley,
Luton
MAY
Sun 24th
Putteridge Recreation Centre,
Putteridge Lane, Stopsley,
Luton

Berkshire
MAY
Sat 2nd-4th
The East Berkshire Antiques
Fair, Hall Place, Burchett's
Green, Maidenhead
Tel: (0628) 824388

Fri 15th-17th
Antiques Fair, Highclere
Castle, Newbury

Buckinghamshire
APRIL
Fri 17th-20th
Antiques Fair, Stowe School
Tel: (0277) 362662
MAY
Sun 24th-25th
Fine Art & Antiques Fair,
Bellhouse Hotel, Beaconsfield
AUGUST
Sun 30th-31st
Fine Art & Antiques Fair,
Bellhouse Hotel, Beaconsfield

Cheshire
MAY
Fri 8th-10th
The Tatton Park 19th & 20thC
Paintings Fair, Knutsford
JULY
Thurs 23rd-25th
The Game Fair, Antiques Fair,
Tabley Park

Cornwall
APRIL
Fri 17th-18th
Truro Antiques & Collectors
Fair, City Hall, Truro
Tel: (0364) 52182

AUGUST
Fri 14th-15th
Truro Antiques, Collectors &
Book Fair, City Hall Truro
Tel: (0364) 52182

Cumbria

MAY
Wed 13th-17th
3rd Spring Grasmere Antiques Fair, Grasmere
Tel: (0748) 824095

Derbyshire

APRIL
Sat 4th-5th
Antiques Fair, Pavilion Gardens, Buxton
Tel: (04868) 22562

Sun 19th-20th
Antiques Fair, Elvaston Castle
Tel: (0602) 459321

MAY
Sat 9th-16th
28th Buxton Antiques Fair, Pavilion Gardens, Buxton
Tel: (04868) 22562

Sun 24th-25th
Antiques Fair, Elvaston Castle
Tel: (0602) 459321

JUNE
Sat 6th-7th
Antiques Fair, Pavilion Gardens, Buxton
Tel: (04868) 22562

JULY
Sat 11th-12th
Antiques Fair, Pavilion Gardens, Buxton
Tel: (04868) 22562

AUGUST
Sat 29th-30th
Antiques Fair, Pavilion Gardens, Buxton
Tel: (04868) 22562

Sun 30th-31st
Antiques Fair, Elvaston Castle
Tel: (0602) 459321

Devon

APRIL
Sun 19th-20th
Exmouth Easter Antiques & Collectors Fair, The Pavilion, The Sea Front, Exmouth

Thurs 23rd-24th
Exeter Spring Antiques Fair, The Imperial Hotel, St. Davids Hill, Exeter
Tel: (0364) 52182

MAY
Sun 3rd-4th
Exmouth Bank Holiday Antiques Fair, The Pavilion, The Sea Front, Exmouth

Fri 23rd-24th
Newton Abbot Giant Antiques, Collectors & Book Fair, The Racecourse, Newton Abbot
Tel: (0364) 52182

Thurs 28th-29th
The 25th Annual North Devon Antique Dealers Fair, Queens Hall, Barnstaple
Tel: (0364) 52182

JUNE
Sat 13th-14th
Antiques Fair, Haldon Hotel, Dunchideock

Sat 27th-28th
Antiques Fair, Westpoint Exhibition Centre, Exeter
Tel: (0363) 82571

JULY
Sat 18th-19th
Antiques Fair, Blundell's School, Tiverton
Tel: (0363) 82571

AUGUST
Sun 30th-31st
Exmouth Antiques Fair, The Pavilion, Exmouth

Dorset

MAY
Sat 16th-17th
Mammoth Fair, Exhibition Centre, Bournemouth

Essex

JULY
Tues 30th-1st Aug
Essex Euro Antiques Fair, County Showground, Great Leighs
Tel: (0565) 634614

Gloucestershire

APRIL
Sat 11th-12th
South Cotswolds Antiques Fair, Westonbirt School

MAY
Sat 2nd-3rd
Cotswold Antiques & Collectors Fair, Cheltenham Racecourse
Tel: (0934) 624859

JULY
Sat 18th-19th
North Cotswolds Antiques Fair, Stanway House

AUGUST
Sat 15th-16th
South Cotswolds Antiques Fair, Westonbirt School

Hampshire

JUNE
Thurs 4th-6th
Petersfield Antiques Fair, Petersfield
Tel: (0452) 862557

Hereford & Worcester

JULY
Fri 10th-12th
Antiques Fair, Hagley Hall

Hertfordshire

APRIL
Fri 24th-26th
Porcelain & Jewellery Fair, Hatfield House
Tel: (0277) 362662

MAY
Fri 29th-31st
Antiques Fair, Bushey School

Kent

JULY
Sat 25th-26th
Mammoth Fair, Kent Showground, Maidstone

Leicestershire

MAY
Sat 9th-10th
Mammoth Fair, Donington Park

Lincolnshire

MAY
Fri 22nd-25th
Antiques Fair, Harlaxton Manor, Grantham
Tel: (0277) 362662

Norfolk

APRIL
Thurs 15th-18th
25th Annual Norfolk Easter Antiques Fair, St. Andrew's Hall

Sat 25th
Corn Hall, Diss, Tradex Organization
Tel: (0728) 79531

Northamptonshire

JUNE
Mon 15th-16th
Mammoth Fair, Showground, Peterborough

JULY
Tues 21st-23rd
Antiques Fair, Showground, Peterborough

Northumberland

JUNE
Fri 12th-14th
Antiques Fair, Alnwick Castle
Tel: (0937) 845829

Nottinghamshire

JUNE
Fri 19th-21st
The Thoresby Antiques Fair, Nr Ollerton
Tel: 081-644 9327

Oxfordshire

APRIL
Fri 17th-18th
Antiques Fair, Spread Eagle, Thame
Tel: (0844) 213661

AUGUST
Sat 1st-2nd
5th Annual Radley College, Antiques Fair & Staffordshire Figures Fair, Radley College, Nr Abingdon
Tel: (0273) 423355

Shropshire

JUNE
Thurs 18th-21st
Antiques Fair, Moathouse, Telford

Somerset

APRIL
Sat 11th-12th
Antiques Fair, Millfield School, Street
Tel: (0363) 82571

Sat 25th-26th
Antiques Fair, Showground, Shepton Mallet
Tel: (0278) 691616

MAY
Fri 15th-16th
Wells Antiques, Collectors & Book Fair, The Star Hotel, Wells

JULY
Sat 11th-12th
Antiques Fair, Showground, Shepton Mallet
Tel: (0278) 691616

Fri 17th-18th
Wells Antiques, Collectors & Book Fair, The Star Hotel, Wells

AUGUST
Sat 22nd-23rd
Antiques Fair, Downside School

Surrey

APRIL
Fri 3rd-5th
Antiques Fair, Cranleigh School
Tel: (0634) 723641

Thurs 9th-12th
Thames Valley Antiques, Eton College
Tel: (0865) 340028

Sun 19th-20th
Ceramics Fair, Oatlands Park, Weybridge

JULY
Fri 31st-2nd Aug
Antiques Fair, Charterhouse School, Godalming

AUGUST
Sun 30th-31st
Antiques Fair, Dorking Halls, Dorking, Surrey
Tel: 081-874 3622

East Sussex

MAY
Fri 22nd-25th
Sussex Oak and Country Fair, Barkham Manor Barn, Piltdown

AUGUST
Fri 21st-23rd
Petworth Antiques Fair, Seaford College
Tel: (0277) 362662

West Sussex

MAY
Sun 3rd-4th
Ceramics Fair, Felbridge Hotel, East Grinstead
Tel: (0634) 723461

AUGUST
Fri 28th-29th
Antiques Fair, King Edward Hall, Lindfield
Tel: (0273) 423355

Staffordshire
JUNE
Fri 19th-21st
Giant Antiques Fair, Bingley
Hall, County Showground,
Stafford
Tel: (0532) 843333

AUGUST
Fri 14th-16th
Giant Antiques Fair, Bingley
Hall, County Showground,
Stafford
Tel: (0532) 843333

Suffolk
APRIL
Mon 20th
St Felix School, Southwold
Tradex Organization
Tel: (0728) 79531

MAY
Mon 4th
Jubilee Hall, Aldeburgh
Tradex Organization
Tel: (0728) 79531

Sun 10th
Snape Maltings
Tradex Organisation
Tel: (0728) 79531

Sun 24th-25th
St Felix School, Southwold
Tradex Organization
Tel: (0728) 79531

JUNE
Sun 7th
Snape Maltings
Tradex Organization
Tel: (0728) 79531

Sat 20th
St Edmunds Hall, Southwold
Tradex Organization
Tel: (0728) 79531

Sat 27th-28th
Antiques Fair, Horsedriving
Trials, Sandringham

JULY
Sun 12th
Snape Maltings
Tradex Organization
Tel: (0728) 79531

Sun 19th
St Felix School, Southwold
Tradex Organization
Tel: (0728) 79531

Wed 22nd-25th
26th Annual Snape Antiques
Fair, The Maltings, Snape
Tel: (0986) 872368

Sat 25th
Jubilee Hall, Aldeburgh
Tradex Organization
Tel: (0728) 79531

AUGUST
Sun 9th
Snape Maltings
Tradex Organization
Tel: (0728) 79531

Sun 30th
Jubilee Hall, Aldeburgh
Tradex Organization
Tel: (0728) 79531

Tyne & Wear
APRIL
Sat 11th-12th
Antiques Fair, Gosforth Park,
Newcastle-upon-Tyne

Warwickshire
MAY
Sun 3rd-4th
The Sutton Coldfield Antiques
Fair, Penn's Hall, Hotel
Tel: (0952) 595622
JUNE
Fri 26th-28th
Antiques Fair, National
Motorcycle Museum, Solihull

West Midlands
APRIL
Thurs 9th-15th
British International Antiques
Fair, National Exhibition
Centre, Birmingham
Tel: 021-780 4141

Wiltshire
APRIL
Thurs 23rd-24th
Bradford-on-Avon Antiques
Fair

Yorkshire
APRIL
Fri 10th-12th
Antiques Fair, Ampleforth
College
Fri 24th-26th
Antiques Fair, Gt Yorkshire
Showground, Harrogate
JULY
Tues 28th-29th
Antiques Fair, Gt Yorkshire
Showground, Harrogate

Scotland
APRIL
Thurs 2nd-4th
Scottish Antiques Fair,
Roxburghe Hotel, Edinburgh
Fri 3rd-4th
Antiques Fair, Scottish
Exhibition Centre, Glasgow
JUNE
Tues 9th-11th
Perthshire Antiques Fair, Lovat
Hotel, Perth
AUGUST
Sat 1st-2nd
Mammoth Fair, Showground,
Kelso
Tues 4th-5th
Mammoth Fair, Edinburgh

Wales
MAY
Sat 30th-31st
North Wales Antiques Fair,
Bodelwyddan Castle, Clywd
Tel: (0273) 423355

DIRECTORY OF MARKETS & CENTRES

This directory is in no way complete. If you wish to be included in next year's directory or if you have a change of address or telephone number, please could you inform us by December 31st 1992. Entries will be repeated in subsequent editions unless we are requested otherwise.

London

Alfies Antique Market,
13-25 Church Street, NW8
Tel: 071-723 6066
Tues-Sat 10-6pm

Angel Arcade,
116-118 Islington High Street,
Camden Passage, N1
Open Wed & Sat

Antiquarius Antique Market,
135/141 Kings Road,
Chelsea, SW3
Tel: 071-351 5353
Open Mon-Sat 10-6pm

Antiques & Collectors Corner,
North Piazza, Covent Garden,
WC2
Tel: 071-240 7405
Open 9-5pm every day

Bermondsey Antiques Market,
corner of Long Lane and
Bermondsey Street, London, SE1
Tel: 071-351 5353
Friday 5am-2pm

Bermondsey Antique Warehouse,
173 Bermondsey Street, SE1
Tel: 071-407 2040/4250
Open 9.30-5.30pm, Thurs 9.30-8pm,
Fri 7-5.30pm. Closed Sat and Sun

Bond Street Antiques Centre,
124 New Bond Street, W1
Tel: 071-351 5353
Open Mon-Fri 10-5.45pm,
Sat 10-4pm

Camden Antiques Market,
Corner of Camden High Street,
and Buck Street, Camden Town,
NW1
Thurs 7-4pm

Camden Passage Antique Centre,
12 Camden Passage, Islington, N1
Tel: 071-359 0190
Stalls open Wed 8-3pm (Thurs
Books 9-4pm), Sat 9-5pm

Chapel Street Market,
Jubilee Shopping Hall,
65-67 Chapel Market, Islington,
N1
Tel: 071-278 9942
Open Wed, Fri, Sat & Sun

Chelsea Antiques Market,
245-253 Kings Road, SW3
Tel: 071-352 5689/9695/1424
Open 10-6pm

Chenil Galleries,
181-183 Kings Road, SW3
Tel: 071-351 5353
Mon-Sat 10-6pm

Corner Portobello Antiques
Supermarket,
282, 284, 288, 290 Westbourne
Grove, W11
Tel: 071-727 2027
Open Fri 12-4pm, Sat 7-6pm

Covent Garden Antiques Market,
Jubilee Market, Covent Garden
Piazza, WC2
Tel: 071-240 7405
Mon only 6-4pm

Cutler Street Antiques Market,
Goulston Street, near Aldgate
End, E1
Sun 7-2pm

Crystal Palace Collectors Market,
Jasper Road, Westow Hill,
Crystal Palace, SE19
Tel: 081-761 3735
Open Wed 9-4pm, Fri 9-5pm,
Sat 9-4pm, Sun 11-4pm

Dixons Antique Centre,
471 Upper Richmond Road West,
East Sheen, SW14
Tel: 081-878 6788
Open 10-5.30pm, Sun 1.30-5.30pm.
Closed Wed

Franklin's Camberwell Antiques
Market,
161 Camberwell Road, SE5
Tel: 071-703 8089
Open 10-6pm, Sun 1-6pm.

Georgian Village Antiques
Market,
100 Wood Street, Walthamstow,
E17
Tel: (0304) 853418
Open 10-5pm. Closed Thurs

Georgian Village,
Islington Green, N1
Tel: 071-226 1571
Open Wed 10-4pm, Sat 7-5pm

Good Fairy Open Market,
100 Portobello Road, W11
Tel: 071-351 5950/071-221 8977
Sats only
Open Sat 5-5pm

Grays Antique Market,
58 Davies Street, W1
Tel: 071-629 7034
Open Mon-Fri 10-6pm

Grays Mews,
1-7 Davies Street, W1
Tel: 071-629 7034
Open Mon-Fri 10-6pm

Grays Portobello,
138 Portobello Road, W11
Tel: 071-221 3069
Open Sat 7-4pm

Greenwich Crafts Market,
Burney Street Car Park,
Greenwich, SE10
Tel: 071-240 7405/6
Open Sat (& Sun Summer)

Greenwich Flea Market,
Burney Street Car Park,
Greenwich, SE10
Tel: 071-240 7405/6
Open Sat & Sun

Hampstead Antique Emporium,
12 Heath Street,
Hampstead, NW3
Tel: 071-794 3297
Open 10-6pm. Closed Mon & Sun

Jubilee Market,
Covent Garden, WC2
Tel: 081-836 2139
Open Mon

L'Aiglon Galleries,
220 Westbourne Grove, W11
Tel: 071-727 6596

The London Silver Vaults,
Chancery House,
53-65 Chancery Lane, WC2
Tel: 071-242 3844
Open 9-5.30pm. Sat 9-12.30pm

The Mall Antiques Arcade,
Camden Passage, Islington, N1
Tues, Thurs, Fri 10-5pm,
Wed 7.30-5pm, Sat 9-6pm

Northcote Road Antiques Market,
155A Northcote Road, Battersea,
SW11
Tel: 071-228 6850
Open Mon-Sat 10-6pm,
Sun 12-5pm

Old Church Galleries,
320 Kings Road, SW3
Tel: 071-351 4649
Open Mon-Sat 10-6pm
Closed Sun & Bank Holidays

Peckham Indoor Market,
Rye Lane Bargain Centre,
48 Rye Lane, Peckham, SE15
Tel: 081-639 2463
Open Tues-Sat

Pierrepoint Arcade,
Camden Passage, N1
Tel: 071-359 0190
Open Wed & Sat

Portobello Road Market,
London, W11
Open Sat 5.30-5pm

Rochefort Antique Gallery,
32/34 The Green,
Winchmore Hill,
London, N21

Buckinghamshire

Amersham Antique Collectors
Centre, 20-22 Whieldon Street,
Old Amersham
Tel: (0494) 431282
Open Mon-Sat 9.30-5.30pm

Antiques at Wendover,
The Old Post Office, Wendover
Tel: (0296) 625335
Open Mon-Sat 10-5.30pm,
Sun 11-5.30pm

Bell Street Antiques Centre,
20/22 Bell Street, Princes
Risborough
Tel: (084 44) 3034
Open 9.30-5.30pm, Sun 12-5pm

Market Square Antiques,
20 Market Place, Olney
Tel: (0234) 712172
Open Mon-Sat 10-5.30pm,
Sun 2-5.30pm

Olney Antiques Centre,
Rose Court, Olney
Tel: (0234) 712172
Open 10-5.30pm,
Sun 12-5.30pm

Tingewick Antiques Centre,
Main Street, Tingewick
Tel: (0280) 848219
Open 10.30-5 inc. Sun

Winslow Antiques Centre,
15 Market Square, Winslow
Tel: (0296) 714540/714055

Cambridgeshire

Collectors Market,
Dales Brewery, Gwydir Street
(off Mill Road), Cambridge
Open 9.30-5pm

Willingham Antiques &
Collectors Market,
25-29 Green Street, Willingham
Tel: (0954) 60283
Open 10-5pm. Closed Thurs

Cheshire

Davenham Antique Centre,
Northwick
Tel: (0606) 44350
Open Mon-Sat 10-5pm,
Closed Wed

Nantwich Antique Centre,
The Old Police Station, Welsh
Row, Nantwich
Tel: (0270) 624035
Open 10-5.30pm. Closed Wed

Melody's Antique Galleries,
32 City Road, Chester (towards
railway station)
Tel: (0244) 341818/328968
Open Mon-Sat 10-5.30pm

Stancie Cutler Antique &
Collectors Fairs,
Nantwich Civic Hall, Nantwich
Tel: (0270) 624288
Open 1st Thurs each month
12-9pm except May — 1st Wed,
Bank Hol Mons & New Year's
Date 10-6pm, 3rd Sat of each
month 9-4pm

Cornwall

New Generation Antique Market,
61/62 Chapel Street, Penzance
Tel: (0736) 63267
Open 9.30-5pm

Waterfront Antique Complex,
1st Floor, 4 Quay Street, Falmouth
Tel: (0326) 311491
Open 9-5pm

Roger's Antiques Gallery,
65 Portobello Road, W11
Tel: 071-351 5353
Open Sat 7-4pm

Steptoes Yard
52A Goldhawk Road, W12
Tel: 071-240 7405
Open Sat & Sun 6-5pm

Streatham Traders & Shippers
Market,
United Reform Church Hall,
Streatham High Street, SW16
Tel: 071-764 3602
Open Tues 8-3pm

Wimbledon Market, Car Park,
Wimbledon Greyhound Stadium,
Plough Lane, SW19
Tel (0774) 258115
Open Sun

Willesden Market, Car Park,
White Hart Public House,
Willesden, NW10
Tel: 071-240 7405/6
Open Wed & Sat

World Famous Portobello Market,
177 Portobello Road and
1-3 Elgin Crescent, W11
Tel: 071-221 7638/229 4010
Open Sat 5-6pm

York Arcade,
80 Islington High Street, N1
Tel: 071-837 8768
Open Wed & Sat 8-5pm, Tues,
Thurs, Fri 11-3pm

Avon

Bartlett Street Antique Centre
5-10 Bartlett Street, Bath
Tel: (0225) 466689/446322
Mon-Sat 9.30-5pm, Wed Market
8-4pm

Bath Antiques Market,
Guinea Lane, off Lansdown Road,
Bath
Open Wed 6.30-2.30pm

Bristol Antique Market,
St Nicholas Markets,
The Exchange, Corn Street
Tel: (0272) 260021
Open Thurs & Fri 9-4pm

Clifton Antiques Market,
26/28 The Mall, Clifton, Bristol
Tel: (0272) 741627
Open 10-6pm. Closed Mon

Great Western Antique Centre,
Bartlett Street, Bath
Tel: 081-886 4779/081-363 0910
Open 10-6pm, Closed Wed & Fri
Tel: (0225) 424243/42873/310388
Open Mon-Sat 10-5pm,
Wed 8.30-5pm

Bedfordshire

The Woburn Abbey Antiques
Centre,
Woburn
Tel: (0525) 290350
Open every day 11-5pm Nov to
Easter. 10-5.30pm Easter to Oct

Reading Emporium,
1A Merchant Place (off Friar
Street), Reading
Tel: (0734) 590290
Open 10-5pm

Berkshire

Hungerford Arcade,
High Street, Hungerford
Tel: (0488) 683701
Open 9.30-5.30pm, Sun 10-6pm

Twyford Antiques Centre,
1 High Street, Twyford
Tel: (0734) 342161
Open Mon-Sat 9.30-5.30pm,
Sun 10.30-5pm, Closed Wed

Dorset

The Antique Centre,
837-839 Christchurch Road,
Boscombe East, Bournemouth
Tel: (0202) 421052
Open Mon-Sat 9.30-5.30pm

Barnes House Antiques Centre,
West Row, Wimborne Minster
Tel: (0202) 886275
Open 10-5pm

Bridport Antique Centre,
5 West Allington, Bridport
Tel: (0308) 25885
Open 9.30-5pm

LONDON'S ANTIQUE VILLAGE

Camden Passage

AT THE ANGEL, ISLINGTON

Market Days:
Wednesday and Saturday

Books on Thursdays

Enquiries:
Sara Lemkow
Tel: 071-359 0190

**Pierrepoint Arcade, Gateway Arcade
Angel Arcade and The Georgian Village**

Gold Hill Antiques & Collectables,
3 Gold Hill Parade, Gold Hill,
Shaftesbury
Tel: (0747) 54050

Sherborne Antique Arcade,
Mattar Arcade, 17 Newlands,
Sherborne
Tel: (0935) 813464
Open 9-5pm

R. A. Swift & Son
Antiques Centre,
4B Wolverton Road (Off
Christchurch Road), Bournemouth
Tel: (0202) 394470

Wimborne Antique Centre,
Newborough Road, Wimborne
Tel: (0202) 841251
Open Thurs 10-4pm, Fri 8.30-5pm,
Sat 10-5pm, Sun 9.30-5pm

Cumbria

Carlisle Antique & Craft Centre,
Cecil Hall, Cecil Street, Carlisle
Tel: (0228) 21970
Open Mon-Sat 9-5pm

Cockermouth Antiques Market,
Courthouse, Main Street,
Cockermouth
Tel: (0900) 824346
Open 10-5pm

Devon

The Antique Centre on the Quay,
The Quay, Exeter
Tel: (0392) 214180
Open 10-5pm, Sun 11-5pm

The Antique Centre,
Abingdon House, 136 High Street,
Honiton
Tel: (0404) 42108
Open Mon-Sat 10-5pm

Barbican Antiques Market,
82-84 Vauxhall Street, Barbican,
Plymouth
Tel: (0752) 266927
Open 9.30-5pm

Dartmoor Antiques Centre,
Off West Street, Ashburton
Tel: (0364) 52182
Open Tues 9-4pm

Essex

Battlesbridge Antiques Centre,
The Green, Chelmsford Road,
Battlesbridge, Nr Wickford
Tel: (0268) 764197
Open all weekend & most
weekdays

Kelvedon Antiques Centre,
139 High Street, Kelvedon
Tel: (0376) 70896
Open Mon-Sat 10-5pm

Trinity Antiques Centre,
7 Trinity Street, Colchester
Tel: (0206) 577775
Open 9.30-5pm

Gloucestershire

Cirencester Antique Market,
Market Place, Cirencester
Tel: 071-240 0428
Open Fri

Gloucester Antiques Centre,
Severn Road, Gloucester
Tel: (0452) 29716
Open Mon-Fri 9.30-5pm,
Sat 9.30-4.30pm, Sun 1-5.30pm

Hampshire

Folly Antiques Centre,
College Street, Petersfield
Tel: (0730) 64816
Open 9.30-5pm, Thurs 9.30-1pm

Hereford & Worcester

Leominster Antiques Market,
14 Broad Street, Leominster
Tel: (0568) 2189
Open Mon-Sat 10-5pm

Worcester Antiques Centre,
Reindeer Court, Mealcheapen
Street, Worcester
Tel: (0905) 610680/1

Hertfordshire

By George! Antiques Centre,
23 George Street, St Albans
Tel: (0727) 53032
Open 10-5pm

The Herts & Essex Antique Centre,
The Maltings, Station Road,
Sawbridgeworth
Tel: (0279) 722044
Tues-Fri 10-5pm, Sat & Sun
10.30-6pm, Closed Mon

St Albans Antique Market,
Town Hall, Chequer Street,
St Albans
Tel: (0727) 50427
Open Mon 9.30-4pm

Humberside

New Pocklington Antiques Centre,
26 George Street, Pocklington
near York
Tel: (0759) 303032
Open Mon-Sat 10-5pm

Kent

The Antiques Centre,
120 London Road, Sevenoaks
Tel: (0732) 452104
Open 9-1pm, 2-5.30pm

Burgate Antiques,
10 Burgate, Canterbury
Tel: (0227) 456500
Open Mon-Sat 9.30-5.30pm

Castle Antiques Centre,
1 London Road, Westerham
Tel: (0959) 62492
Open Mon-Sat 10-5pm

Folkestone Market,
Rotunda Amusement Park,
Marine Parade, Folkestone
Tel: 081-981 0797/081-278 9942
Open Sun

Hythe Antique Centre,
5 High Street, Hythe
Tel: (0303) 269043
Open 10-4, Sat 10-5pm, Closed
Wed & Sun

Malthouse Arcade,
High Street, Hythe
Tel: (0303) 260103
Open Fri & Sat 10-6pm

Noah's Ark Antiques,
5 King Street, Sandwich
Tel: (0304) 611144
Open 10-4.30pm, Closed Wed &
Sun

Rochester Antiques & Flea
Market,
Corporation Street, Rochester
Tel: 071-240 0428
Open Sat 9-2pm

Sandgate Antiques Centre,
61-63 High Street, Sandgate
Tel: (0303) 48987
Open 10-6pm, Sun 11-6pm

Tenterden Antiques Centre,
66-66A High Street, Tenterden,
Kent
Tel: (058 06) 5655/5885

Tudor Cottage Antiques Centre,
22-23 Shipbourne Road,
Tonbridge
Tel: (0732) 351719
Open 10-5.30pm

Tunbridge Wells Antique
Centre,
Union Square, The Pantiles,
Tunbridge Wells
Tel: (0892) 33708
Open Mon-Sat 9.30-5.30pm

Lancashire

Bygone Times Antiques,
Eccleston (6 mins from J27, M6)
Tel: (0257) 453780
Open 7 days a week 8-6pm

Darwin Antique Centre,
Provident Hall, The Green,
Darwin
Tel: (0254) 760565 (Closed
Tuesdays)

Last Drop Antique & Collectors
Club,
Last Drop Hotel, Bromley Cross,
Bolton
Open Sun 11-4pm

Levenshulme Antiques
Hypermarket,
Levenshulme Town Hall,
965 Stockport Road,
Levenshulme, Manchester
Tel: 061-224 2410
Open 10-5pm

MALTHOUSE ARCADE HYTHE, KENT

37 varied stalls and café in ancient brewery building in centre of Hythe.

All kinds of antiques, pictures, linen, militaria, furniture, china, cradles and dolls, post-cards, books, silver, jewellery, brass, copper, crafts. Lively atmosphere in building laid out as a row of miniature shops downstairs, and an open gallery upstairs, with doors leading to garden and café. Established 1974

Open Fridays and Saturdays 10-6;
Bank Holiday Mondays 10-6
Owners Mr. & Mrs. R. M. Maxtone Graham
Enquiries (0304) 613270 or at MALTHOUSE (0303) 260103

Under same ownership; established 1978
NOAH'S ARK ANTIQUE CENTRE, SANDWICH
Staffordshire, china, glass, antiquaria, books, paintings, jewellery, furniture. Tel: (0304) 611144.
Mon-Sat, 10am-4.30pm. Closed Wednesdays

Preston Antique Centre,
The Mill, New Hall Lane, Preston
Tel: (0772) 794498
Fax: (0772) 651694
Open Mon-Fri 8.30-5.30pm,
Sat 10-4pm, Sun 9-4pm or by appointment

Royal Exchange Shopping Centre,
Antiques Gallery, St Ann's
Square, Manchester
Tel: 061-834 3731/834 1427
Open Mon-Sat 9.30-5.30pm

Walter Aspinall Antiques,
Pendle Antique Centre, Union
Mill, Watt Street, Sabden near
Blackburn
Tel: (0282) 76311
Open Mon-Thurs Summer
9-8pm, Winter 9-6pm
All year Fri 9-5pm, Sat 10-5pm,
Sun 11-4pm

Leicestershire
The Antiques Complex,
St Nicholas Place, Leicester
Tel: (0533) 533343
Open 9.30-5.30pm

Oxford Street Antiques
Centre Ltd,
16-26 Oxford Street, Leicester
Tel: (0533) 553006
Open Mon-Fri 10-5.30pm,
Sat 10-5pm, Sun 2-5pm

Lincolnshire
Boston Antiques Centre,
12 West Street, Boston
Tel: (0205) 361510
Open 9-5.30pm

Hemswell Antique Centre,
Caenby Corner Estate,
Hemswell Cliff near
Gainsborough
Tel: (042 773) 389
Open 10-5pm 7 days-a-week

The Lincolnshire Antiques
Centre, 26 Bridge Street,
Horncastle
Tel: (0507) 527794
Open Mon-Sat 9-5pm

Talisman Antiques,
51 North Street, Horncastle
Tel: (0507) 526893
Open 10.30-5pm. Closed Mon

Talisman Antiques,
Regent House,
12 South Market, Alford
Tel: (0507) 463441
Open 10.30-4.30pm,
Closed Thurs

Norfolk
Angel Antique Centre,
Pansthorn Farmhouse,
Redgrave Road,
South Lopham, near Diss
Tel: (037 988) 317
Open 9.30-6pm inc Sun

Antique & Collectors Centre,
St Michael at Plea, Bank Plain,
Norwich
Tel: (0603) 619129
Open 9.30-5.00

Cloisters Antiques Fair,
St Andrew's & Blackfriars Hall,
St Andrew's Plain, Norwich
Tel: (0603) 628477
Open Wed 9.30-3.30pm

Coltishall Antiques Centre,
High Street, Coltishall
Tel: (0603) 738306
Open 10-5pm

Fakenham Antique Centre,
Old Congregational Chapel,
14 Norwich Road, Fakenham
Tel: (0328) 862941
Open 10-5pm, Thurs 9-5pm

Norwich Antiques & Collectors
Centre,
Quayside, Fye Bridge, Norwich
Tel: (0603) 612582
Open 10-5pm

The Old Granary Antique &
Collectors Centre,
King Staithe Lane,
(off Queens Street), King's Lynn
Tel: (0553) 775509
Open Mon-Sat 10-5pm

Wymondham Antique Centre,
No 1 Town Green, Wymondham
Tel: (0953) 604817
Open 10-5pm

Northamptonshire
Antiques & Bric-a-Brac Market,
Market Square, Town Centre,
Wellingborough
Tel: (0905) 611321
Open Tues 9-4pm

Finedon Antiques Centre,
Church Street, Finedon, Nr.
Wellingborough
Tel: (0933) 681260

The Village Antique Market,
62 High Street, Weedon
Tel: (0327) 42015
Open 9.30-5.30pm,
Sun 10.30-5.30pm

Northumberland
Colmans of Hexham,
15 St Mary's Chare, Hexham
Tel: (0434) 603811/2
Open Mon-Sat 9-5pm

Nottinghamshire
Castle Gate Antiques Centre,
55 Castle Gate, Newark
Tel: (0636) 700076
Open 9-5.30pm

Newark Antiques Centre,
Lombard Street,
Newark-on-Trent,
Tel: (0636) 605504
Open 9.30-5pm

Newark Antique Warehouse,
Kelham Road, Newark
Tel: (0636) 74869
Open 9-5.30pm

Nottingham Antique Centre,
British Rail Goods Yard, London
Road, Nottingham
Tel: (0602) 504504/505548
Open 9-5pm. Closed Sat

Top Hat Antiques Centre,
66-72 Derby Road, Nottingham
Tel: (0602) 419143
Open 9.30-5pm

Oxfordshire
Antique & Collectors Market,
Town Hall, Thame
Tel: (0844) 28205
Open 8.30-3.30pm. Second Tues
each month

Cotswold Gateway Antique
Centre,
Cheltenham Road, Burford
Roundabout, Burford
Tel: (099 382) 3678
Open 10-5.30pm,
Sun 2pm-5.30pm

Chipping Norton Antique
Centre,
Ivy House, Middle Row,
Chipping Norton
Tel: (0608) 644212
Open 10-5pm inc Sun

Deddington Antique Centre,
Laurel House, Bull Ring,
Market Square, Deddington
Tel: (0869) 38068
Open Mon-Sat 10-5pm

The Lamb Arcade,
High Street, Wallingford
Tel: (0491) 35166
Open 10-5pm, Sat 9.30-5pm,
Wed 10-4pm

Oxford Antiques Centre,
The Jam Factory, Oxford
Antiques Centre,
27 Park End Street,
Oxford (opp the station)
Tel: (0865) 251075
Open Mon-Sat 10-5pm &
1st Sun every month

Span Antiques,
6 Market Place, Woodstock
Tel: (0993) 811332
Open 10-1pm, 2-5pm.
Closed Wed

Shropshire
Ironbridge Antique Centre,
Dale End, Ironbridge
Tel: (0952) 433784
Open 10-5pm, Sun 2-5pm

Pepper Lane Antique Centre,
Pepper Lane, Ludlow
Tel: (0584) 876494
Open Mon-Sat 9.30-5pm

Shrewsbury Antique Market,
Frankwell Quay Warehouse,
Shrewsbury
Tel: (0743) 50916
Open 10-5.30pm, Sun 12-5pm

Shrewsbury Antique Centre,
15 Princess House,
The Square,
Shrewsbury
Tel: (0743) 247704
Open Mon-Sat 9.30-5pm

St Leonards Antiques,
Corve Street, Ludlow
Tel: (0584) 875573
Open Mon-Sat 9-5pm

Stretton Antiques Market,
36 Sandford Avenue, Church
Stretton
Tel: (0694) 723718
Open Mon-Sat 9.30-5.30pm,
Sun 10.30-4.30pm

Telford Antique Centre,
High Street, Wellington, Telford
Tel: (0952) 56450
Open Mon-Sat 10-5pm,
Sun 2-5pm

Somerset

County Antiques Centre,
21/23 West Street, Ilminster
Tel: (0460) 54151
Open 10-5pm

Dulverton Antique Centre,
Lower Town Hall, Dulverton
Tel: (0398) 23522
Open Mon-Sat 9.30-5pm

Guildhall Antique Market,
The Guildhall, Chard
Open Thurs 8-4pm

Taunton Silver Street Antiques
Centre,
27/29 Silver Street, Taunton
Tel: 071-351 5353
Open Mon 9-4pm

Staffordshire

The Antique Centre,
128 High Street, Kinver
Tel: (0384) 877441
Open 10-5.30pm

Antique Market,
The Stones, Newcastle-under-
Lyme
Tel: (088 97) 527
Open Tues 7-2pm

Barclay House Antiques,
14-16 Howard Place, Shelton,
Stoke-on-Trent
Tel: (0782) 274747
Open Mon-Sat 9.30-6pm

Rugeley Antique Centre,
161/3 Main Road, Brereton near
Rugeley
Tel: (08894) 77166
Open 10-5pm

Tutbury Mill Antiques,
6 Lower High Street, Tutbury
near Burton-on-Trent
Tel: (0283) 815999
Open 7 days 9-6pm

Walsall Antiques Centre,
7A The Digbeth Arcade, Walsall
Tel: (0922) 725163/725165

Suffolk

The Barn,
Risby, Bury St Edmunds
Tel: (0284) 811126
Open 7 days-a-week

Debenham Antique Centre,
The Forresters Hall,
High Street, Debenham
Tel: (0728) 860777
Open 9.30-5.30pm

Long Melford Antiques Centre,
The Chapel Maltings, Long
Melford
Tel: (0787) 79287
Open Mon-Sat 9.30-5.30pm,
Closed Bank Holidays

Old Town Hall Antiques Centre,
High Street, Needham Market
Tel: (0449) 720773
Open 10-5pm

Waveney Antiques Centre,
Peddars Lane, Beccles
Tel: (0502) 716147
Open Mon-Sat 10-5pm

Surrey

Antiques Arcade,
22 Richmond Hill, Richmond
Tel: 081-940 2035
Open Tues, Thurs, Fri 10.30-
5.30pm, Sun 2-5.30pm

Antiques & Interiors,
34 Station Road East, Oxted
Tel: (0883) 712806
Open Mon-Sat 9.30-5.30pm

Victoria & Edward Antiques
Centre,
61 West Street, Dorking
Tel: (0306) 889645
Open Mon-Sat 9.30-5.30pm

The Antiques Arcade,
77 Bridge Road, East Molesey
Tel: 081-979 7954
Open 10-5pm

The Antiques Centre,
22 Haydon Place corner of Martyr
Road, Guildford
Tel: (0483) 67817
Open 10-5pm. Closed Mon, Wed

Fern Cottage Antique Centre,
28/30 High Street, Thames Ditton,
Tel: 081-398 2281
Open 10-5.30pm

Maltings Monthly Market,
Bridge Square, Farnham
Tel: (0252) 726234
First Sat monthly

The Old Smithy Antique Centre,
7 High Street, Merstham
Tel: (073 74) 2306
Open 10-5pm

Reigate Antiques Arcade,
57 High Street, Reigate
Tel: (0737) 222654
Open 10-5.30pm

Surrey Antiques Centre,
10 Windsor Street, Chertsey
Tel: (0932) 563313
Open 10-5pm

Sutton Market,
West Street, Sutton
Tel: 01-661 1245
Open Tues & Sat

Wood's Wharf Antiques Bazaar,
56 High Street, Haslemere
Tel: (0428) 642125
Open Mon-Sat 9.30-5pm

Sussex East

Bexhill Antiques Centre,
Quakers Mill, Old Town, Bexhill
Tel: (0424) 210182/221940
Open 6 days, 10-5.30pm

Brighton Antiques Gallery,
41 Meeting House Lane, Brighton
Tel: (0273) 26693/21059
Open 10-5.30pm

Brighton Market,
Jubilee Shopping Hall,
44-47 Gardner Street, Brighton
Tel: (0273) 600574
Open Mon-Sat

Chateaubriand Antiques Centre,
High Street, Burwash
Tel: (0435) 882535
Open 10-5pm, Sun 2-5pm

The Collectors Market,
The Enterprise Centre, Station
Parade, Eastbourne
Tel: (0323) 32690

George Street Antiques Centre,
47 George Street, Old Town,
Hastings
Tel: (0424) 429339, Open 7 days a
week 9-5pm, Sundays 11-4pm

Kollect-O-Mania,
25 Trafalgar Street, Brighton
Tel: (0273) 694229
Open 10-5pm

Lewes Antique Centre,
20 Cliffe High Street, Lewes
Tel: (0273) 476148
Open 10-5pm

Mint Arcade,
71 The Mint, Rye
Tel: (0797) 225952
Open 10-5pm every day

Newhaven Flea Market,
28 South Way, Newhaven
Tel: (0273) 517207/516065
Open every day

Prinnys Antique Gallery,
3 Meeting House Lane,
Brighton
Tel: (0273) 204554
Open Mon-Sat 9.30-5pm

Seaford's "Barn Collectors"
Market & Studio Book Shop,
The Barn, Church Lane,
Seaford
Tel: (0323) 890010
Open Tues, Thurs &
Sat 10-4.30pm

Sussex West

Antiques & Collectors Market,
Old Orchard Building,
Old House,
Adversane near Billingshurst

Copthorne Group Antiques,
Copthorne Bank, Crawley
Tel: (0342) 712802
Open Mon-Sat 10-5pm

Eagle House Antiques Centre,
Market Square, Midhurst
Tel: (0730) 812718
Open daily except Sun

Mamies Antiques Market,
5 River Road, Arundel
Tel: (0903) 882012
Open Sat 9-5pm

Midhurst Antiques Market,
Knockhundred Row, Midhurst
Tel: (0730) 814231
Open 9.30-5.30pm (winter 5pm)

Shirley, Mostyns Antique
Centre,
64 Brighton Road, Lancing
Tel: (0903) 752961
Open Mon-Fri 10-5pm or by
appointment

Petworth Antique Market,
East Street, Petworth
Tel: (0798) 42073
Open 10-5.30pm

Tyne & Wear

Antique Centre Newcastle,
8 St Mary Place East,
Newcastle- upon-Tyne
(opp Civic Centre)
Tel: 091-232 9832
Open Tues-Sat 10-5pm

Vine Lane Antique Market,
17 Vine Lane, Newcastle-upon-
Tyne
Tel: 091-261 2963/232 9832
Open 10-5.30pm

Warwickshire

The Antiques Centre,
High Street, Bidford-on-Avon
Tel: (0789) 773680
Open 10-5pm, Sun 2-5.30pm.
Closed Mon

Antiques Etc,
22 Railway Terrace, Rugby
Open 10-5pm. Closed Tues & Wed

The Antique Arcade,
4 Sheep Street, Stratford-upon-Avon
Tel: (0789) 297249
Open 10-5.30pm

Dunchurch Antique Centre,
16/16A Daventry Road,
Dunchurch near Rugby
Tel: (0788) 817147
Open 7 days 10-5pm

Smith Street Antiques Centre,
7 Smith Street, Warwick
Tel: (0926) 497864
Open 10-5.30pm

Spa Antiques Market,
4 Windsor Street, Leamington Spa
Tel: (0926) 22927
Open 9.30-5.30pm

Stratford Antiques Centre,
60 Ely Street, Stratford-upon-Avon
Tel: Mike Conway (0789) 204180
Open 10-5.30 every day

Vintage Antique Market,
36 Market Place, Warwick
Tel: (0926) 491527
Open 10-5.30pm

Warwick Antique Centre,
20-22 High Street, Warwick
Tel: (0926) 495704
Open 6 days-a-week

West Midlands

Birmingham Antique Centre,
141 Bromsgrove Street,
Birmingham
Tel: 021-692 1414/622 2145
Open every Thurs from 9am

The City of Birmingham
Antique Market,
St Martins Market, Edgbaston
Street, Birmingham
Tel: 021-267 4636
Open Mon 7-2pm

Stancie Cutler Antique &
Collectors Fair,
Town Hall, Sutton Coldfield
Tel: (0270) 624288
Open Wed monthly 11-8pm

Walsall Antiques Centre,
7a The (Digbeth) Arcade,
Walsall
Tel: (0922) 725163/5

Wiltshire

Antique Market,
37 Catherine Street, Salisbury
Tel: (0722) 26033
Open 9-6pm

The Avon Bridge Antiques &
Collectors Market,
United Reformed Church Hall,
Fisherton Street, Salisbury
Open Tues 9-4pm

London House Antique Centre,
High Street, Marlborough
Tel: (0672) 52331
Open Mon-Sat 9.30-5.30pm

The Marlborough Parade
Antiques Centre,
The Parade, Marlborough
Tel: (0672) 55331
Open 10-5pm

Mr Micawber's Attic,
73 Fisherton Street, Salisbury
Tel: (0722) 337822
Open 9.30-5pm. Closed Wed

Yorkshire North

The Ginnel,
Harrogate Antique Centre
(off Parliament Street),
Harrogate
Tel: (0423) 508857
Open 9.30-5.30pm

Grove Collectors Centre,
Grove Road, Harrogate
Tel: (0423) 61680
Open 10-5pm

Micklegate Antiques Market,
73 Micklegate, York
Tel: (0904) 644438
Open Wed & Sat 10-5.30pm

Montpelier Mews Antique
Market, Montpelier Street,
Harrogate
Tel: (0423) 530484
Open 9.30-5.30pm

West Park Antiques Pavilion,
20 West Park, Harrogate
Tel: (0423) 61758
Open 10-5pm. Closed Mon

York Antique Centre,
2 Lendal, York
Tel: Peter Banks (0904) 641445
Open Mon-Sat Winter 10-5pm,
Summer 9.30-5.30pm

Yorkshire South

Treasure House Antiques Centre,
4-10 Swan Street, Bawtry near
Doncaster
Tel: (0302) 710621
Open 10-5pm inc Sun

Yorkshire West

Halifax Antiques Centre,
Queens Road/Gibbet Street,
Halifax
Tel: (0422) 366657

Scotland

Bath Street Antique Galleries,
203 Bath Street, Glasgow
Open 10-5pm, Sat 10-1pm

Corner House Antiques,
217 St Vincent Street, Glasgow
Tel: 041-248 2560
Open 10-5pm

The Victorian Village,
53 & 57 West Regent Street,
Glasgow
Tel: 041-332 0808
Open 10-5pm

Wales

Cardiff Antique Centre,
69-71 St Mary Street, Cardiff
Tel: (0222) 30970

Crew Market,
Crew Airfield on A477
(Carmarthen to Pembroke Road),
Port Talbot
Tel: (0639) 884834
Open Sun

Jacobs Antique Centre,
West Canal Wharf, Cardiff
Tel: (0222) 390939
Open Thurs & Sat 9.30-5pm

Offa's Dyke Antiques Centre,
4 High Street, Knighton, Powys
Tel: (0547) 528634/528940
Open Mon-Sat 10-1pm, 2-5pm,
Wed 10-1pm

Pembroke Antique Centre,
The Hall, Hamilton Terrace,
Pembroke
Tel: (0646) 687017
Open 10-6pm

Port Talbot Market,
Jubilee Shopping Hall,
64-66 Station Road, Port Talbot,
Glamorgan
Tel (0639) 883184
Open Mon-Sat

Swansea Antique Centre,
21 Oxford Street, Swansea
Tel: (0792) 466854

Channel Islands

Union Street Antique Market,
8 Union Street, St Helier,
Jersey
Tel: (0534) 73805/22475
Open 9-6pm

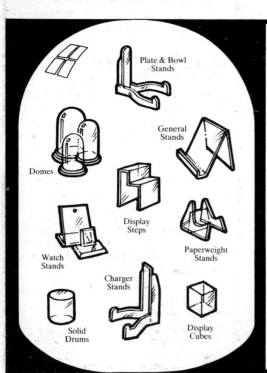
510